always up to date

The law changes, but Nolo is on top of it! We offer several
ways to make sure you and your Nolo products are up to date:

1 **Nolo's Legal Updater**

We'll send you an email whenever a new edition of this book is
published! Sign up at **www.nolo.com/legalupdater**.

2 **Updates @ Nolo.com**

Check **www.nolo.com/update** to find recent changes
in the law that affect the current edition of your book.

3 **Nolo Customer Service**

To make sure that this edition of the book is the most
recent one, call us at **800-728-3555** and ask one of
our friendly customer service representatives.
Or find out at **www.nolo.com**.

please note

We believe accurate, plain-English legal information should help you solve many of your own legal problems. But this text is not a substitute for personalized advice from a knowledgeable lawyer. If you want the help of a trained professional—and we'll always point out situations in which we think that's a good idea—consult an attorney licensed to practice in your state.

1st Edition

The Progressive Discipline Handbook

Smart Stategies for Coaching Employees

by Margie Mader-Clark and Lisa Guerin

FIRST EDITION   JANUARY 2007

Book Design   TERRI HEARSH

Proofreading   JOE SADUSKY

Index   BAYSIDE INDEXING SERVICE

Printing   CONSOLIDATED PRINTERS, INC.

Mader-Clark, Margie.
    The progressive discipline handbook : smart strategies for coaching employees/ by Margie Mader-Clark and Lisa Guerin
       p. cm.
     ISBN-13: 978-1-4133-0561-6 (alk. paper)
     ISBN-10: 1-4133-0561-X (alk. paper)
     1. Labor discipline--Handbooks, manuals, etc. 2. Supervision of employees--Handbooks, manuals, etc. I. Guerin, Lisa, 1964- II. Title.
     HF5549.5L3M33 2007
     658.3'14--dc22   2006046800

For information on bulk purchases or corporate premium sales, please contact the Special Sales Department. For academic sales or textbook adoptions, ask for Academic Sales. Call 800-955-4775 or write to Nolo, 950 Parker Street, Berkeley, CA 94710.

Acknowledgments

In the spirit of our future president's "It takes a village…," I'm happy to announce that writing this book took a freakin' universe! This book represents the efforts of my stellar coauthor, Lisa Guerin, who can take absolute convolution in both idea and word and turn it into convincing prose; our ever-patient editor, Alayna Schroeder, without whom we would be on our 400th chapter and still waxing poetic; Sigrid Metson, our Advisory Board member, who not only helped to craft the concept for this book, but pointed out both the obvious and the sublime—making it a better book; Mollie Sullivan, my extremely bright and insightful adviser on human nature, who added a ton in helping us understand employee reactions to discipline; and, of course, all the members of our esteemed Advisory Board, who provided advice and encouragement along the way.

I want to especially thank George, my neighbor, whose pre-dawn wanderings gave me faith that I wasn't the only creature alive at the ungodly hour in which this book was written. But most of all, to my love, Austin and our son, Calvin—who put up with an absent spouse and mother throughout this long process. You two are my reasons for being, and I thank you from the bottom of my heart for your support and love.

Margie Mader-Clark

About the Advisory Board

Booker McClain

Booker McClain serves as the human resources director for the Continuing Education of the Bar (CEB), University of California. CEB is a legal book publisher and the largest continuing legal education provider in the state. In his 30+ years in human resources, Mr. McClain has held of variety of leadership roles in human resources at the University of California, Los Angeles and at the UC's Office of the President.

Sigrid Metson

Sigrid Metson has held senior management positions at leading publishers including Nolo, West, Bancroft-Whitney (the Thomson Corporation), CareThere, and Reference Software. With expertise in building high-performance teams and process reengineering, she has introduced more than 30 information-based products to market. Ms. Metson also played leadership roles in the acquisition and integrations of Legal Solutions, The Rutter Group, Barclay's, and West Publishing. In addition, she has edited several titles herself, including *Secrets of Successful Writing* (RSI).

Mollie Sullivan

Mollie Sullivan is a psychotherapist working in private practice and at New Leaf Services, where she specializes in substance abuse treatment. Ms. Sullivan holds an M.S. in Clinical Psychology from San Francisco State University and a B.A. in Psychology from the University of Michigan, Ann Arbor. She is currently pursing a license as a Marriage and Family Therapist.

Mary Walti

Mary Walti is currently the director of human resources and organization development at Kodak EasyShare Gallery, formerly Ofoto, Inc., a wholly owned subsidiary of Eastman Kodak Company. She partners with Kodak's HR team on initiatives such as executive talent exchange, succession planning, and retention. Prior to this, she was employed by early stage start-up companies funded by Mayfield, Institutional Venture Partners, and Kleiner Perkins Caufield and Byers. Before that she worked in the wine business running a boutique wine and spirits importing business. She received her undergraduate degree from the University of California, Santa Barbara in Political Science, and completed the Executive/Professional M.B.A. program at the University of San Francisco.

About the Authors

Margie Mader-Clark

For the last 17 years, Margie Mader-Clark has worked in the fields of human resources and effectiveness consulting, primarily in the fast-paced world of the Silicon Valley. She has experienced first-hand the power of good management—and sadly, the devastating impact of poor management. She practices a simple, commonsense approach to her work, and this book takes the same philosophy. While working through disciplinary issues is difficult, mastering these skills builds a quality workforce, minimizes expensive replacements costs, and breeds long-term success. Mader-Clark has implemented and taught these basic principles in companies like Netscape Hyperion Solutions, and a number of Internet start-ups. She is the author of *The Job Description Handbook* and has contributed to other Nolo publications, including *The Manager's Legal Handbook*, *The Performance Appraisal Handbook*, and Nolo's online library.

Lisa Guerin

Lisa is an editor at Nolo specializing in employment law. She is the author or coauthor of several Nolo books, including *The Manager's Legal Handbook*, *Dealing With Problem Employees*, *Federal Employment Laws*, *Workplace Investigations*, *Create Your Own Employee Handbook*, and *Nolo's Guide to California Law*. Lisa has practiced employment law in government, public interest, and private practice, where she represented clients at all levels of state and federal courts and in agency proceedings. She is a graduate of Boalt Hall School of Law at the University of California at Berkeley.

Table of Contents

Introduction

Part I: An Overview of Progressive Discipline

1 Progressive Discipline Basics

2 Principles of Effective Progressive Discipline

3 Avoiding Legal Trouble

Part II: Is It Time for Discipline?

4 Identifying Potential Problems

5 Deciding What Action to Take

Part III: Smart Discipline Skills

6 Why Discipline Is Hard

7 Smart Talk: How to Discuss a Discipline Problem With an Employee

8 Smart Ways to Deal With Difficult Employee Reactions

9 Smart Documentation

10 Smart Collaboration: Involving the Right People at the Right Time

Part IV: The Disciplinary Steps

11 Step 1: Coaching

12 Step 2: Verbal Warnings

13 Step 3: Written Warnings

Part V: If Discipline Fails

14 Termination

15 Life After Discipline

Appendixes

A Tools, Checklists, and Summaries

B Sample Documentation

Index

Introduction

I f you're like most managers, you don't look forward to telling employees that they aren't meeting the company's expectations. Nobody wants to be "the bad guy," and most of us are at least a bit averse to the confrontation inherent in correcting behavior and performance. You might avoid the conversation, hoping that your wayward employee will somehow improve without your intervention. When you do finally sit down with the employee, you might feel unsure about what to say and how to say it, anxious about how the employee will react, or uncertain of how you should document the meeting and follow up afterward. You might even be worried that disciplining the employee could lead to legal problems.

Unfortunately, even though managing performance and conduct is a very important part of a manager's job, many managers receive precious little guidance on handling employee discipline. While many companies have a progressive discipline system or policy in place, they don't always take the time to train their managers in the nuts and bolts of *how* to discipline employees in a way that gets results. And even when companies do provide some disciplinary guidelines, managers are left alone to face the stress, uncertainty, and difficult emotions that accompany most discipline situations.

That's where this book comes in: It provides all of the information you need to handle employee discipline confidently, fairly, and effectively. In the chapters that follow, you'll learn how to decide when discipline is necessary; how to plan for a disciplinary meeting; what to say to the employee; how to react to an employee who responds with tears, anger, or defensiveness; how to document a disciplinary meeting; how to follow up to make sure that the employee is improving; how to handle terminations; and much more. The tools, techniques, and strategies we provide in this book will help you identify and correct performance, attendance, and conduct problems, through a collaborative, respectful process that will work within any company's disciplinary system. Using this process will protect you and your company from legal trouble—and allow you to rest assured that you've handled disciplinary issues fairly, consistently, and constructively.

What Is Progressive Discipline?

You're probably already familiar with the concept of progressive discipline. At the most basic level, progressive discipline is any employee discipline system that provides a graduated range of responses to employee performance or conduct problems. These disciplinary measures range from mild to severe, depending on the nature and frequency of the issue. For example, an informal coaching session or verbal warning might be appropriate for an employee who violates a minor work rule, while a more serious intervention—even termination—might be called for if an employee commits serious misconduct (such as sexual harassment) or does not improve a performance or conduct problem after receiving several opportunities to do so.

Most large companies use some form of progressive discipline, although they don't necessarily call it by that name. Whether they are called positive discipline programs, performance improvement plans, corrective action procedures, or something else, these systems are similar at their core, although they can vary in the details. For example, companies might adopt different types of disciplinary measures (or different names for these measures), might require managers to give employees a certain number of opportunities to improve before termination becomes an option, or might require particular forms of documentation. However, all progressive discipline systems are based on the same principle: that the company's disciplinary response should be appropriate and proportionate to the employee's conduct.

The Benefits of Progressive Discipline

If you are familiar with the benefits a coach can confer on a team or individual team members, you will instantly understand how progressive discipline can help you turn an uneven performer into a star player. Using progressive discipline can help you get employees back on track and thereby avoid the consequences of continued poor performance or misconduct or expensive replacement costs. Done right, progressive discipline can:

- allow managers to intervene and correct employee behavior at the first sign of trouble
- enhance communication between managers and employees
- help managers achieve higher performance and productivity from their employees
- improve employee morale and retention by demonstrating that there are rewards for good performance and consequences for poor performance
- avoid expensive replacement costs
- ensure consistency and fairness in dealing with employee problems, and
- lay the groundwork for fair, legally defensible employment termination for employees who cannot or will not improve.

If those benefits aren't enough to convince you that discipline is a tremendously important part of your job, consider what could happen if you don't step in to correct an employee's problems. Unless you intervene, the employee may not know that his or her behavior or actions are unacceptable. Your company will suffer the direct consequences of the employee's actions: reduced productivity; quality control problems; dollars, opportunities, or customers lost; or worse. There may also be indirect consequences, such as low employee morale, lack of confidence in your management skills, and high turnover. If you multiply these effects by the number of managers in your company, you can see the true cost of failing to discipline effectively.

Getting Results With Progressive Discipline

While company policy or practice often dictates the level of discipline to be imposed for particular problems or infractions, there's a lot more to the success of the discipline process. A progressive discipline system or policy provides a basic framework for handling employee problems fairly and consistently, but a policy is only a start: To get the best results with progressive discipline, you can't just move mechanically from one step in the discipline process to the next, until it's time to fire the employee. Instead, you must involve the employee in the process. The employee's engagement in improving his or her performance, behavior, or attitude will ultimately determine whether progressive discipline is successful.

This book will teach you a variety of techniques and strategies for working collaboratively with your employees to find solutions to disciplinary problems. You'll learn how to communicate your expectations clearly, help your employee understand why improvement is necessary and important to the company's success, work together to develop solutions, provide the resources necessary for the employee to succeed, and monitor the employee's progress toward his or her goals. By collaborating with the employee to resolve disciplinary problems, you will enhance the employee's sense of commitment to the solution and to the company's overall success.

Avoiding Legal Trouble

Mishandled employee discipline can lead to serious legal problems, including discrimination lawsuits, claims of wrongful termination, retaliation charges, and more. And it's not only your company that's at risk: In some situations, employees can also sue individual managers for damages. We don't have to tell you that being sued—or creating legal exposure for your company—can have devastating consequences for you, your reputation, your career, and even your personal finances.

Fortunately, it's not difficult to avoid making the mistakes that lead to lawsuits. We provide the information you need to stay out of legal trouble in each chapter, calling your attention to any important legal principles and consequences you should consider as you prepare for, dispense, document, and follow up on employee discipline. We also devote an entire chapter (Chapter 3) to legal issues that may arise when disciplining employees. Armed with this information, you will know that you're on safe legal ground when managing performance and behavior problems.

As you read through the chapters that follow, you'll also learn the many ways that using progressive discipline can actually protect your company from legal trouble. The techniques we advocate will help you let employees know what you expect; be fair, consistent, and objective in using discipline; include employees in the process of improvement; and document your actions and decisions properly. If you follow these strategies, employees who are unable or unwilling to improve won't have the legal ammunition necessary to fuel a lawsuit. And, if you consistently use the respectful, collaborative process we advocate, very few employees will be motivated to sue.

Who Should Read This Book

Anyone who supervises employees can use this book to improve performance, enhance communication and teamwork, minimize behavior and conduct problems, and avoid legal trouble. It can be used by:

- supervisors and line managers
- senior managers and executives
- business owners, and
- human resource professionals.

This book is primarily for managers and supervisors who work for private sector companies. If you work for the federal, state, or local government, you may have to follow a long list of required procedures when disciplining employees, and those procedures may differ from what we describe here. Even in this situation, you will still find much of this book useful, particularly in helping you communicate with your employees.

If your workplace is unionized, you may have to use a disciplinary process that differs significantly from the one presented in this book. In a union workplace, the collective bargaining agreement (CBA)—the contract between a union and the company that defines the rights and obligations of each—usually dictates how and when managers may discipline employees. The CBA may state when discipline is appropriate, which types of discipline apply to which types of offenses, and what rights the employee has throughout the disciplinary process. Typically, CBAs also give employees the right to file a grievance over disciplinary issues, to be ultimately decided in arbitration if the company and union can't reach an agreement. Because of these complications, you should talk to a lawyer to find out exactly what's allowed (and what isn't). This book provides plenty of techniques and strategies that you can put to use within the disciplinary options available to you, but it cannot help you interpret your company's collective bargaining agreement.

How to Use This Book

To help you understand each stage of the discipline process, we have divided this book into parts. Here's what you'll find in each:

- **Part I: An Overview of Progressive Discipline** describes what progressive discipline is, how it works, and how to stay out of legal trouble when disciplining employees.
- **Part II: Is It Time for Discipline?** explains how to decide whether discipline is necessary, including how to identify problems, evaluate their severity, and choose an appropriate response.
- **Part III: Smart Discipline Skills** teaches you the techniques you need to effectively communicate with employees, handle typical reactions, document discussions and decisions, and involve others in the company.
- **Part IV: The Disciplinary Steps** explains how and when to use each of the disciplinary measures available in typical progressive discipline systems, from informal coaching sessions to written warnings.
- **Part V: If Discipline Fails** describes how to terminate employment when necessary, and how to help your company and team move on after an employee's departure.

This book is intended as a companion to your company's discipline procedures. By following the strategies and tools we describe, you can make your use of discipline more effective, collaborative, and results-oriented, all while staying out of legal trouble.

To illustrate the concepts we describe, this book uses a model progressive discipline system, with steps ranging from informal coaching to termination of employment. We've chosen this system—and offered forms and samples for use with it—because it includes all of the steps you are likely to find in your company's own progressive discipline procedures. If you do not have a progressive discipline system in place in your company, you can use this as a model to develop one. However, if your company does have a system and it differs from the one we describe, or if your company requires you to use particular forms or terminology, you should adhere to your company's requirements. If, after reading this book, you believe that your company's system could create some legal exposure or simply could stand some improvement, raise the issue with your manager, human resources department, or legal counsel.

Icons Used In This Book

 This icon alerts you to a practical tip or good idea.

 This icon is a caution to consider potential problems you may encounter.

 This icon refers you to related information outside of this book, in other Nolo books or additional resources.

 This icon means there is an accompanying audio segment on the CD included with this book.

 This icon indicates that there is a relevant form on the CD included with this book.

An Overview of Progressive Discipline

Progressive Discipline Basics

P rogressive discipline gives managers a flexible structure for handling any employee problem, from poor performance to spotty attendance to misconduct. That's why so many companies use some form of progressive discipline to manage employees who are not meeting expectations. Because these systems vary in details, however, it can be tough to get a handle on exactly what progressive discipline is and how it works.

Although they may go by different names, all true progressive discipline systems have a few things in common:

- They offer a range of disciplinary measures to respond appropriately to employee problems.
- They are systems of proportional response, in which the severity of the discipline depends on the severity of the problem.
- They give employees a meaningful opportunity to improve when problems arise, unless the employee's behavior is so extreme that immediate termination is required.

This chapter explains what a progressive discipline policy should look like and gives you a step-by-step guide to help you most effectively use a progressive discipline system. For those whose companies have already adopted a policy, we also provide some tips on using this book to stay safe and legal in conjunction with that policy.

What a Progressive Discipline Policy Should Look Like

Before you can begin to use a progressive discipline policy to maximize employee performance, you need to know what a good policy should include. This information will help you understand the basic tools available to you. If your company doesn't have a written progressive discipline policy, you can use this information, and the sample policy in Appendix A, to create one.

⚠ Follow your company's policy. We can't say it enough times: If your company already has a progressive discipline policy that differs from the model policy we use in this book, you must adhere to your company's policy. If you believe, after reading this book, that your company's policy could create legal exposure, we encourage you to raise that issue with the appropriate people, such as your manager, human resources department, and/or legal counsel.

Effective progressive discipline systems offer the best of both worlds: They give managers the structure they need to treat employees consistently, with the flexibility to take unique situations and problems into account. In most progressive disciplinary systems, managers deal with first-time problems by administering a verbal coaching or warning, then escalate to more serious measures if the problem continues or the employee develops other problems. For more serious issues, the manager can start the process at a higher disciplinary level—even termination, for very significant offenses.

These are the disciplinary measures typically available in most companies' policies (although they might go by different names):

- coaching
- verbal warning
- written warning
- termination

Coaching

In today's workplace, most managers know that creating successful employees isn't always about directing and controlling, it's often about encouraging and developing. This process is often referred to as coaching. In this context, coaching is a manner of relating to and managing your employees to help them maximize their performance and build their skills and competencies. As such, coaching is not simply—or even primarily—a disciplinary measure, but is instead a management approach that emphasizes communication, collaboration, goal setting, mentoring, and assistance to help your employees realize their full potential.

In this book, however, we use the term "coaching" in a more limited sense, to refer to the first step of a progressive discipline system. Although you might be coaching your employees in the broader sense all the time, you are coaching under our definition only when you are using your collaborative and communication skills to correct a disciplinary problem. While it requires the same set of skills, coaching in the disciplinary system ensures specified goals are reached and gives you options to escalate discipline if they aren't.

Considered the least harsh disciplinary measure, coaching can be used at the first sign of relatively minor trouble. The purpose of coaching is to work through and correct an action or behavior before it becomes a larger problem. Coaching is typically handled in a face-to-face meeting. Done well, coaching can nip potential problems in the bud while conveying to the employee that his or her performance and conduct matter to you and the company. You'll find strategies and step-by-step instructions for coaching employees in Chapter 11.

⚠ **Keep track of your coaching sessions.** In many companies, managers are free to coach employees as many times as they wish, even on the same disciplinary issue, before they decide that the employee should formally enter the company's progressive discipline system with an official verbal warning. The problem with this practice is that it allows for inconsistent treatment among employees, with all of the possible legal problems that this can create (see Chapter 3 for more information on the dangers of inconsistency). That's one reason to treat coaching as a distinct step in the disciplinary process, and to document it. Although you don't have to tell the employee you're coaching that your conversation constitutes a form of discipline, you should make some notes on the conversation and escalate to a verbal warning if the situation doesn't improve. (You'll find information on documentation in Chapter 9.)

Verbal Warning

If a problem continues despite your coaching efforts, a formal verbal warning is often the next step. Typically, a manager delivers a verbal warning in a formal meeting, where the employee is told that the behavior or action is unacceptable. The term "warning" is used to communicate that there is a real problem, one which must be resolved if the employee is to get back on track. Verbal warnings differ from coaching because they are more formal. The employee is notified that he or she is being disciplined, and the incident is usually documented

in the employee's personnel file. Verbal warnings are covered in
Chapter 12.

Written Warning

You have coached your employee and given a formal verbal warning
that he or she must improve, but the problem continues. Or, an
employee's behavior is serious enough to warrant an immediate, forceful
response, but not so extreme as to require termination. Providing a
written warning conveys that the employee's job is at risk unless the
problem is solved. Often, company polices require the manager to
involve higher management or the human resources department when
giving a written warning. We cover how to prepare for, give, and
document a written warning in Chapter 13.

Termination

Nothing has worked. All attempts to correct the employee's performance
or behavior have failed. The employee's unacceptable actions, despite
numerous warnings, continue. Or, the employee has done something
so egregious that immediate termination is appropriate (for example,
stealing from the company or coworkers, or committing violence).

Termination of employment isn't really a disciplinary measure: It
represents the failure of the disciplinary process. If discipline doesn't
work despite your best efforts to help the employee improve, you know
that there's nothing more you can do. We discuss terminations in more
detail in Chapter 14.

Why Disciplinary Policies Should Be in Writing

Some employers tell us that they don't want to adopt a written progressive discipline policy and distribute it to their employees. Usually, companies go this route because they fear lawsuits by employees claiming that they are entitled to every step in a written policy and can't be fired unless the company proceeds through all the steps.

However, refusing to write down a progressive discipline policy won't protect a company from this type of claim. If a company uses a progressive discipline system—even if it never puts its policy in writing—the employee could argue that the employer's practices created an *implied contract*. (For more on implied contracts, see Chapter 3.) In this situation, the employee could use the employer's actions against it to argue that, because the employer always applied particular disciplinary measures to particular offenses, the employee was contractually entitled to the same treatment.

A properly written disciplinary policy will guard against this type of lawsuit by reiterating that the company is an at-will employer and reserves the right to discipline as it sees fit. The sample policy we provide in Appendix A demonstrates how to both convey the company's intent to provide progressive discipline and reserve the company's right to terminate employment at will.

How Progressive Discipline Works

Many companies either have a progressive discipline policy in place or follow one in practice. And it's not hard to see why: Used properly, progressive discipline gives managers the tools they need to make fair, consistent, and legally defensible disciplinary decisions. Because it is based on communication and collaboration, true progressive discipline also helps employees improve—the ultimate goal of any disciplinary system.

"All well and good," you might be thinking, "but how do I do it?" How do you decide what type of discipline is appropriate in any given situation? And how do you deliver that disciplinary message in a way that produces actual improvement?

When you confront a situation that might call for discipline, follow these steps:

1. **Gather information.** Before you act, make sure you know what happened.

2. **Assess the severity.** Consider how the problem is affecting the employee, the team, and the company.

3. **Decide how to respond.** Choose the appropriate disciplinary measure, based on the severity and frequency of the problem and how your company has addressed similar issues in the past.

4. **Prepare to talk to the employee.** Plan your disciplinary meeting, including what you will say and how you will say it.

5. **Meet with the employee.** Talk about what has happened and collaborate to create an improvement plan.

6. **Document.** Make a written record of the discipline imposed and the improvement plan.

7. **Follow up.** Check back in to make sure the employee is meeting his or her commitments.

Gather Information

Before you jump in to take action, you have to understand what is really going on. Some situations are relatively clear cut—for example, an employee has been showing up late to work, missed a deadline, or failed to follow required safety procedures. You might not know all of the reasons for the employee's actions until you talk to him or her, but you do know that a rule was violated or a performance standard wasn't met, and that the employee is responsible. In this scenario, you can move on to assessing the severity of the problem.

Other situations are trickier to untangle, especially if more than one employee is involved. If, for example, your team is not meeting its performance goals, you might not know exactly who or what caused the problem. Or, if one employee accuses another of misconduct (like harassment or threats of violence), you may need to gather more information before deciding what to do. If you can't figure out who is responsible for a problem, you might need to investigate before you take action. (For detailed information and step-by-step instructions for investigating, see *Workplace Investigations*, by Lisa Guerin (Nolo), available for electronic download at www.nolo.com.)

Don't just respond to problems—prevent them. The best managers know that they can't get the most out of their teams just by stepping in when disaster strikes. Instead, they continuously manage employee performance by communicating frequently with their teams, giving regular feedback, and providing the resources necessary for success. You'll find tips and techniques for this type of performance management in Chapter 4.

Assess the Severity

Before you decide whether or what type of discipline is in order, you need to know how the problem is affecting you, your teams, and your company. There are several important reasons for doing this:

- The disciplinary measure you impose should depend, in large part, on how serious the problem is. If the employee's behavior is having or could have a direct and significant impact on the company's ability to get out its products or serve its customers, a higher level of discipline may be in order.

- It will be easier to leave your emotions at the door and make objective, fair disciplinary decisions if you focus on the effect of the employee's behavior—and not on your own anger or disappointment. It's easy to let negative feelings enter into your decisions, especially if the employee's actions have undermined your authority or caused you to miss your own performance goals.

- Knowing how the problem is affecting the team and the company— and having a few examples ready when you meet with the employee—communicates the importance of the issue and gives the employee the proper context within which to understand the problem. It demonstrates that the employee is a crucial member of the team and that his or her performance plays an important role in the company's success. And it will help both of you troubleshoot the solutions you come up with, to make sure that they address both the employee's concerns and the needs of the company.

EXAMPLE: You sit your accounts payable clerk down and say, "Your lack of attention to detail is causing us to have to double check your work, and making our customers suspect the integrity of their invoices. This is costing the company money and time, and we need to figure out a way to fix it." His first response is to ask for more information: What lack of detail? Who has had to go over the work, in which accounts? Which customers are upset?

Because you took the time to consider the impact of the clerk's problem, you are armed with a few examples, such as, "The Jones Company has found errors in their invoices twice. This means that the sales rep, Tom, has had to spend his time on the phone with them assuring them that we will correct the invoice and are not charging them for product they didn't order. This embarrasses our company and hurts our reputation, but it also hurts our future business. Because Tom's time with them is limited, this means we're using it to correct a problem we shouldn't have had instead of giving Tom the opportunity to sell them more product. Long-term, persistent errors like this make the company look as though it doesn't take its billing or its invoicing seriously—sending the signal that clients shouldn't take our invoices seriously, either."

Once the clerk understands that his performance actually endangered the company's relationship with a customer, wasted a coworker's time, and squandered a chance for the company to make more money, he can see how important it is for him to do his job right—and will better understand why you feel the need to intervene. Now, you can begin to collaboratively find a solution.

When the measure you take is based on how an employee's problems are affecting the company, and you focus your corrective efforts on changing that situation, you and your employee will be on the same page: Working to improve the situation, rather than arguing about what happened and whether it's really a problem. The employee will see that you are acting fairly and will be less likely to respond with defensiveness or anger. You'll find specific strategies for assessing the impact of an employee's performance or behavior problems in Chapter 5.

Decide How to Respond

The whole point of progressive discipline is proportionate response: In other words, the disciplinary measure you choose should reflect how serious the problem is. If, for example, your employee has been late to the office one time, a written warning is probably too harsh. A simple coaching session—even a brief chat at the employee's desk—will probably do the trick.

When trying to figure out how serious a particular problem is—and therefore, what type of disciplinary measure to impose—there are several factors to consider:

- **The effect of the behavior.** Understanding how an employee's problem affects other employees, customers, and business opportunities is fundamental to deciding how to respond.
- **The frequency of the behavior.** When one employee misses a single deadline after years of on-time delivery, it is less worrisome than when another is routinely late with assignments. A repeat problem means that the employee doesn't understand your expectations, doesn't know how to meet them, doesn't have the resources to meet them, or simply has entrenched behaviors—like procrastination, in the case of the employee who keeps missing deadlines—that must be improved.
- **Disciplinary history.** If you've already met with the employee about the issue and come up with a reasonable action plan that hasn't been executed, tougher discipline will be necessary.
- **The legality of the behavior.** If the employee has done something illegal, such as harassed or threatened another employee, misrepresented the company's financials to shareholders, or used company computer equipment to download pirated software, a very serious response is in order. In these situations, how the company responds could determine its liability to a third party.

EXAMPLE: Steve asks Claudia out several times, but she turns him down. When Steve asks her to be his date at a company party, Claudia says, "Look, I've tried to be polite about this, but I just don't want to go out with you. Please stop asking me; I'm not going to change my mind." Steve then begins leaving romantic notes on the windshield of Claudia's car in the company parking lot, and on her desk. Claudia tells him to stop and reports his behavior to John, the human resources manager.

John gives Steve a verbal warning and tells him to stop bothering Claudia. Steve stops leaving notes for Claudia but begins going out of his way to see her. He times his arrival and departure from the office to coincide with hers, he hangs out in the hallway outside of her office and stares at her, and he "just happens" to cross her path during her twice weekly lunchtime walks on a nearby bike path. Claudia again complains to John, who gives Steve another verbal warning.

What's wrong with this picture? Steve is stalking Claudia and is receiving nothing more than a slap on the wrist. The company hasn't let Steve know that his actions are inappropriate and will not be tolerated. Claudia will be able to argue that the company should be legally responsible for any harm she suffers as a result of Steve's actions, including her emotional distress.

Prepare to Talk to the Employee

Even if you will just be engaging in simple coaching, spend a little time preparing your approach. Planning will give you some important breathing space, so you won't respond emotionally. It will also help you get all your ducks in a row prior to taking action, so you can explain the problem and its effects to the employee.

The keys to good preparation are:

- **Get the facts you need.** When you discipline an employee, it's very important to be specific. Be prepared to offer concrete examples of the issue you want to correct and to explain how this behavior falls short of your expectations. You should also be prepared to explain clearly what the employee needs to improve and why— you might find it helpful to bring a copy of particular company policies, the employee's job description, performance appraisals, or other documents where these expectations are expressly stated. The more general you are, the more likely the employee will be to respond by challenging you or being defensive, rather than understanding the problem. If the employee doesn't see exactly what needs to improve and why, you won't be able to craft a solution together.

- **Gather feedback from others, if necessary.** Some companies require managers to get permission—from their manager or the human resources department, for example—before imposing a verbal or written warning. Of course, you should do this if your company requires it, but there are good reasons to seek out feedback, even if you don't have to. You can get ideas on what to say, how to say it, and what solutions might work. You can also find out how similar situations have been handled in the past—a critical factor in making sure that your disciplinary decisions can withstand legal scrutiny.

- **Think about what you will say.** No matter what type of discipline you're using, you'll have to sit down with the employee and talk about it. Script your first few sentences—what are the most important points you want to make? Because the meeting should be a collaborative exchange between you and the employee, you shouldn't write out everything you plan to say; just consider how you'll open the conversation and make a list of key issues to cover.

- **Prepare for possible responses.** Will this employee take responsibility and immediately move to solving the problem? Or will you be met with resistance? If you're uncomfortable about emotional confrontations, plan how you will respond if the employee reacts with anger or tears. (You can find much more about preparing for an employee's reaction in Chapter 8.)

Meet With the Employee

Now you are ready to address the issue face to face with your employee. This is where your preparation will pay off in an honest, respectful session that paves the way for improvement. In a typical meeting, you will progress through these steps:

- **State the issue.** At the outset, you should tell the employee exactly what you are there to discuss. This will help you set the stage for an honest conversation and avoid making the employee feel sandbagged. Follow up with a sentence or two explaining the impact on others or the company.

EXAMPLE: "Karen, I wanted to meet with you today to talk about your attendance. You were at least half an hour late twice last week, on Tuesday and Wednesday. On both days, Mark tried to cover your phone, but he wasn't able to take all of your calls along with his own. This means customers had to wait longer to talk to a representative, which doesn't reflect well on us."

- **Review previous discussions, if any.** If you and the employee have already talked about this issue—whether in a disciplinary meeting or a casual conversation—briefly summarize those discussions. This will remind the employee that he or she knew about the problem and agreed to improve. It helps justify your continued attention to the problem and focus the employee on what needs to change.

    EXAMPLE: "You and I discussed tardiness several months ago, after you were late for the first time. As you'll recall, I reminded you that one of your job requirements is to be at work promptly at 9:00 a.m., every morning. You agreed that you would arrive on time from then on."

- **Get the employee's buy-in.** Before you move on, make sure the employee agrees about what happened. If you're wrong about the facts, you should find out right away, before you try to begin solving a problem you might not have. And, if the employee reacts defensively or with anger, you'll want to make sure that you can at least agree about what happened, even if you disagree about why.

    EXAMPLE: Karen responds to the statement above by saying, "I don't think I was that late. Besides, I had to drop my daughter off at her grandmother's house those days."

Rather than arguing, simply restate the facts and ask the employee to agree to them. "Karen, the time clock shows that you punched in at 9:40 on Tuesday and 9:45 on Wednesday. As you know, you are scheduled to start work—and that means be at your desk, ready to answer phones—at 9:00. So before we start talking about why you were late, I want to make sure you agree that you were late on those days."

- **Hear the employee out.** Once you and the employee agree on the facts, the employee will probably want to offer reasons (or excuses) for his or her behavior. Listen carefully to what the employee says—you may learn things you didn't know about the situation, or about how your employees get along or understand their work assignments. Show that you're listening by repeating back what you hear.

> **EXAMPLE:** Karen says, "I didn't realize I was that late; I'm sorry. I had to take my daughter to her grandmother's house because she was sick and couldn't go to school. It's so far out of my way, and I got caught in traffic."
>
> You respond, "So you were late because you hit traffic and had to drive farther than usual, in order to take your daughter to her grandmother's house?"

- **Start working together on solutions.** During this process, you'll want to help the employee come up with ways to solve the problem and offer any resources or help you can.

> **EXAMPLE:** You move the conversation to problem solving by saying, "Karen, I think I understand why you were late last week. But we need you here on time, every day, so our customers get the service we promise them. What can you do to make sure you get here on time?"

- **Decide on a plan.** Sometimes, you and the employee will come up with several ideas; other times—particularly if you are dealing with misconduct—the only solution is for the employee to stop the problem behavior. Either way, once you determine the best course of action, restate it so you both understand what will happen next.

EXAMPLE: Karen says, "Well, I'm hoping this won't be an issue, but I suppose my daughter could get sick again. I guess I could leave earlier, now that I know how long it takes to get here from her grandmother's house. Or, if I'm running late, I could ask my husband to drop her off on his way to work; after all, it's his mother!"

You respond, "Those sound like good ideas. So next time your daughter has to go to her grandmother's, you'll either leave earlier so you can get here on time or have your husband take her."

- **Decide what will happen next.** If you're managing a performance problem, state what you want to see change, and by when. Also plan to check in with the employee in the interim, to make sure things are moving forward as planned.

EXAMPLE: In Karen's case, very little follow up will be required, although you might want to ask her to check in with you the next time her daughter is sick, to make sure that her ideas for arriving on time worked.

You'll find detailed information on how to hold coaching sessions and give verbal and written warnings in Chapters 11 through 13, and strategies for communicating effectively with employees in Chapter 7.

Document

It is vitally important to document disciplinary matters. Of course, you'll want written proof that the employee was aware of the problem and was given a fair chance to improve, should the issue ever end up in court. But there are many other reasons to put your disciplinary decisions and actions in writing:

- It helps you make sure that you and the employee agree on what happened, what is expected, how the employee will improve, and by when.
- It creates a record for you or the employee's future managers to use if discipline becomes necessary again.

- It can help you identify patterns on your team. For example, if several of your reports have trouble meeting deadlines, you might want to examine your own scheduling practices. Are you giving people enough time? Does your team know why these deadlines are important? Does the team have enough resources to get the job done? Do you need to create a calendaring system, send out email reminders, or come up with another way to keep everyone on track?

You'll find detailed instructions on how to document, including a sample form you can use, in Chapter 9.

Follow Up

Now that you've completed the difficult meeting and have an action plan for fixing the problem, you may just want to sit back and congratulate yourself on handling a difficult issue well. But remember, the ultimate goal of workplace discipline is to fix the problem and improve the employee's performance. The only way to do this is to adhere strictly to your agreements, stay on top of the employee's performance going forward, check in often on the status of the action plan, and work closely with your employee to ensure a positive outcome. Progressive discipline is a process, not a single meeting or document. To get the most out of the process, you need to stay involved until the problem is truly resolved.

Using This Book With Your Company's Policy

The techniques described above are universal: You can use them to assess and deal with any problem and to apply any of the disciplinary measures available in a progressive discipline system. If your company already has a progressive discipline policy, you can apply these strategies within your company's rules to make the system—and your management skills—more effective.

This doesn't mean you can ignore your company's requirements, however. Your company's policies dictate its relationship with its employees: They reflect how the company wants and expects you to deal with workers. Deviating from established company policies can create legal risks for the company—and obviously, can get you into trouble at work, as well.

Here are some tips to get the most out of this book while complying with your company's rules:

- **When in doubt, follow company policy.** If the terms, forms, or advice we use are different from your company's policy, follow the policy. If you have questions about what you should do or whether the policy is fair or legal, talk to your human resources department.

- **Pay close attention to terminology.** For example, your company might have a disciplinary measure it calls an "oral reprimand," which is in all ways identical to what we refer to as a "verbal warning." If it's clear that we're all talking about the same thing, you can follow the advice we provide on verbal warnings to give an oral reprimand. If you aren't certain, follow your company's policy.

- **Focus on strategy.** Even if your company's policy is different from our model, you can apply the planning, communication, collaboration, documentation, and follow up techniques we provide here. Your company's policy provides the structure for discipline (the disciplinary measures available and when they should be used); we provide strategies to make your discipline most effective no matter what form of discipline your company requires.

Progressive Discipline Basics: Smart Summary

● If your company has a discipline policy, you should follow it. The techniques in this book, including planning, communication, collaboration, documentation, and follow up, can be used in conjunction with that policy. When in doubt about what to do, what your company policy requires, or whether the policy creates legal risks for the company, you should talk to your manager, human resources department, or legal counsel.

● A carefully written discipline policy notifies employees that they'll be disciplined for violating company policy, gives managers guidance about how to apply company policy, tells employees that they'll have fair opportunity to improve the problem performance or behavior, and reserves the right to deviate from the policy when appropriate and to terminate employment at will.

● When faced with a problem requiring discipline, you'll have to gather information, assess the severity, decide how to respond, meet with the employee, document, and follow up.

● Discipline should be proportionate to the seriousness of the problem, considering things like the effect of the behavior, the frequency of the behavior, the employee's disciplinary history, and the legality of the employee's conduct.

Principles of Effective Progressive Discipline

Today, most large companies use some form of progressive discipline to manage performance and other problems. But it hasn't always been so: Fifty or sixty years ago, workers were routinely fired, without warning or discussion, for slow production, absenteeism, insubordination, or just rubbing the boss the wrong way. Workers served primarily as cogs in a manufacturing assembly line—if a cog was "broken," it made more sense to replace it than to spend time and energy trying to fix it. Managers also played a different role: Rather than offering direction, coaching, and support, bosses and masters issued demands and directions—and if orders weren't followed, then punishment did.

A lot has changed since then. Along with the advent of civil rights, the maturing of human resources as a profession, and the accumulation of labor laws and other worker protections, significant technological innovations have transformed the way we work. The late Peter Drucker, a well-known management guru, coined the term "knowledge workers" in the late 1960s to refer to people who do their jobs primarily with their brains (as opposed to manual labor). As technology has developed, so has the number of knowledge workers, and with this change has come a shift in the skills, abilities, and expectations of the average worker.

Knowledge workers expect to be treated as individuals who have unique and valuable contributions to make. Because their work product is so often intangible—there's no cog produced anymore—knowledge workers understand their roles when they see how their performance affects the overall product and the company as a whole. Gone are the days of making life decisions for your employees, tightly controlling their activities, and rigidly maintaining their hours. Flexibility in working with individual employees is critical in today's workplace.

As a result, the job of a manager has shifted from a purely supervisory role—watching, monitoring, and punishing behaviors—to more of a mentoring role—identifying goals collaboratively, providing the resources necessary to accomplish them, and removing roadblocks along the way. This "management edge" can make or break a company. How well you as a leader respond to the challenges of managing your team of knowledge workers will define your success (and your company's as well). As Jack Welch, General Electric's legendary former CEO, explains,

"[I]f you pick the right people and give them the opportunity to spread their wings and put compensation as a carrier behind it you almost don't have to manage them." This enlightened management style helped to take General Electric from a sleepy "Old Economy" company with a market capitalization of $4 billion to a dynamic new one worth nearly half a trillion dollars.

Progressive discipline has developed and changed in response to these kind of shifts. Although the term "progressive discipline" has been around for a while, particularly in unionized settings, it used to refer to a rigid system in which particular punitive measures were required for particular types of misconduct. In contrast, today's progressive discipline embraces the "manager as coach" model of the modern workplace.

This chapter explains the principles on which modern progressive discipline is based. Understanding these fundamentals will help you stay on track and keep the big picture in mind as you employ progressive discipline.

Principle 1: Your Goal Is Retention—Not Termination

Many people mistakenly believe that the purpose of discipline is to build a case to fire employees down the road. Of course, handling disciplinary issues properly, as described in this book, will help you preserve your right to end the employment relationship legally, if an employee can't improve. But that's just one of the benefits of the system, not its purpose.

As a manager, your goal when dealing with employees who've gotten off track isn't to fire them, but to help them improve their performance and develop a renewed dedication to the job. Termination is seldom the best outcome for the business. The potential downsides of firing an employee rather than helping the employee improve include:

- real dollars and time: the cost of hiring and training a new employee
- morale and productivity: a feeling among your remaining team members that they may be "next," resulting in lower productivity, increased anxiety, and unwanted transfers or resignations
- competition for talent: difficulty replacing the employee quickly in today's ever-more-competitive hiring landscape

- opportunity cost: increased expenses and lost revenues associated with having an open position for a period of time, and
- legal expenses and problems: legal exposure for both you and the company, if the employee challenges the termination.

Principle 2: Discipline Should Be Proportionate

Progressive discipline requires you to respond to an employee's behavior by choosing a disciplinary measure of corresponding seriousness. Responding to a relatively minor issue with an informal coaching session lets an employee know that you've identified a problem and that you want to give him or her every chance to improve. Similarly, giving a written warning to an employee who has engaged in serious misconduct indicates that the behavior is unacceptable and must stop immediately. In either case, the employee you discipline is not the only audience for your action: Other employees will also see (or hear about) how you handle these issues and will get a better understanding of what you and the company expect.

As you'll learn in Chapter 5, there are many ways to measure how serious a problem is. One important consideration, both in deciding how to deal with the problem and in communicating with the employee, is how it affects coworkers, your team, and the rest of the company. Figuring out the impact an employee's problem is having on the company will help you be certain that you're not overreacting to—or downplaying—the employee's behavior. It will also allow your employees to see the direct effects of their behaviors or actions, which not only conveys that they are important to the company, but also explains why continued problems cannot be tolerated. Communicating how the employee has affected the company will also help you maintain your focus on the business, which will help you avoid personalizing the issue and reacting emotionally.

Principle 3: Have the Facts at Your Fingertips

Before you meet with your employee to discuss a problem, you'll need to be ready to explain why correction is necessary. Employees need to understand the scope of the problem and to be included in the decision-making process. This means you can't just hand over a written warning; instead, you have to be prepared to explain the problem clearly, with pertinent examples and potential solutions.

Principle 4: Listen to Your Employees

Your ability to listen to your employee as you discuss performance or conduct issues will make or break the discipline process. If you monopolize the conversation or ignore your employee's effort to explain his or her side of the story, your relationship with the employee might be damaged beyond repair—and you may not solve an otherwise solvable problem. Steven Covey, author of the enormously successful *Seven Habits of Highly Effective People*, says, "When another person is speaking, we usually 'listen' at one of four levels: ignoring, pretending, selective listening, or attentive listening. We should be using the fifth, highest form of listening—empathic listening .... Empathic listening is listening with intent to understand the other person's frame of reference and feelings. You must listen with your ears, your eyes and your heart."

Empathic listening allows you to understand the root of the problem and gives you and the employee common ground for coming up with a solution. It will also help you make sure that you've chosen the right corrective response. Moreover, an employee who feels heard and understood is often more willing to engage in the corrective process and move forward with a positive attitude; an employee who feels ignored, on the other hand, is more likely to feel resentful, angry, and antagonistic toward you and the company.

Principle 5: Collaboration Is the Key to Success

After you have explained how the employee's behavior is affecting the company and listened to the employee's side of the story, it's time to work together to develop an action plan for improvement. This collaboration allows the employee to feel some ownership of the resolution and take responsibility for making it happen. If you come into a disciplinary meeting with all the answers, your employee won't have to actively participate—and is more likely to disengage emotionally.

Remember, you hired your employees for their smarts and skills. If you ignore those qualities so you can dictate a specific remedy for the problem at hand, you could lose not only the employee's emotional dedication to the job, but also his or her willingness to share ideas about the problem and possible solutions. An employee who has a voice in the process is more engaged and feels more responsible for a successful outcome. This principle holds true no matter what position the employee holds or how pervasive the problem is.

Principle 6: Be Flexible Within a Consistent Framework

Progressive discipline systems are fair because they require consistency. These systems require managers to treat similar problems alike and to differentiate between less serious and more serious issues. This framework gives you a solid basis for making disciplinary decisions and deciding how to handle all of the particular and unique issues that might come up on your team.

However, because progressive discipline is rooted in collaboration, you must be flexible in handling disciplinary discussions, coming up with potential solutions, and working with employees to help them improve. Although the particular disciplinary measure you use will typically be dictated by the employee's behavior, the way you apply the techniques and tactics described in this book will depend on the employee and the situation.

> **EXAMPLE:** Lauren supervises a team of technicians who service the company's technology needs. They handle problems with the company's computers, servers, telephone system, website, and so on. Lauren has received similar complaints about two of her reports: Yasmin and Stefan. In each case, the technician was slow to respond to an employee's request for help with a computer problem. Because neither Yasmin nor Stefan has had any problems before, and because the complaints don't seem overly serious, Lauren decides to coach each of them.
>
> Lauren sits down with Yasmin and says, "I need your help with a problem. Phil in Sales told me that he asked you for help when

he couldn't get his spreadsheet software to work properly, and you didn't provide that help until late the next afternoon. This caused lots of problems for him because he was trying to generate a price quote for a client, who had to wait until the following week to get the information. What happened?" Yasmin responds, "I was so busy with a server problem that I didn't have any time for Phil. I told him he could ask someone else for help, but I guess he didn't do that." Lauren says, "Yasmin, it's our responsibility to provide help when employees ask for it. If there's a problem that you can't handle on the day someone asks you for help, I expect you to let me know. That way, I can decide how important the problem is and juggle workloads to free up someone to work on it, if necessary." Yasmin says, "Wow, I didn't know that. I'll be happy to do that from now on—it will really help me manage my workload."

Next, Lauren sits down with Stefan. She says, "Stefan, I need to talk to you about something. Dayna told me that she had to wait two days for you to help her with a website problem. She needed to change the content on several pages, and she couldn't do it without your help. This set her whole team back on their schedule for the website transition. Why did this happen?" Stefan says, "Geez, I didn't know it was such a big rush—and now she's talking about me behind my back?" Lauren responds, "Stefan, our team has a reputation for providing fast, excellent service to the rest of the company. Dayna was counting on that when she had the website problem, and she didn't get it. She's entitled to talk to me about it—in fact, I want all of the company managers to let me know how we're doing. The problem isn't Dayna: It's the slow response time. What happened here? Why was there a delay?" After a few more exchanges, Stefan finally admits that he's not really up to speed on the company's website content program, and he had to take some time to read up on it before he could help Dayna. Lauren says, "Because we all have to pitch in when problems come up, the whole team has to understand the basics of every program the company uses. I know that website software is complicated, and I'd be happy to send you to a training program on it." Stefan agrees that this would help solve the problem.

Principle 7: Some Employment Relationships Don't Work Out

Although the goal of progressive discipline is to help employees improve, some employment relationships were just not meant to be. If an employee really can't or won't take the necessary steps to solve a problem, progressive discipline lays the proper foundation for a fair and legal termination process.

Many managers say that terminating employees is their least favorite part of the job, but it's much easier if you have used progressive discipline. As Jack Welch of General Electric described, "[M]y main job was developing talent. I was a gardener providing water and other nourishment to our top 750 people. Of course, I had to pull out some weeds, too." An employee who has not improved after being given opportunities to understand the impact of his or her behavior; participate in coming up with a solution; and get the time, resources, and coaching necessary to improve, has basically self-selected out of the company. Because you've done all you can, you can now terminate employment and replace the employee with a clear conscience.

You will also have plenty of legal protection. Because progressive discipline requires you to be consistent and proportionate, fired employees will have a tough time arguing that they were treated unfairly, discriminated against, or wrongfully terminated. You will have all of the documentation you need to prove that you had legitimate, job-based reasons for your actions. And chances are good that you won't ever see the inside of a courtroom: Employees who have had the benefit of progressive discipline generally feel fairly treated (and, therefore, don't feel motivated to sue), even if the job doesn't work out.

Principles of Effective Progressive Discipline: Smart Summary

⬤ The number one goal of progressive discipline is retention—not termination. That means working collaboratively with your employees to solve problems, not mechanically going through the progressive discipline steps until you terminate employment.

⬤ Imposing proportionate discipline communicates to the employee how serious the problem is; it also tells other employees what the company expects.

⬤ Listening to your employees is a fundamental part of the progressive discipline process. If you do all the talking, you won't understand the basis of the employee's thoughts or actions, and you'll have a hard time addressing the problem with a relevant solution.

⬤ Today's workers expect to be treated as individuals with unique and valuable contributions to make. That's why, in the progressive discipline process, it's important to enlist the employee's help in crafting a solution.

⬤ Progressive discipline gives you the flexibility to develop solutions relevant to individual employees and their working styles. However, at the same time, it's important to administer discipline consistently—to impose similar discipline for similar problems.

■

Avoiding Legal Trouble

One of the reasons managers find discipline stressful is that mishandling a disciplinary situation could lead to a lawsuit. But if you're tempted to alleviate this stress by avoiding discipline altogether, think again. Failing to discipline can lead to legal exposure, too—and it allows workplace problems to grow unchecked. The only way to successfully lead and manage the employees who report to you is by setting reasonable expectations and encouraging employees to meet them, through recognition, rewards, mentoring, and—when necessary—discipline.

The good news is, once you understand the basic legal principles explained in this chapter, you can discipline without the constant worry that you'll have to explain yourself in court. By following the strategies explained in this book, you'll help protect your company— and yourself—from legal liability for employee discipline. To use progressive discipline effectively, you must have legitimate, objective reasons for your actions; be fair and consistent in applying disciplinary measures; consider the employee's situation carefully; communicate your expectations clearly; and document your discussions and decisions thoroughly. All of these practices will help ensure that you stay on safe legal ground when disciplining employees.

What's more, employees who are treated fairly and respectfully—as smart progressive discipline requires—are unlikely to sue. Even employees who eventually have to be fired because they couldn't (or wouldn't) get back on track will at least feel that they were given a fair shake, and will be less motivated to seek revenge in the courtroom.

However, there are no guarantees. Even though employment lawsuits are relatively rare, and even though using the progressive discipline techniques we describe will help you limit your company's exposure, there is always the chance that the problem employee you had to fire will decide to sue. For the unlucky managers who find themselves in this situation, how they handled disciplinary issues takes center stage in the courtroom. The judge and jury will consider questions like these:

- Did the manager apply the company's policies and rules fairly and consistently, or was the employee singled out?
- Was the employee given a real opportunity to improve, or did the manager set the employee up for failure?

- Did the manager have legitimate, business-related reasons for disciplining and firing the employee, or was the termination motivated by prejudice or the desire to retaliate?
- Did the manager document the employee's problems as they happened, or was the employee taken by surprise by the termination? (Or worse, does it look like the company fabricated evidence, after the fact, to try to justify the termination?)

Mishandled discipline—especially if the employee is eventually terminated—is a major source of employment litigation. Typically, the employee uses disciplinary actions as evidence that the company singled out the employee for poor treatment for an illegal reason (for example, because of the employee's race, gender, or disability; because the employee recently complained of sexual harassment or shareholder fraud; or because the employee took leave to serve in the military or care for an ailing family member). In essence, the employee claims that the discipline was not a legitimate company response to poor performance or misconduct but was instead a punishment unfairly imposed for illegal discriminatory or retaliatory reasons.

You could be targeted in a lawsuit. Some employment laws— including the Family and Medical Leave Act (FMLA) and the antidiscrimination laws of some states—allow employees to sue individual managers for damages. Employees can also name managers in certain other types of lawsuits (defamation is a common example). Although the company almost always has "deeper pockets," the supervisor or line manager—who represents the company in day-to-day dealings with the employee—is the more likely object of the employee's anger or hurt feelings over being fired.

This chapter provides ten valuable strategies that will help you avoid legal traps—and fulfill your legal obligations—when disciplining employees. It will explain all you need to know about the law as it applies to employee discipline and keep you on the right side of the law. It covers some common mistakes managers make and how to avoid them. And, if you have to fire an employee at the end of the disciplinary process, the information in this chapter will help you make sure that you've followed the rules—and can prove it in court, if it comes to that.

Strategy 1: Don't Compromise At-Will Employment

Most managers and human resource specialists are familiar with the term "employment at will." If you need a quick refresher, workers who are employed at will can quit at any time, for any reason, and they can be fired at any time, for any reason *that isn't illegal*. An illegal reason is one that violates certain employee rights. For example, you may not fire employees because of their race or ethnicity, because they were called to serve on a jury, or because they have raised concerns about workplace safety. You don't need good cause—such as poor performance or serious misconduct—to fire at-will employees.

Of course, most savvy companies don't fire employees for frivolous reasons, even if they have the right to do so. It doesn't make good business sense to fire without a good reason, and it leads to poor morale and expensive replacement costs. And any employment lawyer will tell you that firing for no apparent reason can also lead to lawsuits, simply because workers who feel they were treated unfairly are more motivated to sue—often, because they suspect that the company must have had a hidden, illegitimate reason for firing them. Even when employees lose these lawsuits, they are expensive, time consuming, and stressful for the company.

Nonetheless, the right to fire at will is very important, even if your company wisely chooses not to exercise it. If your company is sued by an at-will employee, you don't have to prove that you had good cause to fire; you only have to prove that your reasons were not illegal. You won't have to argue over whether the employee's performance, conduct, or attitude was *really* bad enough to justify termination. In fact, chances are good that this type of case will never see the inside of a courtroom, simply because few lawyers are willing to represent an at-will employee who doesn't have some proof that he or she was wrongfully fired.

> **EXAMPLE:** Jackie manages a team that develops national advertising and branding campaigns for their clients' products and services. Brian, one of her reports, just doesn't seem to have the creativity necessary for the job. The rest of the team isn't excited by his ideas, and the few concepts he's presented to clients have fallen flat. Jackie has coached him on developing new ideas, partnered with him on a project, and addressed the problem through the company's

progressive discipline system, but Brian hasn't improved. Although Brian is very skilled at graphic design, turns in all of his projects on time, and is well-liked in the company, Jackie wants to replace him with someone who can come up with interesting, new ways to bring in new customers for their clients. So she fires him. Brian is angry and decides to sue the company.

If Brian was not an at-will employee, but instead had an employment contract, the company will have to prove that it had good cause to fire him. The company will have to show that Brian's creativity measurably lagged behind the rest of the team, and that this gap was significant enough to justify firing him. To prove this, the company might have to ask Brian's coworkers—or worse, its clients—to testify on its behalf. And what if Brian can show that other team members missed deadlines, had trouble with the technical aspects of graphic design, or occasionally came up with a concept that missed the mark? As you can see, it can be hard to win an argument over whether conduct or performance was "bad enough" to justify firing.

Now assume that Brian was an at-will employee. The lawyer he talks to will try to find out whether the company had an illegal reason for firing him. If there is no evidence of discrimination, retaliation, or another improper motive, the lawyer will most likely send Brian on his way after advising him that he won't win a lawsuit. And, even if Brian finds a lawyer willing to take the gamble, the case will probably be thrown out before it ever gets to trial.

Who Works at Will

Most employees work at will unless they have a contract that limits the company's right to fire. For example, many companies lure top executives with an employment contract that promises employment for a set term (for example, one or two years) as long as the employee doesn't commit specified types of misconduct. The purpose of these contracts is to attract and retain employees who are vital to the company's success—and who would probably be hot commodities on the open market. The contract binds the employee to the company and vice versa.

During the contract's term, these employees can be fired only for the reasons described in the contract.

Not every contract is in writing. For example, an employee might have an oral contract, based on statements made during the hiring process. An oral agreement is every bit as binding as a written agreement, although it can be much harder to prove. If there's a later dispute over an oral contract, it will be the employee's word against the company's. Although we advise against them, oral contracts do exist and can limit a company's right to fire. For example, imagine that the company president said this to a candidate for the position of department manager: "If you'll make a one-year commitment to the company, we'll give you that long to turn this department around." The company is bound to the agreement, just as if it were written down and signed—and the company would be on shaky legal ground if it fired the manager for poor performance during that first year.

The trickiest type of contract, from a legal point of view, is an implied contract. An implied contract is neither written down nor explicitly stated aloud. Instead, it is implied from the words and actions of the parties. If you or other company managers give employees the idea that they have job security, you can create an implied contract. And this is something you don't want to do, because it ties your hands in future dealings with your employees.

How Discipline Can Erode At-Will Employment

There are two ways discipline can undermine the at-will relationship: through company policies, and through the actions of individual managers. If a company's discipline policy appears to require particular disciplinary responses to particular actions, that might be enough to create an implied contract that the employee will not be fired unless and until he or she has had the benefit of every disciplinary step in the company's system. Similarly, if the policy reserves termination only for a list of serious offenses, that might give an employee the right not to be fired unless he or she commits one of the specified acts. Most larger companies have disciplinary policies that have been carefully vetted by lawyers to avoid these traps, but if yours does not—or if you'd like to troubleshoot your company's policy—compare it to the sample policy in Appendix A.

Even if your company's policy doesn't create any legal problems, your own actions might. If you say, do, or write anything while imposing discipline that appears to promise continued employment, you could be undermining the at-will relationship. Typically, this comes up when managers are discussing the consequences of continued poor performance or misconduct or the rewards of improving. Employees might argue that your comments gave them a contractual right either to be fired only for certain reasons or to receive the rewards you promised for improvement.

Of course, the ultimate goal of progressive discipline is to improve employee performance. To improve performance while maintaining accountability, you must set measurable goals, with deadlines for meeting them. However, some managers make the mistake of adding on a threat or a promise, to make sure the employee understands why the goals must be met. This is where managers run the risk of undermining the company's at-will rights. Some examples are shown below.

Statement	But What If ...	Problem	So Say ...
"Tom, I can't promise you a future here unless you can bring your sales numbers up."	Tom improves his numbers, but does so by stealing clients from coworkers.	Tom might claim he was promised a future with the company if he brought his numbers up and can't be fired because he did bring them up.	"Tom, the company requires its sales representatives to bring in $10,000 in business per month, and you are currently falling short of that mark. You must bring up your numbers to meet this job requirement."
"Mary, the company would like to promote you to my position when I retire, but you'll have to improve your communication skills."	Mary improves her communication skills, but a more qualified external candidate is hired for the job.	Mary can argue that she did what she was told she needed to in order to get the job and is therefore entitled to the position.	"Mary, your position as marketing manager requires that you have excellent communication skills, so that you can market our products to potential purchasers. The feedback we've received from customers so far is that it's very difficult to talk to you because you don't seem to be paying attention when others are speaking, and you cut people off abruptly. This behavior needs to improve. "

Statement	But What If ...	Problem	So Say ...
"David, you are on a one-year probation period. If I receive one more complaint from a customer about your attitude, I'll have no choice but to let you go."	David receives no more customer complaints in the next year, but coworkers complain about how David treats them.	David can contend that he is a "permanent" employee and can't be fired—he did what he was told was necessary to finish probation.	"David, I have received three complaints from customers that you were rude and raised your voice during a call. That behavior isn't acceptable. For the next month, I will randomly monitor five of your calls per week. You will also repeat the customer service training for new telephone representatives."
"Bob's records show that he scans and delivers an average of 30 packages a day, while his coworkers average 50 packages. I've told him that if he can't improve his productivity, I'll have to put him on written warning."	Bob's productivity dips even lower, and he starts delivering 10 packages a day.	The company might have to give Bob a written warning because his productivity hasn't improved, instead of terminating his employment.	"Bob's records show that he scans and delivers an average of 30 packages a day, while his coworkers average 50 packages. I have told him that he must scan an average of 50 packages a week, starting February 1. In the interim, Claire will work with him every Monday morning to make sure he understands proper scanning procedures."

All these statements could lock the company into one course of action, rather than allowing it the flexibility provided by at-will employment. As you can see, it's all too easy to inadvertently make promises that undermine the at-will relationship. Happily, the solution is just as easy: Don't make any promises about what the future will bring, for better or for worse. Explain the goal you want the employee to reach, not what you or the company plan to do if that goal is or is not met.

Takeaway Tips

➡ The right to fire employees at will is very valuable, even if your company never terminates employees without good reason.

➡ Managers can undermine at-will employment by making statements that appear to promise continued employment—including statements about the employee's future at the company, comments that seem to promise that the employee will be fired only for certain reasons, or statements that lock the company into following a particular course of action when disciplining employees.

➡ Avoid creating implied contracts by explaining only the goals you want employees to meet, not what you or the company plan to do if those goals are or are not met.

Strategy 2: Be Consistent

Done properly, progressive discipline offers a lot of flexibility: You and the employee work together to come up with ways to solve whatever problem the employee is having. This allows you to craft a plan that takes into account the employee's unique situation and perspective, as well as the needs of the company.

But with flexibility comes the responsibility to be consistent. You must adhere to the basic disciplinary steps, and your company's discipline policy, whenever you have to deal with an employee whose performance or conduct is unacceptable. You can still work with your employees to come up with customized, flexible solutions for improving performance, but the basic disciplinary measures you impose—whether it's an informal coaching session or a written warning—should be the same for similar problems.

If you are seen as playing favorites, you'll quickly lose the benefits of progressive discipline. Employees won't feel treated fairly or respected, and they won't understand the consequences of poor performance or behavior. Instead, they'll believe the system is rigged in favor of some employees—and against others. They'll believe that punishments and rewards flow from being on your good side, not from doing what the company needs them to do.

The biggest danger of inconsistency, from a legal point of view, is that it can lead to discrimination lawsuits. Employees who are treated differently quickly start to wonder why. And if employees have any reason to believe that your inconsistent treatment is based on a protected characteristic—a characteristic that federal or state law dictates may not be the basis of employment decisions—you could be facing major legal trouble.

Federal law prohibits discrimination based on race, national origin, gender (including pregnancy), religion, disability, and age (if the employee is at least 40 years old). Typically, federal antidiscrimination laws apply to all but very small employers; see "Which Federal Antidiscrimination Laws Apply to Your Company?," below, for more information.

Which Federal Antidiscrimination Laws Apply to Your Company?

Not every antidiscrimination law applies to every employer. Federal anti-discrimination laws apply only to employers with more than a minimum number of employees—and this minimum number is different for each law.

Name of Law:	Discrimination Prohibited on the Basis of:	Applies to:
Title VII	Race, national origin, religion, sex	Employers with 15 or more employees
Age Discrimination in Employment Act	Age (against employees age 40 and over only)	Employers with 20 or more employees
Americans With Disabilities Act	Physical or mental disability	Employers with 15 or more employees
Equal Pay Act	Sex (applies only to wage discrimination)	All employers
Immigration Reform and Control Act	Citizenship status, national origin	Employers with 4 or more employees

Virtually every state also has an antidiscrimination law. Some of these laws apply to smaller employers, and some prohibit additional types of discrimination, such as discrimination based on marital status, sexual orientation, or weight. (For more information on state antidiscrimination laws, see "State Laws Prohibiting Discrimination in Employment," in Appendix C.)

If you discipline employees inconsistently, and there appears to be a link between the employees' race, gender, or other protected characteristic and the degree or type of discipline you impose, you could be accused of discrimination.

EXAMPLE: Tanya manages a large group of warehouse workers. Some of the workers have been at the company for years and don't always follow safety rules to the letter. Because they're good at their jobs and haven't had any accidents, Tanya lets it go.

One day, Tanya notices a newer employee using the forklift incorrectly, and she's worried that he might damage the property he's moving. She realizes that she needs to enforce the safety rules, because the more senior workers are passing their bad habits down to new employees. She schedules a disciplinary meeting with the employee who misused the forklift. At the meeting, he complains that other workers haven't been disciplined for ignoring safety rules. Even though Tanya has a valid reason for discipline, she could face some problems if, for example, she and the more senior workers are white and the newer worker she chose to discipline is Latino. He might wonder whether his race played a role in her decision, and other workers might start to question her impartiality. This suspicion could lead to a lawsuit, and Tanya's decision to impose discipline would be scrutinized.

Takeaway Tips

➡ Consistent application of the company's policies and rules is the key to avoiding discrimination claims.

➡ If you make an exception to the rules for one employee, expect that your other reports will learn about it—and demand the same leeway for themselves, if they ever need it.

➡ It can be tough to balance the need to be flexible in dealing with employee concerns with the need to be consistent. The best course of action is to be consistent in applying discipline—that is, impose the same discipline for the same infractions or problems—and be flexible in working with your employees to come up with ways to help them meet the company's expectations.

Strategy 3: Be Objective

To discipline effectively, you must be objective. This means you have to stay above the fray, figure out what happened and why, then decide on the appropriate disciplinary measure based on the facts—not based on your feelings or frustrations, and not based on what you privately think of the employees involved. This can be harder than it sounds.

It's human nature to develop personal opinions of the people we work with, to like some and dislike others. It's also quite natural to be at least a little upset when you have to impose discipline on an employee who has failed to meet your expectations, acted inappropriately, or perhaps even affected your ability to meet your own performance goals. But allowing these feelings to enter into employment decisions can lead to all sorts of problems, from accusations of favoritism to charges of discrimination.

Making objective, business-based decisions about discipline has two important legal benefits. First, it eliminates potential discrimination claims. Employees won't be able to claim that you had illegitimate motives for your decisions if you can point to sound, objective reasons for imposing discipline or the program. Second, if you ever have to prove that you had good cause for discipline, it's much easier to prove objective facts than subjective opinions. (See "Strategy 10: Document Everything," below, and Chapter 9 for tips on documenting factual reasons for discipline.)

Making decisions based on the company's business needs is also a core element of smart discipline. As explained in Chapter 5, you must consider—and explain to the employee—how the employee's actions have affected the company. This will help you focus on the objective, measurable reasons for discipline and avoid acting on your emotions.

> **EXAMPLE:** Maureen is 65 years old and has worked in the accounts receivable department for many years. She frequently challenges her supervisor, Alan, who is 35 years old. Maureen tells Alan that she should have been supervisor of the department, and that he should not tell her how to do her job. Alan's department runs into major trouble when Maureen doesn't meet an important deadline for entering customer information into a new software program. Maureen tells him that she thinks the company should keep using the old software, and that she is in no rush to convert to the new program. Alan decides it's time for discipline.
>
> Here's a portion of what Alan planned to write in Maureen's written warning: "Maureen has a bad attitude and is insubordinate. I know she is unhappy about having to report to a younger

supervisor, but that's no excuse. She thinks she knows everything, but in fact she is unable to keep up with new technology and the changing needs of our customers. She insists on doing things the same way she's been doing them for the last 30 years. If she can't handle changes in the field, she should consider retirement."

You can probably see why Alan thought about writing this—and, hopefully, you can also see why he shouldn't. First of all, this document would be Exhibit A in Maureen's age discrimination case against the company: It sounds like Alan is saying that this old dog is unwilling to learn a new trick. Second, Alan has used subjective terms like "bad attitude" and "insubordinate" without explaining what he means. He won't be able to prove that he had good reason for disciplining Maureen if he has to rely on this warning.

Once Alan's had some time to cool off, he writes this instead: "Maureen missed her March 15 deadline to enter customer information into the department's new *BillItNow* software program. As a result, all of our invoices for the month went out two weeks late, and we were unable to meet our deadline for the company's quarterly report. At our team meetings in January and February, I talked about the importance of making this deadline and urged anyone who was having trouble learning the new program to talk to me. Maureen never informed me that she would have any trouble with the deadline. When I asked Maureen what happened, she told me that she did not agree with the decision to purchase new software and did not feel that it was important to meet the deadline."

This is much better. Instead of characterizing Maureen's behavior, Alan simply reports it factually. He explains what he said and did, what Maureen said and did, and the consequences of her actions. This is also a more effective way to get his point across: He doesn't have to come right out and say that Maureen is insubordinate, because the last sentence of his documentation makes that painfully obvious.

Takeaway Tips

⇨ Leave your emotions at the door when it's time to discipline employees. Losing your objectivity (or your temper) will make it much harder for you to get the results you want—and will virtually guarantee that your employees respond defensively or with anger.

⇨ If you don't know who's to blame for a problem, investigate before you take action.

⇨ When you talk to employees and document disciplinary actions, rely on the facts, not on opinions or characterizations of the employee's conduct. Facts can be proved or disproved; opinions cannot.

Strategy 4: Don't Retaliate

Many employment laws prohibit retaliation against employees who exercise their rights under those laws. Typically, employers are prohibited from retaliating against an employee who takes advantage of the rights provided by the law (for example, an employee who takes protected family medical leave) and against an employee who complains that the employer violated the law (for example, an employee who files a sexual harassment complaint). Most employment laws prohibit retaliation for a very simple reason: If they didn't, there would be no way for employees to enforce their rights under the law, and the rights would be meaningless. If an employer was free to fire any employee who complained of harassment, for example, employees would quickly learn that they had to put up with harassment if they wanted to keep their jobs.

⚠ **You may not make employment decisions based on an employee's litigiousness.** Some managers believe that they are perfectly within their rights to turn the cold shoulder to an employee who has sued, or threatened to sue, the company. After all, the employee has mistreated the company, so the company can return the favor. Right? Wrong. It is retaliation to treat an employee less favorably (for example, to discipline, refuse to promote, or route unpopular assignments to the employee) because he or she has filed or talked about filing a lawsuit. This is true even if you believe that the lawsuit is groundless, and even if the lawsuit is against a previous employer.

Here are some of the most frequently invoked retaliation protections:

- **Antidiscrimination laws.** Employers may not retaliate against an employee who complains of harassment or discrimination, whether the employee makes that complaint within the company (to the human resources department, for example) or to a court or government agency.
- **Leave laws.** Virtually all laws that allow employees to take time off for certain reasons also prohibit employers from disciplining or firing an employee who takes leave for those reasons. (For more information on leave laws, see "Strategy 6: Be Careful When Disciplining for Absences," below).
- **Health and safety laws.** The Occupational Safety and Health Act and similar state laws prohibit employers from retaliating against employees who complain of unsafe working conditions.
- **Whistleblower prohibitions.** Whistleblower laws prohibit employers from punishing employees who come forward, either to company managers or to government enforcement agencies, with complaints that the company has done something illegal or unethical. The whistleblower law that's gotten the most press in recent years is the Sarbanes-Oxley Act of 2002, which prohibits publicly traded companies from retaliating against employees who raise good faith complaints about shareholder fraud. And many state courts have found that employees who are fired for raising legitimate concerns about company illegalities may be able to sue for wrongful termination.

Even if you have perfectly legitimate reasons for disciplining an employee, the timing of the discipline can create problems. If you discipline after an employee has exercised a legal right or made a complaint, the employee may claim that you imposed discipline to punish him or her—in other words, that your discipline was retaliatory. Of course, nothing prevents you from disciplining an employee—even an employee who has just filed a lawsuit—for violating workplace rules or poor performance. But you must make sure that you'll be able to prove that you would have taken the same action if the employee hadn't complained or exercised rights, preferably through documents showing that the employee's problems predated his or her protected activity.

Proceed with caution—and preferably, only after getting the green light from your legal counsel—if you want to discipline an employee in these circumstances:

- The employee recently revealed that he or she wants to take protected leave—for example, to give birth, care for a seriously ill family member, or serve in the military.
- The employee recently requested a reasonable accommodation for a disability (see "Strategy 5: Make Reasonable Accommodations for Employees With Disabilities," below, for more information).
- The employee recently filed a workers' compensation claim.
- The employee recently made a complaint, within the company or to an outside agency, of harassment, discrimination, health and safety violations, or other allegedly illegal conduct.
- The employee recently assisted another employee who made a complaint, testified, acted as a witness, or otherwise participated in an investigation into workplace misconduct.
- The employee recently filed a lawsuit against the company.

Retaliation claims are a clear and present danger. Employers have a very real reason to be concerned about retaliation claims. Juries seem to be particularly suspicious when employers discipline employees who are trying to serve the public good and often are willing to award large damages to employees who bring these claims, especially if the employee claims to have been fired for complaining of illegal conduct. And these cases can be tough for employers to win: Even if the employer can prove that the underlying claim—of sexual harassment or unsafe working conditions, for example—isn't valid, it can still lose the retaliation case.

Takeaway Tips:

 Employees are protected from retaliation for exercising their legal rights and for reporting or making a complaint that the employer violated a law.

Timing is the key to winning or losing a retaliation case. If an employee can show that you imposed discipline immediately after he or she exercised a right or made a complaint, that employee has a stronger case. On the other hand, if you can show that you documented the employee's problems before the employee took any protected action, you are in the better position.

Strategy 5: Make Reasonable Accommodations for Employees With Disabilities

If an employee's performance or conduct problems are the result of a disability, you have special obligations. You cannot simply ignore the employee's disability and proceed with your disciplinary actions. Instead, you must consult with the employee to figure out whether some accommodation would help him or her do the job successfully. On the other hand, you are not required to lower your standards or avoid disciplining disabled employees who cannot meet the company's expectations. This section explains the rules for accommodating employees with disabilities.

Your Legal Obligations to Employees With Disabilities

The Americans With Disabilities Act (ADA) prohibits private employers with at least 15 employees from discriminating against a person with a disability. (42 U.S.C. §§ 12101–12213.) However, the ADA doesn't require companies to hire or retain workers whose disabilities make them unable to do their jobs. Only qualified workers with disabilities—those who can perform the essential functions of the job, with or without a reasonable accommodation—are protected from discrimination.

The ADA can be a difficult law to understand, partly because of how it defines basic terms. You may think you know what a disability or an accommodation is, for example, but the ADA uses its own very specific definitions. Here is a quick introduction to some common ADA terms:

- **Person with a disability.** Under the ADA, there are three ways someone might qualify as a person with a disability:
    - The person has a long-term physical or mental impairment that substantially limits a major life activity (such as the ability

to walk, talk, see, hear, breathe, reason, work, or take care of oneself). Temporary impairments (such as a broken arm or leg) are not disabilities.

- The person has a history of disability (for example, he or she suffered depression or cancer in the past).
- The person is regarded as having a disability. This sometimes comes up when a worker has an obvious impairment, such as a limp, that is not disabling but appears so to the employer.

• **Qualified worker.** A worker is qualified if he or she has the necessary experience, skills, training, licenses, and so on to do the job and can perform its essential functions with or without a reasonable accommodation.

• **Essential functions.** Essential job functions are the fundamental duties of the position, those things that the person holding the position absolutely must be able to do.

• **Reasonable accommodation.** Reasonable accommodations include assistance or changes to the job or workplace that will enable an employee with a disability to do the job. Examples include a lowered desktop or accessible washroom for an employee who uses a wheelchair; voice-recognition software for an employee who has carpal tunnel syndrome, severe learning disabilities, or limited vision; or a temporary part-time schedule for a worker who is getting chemotherapy or radiation treatment for cancer.

• **Undue hardship.** An accommodation creates an undue hardship if it would involve significant difficulty or expense for the employer or if it would fundamentally alter the nature or operation of the business. Whether an accommodation creates an undue hardship depends on a number of factors, including:
  - the accommodation's cost
  - the size and financial resources of the business
  - the business structure, and
  - the effect the accommodation would have on the business.

If a reasonable accommodation creates an undue hardship, the employer doesn't have to make the accommodation.

Disabilities and Discipline

Many managers are understandably confused by the interaction of two of the ADA's basic principles. On the one hand, the ADA protects workers only if they can do the job's essential functions; you are not legally required to lower production or performance standards for workers with disabilities. On the other hand, you may have a legal obligation to accommodate a worker's disability, if it doesn't create an undue hardship. When an employee's performance or conduct is falling short because of his or her disability, it can be tough to figure out whether the employee is capable of doing the job's essential functions, and whether a reasonable accommodation will make a difference.

Your job is easiest at the extremes: if a simple accommodation would allow the employee to meet your expectations, or if there's simply no way for the employee to do the job.

EXAMPLE 1: Leroy, a retail merchandiser, uses a wheelchair. His numbers are missing the mark. When his supervisor, Loretta, talks to him about it, she learns that it's very time-consuming for him to load product samples each morning because there's no accessible parking near the warehouse, and he can only carry one or two boxes of samples at a time. Loretta creates a parking space for him by the loading bay door and arranges for a warehouse worker to meet him there at a set time each morning to load the samples in his van. This saves Leroy time, making it possible for him to make more sales calls. His numbers go up immediately. Problem solved.

EXAMPLE 2: Now assume that Leroy doesn't have any trouble loading samples but still isn't making his numbers for a different reason. Leroy's company sells camping gear to outdoor supply companies. Part of his job is to demonstrate how easy it is to set up the company's tents. The problem is that it's fairly difficult and time-consuming for Leroy to set up the tents. And Leroy can't demonstrate the tents' cool interior features, because his wheelchair won't fit inside. Leroy's stores aren't buying because Leroy's disability makes it almost impossible for him to effectively present this product, and it's hard to come up with a reasonable accommodation that wouldn't pose an undue burden. This job is probably just a bad fit for Leroy.

As long as you've met your obligation to provide a reasonable accommodation (if one is available), it is perfectly acceptable to discipline an employee with a disability for failing to meet performance or conduct standards. In some cases, it might be a reasonable accommodation to change a workplace rule, if doing so is feasible and does not pose an undue hardship to the company. For example, an employee might be groggy in the morning after taking antidepressive medication. You might allow this employee to come in a couple of hours late as a reasonable accommodation, if it doesn't really matter when he or she works. On the other hand, if the employee is a dispatcher for your delivery team and must be at work by 8 a.m. to get the trucks on the road, it would probably be an undue hardship to let him or her come in late.

Hidden Disabilities

If your employee is blind or uses a wheelchair, you know that he or she has a disability. Other disabilities are not so obvious, however. In fact, you might learn of an employee's disability only after you decide to impose discipline.

If an employee tells you that his or her performance or misconduct problems are related to a disability, you have an obligation to explore the possibility of providing a reasonable accommodation. However, you don't have to rescind discipline you've already imposed. The duty to accommodate exists only after you know of the employee's disability.

More information on the ADA and reasonable accommodation. The ADA is enforced by the federal Equal Employment Opportunity Commission (EEOC). You can find lots of free information on the ADA at the EEOC's website, www.eeoc.gov. Click "Disability" for some basic information and a list of links to EEOC factsheets and enforcement guides.

Takeaway Tips:

➡️ If an employee's disability is creating performance or conduct problems, talk to the employee about reasonable accommodations. Start by asking the employee what would help him or her do the job. You do not have to provide the accommodation that the employee requests, if you can provide an alternate accommodation that is reasonable.

➡️ An employee whose disability makes it impossible for him or her to perform the job's essential functions, even with an accommodation, is not qualified for the position. You have no obligation to treat that employee any differently than you would treat a nondisabled employee who can't do the job.

➡️ Give your disabled employees a chance. If you disciplined an employee before learning that his or her problems were related to a disability, you aren't legally required to "undo" the discipline. But it might be a good idea to give that employee a clean slate, especially if there might be a reasonable accommodation that would solve the problem.

Strategy 6: Be Careful When Disciplining for Absences

Attendance is a very basic requirement of many jobs: If the employee doesn't show up regularly, the work won't get done. Recognizing this, many companies have adopted attendance policies. Typically, these policies provide that employees who exceed a certain number of absences, regardless of the reason, will be subject to discipline, up to and including termination. Even companies that don't have a written attendance policy follow one in practice: Employees are disciplined when their absences reach a certain number.

There are several traps lurking here for the unwary manager. First, if you discipline employees for taking leave to which they are legally entitled, you have broken the law and could face an enforcement action by a government agency, or even a lawsuit. Second, even though it's very easy to bend the rules on absences when employees seem to have an urgent need for leave, granting exceptions means treating employees differently, which could lead to discrimination claims. And third, you've got to initiate discipline at the first sign of trouble, not after an employee has racked up piles of unexcused absences.

Legally Protected Absences

Many types of absences are legally protected. State and federal laws give employees the right to take a limited amount of time off for a variety of reasons, from attending school conferences or National Guard training to giving birth or healing from a workplace injury. If you penalize employees for taking a protected absence—even if the protected absence follows a long string of unexcused and unprotected days off—you have violated the law.

Here are some of the most common types of protected absences:

- **Family medical leave.** Under the federal Family and Medical Leave Act (FMLA), covered employees are entitled to take up to 12 weeks of unpaid leave each year (1) for the birth, adoption, or placement of a child; (2) to care for a family member with a serious health condition; or (3) to recover from their own serious health condition. Employers may not discipline or fire employees for taking FMLA-protected leave and must reinstate returning employees to the position they held prior to taking leave. Although the FMLA applies only to employers that have at least 50 employees, some states have similar laws that cover smaller companies and/or provide more generous leave benefits; a handful of states allow employees to take protected leave for specified reasons, such as to donate bone marrow or take a child or elderly relative to the doctor or dentist.

- **Military leave.** The federal Uniformed Services Employment and Reemployment Rights Act (USERRA) prohibits discrimination against members of the armed services and requires employers to reinstate employees who take up to five years of leave for military service. Many states have similar laws that protect those who serve in the state guard or militia. Employers may not discipline or fire employees for taking protected leave under these statutes.

- **Jury duty.** Almost every state prohibits employers from disciplining or firing an employee who takes time off to attend jury duty or serve on a jury. Typically, the employee must meet certain requirements, such as providing advanced notice of the need for leave. Some states require employers to pay for all or some of this time; others do not.

- **Voting.** Many states require employers to allow employees to take a few hours off to vote, if the employee otherwise would not be able to get to the polls while they were open. An employer may not fire or otherwise discipline an employee for taking this time off, as long as the employee meets any requirements imposed by the law (for example, the employee may have to give notice in advance or provide proof, upon returning to work, that he or she actually voted).

- **School events.** Some states prohibit employers from disciplining or firing employees who take time off for certain school activities, such as responding to a child's emergency, attending parent-teacher conferences, or volunteering in the classroom. The amount of protected time off varies, as do the reasons leave may be taken.

- **Domestic violence.** Some states require employers to allow employees to take time off to deal with issues relating to domestic violence, such as medical appointments, counseling, attending legal proceedings, or relocating to a safe environment. Employees may not be disciplined or fired for taking leave for these purposes.

- **Disabilities.** As explained above, the Americans With Disabilities Act (ADA) requires certain employers to provide reasonable accommodations to employees with disabilities. Time off from work might be such an accommodation if the employee needs the time for required medical treatment or recuperation from a disability-related illness, for example. An employer may not discipline or fire an employee for taking leave as a reasonable accommodation. And the employer may not otherwise penalize the employee for taking leave—for example, by refusing to take the leave into account when calculating the employee's annual productivity numbers.

- **Work-related injuries and illnesses.** Most companies are required to carry workers' compensation insurance, which reimburses employees for medical expenses incurred and wages lost due to on-the-job injuries and illnesses. Virtually all states prohibit companies from discriminating or retaliating against an employee for filing a workers' comp claim, and some states interpret this prohibition to include disciplining or firing a worker because he or she is on leave due to an injury covered by workers' compensation.

> ⚠️ **Get help untangling leave requirements for injured, ill, or disabled employees.** There is plenty of overlap among the ADA, FMLA, and workers' compensation laws. Although these laws have different purposes and requirements, they regulate some of the same issues, which can lead to confusing—and sometimes conflicting—obligations for employers. If you're faced with a difficult question regarding an injured, ill, or disabled employee and you're not absolutely clear on your obligations, talk to a lawyer.

Making Exceptions

Consistency can also be a problem when disciplining for absences. As a manager, you know that you must be consistent in imposing discipline. As a human being, however, you will undoubtedly have more sympathy for an employee who misses work because his friend was in a serious car accident than one who misses work to watch a favorite actor appear on a daytime soap.

Although you have to apply company policies consistently, this doesn't mean that you have to turn a blind eye to significant events in an employee's life, even if they don't come with a legally protected right to take time off. It's certainly acceptable to allow an employee to take time off beyond what would ordinarily be allowed under your company policies for a reason that's compelling but not legally protected. If you do, however, remember that you'll have to be ready to grant that same privilege to other employees who have a legitimate need for leave, or risk being accused of playing favorites or, much worse, discriminating.

> **EXAMPLE:** Rob's ex-wife, with whom he shares custody of their young daughter, must move to another state immediately to care for her dying father. Rob calls in Monday morning and asks for permission to take the week off so he can spend time with his daughter and take care of her while his ex-wife prepares to move.

Although Rob didn't follow company policies that require written notice before taking leave for personal reasons, John, Rob's manager, decides to grant the request. Rob is generally reliable and seems to have a good reason for taking time off.

Carla, another employee who reports to John, is upset when she finds out about Rob's leave. John gave Carla a verbal warning when she failed to give written notice to take personal leave when her teenage son was chosen at the last minute to compete in a regional spelling bee out of state. Now John could be in trouble: Although Rob's request seems more urgent than Carla's, John has bent the rules for a father and enforced them against a mother. If this starts to look like a pattern of disciplining women and not men for leave violations, the company could be looking at a discrimination claim—not to mention some angry female employees.

Here's another very good reason to be careful when granting exceptions to your usual leave rules: Courts will consider your company's past practices when deciding whether an employee is entitled to leave as a reasonable accommodation. You really can't argue that it would be an undue hardship to allow an employee to take four months off to recover from surgery related to a disability if you gave another employee the same amount of leave to go on a trek in the Himalayas.

Don't Let Absences Slide

Some managers don't pay much attention to employee absences until they start creating real trouble in the workplace. For example, let's say you have a report who routinely extends his vacations by a few "sick" days and tends to also take ill on the day after a long weekend. Clearly, you have reason to believe this employee is abusing the company's sick leave policy, but it might not cause you any real grief until the team starts missing deadlines or production quotas because of these absences. If you initiate corrective action only after a handful of unexcused absences, you've done your company a real disservice, for several reasons:

- Coworkers have noticed the free ride this employee got, and they are undoubtedly resentful at having to pick up the extra work he left undone on his "sick" days. Some of them have probably also decided that they could use an extra day or two off themselves, especially when they see that there are no consequences for abusing sick leave.

- If you decide to be more vigilant about employee absences from now on, you will have a consistency problem—and therefore, a potential discrimination problem. Employees who face discipline after their first unexcused absence will have a legitimate gripe that they were treated less favorably than the employee who got away with all those extra sick days.

- You still can't impose discipline for legally protected absences, and that can be very frustrating if an employee has already taken a lot of time off for other reasons. For example, let's say your employee racked up several weeks' worth of unexcused absences before you decided it was time for a verbal warning. The employee then informs you that he plans to take two more months off after his wife has a baby. You might think, "Enough is enough! This guy has some nerve, responding to my warning with a request for more time off!" But if the leave is protected, you can't discipline him for it. On the other hand, if you had stepped in right away and begun the discipline process after the first unexcused absence, he would either have shown up for work on the days he missed or be looking for another job after you terminated employment.

Takeaway Tips:

➡ **Don't discipline employees for taking legally protected leave.** If an employee needs leave for reasons related to a workplace injury, illness, or disability, tread very carefully—and get some guidance from your legal department or outside counsel.

➡ **Enforce your company's leave policies consistently;** you should have compelling, legitimate reasons for any exceptions.

➡ **Don't let employees abuse your company's leave policies.** Step in at the first sign of trouble to avoid escalating problems.

Strategy 7: Deal With Dangerous Situations Right Away

If an employee is endangering coworkers or company property, you must step in. There are, of course, many practical reasons for doing so, from maintaining morale to keeping workers safe. But there is also a very important legal reason to take action: Any harm a dangerous worker causes after the company becomes aware of the problem may be legally attributable to the company. Failing to act in these situations will almost certainly make the situation worse.

Here are some allegations of misconduct that should result in immediate action by the company:

- severe harassment or discrimination
- health or safety violations that could cause significant harm to workers or company property
- illegal conduct that could affect the company's customers, clients, or shareholders
- theft of the company's intellectual or other property
- threats to harm someone, stalking, fights, bringing weapons to work or threatening to use a weapon, and other types of violence
- vandalism or sabotage of company property
- use of company property for an illicit purpose
- stealing from the company's customers or clients, or
- substance abuse that affects an employee's ability to work safely and efficiently.

Your Company's Liability for Illegal Conduct

If an employee does something illegal, how you respond could have very serious ramifications. Your response must clearly communicate that the employee's actions are unacceptable and that the company will not condone illegal behavior. If you decide not to fire the employee—for example, because the employee violated the law inadvertently or otherwise didn't understand the situation—you must make very sure that your response stops the problem.

The reason for this is simple: Your company might be held liable for harm caused by the employee's actions. There are several ways this might happen:

- Under a legal theory called "respondeat superior," the employer is generally liable for harm its employees cause to third parties when acting within the course and scope of employment.
- Some states allow third parties to sue an employer for negligent hiring or supervision of an employee, if the employer knew or should have known that the employee was unfit for the job, yet failed to take action.
- The U.S. Supreme Court has held that employers are legally liable for certain types of harassment if they fail to take reasonable steps to discover, investigate, and end the harassment.

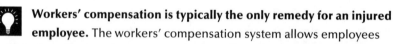 **Workers' compensation is typically the only remedy for an injured employee.** The workers' compensation system allows employees to claim benefits for most injuries suffered on the job, no matter who caused the injury. However, it also imposes a limitation on employer liability for these injuries: Employees may not sue their employers for workplace injuries unless the employer intentionally caused the harm. Although this rule does not prevent employees from suing for harassment or discrimination, it does effectively prevent most personal injury claims by employees against their employers.

If You Don't Know All the Facts

If you learn of potentially dangerous behavior, you must intervene right away to keep other employees and company property safe. However, you may not have enough information to discipline or fire the allegedly dangerous employee. The best course of action in these circumstances is to suspend the employee immediately, with pay. That will give you time to investigate and figure out exactly what happened—and what you should do about it. For detailed information on investigating misconduct, see Nolo's *Workplace Investigations,* by Lisa Guerin (available for download at www.nolo.com).

Don't suspend employees without pay while you investigate. No matter what an employee is accused of doing, it's always a bad idea to suspend employees without pay pending an investigation. An unpaid suspension signals that you believe the employee is probably guilty—which can cause bad feelings and potential legal problems. Suspending exempt employees (those who are not entitled to earn overtime) without pay can also lead to wage and hour problems, in some cases. In the long run, it's a better idea to simply pay the employee for a few days off while you figure out what happened.

Handling Safety Rule Violations

An employee who violates a workplace safety rule could be endangering him- or herself and others. This is reason enough to impose discipline, but there's another important reason to discipline safety violations: It could protect your company in an enforcement action by the federal Occupational Safety and Health Administration (OSHA).

OSHA enforces the Occupational Safety and Health Act, a federal law that requires employers to provide a safe workplace and to take certain actions to protect workers. OSHA creates and administers health and safety rules, in part by investigating workplace accidents or incidents in which employees are seriously injured or killed. When it investigates, OSHA looks to see whether the employer established and enforced proper workplace safety rules. If the employee was injured despite the employer's best efforts, the employer might not receive a citation. If, however, the employer didn't adopt safety rules—or didn't take its safety rules seriously—it could face penalties, fines, and even criminal sanctions.

In determining whether an employer is responsible for a workplace injury, OSHA and the courts will consider whether the employer enforced its safety rules effectively. If an employer can show evidence that it consistently enforced its safety rules through training employees and disciplining those who broke the rules, it will have a better chance of escaping liability. If you use progressive discipline for safety violations, imposing more serious measures for repeat offenses or for particularly dangerous behavior, and you document your actions carefully, your company will be well-positioned to fight an OSHA citation.

➡ Failing to discipline an employee who is endangering people or property can lead to huge legal exposure. If the employee winds up actually harming customers, clients, or other employees, it will also make your company look both clueless and callous.

➡ If you aren't completely certain about what happened, suspend the suspected employee with pay while you investigate.

➡ Get expert help. You should certainly talk to counsel before you suspend an employee, and then again before you fire him or her. If you're worried about potential violence, there are plenty of workplace consultants who can help you think through the issues and come up with a plan.

Strategy 8: Keep It Confidential

It's never a good idea to discuss specific instances of employee discipline with anyone who doesn't have a need to know. First and foremost, it shows disrespect for the employee you had to discipline, who certainly doesn't want his or her failures broadcast throughout the workplace. It may also breach the trust you've established through the collaborative process. Once you start talking about an employee's performance problems or misconduct, you can be sure that the rest of your team will too, which can lead to plenty of gossip, potential bad feelings, and loss of productivity.

An employee who believes that you have spread false, damaging information about him or her might have more than hurt feelings—that employee might also have a valid legal claim for defamation. When you discipline an employee, you are communicating that the employee has done something wrong or failed to meet company expectations in some way. If you are wrong about the employee's performance or conduct, or if you make the discipline public in a way that falsely maligns the employee, you might be vulnerable to a defamation claim.

Another danger of talking unnecessarily about discipline is that it compromises employee privacy. Often, personal problems spill into the workplace to create performance problems. So when you meet with an employee to talk about performance or conduct issues, you shouldn't be surprised if you end up hearing more about his or her private life than about the job.

But this doesn't give you carte blanche to repeat that information to others in the company. This not only is disrespectful and very hurtful to the employee who confided in you, but also could lead to legal claims of invasion of privacy. Even though you (hopefully) didn't pry this information out of the employee, you could face a lawsuit if you reveal it to others who have no legitimate need to know about it.

The best practice is to reveal information an employee tells you in confidence only if you must. For example, if you have a coaching session with an employee whose performance is slipping, and she tells you that she's having trouble concentrating at work because a coworker is sexually harassing her, you cannot keep that information confidential. You have a duty to the company and the employee to escalate the complaint appropriately and make sure it's investigated. If, however, the employee tells you that her performance is suffering because her husband is having an affair, that would be something to keep to yourself.

> **EXAMPLE:** Roger has a coaching session with Sherry for poor performance. When Roger asks Sherry why her productivity is flagging, Sherry confides she is preoccupied by her son's recent arrest for drug possession. Roger and Sherry brainstorm together to come up with some short-term solutions, such as allowing Sherry to leave a bit early for the next two weeks and make up the time on the weekend, so she can make sure her son comes straight home from school.
>
> Afterwards, Roger considers what to do with this information. He can't think of any reason why others in the company would need to know about Sherry's son, and he knows that Sherry is deeply embarrassed by the whole situation. He decides that he won't reveal her son's problems. If anyone in the company asks him why Sherry is leaving early, he will simply say, "We've adjusted Sherry's schedule for the time being; she'll make up the time later."

Takeaway Tips

➡ Discipline employees privately, in a place where you won't be seen or heard by others.

➡ Don't talk about employee discipline with anyone who doesn't have a need to know.

➡ Learn to keep confidences. Even if you are a gossip outside of work, you have to fight the urge to blab at work, no matter how strong the temptation.

Strategy 9: Remember: You Represent the Company

Sometimes, you may be called upon to deliver discipline that you don't entirely agree with. This can be especially hard if you have to fire an employee. Maybe you think the company's rules are too harsh or the employee deserves another chance. Maybe you just like the employee and don't want to see him or her go. It's a tough situation to be in, but it's also part of being a manager. Although you might have made a different decision if you were in charge, letting the employee know that can lead to problems.

> **EXAMPLE:** Rich is Eddie's manager and friend. Recently, Eddie has had trouble meeting the company's new productivity standards. These standards are strict, and the company has instructed managers to initiate discipline proceedings immediately with employees who are unable to meet them. After Rich arranged for Eddie to be retrained in the new system, Eddie's numbers improved, but they're still falling short. The company decides to terminate Eddie's employment. There's nothing illegal about this decision, but Rich doesn't like it.
>
> At the termination meeting, Rich tells Eddie the bad news. He also says, "If it were up to me, you'd still have a job here. These new quotas are pretty tough on long-term employees who are used to the old system. Your performance has always been great, and I wish the company had taken that into account." Based on Rich's comments, Eddie might start wondering if the quotas were fair, and if his firing was legally justified.

As a manager, you represent the company. What you say is legally attributable to the company, and can be used against it—even if you intended only to express your personal opinion. If you don't agree with the company's disciplinary decision, raise the issue with higher management, the human resources department, or legal counsel *before* you talk to the employee.

Takeaway Tips

➡ There's a time and place to challenge disciplinary and firing decisions you don't agree with: Before you meet with the employee, discuss it with your supervisor, human resources department, or legal counsel.

➡ If you have a problem with discipline you've been asked to impose, just try to be brief when you meet with the employee, and stick to the facts.

➡ There's nothing wrong with expressing sympathy for the employee's situation or sadness to see the employee go, as long as you don't cross the line into blaming the company for what happened. There's a difference between "I'm sorry to see you go" and "You never should have been fired."

Strategy 10: Document Everything

As a manager, you're probably already aware of the importance of documentation. It's especially important when you discipline an employee, because discipline (especially termination) can lead to lawsuits. Keeping a written record of the reasons you imposed discipline, the employee's response, and the plan of action you and the employee decided on will help you prove that you acted fairly and legally.

Documentation can also help you troubleshoot your own disciplinary decisions—and your managerial skills. For example, do you always impose the same discipline for the same offense? Are you consistent in the way you treat your reports? Do your reports seem to have similar problems, which could indicate that they need some training or other help? Could any of these problems be the result of the way you manage?

Here are some of the additional benefits of documenting discipline:

- It will help jog your memory, if you later have to explain (or testify about) why you imposed discipline.
- It will help dispel claims that you had an improper motive, such as discrimination or retaliation.
- It will help show that you gave the employee notice and a chance to improve. Most jurors are employees rather than employers, and they are very interested in whether you gave the employee a fair shake.
- It will help show that the employee was part of the process, which will take the wind out of an argument that he or she was treated unfairly or taken by surprise.

Chapter 9 explains how to document disciplinary decisions and provides a sample form you can use in preparing your own documentation.

Takeaway Tips

⮕ If you document your decisions carefully, you will help protect yourself and your company from future lawsuits.

⮕ If you don't have documents, you don't have proof. Documents are a great way to show exactly what you did and why. And a jury is going to be suspicious if you don't have any documents to back up your story.

Avoiding Legal Trouble:
Smart Summary

- You can terminate the employment of an at-will employee at any time, for any reason that isn't illegal. Don't undermine at-will employment or lock your company into a specific course of action by threatening or promising an employee certain steps in the discipline process.

- When you discipline, find out how others in the company have handled similar issues in the past. This helps you apply discipline consistently and objectively.

- If you grant leave to employees when it's not required by law, you must do it consistently among employees to avoid looking like you're "playing favorites" or worse, discriminating.

- Dangerous situations can create serious liability for the company, especially if not handled immediately. When an employee does something dangerous, act quickly to put a stop to it.

- Don't promise employees confidentiality, but maintain it when possible. Show your employees you respect their privacy and avoid defamation claims.

- Documenting your discipline decisions serves many purposes. It creates a written record of why you imposed discipline, the employee's response, and the plan of action you and the employee decide on. This may be very important if you ever have to justify your actions in a lawsuit.

Build Your Skills: An Overview of Progressive Discipline

Questions

1. When dealing with an employee problem, progressive discipline requires you to follow these steps: coaching, verbal warning, written warning, and finally, termination. ☐ True ☐ False

2. What is the main purpose of progressive discipline?

3. When disciplining an employee, you should listen to his or her side of the story, and then explain how to solve the problem.

   ☐ True ☐ False

4. Caroline catches one of her employees, Norma, violating a company dress code. Which of these factors should she consider when deciding what level of discipline is appropriate?

   a. Norma works in the food service industry and wears open-toed shoes and shorts to work, which violates health codes.

   b. Norma has never been disciplined for her attire before.

   c. Both A and B.

   d. Neither A nor B.

5. Melissa and Alejandra are caught reading magazines and chatting on the job. Melissa has been disciplined for making personal phone calls during work time; Alejandra has no previous disciplinary history. Should their boss, Ida, impose the same discipline on each of them?

   a. Yes, because they were doing the same thing.

   b. Yes, because it isn't fair to take Melissa's previous disciplinary record into account, since it was for something different.

   c. No, because Melissa has a previous disciplinary history for a similar incident, but Alejandra doesn't.

   d. No, but only if Alejandra apologizes.

6. An at-will employee can be fired at any time, for any reason.

   ☐ True   ☐ False

7. You can create a legal contract without ever writing down an agreement or making a verbal promise.   ☐ True   ☐ False

8. To motivate an employee with a performance problem, it's a good idea to tell the employee what disciplinary measure you'll impose next if the problem doesn't improve.   ☐ True   ☐ False

9. What is a reasonable accommodation?

10. Dalton calls you on Monday morning to ask if he can take the morning off to wait for a contractor; his roof started leaking during a major storm over the weekend, and he needs to have it repaired right away. Although you don't have to allow him the extra time, you understand his situation and tell him that's fine. If Michael calls you to ask for the morning off because his car has broken down and he needs to get it to a mechanic and arrange alternate transportation, which of these reasons justify treating Michael differently?

    a. Dalton has worked for you for a long time, and you trust him, whereas Michael is a new employee.

    b. Michael just took twelve weeks off under the FMLA, and you want him to start catching up on the work that piled up while he was out.

    c. Michael had plenty of time to take his car to the mechanic while he was on FMLA leave.

    d. None of the above.

Answers

1. False. Although coaching, verbal warning, written warning, and termination are the typical steps in a progressive discipline policy, whether you follow this progressive pattern will depend on different factors, including your company's policy and the seriousness of the problem. For example, if an employee steals $10,000 from the company but has never been disciplined before, company policy or common sense should tell you to terminate employment, not to coach the employee.

2. The main purpose of progressive discipline is employee retention and improvement. That means you're constantly working to help your employee meet the job's requirements—not pushing that employee toward termination.

3. False. When you discipline an employee, you should make sure you know all the facts and listen to the employee's side of the story. Once you have done so, you should work *with* the employee to collaboratively find solutions together—not to tell the employee how to solve the problem.

4. C. You should determine the seriousness of a problem—and thus what level of discipline is appropriate—by considering the problem's effect, the severity of the behavior, the employee's disciplinary history, and the legality of the behavior. Here, Norma's behavior violates health codes—a legal factor Caroline will definitely want to take into account. However, she'll also want to consider the fact that Norma's never been disciplined for this behavior before—maybe she doesn't know the rule, or maybe correcting it now can prevent it from occurring again.

5. C. While it is important to administer consistent discipline for similar problems, you should also take into account the employee's unique situation when talking with the employee about the problem. Here, Melissa has already been disciplined for making personal phone calls during work time—which means she's already been caught chatting on the job. In this case, it's fair to take that into account and to impose different discipline on the two women as a result.

6. False. An at-will employee can be fired at any time, for any reason *that isn't illegal.* For example, it is illegal to fire an at-will employee because

he or she is a certain race, has complained to a government agency about illegal behavior, or has taken a legally protected leave of absence.

7. True. Sometimes, contracts can be *implied* by statements or actions. For example, a statement like "If you complete the improvement plan, you'll become a permanent employee" could be interpreted to mean that you are promising permanent employment as long as the improvement plan is carried out. This could limit your right to fire the employee if he or she has other performance problems not addressed in the improvement plan, for example.

8. False. Telling the employee what the next step is could obligate you to provide that step, even if you later decide that a more serious action should be imposed. To maximize flexibility, focus on the immediate problem and solution—not on what might happen down the line.

9. Reasonable accommodations include assistance or changes to the job or workplace that will enable an employee with a disability to do the job. If you know an employee is disabled, your company has a legal duty to provide that employee with a reasonable accommodation to accomplish his or her job duties, so long as that won't create an undue hardship for the business (for instance, because it's so expensive that it would make it difficult for the company to keep operating).

10. D. While it's perfectly acceptable to offer extra time off when it's not legally required, if you do so, you have to be prepared to offer it on an issue-by-issue basis, not an employee-by-employee basis. Here, if you're going to allow Dalton to take time off to take care of an urgent personal matter, you should allow Michael the same. And you can't penalize Michael for taking legally protected FMLA leave.

■

Is It Time for Discipline?

Identifying Potential Problems

Y ou may have been in this situation before: You're dealing with a time-consuming discipline challenge, and suddenly you realize that there were early indications of trouble brewing, which you ignored, failed to take seriously, or weren't even aware of. While some discipline problems truly do blindside us, we often have warning signs that we just don't notice at the time. By paying closer attention, we can intervene sooner—and thereby solve the problem before it causes any real harm or requires a disciplinary solution.

If you're able to identify potential problems early, you can prevent them from becoming more serious, saving you time and avoiding stress. In this chapter, we'll explain the three types of employee problems, so you'll know what to look for. Then we'll discuss methods to identify, and ideally prevent, these problems, including:

- setting clear expectations
- communicating openly with your employees, and
- looking for specific signs of trouble.

Knowing What to Look For: The Three Types of Employee Problems

No two employees are alike, and neither are any two employee problems. Each issue you face will involve slightly different facts. However, virtually all employee problems fit into these three categories:

- poor performance
- attendance problems (absenteeism and tardiness), or
- misconduct.

Some employees have a problem in only one of these areas. For example, an employee who is often late might do excellent work and behave appropriately once he finally shows up. Similarly, an employee might have a perfect attendance record and follow every workplace rule but have difficulty completing work on time. Identifying the type of problem the employee is having will help you keep your conversation focused and come up with an effective solution for that specific issue. It will also allow you to emphasize what the employee is doing well, which should help you encourage the employee to improve his or her problem area.

EXAMPLE: Reed is an editor for a weekly news magazine. His manager, Bernadette, needs to coach him about an attendance problem. Because Reed is an otherwise excellent editor, Bernadette starts the conversation like this: "Reed, I need to talk to you about a problem I've noticed. A couple of times a week, you return late from lunch by ten or fifteen minutes. Your editing is excellent, you get your work done quickly, and you're always willing to help other editors with their stories. These are all great qualities, but the long lunches are causing some resentment among your coworkers and holding us back. When you're late, we have to either start the afternoon story meeting without you or wait for you to return. As a result, we either don't get your input on the stories—which is too bad, because I really value your opinion—or we have to kill time waiting for you to show up."

Unfortunately, some employees have a problem in one area that causes problems in others. For example, an employee who spends a lot of work time sending personal email messages to friends and surfing the Internet (misconduct) might also have trouble getting his or her job done (poor performance) as a result. In these situations, your disciplinary efforts will be effective only if you can identify and deal with the underlying issue. In the Internet example, the employee's performance isn't going to improve until you get him or her offline. You should certainly point out that the employee's Internet use is causing performance problems and that the employee must show improvement there. But you won't be able to come up with an action plan that will really turn things around until you identify the underlying issue.

EXAMPLE: Let's use the example of the employee who spends too much time online, discussed above. Kristen is the employee, a secretary in an accounting firm; Roger is her manager. When Roger meets with Kristen, he might start by saying, "Kristen, I've noticed that when I walk by your workstation, you're often using your private email account or visiting websites that don't seem to be work-related. Two other partners have mentioned this to me, as well. And since we set up Internet access for you, you have missed two important deadlines and fallen behind in some of your basic responsibilities, like filing and returning telephone calls. As you know, company policy restricts personal use of the Internet, except during breaks and other nonworking hours. It seems like your Internet use is affecting your performance, and we need to deal with this right away."

Here are the three basic types of employee problems, with some examples that will help you quickly identify the particular issue you're facing.

Poor Performance

When an employee fails to perform to set expectations, meet his or her goals, operate with the quality required for the position, or fulfill his or her job responsibilities, you have a performance problem. Typical performance problems include:

- missing deadlines (failing to complete assignments or hand in work on time)
- missing productivity targets or other numerical goals (such as failing to make a required number of calls per day or failing to meet sales quotas)
- poor work quality (such as handing in written assignments that are missing important information or contain errors, creating faulty products, or providing poor service to customers and clients)
- failure to follow through (for example, not returning phone calls or responding to email messages in a timely manner, or not completing the proper paperwork), and
- communication problems (such as failing to touch base with other team members working on a project, difficulties interacting with clients or customers, or failure to keep you informed of important developments—any of these issues might rise to the level of misconduct if the employee is rude or insubordinate or if the noncommunication prevents the work from getting done).

What constitutes poor performance depends the job's requirements. For example, a bookkeeper whose job consists entirely of paying bills and tracking company expenses needs good math skills, but might not need exceptional writing or customer service skills. On the other hand, a bookkeeper who also handles collection activities needs to be able to communicate well with customers, on the phone and in writing, to succeed at the job.

What About Personal Problems?

As we all know, it can be tough to do a good job at work when you're worried about trouble at home. A failing relationship, trouble with one's kids, money problems, a seriously ill friend or relative, and other personal problems can make it hard to concentrate on the job and lead to performance issues.

So what can a manager do when an employee is having a personal problem that is affecting his or her performance? First of all, listen. Hear the employee out and express your sympathy. If your company has an employee assistance program (EAP) that might be able to help, offer the employee a referral. If the employee needs to spend some time away from work (for example, to attend therapy sessions) or make a temporary change to his or her schedule (to take a friend to chemotherapy, perhaps), consider whether you can accommodate that need without causing disruption to your operations. Also, explain any leave to which the employee may be entitled, such as a personal leave of absence, bereavement leave, or family medical leave.

As you try to help the employee deal with his or her immediate situation, however, don't lose sight of the fact that the company's work needs to get done with a minimally acceptable level of performance When you talk to the employee, make it clear that the employee needs to figure out a way to do his or her job, even though personal issues are making that difficult. If the employee is unable to improve after you have discussed the issue and made whatever changes you can to the employee's schedule and workload, it's time to move into the disciplinary system.

Attendance Problems

Attendance problems occur when an employee is absent or tardy in violation of company policy. Absenteeism problems arise when employees either exceed their allotment of days off or don't follow required procedures for taking time off. For example, it might violate company policy for an employee to take several sick days without providing a doctor's note, or to take a vacation day without getting permission in advance from a manager. Missed work days result in work not getting done and deadlines not being met.

Some employees don't take entire days off but persist in showing up late, taking long breaks, returning late from lunch, or leaving early. If your employee is required (by the nature of his or her position, or company policy) to work particular hours, and he or she does not meet those requirements, then it will no doubt affect the job. For instance, a receptionist who is supposed to be the face of the company and greet every visitor cannot be repeatedly late for his or her job. This would leave the post unstaffed and the visitors ungreeted.

Misconduct

An employee commits misconduct when he or she violates a workplace rule; treats other employees, customers, clients, or you with disrespect; acts dishonestly; or otherwise behaves inappropriately in the workplace. Unlike poor performance, which involves an employee's failure to work up to your expectations, misconduct often involves the employee's failure to meet company policies or standards of polite behavior, in his or her dealings with other people or with the company itself.

Common types of misconduct include:
- violation of safety rules
- failing to meet dress code, uniform, or grooming requirements
- horseplay
- fighting
- insubordination
- misuse of company property
- harassment
- discrimination
- theft
- excessive personal use of company email, Internet access, phones, vehicles, and so on
- sleeping on the job
- use of alcohol or illegal use of drugs at work, and
- dishonesty.

How to Spot Employee Problems

Once you know what to look for, you can implement techniques to spot employee problems early. While these problems will be obvious once they become full-scale disasters, you might not know how to look for problems in the early stages, before they jump out at you. Here are some techniques that will help.

Set Clear Expectations

One way to identify and prevent problems is to set very clear expectations for your employees. This serves two purposes: It prevents problems by letting employees understand what is expected of them, and it helps you recognize problems by giving you an objective standard by which to measure performance and conduct.

Human resource experts tell us that the number one reason employees fail to meet their employer's expectations isn't that they're lazy, incompetent, or spiteful. Employees don't meet expectations primarily because they don't know what those expectations are. This means that you can reap great benefits—and avoid having to discipline employees in the future—by being very clear about what you and the company expect, right from the start. It also means that you must jump in and correct problems at the first sign of trouble, so you can make sure your employees understand what you want and have a fair opportunity to meet your expectations.

Define Expectations

Many discipline problems start out as simple misunderstandings between manager and employee about what the manager expects to be done and when. Setting clear expectations avoids these mishaps, but it requires deliberate effort on your part. Before you begin communicating your expectations to your team, you need to spend some time clearly defining what your expectations are.

Performance Expectations

Performance management begins with setting goals for your employees. As part of your performance appraisal process, you should sit down with new employees to review job requirements (what you expect anyone holding that job to accomplish) and set performance goals (developmental goals designed to nurture the employee's strengths, work on weaknesses, and build skills).

If you have a job description that lays out the essential functions of the position, that will give you a place to start. Before you meet with the employee, you should review the job description and make a list of the job's requirements.

> **EXAMPLE:** Corey just accepted a position as customer service representative at a call center for a software company. His manager, Judy, meets with him to discuss her performance expectations. Based on the job description for the position, Judy tells Corey that the job requirements are:
>
> - to answer telephone calls from customers with questions or concerns about the company's products
> - to deal with customers in a courteous, cheerful manner
> - to answer an average of at least 20 calls per day
> - to complete required paperwork on customer complaints
> - to process refunds on a same-day basis
> - to pass customers on to Judy if the representative does not know how to handle the customer's issue, and
> - to be at work and available to answer phones from 6 a.m. to 2:30 p.m., Monday through Friday.

Don't forget to explain why. When you tell employees exactly what the job requires, also let them know the purpose of these requirements. Employees are more likely to meet your expectations—and excel in their jobs—if they know why their efforts are important to the company. In the example above, Judy could tell Corey, "Our company distinguishes itself, in part, by its excellent customer service. By answering every call right away and handling complaints and refunds on a same-day basis, we let our customers know that we really value their business."

When you meet with the employee, you should collaborate to come up with some specific performance goals as well. Unlike job requirements, which must be met by everyone who holds that position, performance goals are tailored to each employee individually, to reflect things he or she would like to improve or capitalize on.

EXAMPLE: Judy also wants to develop some performance goals for Corey. She knows, from interviewing Corey and reading his resume, that he is interested in polishing up his Spanish language skills. Because a good portion of the company's customers speak Spanish as a first language, Judy tells Corey that she would like for him to take a Spanish class, with an emphasis on learning technical terms, so he can handle some calls in Spanish. Corey agrees to this goal, which they write as follows:

"Within the next month, Corey will enroll in a Spanish class that includes computer terminology. The company will pay for the class, and Corey may take time off work to attend, if necessary. Within three months, Corey will handle an average of one call in Spanish per work day."

Human resource professionals often use the acronym SMART to define good performance goals:

- **S**pecific: Each goal needs to focus on a very precise task.
- **M**easurable: Each goal must provide an objective means to measure success, such as a completion date, hourly rate, productivity number, or dollar figure.
- **A**chievable: If you set unrealistic goals, not only will the employee not achieve them, he or she might be too discouraged to even try.
- **R**elevant: Each goal should relate to the job's duties and the employee's skills, giving the employee the opportunity to develop professionally.
- **T**ime sensitive: Goals should have deadlines, or they might get lost in the shuffle.

Once you have specified the job requirements and agreed upon performance goals, write them down and give a copy to the employee. This will give both of you a way to measure whether the employee is meeting your expectations. You can use the document to evaluate the employee throughout the year, so you will know right away if the employee's performance starts to slip. You can use it to create the employee's performance appraisal. You can also use it as a starting point to develop goals for the next year.

This is a very brief introduction to a very rich and sometimes complex topic. For help drafting job descriptions and using them as a tool to develop performance expectations, see *The Job Description Handbook*, by Margie Mader-Clark (Nolo). For detailed information on setting and documenting performance objectives, evaluating employee performance, and giving performance feedback throughout the year, see *The Performance Appraisal Handbook*, by Amy DelPo (Nolo).

Behavioral Expectations

Typically, behavioral standards are prescribed by company policy or codes of conduct. For example, your company's employee handbook probably includes rules about professional conduct, harassment, use of safety equipment, dealing with customers, dress codes, and more.

However, if you have expectations of your team that go beyond these basic rules, you must communicate them. Many times, managers have unwritten or unspoken expectations. Sometimes, these expectations may seem so obvious to you that you don't explain them to your team. When thinking about what you expect, consider:

- **How you want your team to work together.** Some managers encourage employees to use each other as resources (to answer questions, provide alternate perspectives, or verify intended courses of action), even when they're not working together on a project. Others prefer that an employee facing a challenge take it right to management for guidance or direction.
- **Timeframe for responses.** If you want phone calls returned or emails answered within a certain timeframe, communicate that to your employees. If it varies based on audience—whether the communication is to you, coworkers, clients, or others—you must explain that expectation as well.
- **Desired work hours.** If you need or want to see your employees at their desks at a particular time, let them know.
- **Resolving differences.** If you want your employees to work to solve problems amongst themselves before bringing them to you, you need to tell them. Likewise, let them know when you expect to be involved.

- **Staying in touch with you.** Are you an email person, do you prefer voicemail, or do you like to mainly discuss things in person? Tell your employees how you like to be contacted.

Likewise, as you think about what you expect of your employees, remember to be consistent in how you treat each of them. It is difficult for employees to understand appropriate behavior when you set double standards. For example, a manager may be friendly with one employee and exchange jokes or personal stories. If that same manager tries to limit that kind of behavior between other employees, though, frustration and confusion will often result.

Lead by example. It's not fair to hold employees to minimum professional standards that you don't meet yourself. If you expect punctuality, you must be punctual. If professional dress is important to you, you must dress professionally. "Do as I say, not as I do" is never an effective leadership strategy.

Sometimes, there are important reasons to maintain different behavioral standards for different employees. For example, you may expect employees who have direct contact with the public, such as receptionists or salespeople, to dress in business attire or put clients at ease with light banter or joking. On the other hand, you may expect employees who work in a warehouse setting to follow safety regulations that don't apply to others, requiring hard hats and limiting joking and horseplay.

While having these different standards is acceptable, make sure they are based on the needs of the job and not on your relationships with the employees. Moreover, you need to communicate to your team why the rules differ. While these reasons may be obvious to you, don't assume the same is true for your employees.

Communicate Expectations to Your Team

Once you have set expectations for performance and behavior, you'll need to communicate them to your team. While you will discuss the details with each employee, particularly for specific performance goals, here is an exercise you can perform with everyone together that will get you started. It will help you understand what your employees currently believe your expectations are and how you have communicated those expectations. It will give you an opportunity to learn about the messages you're sending, consciously or unconsciously, and correct and clarify misconceptions.

After you have had the opportunity to do this group activity, follow it up with individual sessions with each of your employees. At that time, discuss the specific expectations you have for each individual. When communicating expectations, the clearer you are the better. For example, telling an employee "I expect you to finish this project on a reasonable timeline" doesn't give the employee any real idea of when the project needs to be done. "Reasonable" to you could be the next day, and if the employee doesn't complete the project by then, he or she will have let you down without knowing it. However, giving the employee an objective deadline, such as "I expect you to complete the project by next Friday" makes it possible for the employee to meet your goal (or, at least, to let you know if he or she might have trouble doing so).

Follow up the conversation with a written confirmation of those expectations, even in an informal format like email, so that you can make sure you and the employee are on the same page. Be sure that the employee knows he or she needs to inform you if the expectations are unclear or can't be met. Continue to reevaluate your expectations, accounting for the changing needs of the organization, developing skills of the employee, and shifts in team goals.

When you set clear expectations and communicate those to your employees, problems will stick out like a sore thumb. After all, if everyone in your organization knows what is expected, it will be obvious when an employee is not pulling his or her weight. And, because you've already told the employee what you expect, you can discipline quickly and confidently, knowing that the employee won't be surprised to learn that he or she is falling short.

Communicate With Your Employees

One of the best ways to learn about problems is to hear about them directly from your employees. After all, employees who are struggling often want the help or intervention of management, even if they don't always know how or want to ask for it. Moreover, if your team understands that you want to be informed about potential problems,

Skills Enhancement 1: Setting Expectations

Allow 90 minutes to two hours and gather your team in a room with a large writing area (whiteboard or paper posted on the walls). Designate a scribe who will capture everything the team comes up with (you may choose to use an outside facilitator for that task). Tell your team that you are leaving the room for 30 minutes, and during that time, they should write down every question that they can think of relating to you as a manager, such as:

- How do you prefer to communicate with your employees?
- What is your management style?
- When will we know we did a good job?
- When will we know we did a bad job?
- And so on.

You may choose to open up these questions to things your employees may want to know about you as a person—such as your favorite foods or colors or what you like to do with your free time.

After 30 minutes, reenter the room. For the next hour or so, answer each of the questions posed by the group. If there are other important details that you want to communicate to everyone about your expectations, take the opportunity to build on the discussion and share that information.

they'll know to flag them for you when they come up. You can ensure they do this by:

- establishing regular one-on-one communication
- fostering open communication, and
- building a culture of ownership.

Establish Regular One-On-One Communication

"One-on–ones"—regular meetings in which you check in individually with each of your direct reports—keep you up to speed on what employees are doing, how they are doing, and whether any issues require your attention or intervention. For example, an employee can notify you if he or she isn't going to meet a deadline, is struggling with a project, or is having trouble with a coworker.

Ideally, you should meet regularly—perhaps once a week—with each employee that reports to you. Treating these sessions as an ongoing commitment, not a one-time aberration, will not only give you valuable and regular information about the state of your business, but also lets your team know that you are invested in them and committed to their success. They will be accustomed to sharing the status of their work, the challenges they face, and how the team is doing as a whole.

If you're not already meeting with your employees this way, sitting down the first time might feel awkward, for both you and the employee. After all, employees who aren't used to dealing with the boss may think they're in trouble if they get called in. To prevent this from happening—and gossip from spreading—let each report know that you plan to do regular check-ins. Make sure you know something about each person's projects, so you can ask questions about the progress on those projects. As the process becomes more familiar, employees will be ready to fill you on how things are going before you even ask.

You'll quickly be attuned to warning signs of potential problems during these sessions, too. You will notice if there are changes in an employee's behavior—perhaps a formerly forthcoming employee will be reluctant to talk about workload, or a normally positive employee will become sullen, despondent, or angry. Likewise, if you meet with employees regularly and know their schedules, you'll know when deadlines are in danger of being missed and when deliverables are slipping.

Of course, not every employee is the same; one may finish projects far ahead of deadline, while another finishes only at the last minute, for example. As long as the work gets done well and on time without impacting others, neither approach calls for discipline. Spending time with each of your employees allows you to get to know their various work styles. Once you have a baseline, you'll be able to see changes to their usual style and performance, which will clue you in to trouble that may be brewing.

> **EXAMPLE:** Stephen manages a small regional office for a large national mortgage broker. He has four brokers reporting to him, as well as a client group for whom he works directly. Stephen has structured half-hour meetings every week with each of his direct reports. Here is the typical agenda for these meetings:
>
> Ten minutes: Business update—number and amount of loans, potential close dates.
>
> Ten minutes: Forecasting—monthly and annually.
>
> Five minutes: Prospecting—potential new business.
>
> Five minutes: Resources and problems—anything the employee needs to do a better job, or barriers the employee is facing that Stephen can help remove.
>
> At the conclusion of each thirty-minute meeting, Stephen understands what is going on with each employee on his team.

Foster Open Communication

Have you ever heard senior managers whispering to each other in the break room? Do you wonder what is going on when your boss shuts his or her office door? Do you sometimes learn about new policies, developments, or company directions from gossip rather than through official channels? If the answer to any of these questions is "yes," you probably know how debilitating closed, secretive communication can be to the work environment.

Of course, there are perfectly valid reasons to communicate privately, and not every person at a company can be privy to every decision and conversation. But too much secrecy sends a message that says, "I am keeping things from you," or "You are not important enough for me to speak with directly." If you send your reports implicit messages like these, you can be certain that they you'll get the same in return. That means even if your employees are aware of problems, they won't share that information with you—and you'll lose out on valuable opportunities to nip problems in the bud.

On the other hand, if you communicate directly with the people who report to you, they'll recognize that you see their insights and participation as valuable and fundamental to the team's success. That means they'll work to keep you informed about what's going on.

There are several ways you can make sure you are fostering open communication with your employees. These include:

- **Meet regularly with your entire team.** This will send the message that you all work together, and that you solve problems together. It will help all of you keep abreast of the status of each others' workloads and provide a platform to discuss departmental and company-wide goals or problems.

- **Keep the closed door to a minimum.** If you are having a private meeting, keep the door shut. However, if you can be interrupted, stay accessible by keeping the door open and encouraging your employees to talk to you as needed.

- **Treat all team members professionally.** It's natural that you might feel more comfortable with some team members than with others. However, be aware of the perception developing those relationships can create: that you're "playing favorites." Be particularly careful about talking to your employees about each other, even in a strictly professional context.

- **Keep your employees informed about what you're doing.** Avoid resentment by keeping your team informed about what you're up to, too. They'll appreciate that it's a two-way street.

Build a Culture of Ownership

Another way to keep the lines of communication open with your employees is to create a "culture of ownership": An environment where each employee feels responsible for the company's success and takes personal responsibility for both accomplishments and failures. Creating this type of culture gives employees an incentive to share their concerns, because their own success will depend on the success of the company.

If your company offers employees real ownership, through benefits like stock options and profit-sharing plans, that will certainly help. But there are many other ways to create a culture of shared ownership. The best way to start is by making sure that each of your employees understands how he or she fits into the big picture—that is, how doing his or her job well helps the company succeed. Aligning individual goals directly to the company's goals, rewarding performance that supports the company's direction, and engaging your employees in coming up with business solutions are all ways to create shared ownership.

Use the chart below to identify some specific opportunities to create shared ownership in your own company:

	Hierarchy	Shared Ownership
Setting Goals	Manager delegates tasks to be completed within a certain timeframe.	Team looks at shared goals and determines roles and timelines together.
Briefing Upper Management	Manager creates a PowerPoint slide show on team accomplishments and presents it to senior management.	Each team member creates slides showcasing his or her areas of responsibility, and the team presents the slide show to senior management together.
Hiring	The manager tells the team that a new employee has been hired just before—or even after—that person starts work.	The team participates in creating the job description and the interview process and has input on the hiring decision.
Budgeting	Each quarter, employees are told how much money they can spend and what they can spend it on during the next three months.	Each quarter, each employee submits budget requests for proposed projects that include a cost/benefit analysis explaining why the project should be considered.

When you give employees a sense of ownership, you are much more likely to find out about problems and opportunities early. Employees who feel a sense of ownership care about the success of the team as a whole, so they're going to tell you when they think something will inhibit the team. This gives you the opportunity to look into problems that you otherwise might not even have known about.

⚠ **Encourage teamwork, not backstabbing.** Some employees view an information-sharing environment as an invitation to monitor and criticize their coworkers, particularly if each employee's performance will be judged, in part, by how well the team does as a whole. Fostering shared ownership does not mean building a culture where employees try to throw each other under the bus at the first sign of trouble. Make clear to your team that they must work together to accomplish their collective goals and that each team member has a unique contribution to make.

Look for Signs of Trouble

Sometimes, the hardest part of identifying employee problems or potential problems is seeing the signs of trouble that precede them. While communicating with your employees gives you an opportunity to identify problems, you also need to know what specific conduct might signify that trouble is brewing.

Signs of trouble can be categorized in the following ways:
- declining performance
- changed behavior, or
- tension in your team.

Essentially, you should be looking for changes in the way your employees conduct themselves. This means you have to understand how your employees act and behave under normal circumstances, so you can recognize changes when they occur.

Declining Performance

When an employee has a drastic drop in output or suddenly misses every deadline, it's easy to see that there's a problem. Much more difficult to recognize are problems that begin with subtle changes in the performance of a normally good employee. It is easy to ignore declining performance if it is not typical for an employee. You may even be tempted to rationalize away the decline because you don't want to come down too hard on someone who usually does a good job.

> **EXAMPLE:** Justin has been with ABC Mills for four years. His performance reviews show he is one of the highest performers in the company. As a result, his boss, Mary, has made him one of her "go-to" guys. She gives him a large number of complex projects and knows that she can rely on him to get them done.
>
> Justin is fast approaching a project milestone. He needs to have a complete analysis of the milling process documented by Friday, so Mary's team can begin the next phase of the project: looking for ways to streamline and improve the process. Mary meets with Justin on Friday, confident that she will be seeing the process analysis. Justin tells Mary that the analysis is not quite finished and asks for a few more days. She gives him another week.
>
> Mary has complete confidence in Justin, so much so that she neglects to ask him a very important question: Why is he having trouble getting the project milestone done? Her confidence in him is not allowing her to consider that he may need help with the project or that there may be other forces at play that are preventing him from meeting his deadlines.

When an employee's performance declines, make sure you understand why. Talk to the employee about it as soon as you recognize it. If the employee is overworked or overwhelmed, you may need to decrease his or her workload or get additional help or training. On the other hand, if there are no good reasons for the changes, you may need to begin the progressive discipline process.

Changes in Behavior

After you've worked with your employees for awhile, you'll get to know quite a bit about their work styles and personalities. One employee may be naturally extroverted, talking to you and other employees about every aspect of the job. Another may be quiet or shy, reluctant to disturb anyone unnecessarily.

But when an employee's behavior begins to change, you should immediately question why. There can be many different reasons: It may signal that the employee is unhappy with the work environment, coworkers, or the workload. In other instances, it may be related to issues at home. The behavior changes that you need to address are those that either are inappropriate for the workplace or have the possibility of negatively affecting the employee's performance.

Behavioral changes that are warning signs of potential problems include:

- **Withdrawal.** An employee's participation in group meetings, one-on-ones, or other team gatherings decreases.
- **Quick to anger or frustration.** An employee seems to be set off by the smallest things or is easily frustrated.
- **Excessive absenteeism or tardiness.** An employee is out of the office more than normal or shows up later than usual.
- **Discomfort or tension.** An employee who normally seems comfortable interacting with you seems ill at ease around you, and maybe even avoids you.

These are just a few of the changes in behavior that may signal more-serious problems. As mentioned, any unexplained negative change in behavior can be cause for concern. The follow-up step for you whenever you observe a negative behavior change is simple: Talk to the employee. Explain what you see and give examples. Find out if the employee realizes that his or her behavior has changed. Sometimes, an employee isn't aware that his or her thoughts or feelings are being communicated. Other times, the employee may need to discuss the problems or get additional help. He or she may appreciate that you noticed the change.

Tension in the Team

Sometimes, potential problems will manifest themselves not in individual performance or behavior, but in team performance or behavior. At times, your team may operate like a well-oiled machine, everyone knowing the importance of his or her individual role and the role of the team as a whole. At other times, friction may enter the machine and cause the parts to grind together. Employees may treat each other differently, or team objectives may not be met.

When you see this friction, find its source. It may be the pressure of a lot of work or something more insidious, such as a team member who is working against the others. To figure this out, you may have to ask different team members for their perspectives, until you get a full picture.

> **EXAMPLE:** Jerry manages a team of carpenters who are building a custom home on a tight deadline. At the end of each day, the team has a ten-minute status meeting to monitor overall progress. Because steps in the process must be completed in a very specific order—for example, the roof must be laid before the floor is—these meetings keep the team communicating and ensures that they stay on the project timeline.
>
> During a status meeting one day, Jerry notices that the normal joking and teasing amongst the team is not occurring, and that everyone seems sullen or uncomfortable. After the meeting is over, Jerry asks Mike, one of the natural leaders on the team, to stay behind. "What's going on, Mike?" Jerry asks. "It seemed like folks weren't themselves today." Mike is quiet a moment, then replies, "You probably want to ask Leslie that question." Jerry digs deeper and discovers that Leslie has showed up late for three straight days and asked the team not to tell Jerry. Because this could delay the overall project, the team had grown increasingly uncomfortable about having to cover for Leslie.

As this example illustrates, team tension may signal not only problems for the team as a cohesive unit, but problems for individual employees as well. Although the whole team was delayed, the problem here was really Leslie's—and Jerry might not have discovered the problem if he hadn't taken the time to follow up on changed behavior in other team members.

If your employees seem to have trouble working together, and either perform or behave in a way that is unfamiliar and uncomfortable, be sure to find out why. You'd rather know before the problem gets serious, and you're fortunate to have easy access to the very people—your employees—who know this information.

Identifying Potential Problems: Smart Summary

○ There are three broad categories of employee problems: performance problems, attendance problems, and misconduct. Sometimes, an employee will have trouble in one of these areas, and it will affect another. In those instances, make sure your discipline addresses the root of the problem.

○ If your employees don't know what your expectations are, they're likely to disappoint you. Take the time to define your expectations of performance and behavior, giving your employees full opportunity to grow and succeed.

○ Communicating regularly and openly with your employees keeps you up to speed on how they're doing and gives you advance warning of possible problems. At the same time, it gives employees a sense of ownership and investment in their jobs, motivating them to succeed.

○ To help spot employee problems, look for signs of trouble like declining performance, changed behavior, and tension between team members.

Deciding What Action to Take

O nce an employee issue comes to your attention, you must decide whether and how to intervene. In some instances, discipline might not be the right response—you might decide instead to make a note to yourself to monitor the situation or even reconsider the wisdom of a particular rule or policy. Even if you know you'll have to take action (for example, because an employee has made a serious mistake, engaged in obvious misconduct, or been counseled about the same problem already), you'll have to decide what type of corrective measure to use.

In many cases, the appropriate corrective measure is immediately obvious. For extreme misconduct, such as blatant harassment, theft, or violence, termination of employment is often appropriate. For first-time performance issues or minor misconduct, you will typically want to follow each disciplinary measure in your company's policy in sequence, starting with the least serious (coaching, in our model policy). However, there are plenty of employee problems that fall somewhere between these two extremes. And sometimes, you're faced with one employee who exhibits a number of failings, all of which add up to one big problem.

This chapter will help you figure out whether discipline is appropriate in your situation and, if so, what disciplinary measure to use. We'll explain how to decide whether discipline is in order, gauge the effect and seriousness of the problem you're facing, and use that information to come up with the right disciplinary response.

Is Discipline Appropriate?

Before you think about what type of disciplinary measure might be appropriate, you have to decide whether to discipline at all. In some situations, it might not be fair—or legally defensible—to hold an employee responsible for a workplace problem.

To make this decision, you must be able to answer three questions:
1. Did the employee know of the performance, conduct, or other standard that was violated?
2. Did the employee actually violate that standard?
3. Did the employee have a legal right to do so?

In many cases, the answers to these questions will be obvious. For example, let's say you tell an employee to complete an assignment by the end of the month. The employee misses the deadline by a few days and tells you that she's late because she didn't realize how long the assignment would take. Your performance expectations were clear, the employee didn't meet them, and nothing in her explanation demonstrates that she had a legally protected right to blow the deadline. This is probably all you need to know before moving on to consider the severity of the problem and choose a disciplinary response.

In some situations, however, you'll need more information to decide whether discipline is appropriate. What you learn may convince you that there isn't a problem after all—or that the problem really lies with you, the company, or another employee, not with the employee whom you originally thought was at fault.

Did the Employee Know the Rule?

Start by taking a close look at the policy, rule, or standard that appears to have been violated. Did the employee know what you, or the company, expected? As long as the employee was aware of the rule that applied here, it's fair to impose discipline for violating it. On the other hand, if the rule was not obvious, not communicated, not achievable, not consistently applied, or not clear, discipline is probably not a fair response.

Here are some guidelines to determine whether the employee knew—or should have known—that his or her behavior could result in discipline:

- **Written company policies.** Did the employee's conduct violate company policy, as expressed in the employee handbook or other documents distributed to employees?
- **Company practices and procedures.** Did the employee violate a rule or custom known in the workplace, even if not written down?
- **Your instructions.** Did you tell the employee what you required—for example, deadlines for a project, numerical goals or quotas, quality standards, or dress code requirements?
- **Job requirements.** Did the employee understand what to do based on, for example, the job description or orientation process?

- **Performance goals.** Did the employee's performance appraisals or discussions with you about performance state the company's expectations?
- **The law.** Are the employee's actions illegal? If, for example, the employee committed unlawful harassment, stole from the company or its customers, or threatened to harm someone, the employee has violated the law.
- **Common sense.** Was the employee's behavior obviously inappropriate or dangerous, even if it isn't illegal or explicitly prohibited by company policies?

EXAMPLE: Sam is upset with Scott, the warehouse manager, who recently gave him a lukewarm performance appraisal. Sam decides to get back at Scott by playing a prank. He comes in on the weekend, moves all of the furniture and decorations out of Scott's office, and recreates the office on the warehouse floor. Sam's joke disrupts an entire shift of work and creates a hazard for the other warehouse employees; it's also very disrespectful of Scott's authority and personal space. Although this probably isn't illegal, and most companies don't expressly prohibit relocating someone else's workspace, Sam should be disciplined.

If you conclude that the employee had fair notice of the possible consequences of his or her behavior, you can move on to the next step. If not, however, you might have to plan some training, try harder to communicate your expectations, or enforce the rules more consistently. This will lay the groundwork for discipline if the rule is violated in the future—or perhaps even prevent problems in the first place, because your employees will better understand your expectations and the consequences of violating them.

EXAMPLE: Jeanette is heading to a meeting and is waiting impatiently for the agenda to show up on the department's printer. Jeanette has to wait through someone else's print job, a scholarly article on the Amazon rainforest. Because the company produces database software, Jeanette knows the article is not work related.

Sarah, one of Jeanette's reports, shows up to get the article. When Jeanette asks what it's for, Sarah says that her husband, an anthropology student, asked her to print it out for him. Jeanette says, "Sarah, you know that our employee handbook says you can't use company property for personal reasons."

Sarah is flustered, and replies, "Oh, I didn't know that applied to the printer. It seems like everyone uses the printer to print party invitations, directions, and other personal stuff, so I figured it was okay to print this."

Thinking about it, Jeanette realizes Sarah is right. She also realizes she has used the printer and copier for personal items herself. Jeanette decides not to discipline Sarah—in fact, she realizes it wasn't really fair to reprimand her, given the confusion over what the company's policy means. She stops by Sarah's office and says, "You know, Sarah, you're right. The company is sending mixed signals about printer use and it's leading to confusion. I was especially concerned today because I was waiting for an important document and it was delayed because of personal use. I'll talk to human resources so we can figure out what the policy is for everyone." Jeanette then consults with the human resources department to clarify what the policy requires. Once the policy is clarified, Jeanette explains it to her reports and enforces that interpretation consistently.

Did the Employee Violate the Rule?

Once you've determined that the employee knew of your—or the company's—expectations, you must consider whether a particular employee's performance or conduct actually fell short of the mark. To answer this question, you might have to investigate the situation to make sure that you know exactly what happened—that is, that wrongdoing actually occurred and that the employee you plan to discipline is actually responsible for it.

Whenever you are uncertain about key facts, you should investigate. This comes up most often when there is employee misconduct, particularly if anonymous wrongdoing occurs (for example, racist graffiti shows up in the company washroom or an unpopular manager's car is keyed in the parking lot) or if one employee accuses another of harassment, intimidation, or other interpersonal misconduct. In these situations, you'll need to talk to the employees involved, examine any related documents or other evidence, and reach a conclusion as to what actually happened.

Need information on how to investigate? Download *Workplace Investigations*, by Lisa Guerin (Nolo), available at www.nolo.com. It includes step-by-step instructions on investigating misconduct and other problems, with special emphasis on harassment, discrimination, theft, and violence. The book also includes detailed information on how to conduct interviews, gather evidence, decide what to do, and document your findings.

On rare occasions, however, you might have to investigate a performance or attendance issue, too. Again, these occasions typically involve more than one employee. For example, if two employees are known not to get along, and one accuses the other of taking frequent long breaks, you might want to investigate (by keeping an eye on the employee accused of loafing or by talking to both employees) before you decide to discipline. Similarly, if you assigned a project to a team of employees, they might blame each other for missing important deadlines. You might have to sit down with each team member to get to the bottom of things.

Did the Employee Have a Legal Right to Break the Rule?

You may not discipline an employee who violates a workplace rule or standard because he or she is exercising a legal right. For example, an employee has the legal right to take time off for jury duty. If all of your employees are required to go to an important training session on a particular day, and an employee is unable to attend because of jury duty, you may not discipline that employee for failing to show up.

Here are a few situations when an employee might have a legal right to violate a workplace rule or requirement:

- **The employee takes time off for a legally protected reason.** As explained above, you may not discipline an employee for taking legally protected leave, even if the employee is absent longer than your policies ordinarily allow or misses important events as a result. See Chapter 3 for more information on legally protected time off.

- **The employee refuses to work because of unsafe conditions.** Employees have a legal right, pursuant to the Occupational Safety and Health Act (OSH Act), to refuse to work if they believe that they are in imminent danger of serious harm or death due to workplace conditions or procedures. Employees may exercise this right only if the employer refuses to correct the condition and there's no time to address the condition by making a complaint to the Occupational Safety and Health Administration (OSHA).

- **The employee refuses to participate in illegal conduct.** Many states allow employees to sue their current or former employers if they are disciplined or fired for refusing to do something illegal. For example, if an employee is disciplined or fired for refusing to make false statements to the government or misstate the company's income on shareholder documents, that employee probably has a pretty good legal claim against the company.

- **The employee is entitled to a reasonable accommodation.** As explained in Chapter 3, an employee with a disability may be entitled to a reasonable accommodation, which might include bending the usual attendance rules. For example, an employee who is taking antidepressants that make him groggy in the morning might ask to come in to work a couple of hours later. Even if your company requires everyone to report to work at 9:00 a.m., it might be reasonable to allow one person to come in a bit later.

You can find more information on these legal protections in Chapter 3.

How Serious Is the Problem?

Now you know what type of problem you're facing, and you've decided that corrective action is appropriate. Your next step is to figure out how serious the problem is so that you can choose an appropriate disciplinary response: One that communicates the importance of the problem and demonstrates the company's concern with getting it resolved.

Even if you know what disciplinary measure you will use—because it's dictated by company policy, for example—you should still review this section and consider each of the factors listed below. Your meeting with the employee will be more productive if you've organized your thoughts and can explain how the employee's behavior is causing problems for the company and why things need to change. This information will help the employee take responsibility for his or her actions—and help both of you come up with an effective solution.

Here are some factors to consider when analyzing how serious a problem is (each is explained in detail below):

- the effect of the behavior
- the frequency of the behavior
- the employee's disciplinary history, and
- the legality of the behavior.

Effect

How has the employee's misconduct, poor performance, or attendance problem affected the company? Because progressive discipline requires a proportionate response, a problem that has caused major damage should be met with a more serious disciplinary measure than a problem that has had very little impact on anyone.

Here are some things to consider when analyzing how a problem has affected the company:

- **Cost.** How much money has been spent—or how much money has the business not earned—because of the employee's behavior? Putting a price on the employee's behavior will really help the employee see why things need to change.
- **Time.** How much time have you and other employees had to spend dealing with the employee's problem? For example, have coworkers had to put their work aside to cover for a tardy employee or finish a project the employee failed to complete?
- **Lost opportunities.** Sometimes, an employee's behavior botches a future sale, partnership, or other business opportunity.
- **Damage to relationships.** Has the employee's behavior caused tension on your team or soured interactions with a customer or client? Has morale on your team suffered?
- **Damage to reputation.** If the employee's problems caused you or your team to miss an important deadline, do poor-quality work, fail to hit your numbers, or otherwise not pull your weight within

the company, this makes your team look bad (and hurts your reputation as a manager). Even worse, if the problem affects your relationships with customers or clients, the company's reputation could suffer.

- **Legal exposure.** If the employee breached a contract, violated the legal rights of coworkers or customers, or otherwise broke the law, the company might be liable to third parties for damages.
- **Future problems.** Don't limit yourself to considering the immediate effect of the problem. To really get through to the employee, you should also think about what could happen if the problem continues or gets worse: The consequences can become even more serious, and the long-term costs even higher.

> **EXAMPLE:** Ed manages a small group of recruiting profes-sionals, who are responsible for finding and landing candi-dates for open positions in a large multinational company. Each recruiter has a monthly target number of hires. Ed also uses some qualitative standards to ensure the right candidates are brought in for available positions.
>
> Sharon reports to Ed and has consistently maintained excellent recruiting numbers—in fact, she exceeds her monthly targets regularly. However, Ed has heard from another manager, June, that Sharon pushed her very hard to take on a candidate that June didn't feel was fully qualified. This is a red flag for Ed, who knows that when it comes to hiring, it's about quality first and quantity second. Ed talks to the other managers with whom Sharon has placed candidates in the last few months and hears the same criticism from another manager, Sam. The others seem happy with Sharon's work.
>
> Ed considers the effect of Sharon's behavior. If her hires succeed, this demonstrates that Sharon doesn't have a problem with her recruiting skills, but instead with her ability to convey to the managers exactly how a particular candidate will be able to meet their needs. Because Sharon has strained her relationship with June and Sam, Ed could coach her on how to repair her relationships—and communicate more clearly—with the company's managers.

Now assume that one or both of the hires does not work out. This exposes an entirely different—and more significant—problem, with a far greater impact on the company. The company will have to spend time and money trying to help these hires improve through the progressive discipline process. If they cannot improve, they might have to be fired and replacements found, all of which will cost the company tens of thousands of dollars. On top of that, Sharon's bullying tactics and poor judgment in choosing candidates could sour the other managers on the job the recruiters are doing and cause harm to the recruiting team's reputation in the company. In this scenario, Ed might justifiably decide to skip the coaching and move right to a verbal or written warning, to make very clear to Sharon that her behavior is causing the company harm and must stop immediately.

Assessing the impact of an employee's problem will help you come up with a proportionate disciplinary response. While it might seem a bit time-consuming to think this through every time you have to discipline an employee, you'll soon get the hang of it. Once you start thinking about how a problem is affecting the company, you'll find yourself weighing these factors automatically, without having to sit down and consider every item on the list.

Frequency

How many times has the employee exhibited this particular problem? Often, a recurring problem merits stronger discipline, particularly if you've already had to discipline the employee for the same behavior. (See "Disciplinary History," below, for more on this issue.) If the employee simply isn't taking your coaching seriously, or is trying to "get away with" troubling behavior, you need to demonstrate that you will enforce the company's rules through escalating discipline.

However, repeat offenders aren't always asking for stronger discipline. Sometimes, recurring problems are a sign that the employee either doesn't understand what you expect or doesn't understand why. In this situation, your job is to explain exactly what the rules are and why it's important for the employee to follow them.

EXAMPLE: Marissa works for an event planning company. The company puts on parties, conventions, training programs, and other gatherings for corporate clients. The team pulls together events from start to finish, coordinating food, entertainment, media presentations, and so on; supervising outside vendors and contractors; booking the space and making arrangements for those who attend; and working the floor during the event.

When Marissa was hired, she was told that she was to prepare a brief weekly report covering each event's progress for her supervisor, Carrie. During the first few months of her employment, Marissa dutifully handed in her reports every week. However, Marissa's last few reports have been late and haven't included sufficient detail.

Carrie meets with Marissa to discuss the situation. Because this has become a recurring problem, Carrie is thinking of issuing a verbal warning. But when she asks Marissa what's going on, Marissa says, "I didn't know those reports were important. I used to do them right away, and I spent an hour or more on them, but you never said anything about what I wrote. I guess I figured it was just a paperwork requirement. We're so busy right now, and I assumed you'd want me to prioritize the TechnoSoft event and get to the reports later."

Carrie realizes that Marissa doesn't understand why the reports are important—and that Carrie hasn't done a good job of making that clear. Carrie tells her, "I'm sorry that I didn't talk to you about the reports you've already done. I guess I didn't think I had to because they were just what I needed. But it didn't give me a chance to tell you what I use them for and why they're so important. As you know, we have a long list of preferred vendors, contractors, venues, and so on, and one of my job responsibilities is to constantly update that list and stay on top of those relationships. If a person or company on our list is coming in over budget, showing up late, or otherwise not satisfying the client, I need to know right away so I can get involved. I also want to know if there are people or companies that are doing a great job. If they are already on the list, I'll try to throw more work their way. If not, I'll consider adding them."

When Marissa hears this, she understands the purpose of the reports, what she should include in them, and why it's important to hand them in on time. She tells Carrie, "I'm really sorry I didn't run this by you first. I guess I just assumed that this wasn't a priority."

Carrie responds, "It sounds like we had a misunderstanding, and I'm also sorry I wasn't clear about this. I do need for you to prioritize these reports; will you do that for me?" Marissa agrees to get the reports done on time, every week, and the meeting is over. Because Carrie is partially responsible for the situation, she decides to call it a coaching session rather than issue a verbal warning.

Disciplinary History

Of course, you should also consider whether the employee has already been disciplined—by you or a previous manager—when deciding whether and what type of discipline is appropriate in the situation you're currently facing. The weight you give to prior discipline should depend on whether the employee was already disciplined for the same problem or for something else entirely.

Prior Discipline for the Same Problem

If the employee has already been disciplined for the same behavior, it's time to escalate your response. This is where the "progress" in progressive discipline comes from: An employee is met with progressively more serious disciplinary measures as problems continue. Before you proceed, take a hard look at the solutions you came up with last time around, to make sure that the employee had all of the resources and support necessary to succeed. Assuming that you didn't give the employee impossible goals or impose unrealistic requirements, you should take the employee's continued problems after your intervention as a sign that stronger discipline is necessary.

Before you make your final decision, however, you should also consider how long it's been since the problem last happened. Part of helping employees overcome discipline problems is reinforcing the message that problems can be overcome. If you consider problems from the distant past when dealing with an immediate issue, that message can be contradicted. For example, an employee who had an attendance problem several years ago but has since turned things around may be entitled to a clean slate if the issue reoccurs. On the other hand, an employee who persists in taking unauthorized days off month after month should face a more serious disciplinary measure.

To deal with this difficulty, some companies give disciplinary measures a "shelf life." For example, a verbal or written warning might be removed from the employee's file—and not used in future disciplinary decisions—after a year without any further problems. If your company has a policy like this, you shouldn't consider any disciplinary actions taken before the cutoff date.

Prior Discipline for Other Problems

Employees who exhibit a variety of problems on the job can be very tough to manage. On the one hand, every new problem is a new opportunity to coach and correct. The employee might not understand what you expect or might need some help or training to get the job done right. This is why some human resource experts advise managers to treat each new problem as a separate issue and allow the employee to advance through the progressive discipline system on each one.

On the other hand, an employee who exhibits multiple problems can cause a lot of disruption—and take up a lot of your time. It can be very frustrating for a manager to have to restart the clock every time an employee misbehaves. And sometimes, these multiple offenders are really demonstrating one big problem: A lack of respect for your company's rules and/or for you as a manager. In this situation, you're really dealing with insubordination, a serious form of misconduct that must be met with strong discipline.

> **EXAMPLE:** You supervise Ted, an employee who has an attendance problem. After Ted failed to call in on two occasions to explain he wasn't going to be in, as required, you had a coaching session. You issued a verbal warning when Ted continued to violate the company's attendance policy. Now, Ted has failed to complete his portion of a project your team has been working on for a month. Should you escalate to a written warning for Ted's overall failure to meet the job's requirements or plan a coaching session to focus on the performance problem as a separate issue?

The answer depends on the facts. If Ted is showing improvement in other ways, or if solving the earlier problems has led to the current problem, you might want to start again with coaching. Let's say, for instance, that Ted seems to have turned things around. He was having trouble arranging care for his ailing mother and had to take days off unexpectedly. Now, his caretaking situation is worked out, and he's been showing up diligently every day. If his earlier absences led him to miss the deadline for the team project, you might want to have a coaching session. Because he seems to have solved his attendance problem, you could simply point out that missing deadlines is one consequence of unexcused absences, and that you expect things to change now that he's back at work regularly.

Now, consider how you'd respond if the facts were different. Ted's attendance problem is continuing, and he isn't responding to your efforts to help him improve. During your verbal warning session, Ted said, "You know, I need a day off sometimes for personal reasons. If that violates your rules, then I'm sorry."

When he missed the deadline for the team project, Ted reacts angrily to your questions about it, saying, "That deadline was arbitrary anyway. I know you have until Friday to finalize that project. You gave me the hardest part of the work, and you're just going to have to wait until I have time to finish it."

Responding to this with coaching would be irresponsible and ineffective. Ted is blatantly disregarding the company's rules and your authority, and he will continue to do so until he faces serious consequences. Allowing him to continue to behave this way will also do serious damage to your team's morale and opinion of you— and will also cause Ted to believe that such behavior is acceptable. In this case, a written warning is needed.

Legality

If an employee does something illegal, your response must clearly communicate that the employee's actions are unacceptable and that the company will not condone illegal behavior. After all, as discussed in

Chapter 3, your company might be held liable to others for harm caused by the employee's actions.

If you decide not to fire an employee who violates a law—for example, because the employee violated the law inadvertently or otherwise didn't understand the situation—you must make very sure that your response stops the problem. You also need to make sure that you've documented very thoroughly, just in case you have to justify your actions in the future.

> **EXAMPLE:** Ralph works at a large property management company. He supervises a group of employees who find and deal with tenants for the apartment buildings the company manages in Los Angeles. Ralph's employees screen and choose tenants, inspect the apartments, give approval for repairs and improvements, and so on.
>
> Cyrus is one of Ralph's new employees. The company is upgrading the heating and cooling systems in some of its older buildings, so Ralph asks Cyrus to inspect the systems at a building he will be responsible for. Later that day, Ralph receives a phone call from an angry tenant, who complains that Cyrus just entered her apartment without giving any advance notice. Ralph immediately calls Cyrus and tells him to return to the office.
>
> Ralph asks Cyrus to come into his office, and says, "I just got a call from a very distressed tenant, who says that you entered her apartment without any notice or warning. I'm sure you know that this is against the law unless there's an emergency. The company could get in big trouble for this." Cyrus looks panicked and says, "At my last job, our secretary handled all of the appointments with tenants. When you asked me to inspect the building, I guess I just assumed that someone had given the required notices. Oh man, I really screwed this up. I'm so sorry."
>
> Because Cyrus didn't barge in on the tenant on purpose, and because he seems to have a plausible explanation for his error, Ralph decides not to fire him. On the other hand, Cyrus's actions could cause problems for the company—and Ralph doesn't want to invite legal trouble. Ralph gives Cyrus a written warning and explains the company's procedures for entering apartments in detail.

Choosing the Right Response

By this point, you've already done a lot of work. You've identified the problem, determined that discipline is appropriate, and decided how serious the problem is, based on things like how it's affected the company and the employee's disciplinary history. Now, it's time to use all of this information to choose the right disciplinary response.

If you haven't already disciplined the employee for the same problem, you should consider whether it's appropriate to begin with the first step in your company's program: coaching, in our model system. After all, one of the primary purposes of progressive discipline is to give the employee notice of the problem and an opportunity to improve. The best way to do that is to begin with the least severe disciplinary measure and escalate your disciplinary response only if the employee fails to improve.

As you've no doubt learned from the previous sections, however, there are times when it would be irresponsible not to skip to a more serious disciplinary measure. If an employee has harmed someone, cost the company an important client, or damaged company property, for example, coaching the employee would send the message that the company doesn't take this behavior seriously. It could put people and property at risk, damage the company's reputation, bring down employee morale, and expose the company to legal liability. The trick is to figure out when coaching is the right response and when more serious discipline is in order.

Discipline for Poor Performance

Performance problems can often be resolved at the coaching level. In fact, many performance issues can be handled through simple requests or reminders ("I need those records returned to the central file at the end of each day, Bob, so they can be properly logged. Please make sure you don't leave any on your desk when you leave for the evening.") Particularly if a performance problem appears to stem from a misunderstanding about your expectations, coaching is often quite effective at turning things around.

So when should you consider skipping to a verbal or written warning? Here are some situations when moving to a more serious response might be appropriate:

- You (or another manager) already coached the employee on the same issue (for example, an employee transfers from another department where she or he was coached for problems with accuracy or speed, and continues to have the same problems when performing different tasks in your department).
- The employee's performance problem has caused significant harm to the company (for example, the employee's failure to back up certain computer files resulted in important data being lost).
- The employee's poor performance has created legal liability for the company (for example, the employee threw confidential customer information into the garbage rather than shredding or otherwise destroying it).

Discipline for Attendance Problems

Like performance problems, first-time attendance or tardiness problems are typically handled through coaching. If the problem continues, you should escalate to a verbal warning and proceed through the escalating disciplinary measures provided by your company's policy.

In rare instances, however, you might want to skip straight to a verbal warning or a stronger disciplinary measure. Here are some circumstances when you should consider a more serious response:

- You (or another manager) already coached the employee on the same issue.
- The employee has essentially gone AWOL—that is, the employee has taken unauthorized leave and has not checked in with the company or responded to your efforts to reach him or her for more than a day or two. (Some companies deem that an employee has abandoned the job after several days of unexcused absences; in that case, the employee does not need to be disciplined because the employment relationship has ended, though it should be documented.) Unless the employee has a medical emergency or some other very good excuse, this type of behavior warrants a stronger response.

- The employee's absence or tardiness has caused significant damage (for example, the employee shows up an hour late for an important pitch meeting to a potential client, and the client decides to go with another company as a result).

Discipline for Misconduct

Unlike performance and attendance problems, which should almost always be met with coaching for a first offense, first-time misconduct can call for a more serious disciplinary response, depending on the problem. And termination of employment is the only appropriate way to handle certain types of extreme misconduct.

To decide on an appropriate disciplinary measure, you'll have to weigh the factors covered in "How Serious Is the Problem?," above. Typically, you'll want to consider a stronger response in the following cases:

- The employee endangered or actually damaged people or property.
- The employee disregarded important safety rules.
- The employee was insubordinate.
- The employee's misconduct involved dishonesty (for example, falsifying records).
- The Employee's actions were illegal.

When to Consider Immediate Termination

There are some types of misconduct that justify termination of employment, even for a first-time offense. If an employee appears to have engaged in dangerous, illegal, or deceptive actions, you should investigate immediately. If your investigation reveals that the employee is to blame, you should certainly consider terminating employment.

Any of the following types of misconduct might justify immediate termination, without any second chances:

- **Violence.** This includes fighting with coworkers; pushing and shoving; throwing books, furniture, or office items; vandalizing company property; or any other physical acts taken with the intent to harm people or damage property.
- **Threats of violence.** Statements by a worker that he or she will harm, "get," or kill anyone (including him- or herself) or will bring a weapon to work merit immediate attention.

- **Stalking.** This comes up most often in cases of sexual harassment or workplace romance gone awry but can also arise out of pure hostility—an employee may stalk a supervisor or manager in order to intimidate that person, for example.

- **Possession of an unauthorized weapon.** Your workplace policies should clearly spell out that weapons are not allowed in the workplace unless authorized and necessary to perform work duties.

- **Theft or criminal behavior directed towards the company.** This includes embezzling, defrauding the company, or illegally using the company's intellectual property.

- **Dishonesty about important business issues.** The occasional fudge about progress on a project or reasons for taking time off is probably not a firing offense, but an employee who lies about whether orders have been filled, customers have been served, or important business goals have been met must be dealt with.

- **Use of illegal drugs or alcohol at work.** Using drugs or alcohol at work (other than drinking at company events where alcohol is served, such as office parties or happy hours), or showing up at work obviously impaired, is cause for concern. (See "Dealing with Drug and Alcohol Problems," below, for more information.)

- **Harassing or discriminatory conduct.** If an employee is accused of serious harassment—such as touching another employee sexually or insisting on sexual favors—you must look into it immediately. The same is true of discriminatory conduct (for example, using homophobic slurs, treating men and women differently, or refusing to use vendors or contractors of a particular race).

- **Endangering health and safety in the workplace.** An employee who fails to follow important safety rules, uses machinery in a dangerous way, or exposes coworkers to injury—whether intentionally or through lack of care—could be a huge liability.

- **Assisting a competing business.** Revealing your company's trade secrets to a competitor or using its intellectual property to work for or start a competing company is extremely serious misconduct.

Dealing With Drug and Alcohol Problems

Employees who abuse alcohol and drugs (including illegal drugs, prescription drugs, and over-the-counter drugs) can pose significant and wide-ranging problems for their employers and their managers. These employees often have poor performance or productivity and high rates of absenteeism and tardiness. They can also make a workplace more volatile and more dangerous, and they can expose your company to increased legal liability.

Alcohol Use at Work

Your company's policies should clearly state that drinking on the job is not allowed. (If current policies don't speak to this, raise the issue with your manager, human resources, or legal counsel.) If you catch an employee actually consuming alcohol at work, you should impose discipline. The disciplinary measure you use should depend on the circumstances, including whether the employee has to deal with customers or clients, whether the employee has a safety-sensitive position, and how impaired the employee gets.

> **EXAMPLE:** Cynthia manages the bookkeeping department for a chain of department stores. One day, she sees six of the department's secretaries having a party in a conference room, near closing time. When she enters, she sees that they are sharing cake and a bottle of champagne to celebrate a coworker's fiftieth birthday. Although this is against company rules, the secretaries are almost done with their work day, don't deal with customers, and don't have to operate heavy machinery or otherwise carry out potentially dangerous tasks. None of them is drunk. Cynthia decides that a verbal warning is appropriate.
>
> Now, let's say Cynthia supervises the loading dock for the same department store chain. She is at a meeting for company managers all morning. When she returns to the loading dock after lunch, she hears lots of loud noise. She learns that, while she was out, some of the workers picked up a keg of beer, and they are drinking while listening to a World Cup soccer game. They have also invited some of the delivery drivers to join them. These workers drive, operate forklifts and other heavy equipment, and load and unload very heavy items. While none of them seems completely bombed,

Cynthia places all of the workers who have been drinking on immediate suspension and calls cabs to take all of them home. After investigating the incident, she decides to terminate the employment of the two ringleaders and give written warnings to the others who drank.

Use of Legal Drugs

Many employees properly use prescribed or over-the-counter drugs, such as sleeping aids, cold medication, or painkillers. Sometimes, however, an employee's use of legal drugs can affect his or her ability to do the job safely and well. For example, a medication that causes drowsiness might make it dangerous for a worker to do a job that requires driving.

In this situation, federal and state laws that prohibit disability discrimination might limit your options. As explained in Chapter 3, a company has a legal duty to provide a reasonable accommodation to an employee with a disability, and this duty extends to accommodating the employee's use of drugs that are necessary to treat the disability. If you discover that an employee's on-the-job impairment is caused by drugs used to treat a disability, you should discuss the matter with your employee and try to come up with a reasonable accommodation. (You can find lots of helpful information on various types of accommodations at the website of the Equal Employment Opportunity Commission, www.eeoc.gov.)

Often, you will find that an employee who is impaired by an over-the-counter or legally prescribed drug is taking the drug for the first time and didn't know how it would affect him or her. In this situation, it's best to send the employee home (after arranging for safe transportation) and discuss the matter later. As long as this is a one-time occurrence, a coaching session is probably appropriate.

Use and Possession of Illegal Drugs

If an employee is under the influence of illegal drugs at work, disability rights laws do not limit your options. If the employee has not created a safety threat and does not hold a highly sensitive position, a written warning might be appropriate. However, if the employee endangers the physical safety of others, something more drastic is called for. If the employee has a drug abuse problem, one option is to suspend the employee until he or she successfully completes a treatment program. Some employers, however, opt for a zero-tolerance policy.

Because using or selling illegal drugs is a crime, most employers immediately terminate the employment of employees who engage in this type of behavior at work.

Choosing the Right Response		
Type of Problem:	**You Should:**	**Consider Stronger Discipline If:**
Poor performance	Coach	• Employee has already been coached for the same problem • Employee's problem caused significant harm to the company • Employee's problem created legal liability for the company
Poor attendance/ tardiness	Coach	• Employee has already been coached for the same problem • Employee has gone AWOL • Employee's absence has caused significant harm to the company
Misconduct	Determine how serious the problem is	• Employee endangered or actually damaged people or property • Employee disregarded important safety rules • Employee was insubordinate • Employee's misconduct involved dishonesty (for example, falsifying records) • Employee's actions were illegal
Problems relating to drugs and alcohol	Determine how serious the problem is	• Employee deals with customers or clients • Employee holds a safety-sensitive position • Employee endangered or actually harmed other people or property • Employee's actions were illegal

Deciding What Action to Take: Smart Summary

● Before deciding to discipline, make sure the employee knew the rule that was violated, actually violated the rule without good reason to do so, and isn't protected by law from complying with the rule.

● When deciding what level of discipline is appropriate, remember that the discipline should be proportionate to the problem. Consider the effect of the problem, the frequency of the problem, the employee's disciplinary history, and the legality of the behavior.

● In most instances, when an employee first suffers from poor performance, you can begin the discipline process at the very beginning: by coaching the employee.

● Some behavior is so serious that immediate termination of employment should be considered. Typically, this is true when an employee engages in seriously inappropriate misconduct, such as violence, stalking, dishonesty, use of illegal drugs at work, or harassment.

■

Build Your Skills: Is It Time for Discipline?

Questions

1. What are the three types of employee problems?

2. When an employee has a problem in one area that causes problems in another area, you must discipline that employee twice.

    ☐ True   ☐ False

3. Which of these will help you define your expectations of employee performance?

    a. The job description.

    b. Individual performance goals.

    c. Both A and B.

    d. Neither A nor B.

4. Esther tells Fred that she needs a report "on her desk" by Friday. On Friday at 6:30 p.m., Fred puts the report in her "in" basket. Esther is already gone for the day, and she's flying to a regional office on Monday morning—she needs the report for that trip. Since Fred didn't bring it to her until Friday evening, and he didn't email it to her, she wants to discipline him. Is discipline justified?

    a. Yes, because Fred should have known that "by Friday" meant by the close of business—5 p.m.—on Friday.

    b. Yes, because Fred should have emailed her the report.

    c. No, but only if Esther's usual practice was to receive hard copies instead of email.

    d. No, because there was no way Fred could have known that Esther expected him to email the report, if she never told him.

5. When an employee's behavior changes in a negative way, it could mean that a discipline problem is developing.

    ☐ True   ☐ False

6. It isn't fair to discipline an employee for an inappropriate action or behavior if company policy didn't prohibit it—after all, the employee had no way of knowing the behavior wasn't allowed.

☐ True   ☐ False

7. In which of these situations is it probably appropriate to first coach an employee, before moving to a more serious form of discipline?

   a. The employee makes some small calculation errors on a department efficiency analysis report, which goes to the department manager, the employee's boss.

   b. The employee fails to show up to work or call in sick for two days in a row.

   c. The employee plays a practical joke on a coworker, yanking the chair out from under her when she's about to sit down for a meeting. The coworker falls to the ground, injuring herself.

   d. None of the above.

8. You should always give employees a second chance before terminating employment.

☐ True   ☐ False

9. You should terminate the employment of anyone using drugs or alcohol at work.

☐ True   ☐ False

10. If an employee repeats the same mistake over and over, progressive discipline requires you to escalate your response.

☐ True   ☐ False

Answers

1. The three types of employee problems are performance problems, attendance problems, and misconduct.

2. False. Whether an employee needs to be disciplined for one or both problems depends on the facts of the specific situation. Usually, if you identify and fix the underlying problem, both problems will be solved. In the example in Chapter 4, Kristen spent too much time on the Internet in violation of company policy (misconduct), which meant she had a hard time getting her job done (poor performance). However, it's possible that just by disciplining her for using the Internet, her manager also solved her performance problem, because she'll now have more time to do her work.

3. C. A job's objective requirements, and individual performance goals, will help you define performance expectations. The job requirements will tell you what any person holding the position is expected to accomplish. Performance goals are just as important, however—they tell you what specific goals will nurture the employee's strengths, work on weaknesses, and build skills.

4. D. Managers commonly believe that some expectations are so obvious that they don't need to be verbalized—and then they're disappointed when employees don't meet those expectations. Here, Esther expected Fred to get her the report by the close of business Friday or to email it to her. Unless she told Fred either of these things, though, it isn't really fair to discipline him. After all, he did get the report to her by Friday—he even stayed late to do it. Esther needs to be clearer about her expectations, so Fred will have the opportunity to meet them.

5. True. When an employee exhibits a negative behavioral change, you'll want to explore why. It could mean that the employee is having a work-related problem that requires your intervention, or it could mean that the employee is having personal problems that won't affect his or her work or performance. Either way, getting involved shows the employee you care and gives you the opportunity to identify and perhaps prevent a developing problem.

6. False. Although company policies give employees guidelines for acceptable behavior, they're not the only source. Some behavior

that isn't specifically prohibited by company guidelines also justifies discipline—for example, when an employee violates the law or doesn't follow explicit instructions you've given.

7. A. Many employee performance problems can be overcome with coaching. Often coaching provides the opportunity to further educate an employee or find additional resources to help the employee get the job done. In this case, the employee's errors didn't cause too much trouble, because her boss caught them. The boss can use this opportunity to coach the employee and figure out whether additional resources are needed.

8. False. Some behavior is so egregious that it justifies immediate termination—for example, when an employee's acts endanger or damage others or the employee's misconduct involves dishonesty.

9. False. Although you can prohibit employees from drinking alcohol or using illegal drugs at work and can discipline employees for violating those rules, you must be careful when dealing with legal drugs. That's because your duty to provide reasonable accommodation to an employee with a disability may include accommodating the employee's use of drugs to accommodate the disability.

10. False. Sometimes, employees repeat the same behavior because they don't understand what you expect or why. Before escalating discipline, consider whether the rule, and its rationale, were clearly laid out for the employee.

■

Smart Discipline Skills

Why Discipline is Hard

Disciplining employees is not easy. More than most of your other responsibilities, it is fraught with complex emotions. After all, you're dealing with people—people who may be angry, hurt, or critical of you. And it's not only the employee's emotions that affect the process. You will probably struggle with some of your own emotions: the fear of confrontation, the need to be liked, and apprehension about what people might be saying about you.

Because these emotions can be so overwhelming, anticipating and understanding them before you enter the discipline process will help you avoid being stymied by them and allow you to focus on finding a solution to the problem at hand.

Understanding Your Emotions

Even though you probably don't spend too much of your work time actually disciplining employees, discipline is an essential part of your job as a manager. After all, your core responsibility is making sure that your team succeeds on all fronts. In order to maximize performance and efficiency, you have to hire the right people, set clear expectations, provide incentives for doing good work—and, on occasion, discipline employees who are not meeting your (or the company's) standards.

Recognizing that discipline is a necessary part of your job as a manager should help alleviate some of the stress that often accompanies disciplinary meetings. However, you may still feel uncomfortable about imposing discipline. Because discipline involves confrontation and criticism, it can give rise to complicated emotions, both in you and in the employees you correct. Often, what you want on a personal level—for example, to be friendly, be liked, or avoid confrontation—will conflict with your managerial duty.

The best way to deal with these emotions is to anticipate and plan for them. This chapter is designed to help you deal with the stress of the discipline process and integrate smart discipline into your daily practices. It will help you deal with these realities:

- **Confrontation is awkward.** Having to confront someone about a problem can be difficult. It's easy to make excuses to avoid it.

- **It's tempting to be liked.** Who doesn't want to be popular? And giving people bad news, no matter how well deserved, can make you feel like the "bad guy."
- **You want to be fair.** Every situation is a little bit different, and it can be tough to be fair when imposing discipline.
- **The unknown is scary.** It is impossible to accurately predict how someone will react to bad news. Sometimes, when we don't know what to expect, the anticipation can be even more intimidating than the experience itself. What if others second-guess your decision to discipline, or the employee becomes so upset that he or she decides to talk to a lawyer?

This chapter will help you acknowledge these concerns and prepare yourself to deal with them, so you can enter the discipline process confidently.

Confrontation Is Awkward

Webster defines awkward as "Hard to deal with; especially causing pain or embarrassment." If ever a situation fit that definition, the discipline process is it. Nearly every step in the process has the potential to cause pain or embarrassment, often on both sides. You may feel uncomfortable criticizing an employee, especially if it's someone with whom you've always had a good relationship and genuinely like, or you're discussing a mistake you've also made at some point in your career. And the employee probably feels awkward about being confronted with a shortcoming, especially if he or she is already aware of—and insecure about—the problem.

Here are a few dos and don'ts that will help you overcome this awkwardness and confront disciplinary matters head on.

Do:

- **Accept that you may feel uncomfortable.** Don't waste precious time trying to convince yourself that you should feel perfectly at ease—or getting down on yourself for finding the situation awkward. It is a natural reaction, and it would be even more awkward to try to ignore it. Put your energy toward preparing to make the meeting as productive as possible.

- **Know that the employee may also feel awkward.** You may not want to point this out, but you should adapt your communication style to your employee's reaction. If the employee appears to be uncomfortable or embarrassed, you might want to provide an opportunity for him or her to get over that reaction—for example, by saying, "Why don't we take a minute before we continue" or simply by acknowledging that the situation is a bit uncomfortable.
- **Keep the conversation focused.** Even though you both may be uncomfortable, you are there to discipline, and that's what you'll have to do. Using a prefacing sentence can sometimes help to diffuse feelings of awkwardness, such as "I know this conversation is hard for both of us ..." or "I understand that this is uncomfortable, but I want to clearly communicate my concerns ...."
- **Allow enough time.** Don't rush the process. Despite your other pressing demands, allow enough time for you and your employee to work through the problem at hand. Both of you will feel more comfortable if you know that you'll have the opportunity to fully discuss your concerns and ideas.

Don't:

- **Lose the opportunity to collaborate.** Sometimes it's tempting to do anything you can to get out of an awkward situation as quickly as possible, but rushing through the conversation could cost you an otherwise productive dialogue. Listen closely to what your employee has to say. Stay in the moment and let the emotions run their course. You can still draw your employee into a constructive conversation, even if both of you feel a bit uncomfortable.
- **Be afraid of silence or emotions.** Give your employee time to process what you are saying as he or she sees fit (as long as it's appropriate for a work environment), even if that means you have to sit through some awkward silence. Accept that the employee may not say anything while processing, may respond with strong emotions, or might put you on the spot with questions like "Why didn't you tell me this before?" or "What did I do wrong?"

You Like to Be Liked

You've heard it before: "Carol is such a nice girl. She didn't deserve to be fired. I can't believe Chuck let her go. He is such a hard manager." Or, "Can you believe the nerve of that woman? She didn't even give Stan a chance before she wrote him up." When you've disciplined an employee, others who don't have the full story will probably speculate about what's happened—and they might blame you. Particularly if you are disciplining a popular or especially vocal employee, you can expect to be perceived as the bad guy.

It's natural: We all liked to be liked. If you feel that you're being criticized unfairly, your confidence could be eroded and you might even start to second-guess your decisions. This "bad guy syndrome" is also frustrating because you usually don't get the chance to justify your actions or defend yourself.

Even if the gossip doesn't lead to criticism and blame, you may still feel excluded and ostracized as your employees talk to each other about what's going on in the workplace. You've probably participated in these "water cooler" discussions yourself—either earlier in your career, when you gossiped with coworkers, or now, when you have these discussions with other managers. Your employees do the same thing. They spend time catching up on each others' lives, dissecting last night's hit TV show, and speculating on management decisions that they know little about. These discussions—even when critical of management—are a natural occurrence and a necessary outlet. Your employees can and will talk about everything you do, how you do it, and whether you should have done it differently.

As a manager, you have to learn to rise above the chatter. If you are dealing with employee problems fairly and judiciously, and communicating constructively with the employee who is being disciplined, you have to trust your own decisions and overcome the need to be liked. Yours is not to manage the conversation flow out there, nor is it to defend yourself against what you may be hearing. And, as explained in Chapter 10, you could even get in trouble if you reveal too many details about a particular disciplinary situation to employees who don't have a need to know.

So what can you do to ease the pain? Here are some dos and don'ts to help you overcome your need to be liked when disciplining.

Do:

- **Keep your employees focused.** When discipline issues get employees sidetracked, you need to get the team focused on their own ongoing responsibilities and performance. Often, it's necessary to remind your team what you expect and what success looks like. Although this won't entirely stop the gossip, it will provide something more constructive to talk about.

- **Set clear expectations.** When all team members understand your expectations, they will also understand that discipline is the logical consequence of failing to meet them. The chatter and blame will subside when your employees see that the rules are clear and everyone gets a fair shot.

- **Know the facts.** Get all of the information you need to make the right disciplinary decision. If you've worked to thoroughly understand the problem, you can impose discipline confidently, without having to worry that one of your armchair quarterbacks will come up with something you missed.

- **Engage the employee.** If you've taken the time to get the employee's perspective, then you'll know you've also given the employee a fair shot. An employee who knows that you were listening respectfully may even be your best advocate when others second-guess your actions.

Don't:

- **Get defensive.** You do not need to explain your actions to your team, except to the person involved—and then only to demonstrate that discipline is the expected and justifiable response to the problem. Trying to justify your actions to other members of your team will only make you look weak and defensive, perhaps even unsure of the actions you have taken. Moreover, discipline is a confidential matter between the employee and the company—revealing too much to other employees will only lead to distrust and potential legal trouble.

- **Dwell on short-term popularity.** You are doing what you have to do as a manager—improving each person's performance and the overall performance of your team—which is your ultimate goal and responsibility to the company. Remember that objective when you start to worry about whether you are liked or not—and talk to a higher-up, like your boss, when you need reassurance. Don't expect that affirmation from your team members, who don't know all the facts or share your responsibility for the group's performance.

You Want to Be Fair

We all want to be fair, and you probably feel that that means you need to treat employees the same in similar situations. For the most part, you're probably right: There are many good reasons, as we've discussed, to impose consistent discipline.

However, you may have found that treating employees exactly the same isn't always fair. Sometimes, you should treat employees differently. For example, one employee may have a history of performance problems that another does not, or one employee's actions might be justified while another's are not. In these situations, treating employees differently *is* fair—because the situations really are different.

But when you make the decision to treat employees differently, you'll face extra challenges. You have to be able to explain to the employee who is treated differently that there is a justifiable reason for the different treatment—that no two situations are exactly alike, and that the difference justifies your behavior. And you'll have to accept that the situation might not look fair to an outsider who doesn't have all the facts.

In addition to treating employees consistently, as we talked about in Chapter 2, part of progressive discipline is imposing a disciplinary measure that sufficiently addresses the recognized problem without being too harsh. Nothing will cause others to second-guess the fairness of discipline you impose like apparent over- or under-reactions to employee problems. If an employee has really surprised you or let you down, you might react with high emotion, making rash discipline decisions. If you fear the employee's reaction, on the other hand, you might not impose sufficiently stringent discipline. If you discipline proportionately, you can be confident that you're also imposing discipline fairly.

Given how emotionally charged the discipline process is, it's hard to know whether you're being fair. Follow these steps to maintain fairness.

Do:

- **Discipline based on fact.** When you decide to discipline, do it based on fact—not on how you feel about a particular employee.
- **Research how it's been done in the past.** Consider how you, and others in the company, have handled the same or similar issues. If you are acting consistently when you discipline, your actions are much more likely to be fair.
- **Consult a trusted adviser.** Second opinions can provide a clarity that you wouldn't get otherwise. Talk to your boss, human resources department, or legal counsel to get another perspective on the situation, especially if you have strong feelings or emotions. These feelings can cloud your judgment, without you even realizing it.

Don't:

- **Ignore your gut**. If you feel uncomfortable about treating two employees differently or choosing an appropriate disciplinary measure based on the facts in front of you, figure out the source of your discomfort. It may just be that the disciplinary process is inherently uncomfortable—but it may be that the discipline you're considering isn't consistent or proportionate.
- **Assume that you are naturally fair.** Be your own worst critic—explore the fairness of each discipline decision you make, before you make it. Imagine how you would feel if you were the disciplined employee: Would the discipline surprise you? Would you feel you were treated fairly? Ask your boss or human resources department for an alternate perspective to see whether your behavior seems objectively fair, based on the facts.

You Fear the Unknown

Perhaps the hardest thing about discipline is that you simply don't know how the employee will react to it. This can leave you dreading the encounter, wondering if the employee will lash out or withdraw—or even wondering whether there might be lasting repercussions that reflect poorly on you. You may also worry that you'll be so overwhelmed or surprised by the employee's response that you won't know what to do next.

It's not at all unusual for an employee who is unhappy with being disciplined to lash out and try to damage the manager who is responsible. While it's important to acknowledge that this could happen, it's even more important not to let your fear of it prevent you from using the process fairly and consistently. As long as you follow the strategies we explain in this book, even the most disgruntled employee will have very little ammunition to use against you. Stay the course, apply smart discipline techniques, and lasting negative repercussions become a moot point.

Of course, knowing you're doing the right thing won't help you overcome the feelings of dread you might have when it's actually time to do it. Fortunately, you can anticipate the range of potential reactions and prepare yourself to handle any of them. (We address difficult employee reactions in Chapter 8.) While this won't alleviate your fears entirely, it can help you plan for your meeting and prevent you from feeling totally blindsided when an employee's reaction isn't what you expect.

EXAMPLE 1: Grace had been the receptionist at a music distribution company for many years. She has become the "face of the company," knows everyone by name and is known for her sunny personality and kind demeanor. Grace is responsible for answering the phone, maintaining customer records, and managing office logistics.

One of Grace's responsibilities is to keep accurate and up-to-date customer records, which the sales team uses to make customer calls and track sales. Over several months, many salespeople discover that as they make their sales calls, the phone numbers are wrong and some of the customer names are even incorrect. Reluctantly, they report the issue to Grace's supervisor, Jeremy.

Jeremy looks into the issue, finds it to be true, and decides to coach Grace. He's always had a good working relationship with her, so he's confident that she'll understand the problem and respond well to coaching. Jeremy calls Grace into his office and explains the problem. Grace responds quickly, with a raised voice, "It wasn't me." Jeremy is taken aback. Grace is the only one with read and write access to the customer database, and the only one tasked with this job. "What do you mean it wasn't you? Of course it was you!" Jeremy blurts out before he can think. Grace crosses her arms, sits back in her chair, and repeats, "It wasn't me." Jeremy sits silently, without knowing what to say.

Now Grace and Jeremy are at a standstill. Jeremy is caught by surprise at Grace's anger and denial—and he hasn't planned what to do next. He isn't able to coach Grace as originally planned. Even though Jeremy expected and hoped that Grace would react positively to discipline, he shouldn't have taken for granted that her response would be as he desired. If Jeremy had anticipated that Grace might react defensively, he would have been in a better position to deliver the discipline. Now let's look at the same scenario—only this time, Jeremy is prepared to meet with some resistance.

EXAMPLE 2: Grace tells Jeremy that she is not responsible for the errors in the records. "Grace, aren't you the only one who has access to the customer records?" Jeremy asks. "Yes," she agrees reluctantly. Jeremy continues, "And doesn't the customer records database track who makes changes or updates, and when they're made?" "Yes," she replies again. "Did someone else have access to your password?" Jeremy asks. "No," Grace replies.

"Well, I checked the records the sales team reported had errors. All the records were entered or updated by you in the last three months. Can we at least agree that you were the one who made these entries?"

Because Jeremy has prepared ahead of time, he's able to move beyond Grace's reaction. Even if she still isn't willing to acknowledge her responsibility, Jeremy knows his actions are justified, and he hasn't allowed Grace's resistance to convince him otherwise.

To overcome your fear of the unknown, follow these dos and don'ts.

Do:

- **Prepare.** Do your investigation and research. If you know your facts, you can impose fair discipline even when faced with an employee's emotional reaction. Preparing carefully will also help you avoid having your own emotions take over: You don't have to feel defensive or uncertain, because you know that you're doing the right thing.

- **Stay even keeled.** Keep on point, focus on the problem, and keep your personal reactions in check. Use a level, calm voice throughout the session.
- **Stick to the facts.** Don't get sidetracked by emotions—you're there to discuss a problem, and that's what you should do.

Don't:

- **Be a friend.** While you may be tempted to offer comfort to a sad employee or a sympathetic ear to an angry one, you can send a mixed message when you act like a friend, instead of a manager. By all means, offer a tissue or a moment for the employee to regain composure, but don't forget your purpose and role in the meeting.
- **Expect to have all the answers.** You will probably be surprised by a reaction at some point—maybe so surprised that you don't know what to do. Don't let this deter you: If it means you need a break, take one and come back later.

Accept the Challenge

Even if you apply all these principles, you will probably still find the discipline process a challenge. It's never going to be fun to tell employees that they need to improve performance or behavior. Remember, though, that you are ultimately responsible for the success of your individual employees and your team. Both will grow only if challenged to overcome obstacles. You'll do your employees no favors if you ignore problems—instead, you'll see problems grow and watch employee morale dip.

On the other hand, if you work through discipline problems even when you dread them, you'll achieve results: Not only will you overcome the immediate problem, but you will also improve relations with your team generally. Employees will understand what they need to do to meet your expectations, and they'll be motivated to do so without worrying that you might blindside them with discipline. The result will be a team of high performers who trust you to deal openly and fairly with them—and who know that discipline will be imposed only when expectations aren't met.

Why Discipline Is Hard:
Smart Summary

● Accept that discipline might feel awkward, for both you and the employee. Plan to acknowledge and deal with this discomfort.

● Your job isn't to be liked by all your employees—your job is to ensure your team members' success, and that may mean you have to impose consistent and fair discipline at times. Don't allow your desire or need to be liked to affect your disciplinary decisions.

● Know that employees who don't know the whole story may think you're not being fair when you decide to discipline someone. If you have all the facts, evaluate the problem thoroughly, and apply discipline consistently, you know you're being fair—even if your employees don't.

● The only way to know with certainty how an employee will react to discipline is to actually do it and experience the reaction. Prepare yourself for different possibilities, but don't delay discipline because you're dreading the reaction.

● Even though it's uncomfortable to discipline, doing so sets expectations for your team. This will motivate employees to try and meet your expectations and help limit future problems.

Smart Talk: How to Discuss a Discipline Problem With an Employee

Successful progressive discipline depends on your ability to work with your employee to identify the problem, understand its impact, develop solutions collaboratively, and continue to work together until the issue is fully resolved. Typically, the whole process requires a number of conversations—conversations that can be hard to initiate and even more challenging to navigate. How you choose to talk to someone, what you decide to say, and how well you listen to responses are all vital to successfully overcoming a discipline problem. The more thought and preparation you put into a discussion, and the more active listening you do during the discussion, the more likely you are to engage your employee in actually fixing the problem.

This chapter explains how to get your message across and enlist your employee in finding solutions to the problem at hand. The strategies covered here will help you communicate effectively in the progressive discipline process, no matter what type of problem you're facing or which disciplinary measure you're imposing. Those strategies are:

- **Prepare.** Create a rough outline of the points you want to get across, and think about how your points may be received.
- **Guide.** Set appropriate boundaries for the conversation by choosing the right tone at the outset.
- **Demonstrate.** Show an employee what the problem is by giving clear, legitimate examples.
- **Wait.** Allow the employee time to process what you are saying—don't talk just to fill silence, and don't move on until you know the employee understands what is being discussed.
- **Listen.** Listen empathically and communicate to the employee that you hear his or her concerns.
- **Adapt.** Be prepared to deal with new findings. Even though you have prepared for this meeting and anticipated its potential outcomes, you may learn new information, and you may need to adjust your goals based on that information.
- **Act.** End each session with an action plan, crafted by you and the employee.

Prepare

Good preparation doesn't mean going into a disciplinary meeting with a list of things to say, then plodding through each item one by one. Instead, it means taking the time to see the issue from all perspectives (without making assumptions or drawing premature conclusions), preparing your opening few sentences, and thinking about potential reactions. By going into any difficult communication prepared in this way, you can help the employee understand and focus on the problem.

See the Issue From All Perspectives

Effective discipline requires you to understand the issue as fully as you can. Consider the issue from a range of viewpoints: that of the person or people being disciplined, anyone who may have witnessed the event or borne the brunt of the outcome, and anyone who may otherwise be affected by the issue. If you understand what led to the problem in the first place, how it affects others, and how it affects the individual employee, you will be better able to craft an appropriate solution that deals with every aspect of the problem.

In many cases, you may know only the effect of a problem. For example, you may know that your employee missed a deadline, but not why. To fully understand the situation, you may need to talk with others before meeting with the employee or meet with the employee to gather information before deciding whether to administer discipline.

Many sensitive disciplinary issues, such as sexual harassment, discrimination, theft, or workplace violence may require full-blown investigations. These investigations require special expertise, and you should involve your legal counsel and human resources department. We'll discuss them in Chapter 10.

For more information about conducting effective investigations, check out *Workplace Investigations*, by Lisa Guerin (Nolo), available for download at www.nolo.com. This book explains how to legally and fairly investigate problems such as harassment, discrimination, theft, and violence.

Don't Jump to Conclusions

An employee's actions may strike an immediate chord with you, and all your instincts will tell you to nip it in the bud immediately. Indeed, ending the behavior may be necessary. However, you first need to make sure you understand the entire problem. Take the time to make sure your response is measured and thoughtful, rather than a simple knee-jerk reaction.

> **EXAMPLE:** Bob, the finance manager at a small biotechnology company, is going to be out of the office and asks Sean, a senior-level analyst, to deliver a comprehensive financial report to the CFO. When Bob returns the next day, he talks to the CFO and discovers he hasn't received the report. Bob immediately gets upset, calls Sean into his office, and accusingly says, "I asked you to do a simple thing. What could possibly go wrong with that?"
>
> What Bob doesn't know is that in reviewing the report, Sean found serious errors in it. He held off delivering it to the CFO because he wanted to reconcile the errors first and stayed late to do it. Sean left Bob an email to that effect, but in his haste, Bob hadn't read it.
>
> Bob pulled the trigger too quickly and let his emotions and assumptions drive him to the wrong conclusions. By taking the time to calm down—even for just a few moments—Bob might have gained control of those emotions and begun a productive conversation with an open-ended question: "Why didn't you deliver the report?" Instead, his accusatory tone communicated to Sean that his efforts to do a good and thorough job were not valued by his supervisor.

Prepare Your Opening Sentences

Sometimes, the hardest part of a discipline conversation is getting started. A little forethought will help you figure out how to raise the issue and get the conversation off on the right foot. By jotting down a couple of sentences and thinking about how you will begin the conversation, you can make your most important points while you have your employee's full attention.

As the conversation continues, your employee may be processing what you're saying, struggling to understand why you're disciplining at all, internally preparing responses, or reacting emotionally to what you've said. That's why what you say in the first few sentences is so important—it may be the only time in the conversation that you'll have the employee's full attention. Don't waste this valuable opportunity by fumbling your opening line or not knowing where to start. If you begin with small talk or unscripted language, you may confuse your employee, shifting focus away from the real reason for the discussion.

To make the most of your opening lines, write down what you consider your most important points. Craft a sentence or two that captures those points and sets the right tone for the conversation (we'll discuss appropriate tone below). You don't necessarily need to have these notes in front of you as you begin the conversation, but they should be in the forefront of your mind. You might even want to practice out loud, just to overcome any awkwardness or ambiguity that you can't see on paper.

Anticipate Potential Reactions

Sometimes, an employee can surprise you with a strong emotional reaction. You should anticipate this possibility so that you are not distracted and thrown off track in the meeting. Don't script how you might respond to each emotion, as that could make a comfortable dialogue too rigid. But at the same time, you don't want to be so overwhelmed by the employee's emotions that it prevents you both from finding a successful outcome to the problem at hand.

> **EXAMPLE:** Susie has been managing salespeople for more than thirty years. She runs the worldwide sales organization for a large manufacturing company.
>
> Joe works for Susie and has enjoyed two straight years as her top salesperson. But this year is different. Joe has been working his large accounts, talking to the right people, and employing all the sales skills that made him successful in the past, but he's just not closing business. It's been two quarters since Joe has achieved his sales numbers, and Susie knows it's time to talk about it with him.

Skills Enhancement 2: Opening Discussions

Let's take a moment to put together a few sample openings based on a few different scenarios. Take a moment to jot down how you would open the following discussions.

EXAMPLE 1: Terry needs to talk to Jill about continued errors in her reports. As the office administrative assistant, Jill is responsible for delivering accurate reports. Lately she has been forwarding reports without verifying that the sales numbers are accurate. How would you, as Terry, open the discussion with Jill?

EXAMPLE 2: Damon sends out a joke over the office intranet. While some people find the joke funny, it leaves others uneasy, as its central figures are Catholic priests. Tricia manages Damon and wants to talk to him about the boundaries of appropriate humor in the workplace. If you were Tricia, how would you open the conversation with Damon?

In the first example, Terry really needs to know the whole story. He can open the discussion in several ways. While Terry certainly knows the outcome—others in the company don't feel they can rely on the team's sales numbers—he does not know *why* Jill is making the mistakes. And while the reason for Jill's flawed reports won't change the company's need for accurate information, it may change the direction of Terry's discipline.

Based on the need to garner more information, here are a couple of potential opening lines Terry could use:

- Jill, I'd like to talk to you about inaccuracies we've been finding in the sales reports. Can you help me understand why this has been happening?
- Jill, when we don't provide accurate sales figures, others in the company feel that they can't rely on us. You've had inaccurate numbers on the reports a few times and I'm concerned about the negative effect this is having on our team. Can you tell me how we might be able to address this together?

Skills Enhancement 2: Opening Discussions (cont'd)

In the second example above, Tricia has a difficult task. She must communicate to Damon that his joke wasn't appropriate. At the same time, she doesn't want Damon to think that a sense of humor is unappreciated. Here, the goal is not to understand what Damon was thinking, but to let him know that others might find it offensive. A few opening lines might be:

- Damon, I wanted to talk to you about the joke you sent out on the office intranet. The joke wasn't appropriate for the workplace, and some people expressed that it made them uncomfortable. When you think about the joke, do you see how that could have happened?

- Damon, I appreciate your good sense of humor, but the joke you sent wasn't appropriate. A joke that stereotypes different religious groups could really anger or offend some of your coworkers. That's one of the reasons company policy restricts use of the intranet to work-related communications—it's really not a tool to use for personal reasons. Do you understand?

To prepare for the meeting, Susie pulls Joe's sales reports and sales numbers and looks at how he has been doing business. She wants to be able to give him factual, relevant guidance to improve his work. She invites him to breakfast, knowing the casual environment will put him at ease. In Susie's mind, she has prepared well for her meeting with Joe.

At breakfast, Susie starts with some small talk, they order their food, and she begins the coaching discussion, "Joe, it's time to talk about your numbers and how we might go about improving them. I've spent some time reading your sales reports, and I'd like to hear from you about what you think is going on." Joe is silent for a moment. Then he puts his elbows on the table and covers his eyes, his head bowed, his shoulders shaking.

Susie can see that he is upset and immediately begins to comfort him. "Joe, you know you are one of my best salespeople. You've always had strong numbers, and I hate to see you get upset about this conversation. Please don't cry. Can I get you a tissue?" Susie spends the rest of breakfast trying to comfort Joe, and they leave breakfast without further discussing the problem.

In this example, Susie prepared to deal with Joe's poor sales numbers very carefully. She pulled past data, looked at his sales methodologies, and began the conversation with an open-ended question designed to address the problem and find a solution. What Susie didn't do was anticipate Joe's emotional reaction. Because she was caught by surprise, she spent her time comforting instead of coaching. In this role, her goal of improving Joe's performance was put on the back burner. Joe, overcome by emotion, hasn't made any commitment to improve—and Susie, in comforting Joe, hasn't asked for that commitment.

Had Susie thought about Joe's potential emotional reactions, she could have been prepared with a plan for waiting out his grief. When he got upset, she could have said, "Take a minute and compose yourself. Here's a tissue. When you're ready, let's move on to a discussion about how to improve your sales numbers. If you need more time, we can schedule another meeting." Then she could have simply sat quietly until Joe composed himself or they agreed on an alternate meeting time.

We'll talk more about common employee reactions, and how to respond to them, in Chapter 8. However, as you get ready to meet with your employee, be sure to prepare yourself for the possibility of strong emotions.

Guide

To have a productive conversation about a discipline problem, you need to guide the direction of the conversation. The best way to do this is to set the appropriate tone at the outset. Your tone tells the employee how serious the problem is, as well as how committed you are to solving it.

Webster's defines tone two different ways: "the quality of a person's voice" and "the general atmosphere of a place or situation and the effect that it has on people." When considering the appropriate tone, it is critical to think of both of these things.

Tone of Voice

Your tone can convey many things, including nervousness, confidence, anger, determination, concern, caring, and so on. Different tones are appropriate for different conversations. You'll want to choose a tone that is appropriate for your discipline discussion ahead of time, so that you can maintain consistency throughout the session. If your tone of voice doesn't match your point, you'll send mixed messages.

Choose an Appropriate Environment

The location of your meetings also sends a message to the employee. You should pick a location that illustrates the seriousness of the situation and avoids any distractions that might derail the discussion. There is a reason the police interview suspects in windowless rooms with folding chairs and plain tables. This atmosphere says universally, "You are in serious trouble, and you will be provided no distractions as we discuss it." You need to be similarly conscious about how the physical surroundings affect the tone of your meeting.

There are a few basics that always apply:

- You need to be able to hear each other speak.
- You should be facing the employee so you can make eye contact.

Skills Enhancement 3: Choosing Tone of Voice

Consider the following examples and jot down the tone of voice that you would adopt if you were dealing with each issue:

EXAMPLE 1: Rick manages the receptionist in his law firm. She has done an exemplary job of being the "face of the firm." She is friendly and puts people at ease. Rick has noticed that she has been very down the last few days, not her normal welcoming self. He sees that she is treating people who come into the firm differently than she normally would. He decides to discuss it with her.

EXAMPLE 2: Carrie is the CFO of a major corporation. One day she is in the restroom and happens upon a woman curled in the corner of the bathroom, disheveled, sobbing, and with bruises on her wrists and arms. With some careful coaxing, Carrie learns that the woman has been physically assaulted by a coworker after she told him she would not date him any longer. Carrie comforts the woman, gets her medical help, enlists the aid of the legal and human resources departments in investigating the situation quickly and thoroughly, and is ready to sit down with the man in question.

EXAMPLE 3: Rosanne has worked with Maggie for nearly 10 years. She hired Maggie after having worked with her at two different companies. They see each other socially and their families are friendly. Lately, Maggie has been finishing projects late—an issue Rosanne has addressed with Maggie before. Maggie always replies, "Oh, you know me! I'm worth the wait!" Rosanne decides to meet with Maggie to talk about the problem.

How would you handle these situations? There is no "right" answer. The most important thing is to match your tone to the gravity of the situation. If Rick took a cold, authoritarian tone instead of a questioning tone, the receptionist might immediately feel defensive and clam up. Likewise, if Carrie were to sit down with the woman's alleged abuser and use a concerned or friendly tone instead of a stern one, it would send this

Skills Enhancement 3: Choosing Tone of Voice (cont'd)

man the message that the company does not crack down on violence in the workplace.

The example of Rosanne and Maggie is the trickiest. The women have a friendship that extends outside the office and a history of working together. Maggie is letting those lines blur as she gets coached by Rosanne and, thus, is not taking the problem seriously. It is up to Rosanne to assert her leadership position and convey to Maggie that the problem must be dealt with, despite their friendship. Her tone should be firm and professional to get this message across.

- You should not be distracted by other things.
- You should have space to take notes.

Think about what you'll be doing in the meeting. Do you need a desk between you to convey authority? If you need white space to design solutions to issues, go to a conference room with a whiteboard. You may also want to choose your location based on the type of discipline you are administering, selecting progressively more formal environments as the discipline gets more serious. We'll discuss that in greater detail in Chapters 11 to 14.

Demonstrate

We've already discussed the importance of giving employees specific examples of the conduct or performance that warrants discipline. It's important to select examples that are factually correct, easily remembered by the employee, and directly relevant to the point you are trying to make. Otherwise, the employee might go into a defensive, corrective mode, focusing on how the example is inaccurate or unfair instead of dealing with the problem itself.

What kinds of examples are most effective? First, don't bring up things that happened in the distant past (especially if they haven't come up again since) or have already been addressed. It's much easier to discuss problems that have taken place recently and are still fresh in both of your minds. And if you bring up something that happened a long time ago or has already been addressed, the employee may rightfully feel the criticism isn't fair.

Second, make sure your examples are deeply rooted in fact. Make sure you know the who, what, where, when, and why of each example so you do not spend your time arguing over the details instead of creating solutions.

Third, it's best to use examples that you saw or heard yourself. If you are relaying second-, third-, or even fourthhand accounts, chances increase that the facts are incorrect or are presented through someone else's lens. Incorrect facts undermine your point, too.

Here are a couple of instances where examples are used to illustrate the problem in a disciplinary discussion. What works about each of these, and what doesn't?

EXAMPLE: David is talking with Sara about her caustic behavior toward one of her team members, Shelly. Several people have noticed and reported this behavior. David himself has never seen it, but he trusts the reports of others. Sara is defensive when David raises the issue, and replies, "Name one time where I was mean to Shelly."

David tells her, "Several employees told me that last Wednesday, when you were headed to lunch with Dolores, they saw you look back over your shoulder and say to Shelly, 'So sorry you can't come with us. But with that dress size, you probably don't need lunch anyway.'" Sara is quiet a moment, and replies, "Who told you that?"

"Who told me isn't the point, Sara," David replies. "The real issue is how we are going to solve this problem."

In this situation, David has put enough facts into his example to make it almost irrefutable (as evidenced by Sara's silence and subsequent focus on "who did it"). He is using an example from recent memory, so it is still fresh in Sara's mind. While he hasn't witnessed the behavior himself, it was corroborated by several sources. Finally, David avoids dissecting the example, even when Sara tries to, and instead returns to the problem. Now all he has to do is work with Sara to ensure that it doesn't happen again.

EXAMPLE: Libby is meeting with her employee, Jonathan because she has heard that his performance on the factory floor is sub par. If he falls behind, it slows the whole line. While she has never witnessed the problem herself, she knows about it because her boss saw and asked her to address it.

Libby sits down with Jonathan and tells him that she is concerned about his performance. She explains that he is slowing the whole team and costing the company significant money. Jonathan replies, "This is a complete surprise to me. Can you give me an example of what you mean?"

Libby responds, "Well Jonathan, you know we are always watching for workflow across the entire line, and your area seems to be slow." Jonathan is silent for a moment. "When was I slow? What day?" Libby replies, "There isn't a specific day, just an overall sense of slowness." Jonathan looks at her with disbelief.

In this example, Libby didn't do her homework. She tried to communicate the problem to Jonathan, but she couldn't provide a specific example of the problem. As a result, Jonathan just didn't see there was a problem, so he certainly wasn't ready to participate in a solution.

If you are trying to address a pattern of unwanted behaviors or actions (as opposed to a single incident), it's a good idea to have more than one tight, credible example. You don't need to dredge up an exhaustive list highlighting every time the problem ever occurred, but you should be able to show that it's happened more than once. If the employee understands and acknowledges the problem, you may not have to use all of your examples. But you should be ready to discuss a couple of incidents, in case you need to work harder to convince the employee that the situation is serious.

Wait

Silence is an uncomfortable part of any discipline discussion: When an employee doesn't acknowledge what you've said, you're stuck wondering whether the message got across, and what the employee thinks or feels if it did. Occasionally, employees will "stonewall" managers, using silence to undermine collaborative discipline. Far more often, silence is simply an indication that the employee is processing what you've said.

It can be tempting to fill silence. The danger in doing so is not only that you may say the wrong thing, but also that you are not giving your employee a chance to think. It is much better to wait out the silence and look for an indication from your employee that he or she is ready to continue. These signs might include clearing the throat, shifting and leaning forward, or using the hands to signal that he or she is ready to hear more. Hopefully, your employee will eventually just begin to talk.

Another problem with filling silence is that often, you'll be tempted to say the very things that can get you into hot water. Nervous managers often try to justify their decisions, often by raising issues that are better left unsaid. For example, a manager might defensively state that other people have been disciplined for similar problems or blurt out other confidential information that should not be made available to the employee.

Filling silence also undermines the strength of your position. You will sound as though you are second-guessing yourself or doubting the discipline process—signs to the employee that you aren't confident in your decision.

For all these reasons, you should stay silent yourself during legitimate employee silences. If the employee is using silence to undermine the discipline conversation, you will most likely know it. You may even see it on the employee's face. If the employee continues to be silent even after prompting by you to open the discussion, you can address the silence head on or postpone the meeting until the employee is willing to continue collaboratively.

> **EXAMPLE:** Lourdes manages a team of four salespeople who sell accounting software to small businesses. One member of her sales team, Lance, hasn't been returning calls to current customers who have questions about the software. As a result, Lourdes has received several phone calls from dissatisfied customers.
>
> Lourdes sits down with Lance and explains the problem. As she speaks, Lance's arms are crossed in front of his chest, and he's looking at his feet. When Lourdes asks Lance what he thinks they should do to resolve the problem, Lance replies, "I don't know."
>
> Lourdes waits another minute for Lance to elaborate. When he doesn't, she asks again. "Lance, is there anything you think we can do to resolve this?"
>
> Lance refuses to meet her gaze, and instead turns his head to look out the window. He says again, firmly, "I don't know."
>
> Lourdes replies, "Lance, it seems like you're not willing to talk about this right now. Let's postpone this meeting until tomorrow morning. At that time, please be ready to discuss what we can do to solve this problem."

Listen

If a disciplinary conversation occurs and only one person is speaking, you're not working toward a collaborative solution. If you're busy talking, that means you're not doing *any* listening. Even when you do give the employee the chance to speak, you may be so busy trying to figure out what to say next that even though you look very attentive, you're really just listening for a pause that will allow you to begin speaking again.

Failing to listen has a dramatic effect on the disciplinary conversation. While the employee may get the message that he or she is doing something wrong, you won't show the employee that you want to hear the other side or get help in creating the solution. In essence, you could just communicate the same thing in a letter. That makes the most important part of progressive discipline—finding a solution together— nearly impossible.

To listen well, you must:

- **Set the scene for a distraction-free conversation.** Eliminate things that will keep you from focusing on the employee and issue at hand.
- **Play back what you are hearing.** When you respond, begin with statements reflecting that you have heard your employee's viewpoint.
- **Listen empathically.** Imagine you are the person speaking. Don't just think about what that person is saying; think about what he or she is feeling.

Set the Scene for a Distraction-Free Conversation

Although it sounds intuitive, paying attention is one of the most difficult skills to master. And unfortunately, it's easy for others to notice if you aren't doing it well. You've probably seen it many times in others— when a person's mind is full and racing along, especially while someone else is talking, there's an obvious vacancy in the person's eyes.

Of course, that's not the only way lack of attention manifests itself. You'll answer the wrong question. You'll pick up only pieces of what is being said—losing potentially important information along the way. As a result, the conversation will be fragmented and incomplete, and the employee may feel you don't value his or her perspective.

You need to recognize that your attention may wander and set the scene to prevent that from happening. These tips create an environment as free from distractions as possible:

- Turn off your phone.
- Turn your computer screen away from you and turn off the sound.

- Lower the blinds or close the curtains if the view is distracting.
- Shut your door or grab a private room.
- Make it clear to everyone else that you're not to be disturbed, perhaps by posting a sign on the door.
- Sit directly across from the person you are talking to so you can maintain eye contact.
- Clear your mind prior to walking into the meeting—physically and mentally set aside other things you are working on.

Play Back What You Are Hearing

Another way to make sure you are listening attentively is to repeat what the employee has just said. At a natural break in the conversation, say something like:

- "Let me see if I understand what you are saying …"
- "Tell me if I am following you …"
- "What I think you are saying is …"

Follow those openings with a paraphrased version of what you just heard. This tells the employee that you are listening and understanding what is being said. And, if you didn't get the employee's point, he or she can correct you right away.

> **EXAMPLE:** Samantha is the company controller and Del is her boss, the CFO. Del is having a disciplinary conversation with Samantha about her continuing errors in general ledger accounting. Del has prepared well and explained the problem and the impact it is having on the company. He prefaces this portion of the conversation by telling Samantha that he would like to understand better what she believes the problem to be. Samantha replies, "You are asking me to do way too much work in too short of a timeframe. Not only do I have to do general ledger accounting, I am handling receivables, payables, budgeting, and forecasting. With that much to do, mistakes will get made."
>
> Del responds, "If I understand what you are saying correctly, your workload is too heavy, causing you to make mistakes on the general ledger, is that right?"
>
> Samantha adds a previously unspoken, but implied, "My workload would cause *anyone* to make mistakes."

By playing back what he heard Samantha saying, Del conveyed to Samantha that he was listening attentively. In turn, Samantha felt comfortable sharing more about her state of mind—giving Del an opportunity to understand her perspective and see a more complete picture.

When you reiterate what the employee says, play it back straight, without any editorializing or judgment from you. Avoid statements that interpret the employee's motives, thoughts, or feelings. For example, if an employee misses a deadline because he or she forgot about it, don't reply with "You missed the deadline because you just didn't bother to write it down" or "You blew the deadline because you can't handle more than one project at a time." In both these cases, the statements communicate that you're doing more than listening—you're judging. The moment you add anything that smacks of judgment or opinion about what you are hearing, the employee may feel defensive, attacked, or misunderstood.

Listen Empathically

Another key element to good listening is listening empathically. Empathic listening is also called active listening or reflective listening. The American College dictionary describes empathy as "mentally entering into the feeling of a person ...." As you listen to your employee, put yourself in his or her shoes, and work to understand what it's like to *be* the speaker in that moment. This will help you understand why the problem is occurring and what an effective solution might look like.

So how do you listen empathically? What are the steps?

1. **Temporarily set aside your other priorities.** Clear your calendar and your mind to make room for what you are about to hear.

2. **Focus solely and nonjudgmentally on your employee.** Be prepared to hear and understand the issue from the employee's perspective.

3. **From time to time, tell the employee what you are hearing.** Use a few of your own words (don't parrot the employee) to explain what you understand the employee is communicating, without incorporating your own agenda or opinions.

While you will interject your perceptions throughout the discussion, you don't want to interrupt. Think of a butter knife under a stream of water. If the blade is vertical, the water continues by with barely a ripple—this is interjecting. If the butter knife is horizontal, causing the water to change directions and spill over the sides, that is interrupting. When you feed back to your employee what you are hearing by interjecting your own paraphrase of what he or she is feeling, you are signaling not only that you are listening closely, but also that you are working hard to understand and empathize. A few phrases that indicate you are interjecting are:

- "So *you* think that ..."
- "What *you* need now is ..."
- "So *you're* anxious about ..."
- "Seems *you're* unsure of ..."
- "Sounds like *you're* really feeling ..."

You can see by these phrases that you are not agreeing with your employee about the facts or even validating the employee's thoughts, feelings, or beliefs—you are simply summarizing what he or she has said. Each of these phrases indicates that you hear, understand, and empathize, without excusing the behavior.

Why is empathic listening so important? Because:

- Your employee is more likely to keep explaining instead of defending, blaming, shutting down, or withdrawing.
- You will minimize misunderstandings as you signal that you are really hearing what the employee is saying and feeling.
- You may help your employee clarify emotions, ideas, and needs by sharing your periodic nonjudgmental summaries.
- When the employee feels heard and understood, he or she will feel invested in solving the problem.

Adapt

Even if you've done your homework and investigated an issue before you talk to the employee, your discussion may very well bring you new information. In that case, you'll have to be open to changing your plans to account for the new data.

New information you might get could include:

- new facts about what happened
- insight into what motivated the employee or how the employee perceives the situation

- new information about how your team operates
- the role other people might play in creating or exacerbating the problem
- insight into how the employee is understanding and interpreting the signals you send
- an understanding of your employee's commitment to the company and his or her ongoing success, and
- a different perspective on what next steps might effectively solve the problem.

If new facts make you reconsider whether the discipline you've planned to administer will be effective, don't be afraid to walk away and reevaluate. After all, you can always come back to the discussion. And thinking about how the new facts affect the situation make it possible for you craft more effective solutions.

Don't be bullied. There's a big difference between staying open to new facts and allowing an employee to push your around. Some employees will make excuses for their behavior or call your disciplinary decisions into question. Unless the employee raises new information that you should consider, however, you shouldn't let the employee's response change your mind. If you've followed the smart discipline strategies in this book, you've prepared carefully and chosen the appropriate disciplinary measure. Even if the employee has more seniority or experience than you, only you—the manager—can decide when corrective action is in order.

Act

It's safe to say that if you walk out of a discipline meeting without getting a commitment from your employee for future action, it probably wasn't a very successful meeting. Remember that the purpose of progressive discipline is to improve the employee's behavior or performance. If you don't have an action plan, that means there is not a concrete way to measure improvement.

So how do you go about building an action plan? Here are a few steps to get you started:

1. Agree on the facts and the impact of the problem.

2. Define your role—make sure the employee understands that he or she ultimately owns the problem.

3. Brainstorm and negotiate a plan of action.

4. Follow up to ensure that the action plan is working.

This doesn't have to be a lengthy exercise. Indeed, in some cases, the plan may be very quick and obvious. In the case of unwanted actions that don't seem to have a systemic root, the action plan may just be, "Don't do that anymore." Things like tardiness, absenteeism, and misconduct can often be dealt with this way. More detailed action plans may be necessary for dealing with more complicated issues, however.

Agree on the Facts and the Impact

During the difficult conversation you are having, you must make sure not only that you understand the employee's point of view, but also that the employee understands the issue—and his or her responsibility for dealing with it.

> **EXAMPLE:** Chris is a line supervisor for an auto parts manufacturer. His team is responsible for delivering 2,500 carburetors per month. This goal is based on past performance, so the whole team knows that it is achievable, though challenging. Manuel, an employee with more than ten years of experience, is responsible for packaging the carburetors in boxes and sending the boxes to the distribution department. Lately, he has not been completing this task on time, and it is reducing the number of carburetors that go out each day.
>
> Chris sits Manuel down in a conference room to discuss the issue. He explains how Manuel's performance is affecting the whole team and underlines it by saying that they are in danger of not meeting their 2,500-carburetor commitment. Chris listens carefully to Manuel's response, interjecting to signal his understanding and empathy for Manuel's position.
>
> Chris moves on to planning the course of action going forward. He asks Manuel for his ideas. Manuel replies, "I just told you the solution. We need to lower the number of carburetors that we deliver. We cannot continue to work at this pace. Everyone is feeling the pressure."

Chris realizes he has not adequately outlined the importance of meeting the departmental commitment, the genesis of the measurement, nor Manuel's direct and singular role in it. He starts over again, this time working to put ownership of Manuel's performance problem where it belongs: with Manuel.

In the beginning of this example, it seemed like Chris was doing everything right. He went to great lengths to understand Manuel's point of view and engage him in developing a solution. But as you may have seen in poor performers who report to you, Manuel is not taking responsibility for the problem. Instead, he suggests that the whole team has a problem. Chris needs to get back on course with a difficult message: "No, Manuel. This is not a team issue, nor an issue of capacity. This is you not performing up to the standards of the rest of the team. That is what we have to focus on." Manuel also does not understand that the output requirement is not negotiable. It is a business imperative that is put at risk by poor performance. Chris must make these points more clearly.

Once an employee understands his or her personal responsibility in an identified problem, you can focus on fixing it through productive action planning. But don't be surprised if you have to come back to this issue more than once. You may even go so far as to ask outright, "Do you believe that this is your issue to solve?" Keep talking through it until the employee acknowledges his or her personal responsibility—this is the only way to make sure that the employee is truly committed to improvement.

Define Your Role

In the process of acknowledging ownership and working to craft a solution, the employee needs to understand what your role is. You are a coach. You provide methods, game plans, resources, and ideas. You decide who plays when, and you set the direction for the entire team. You monitor performance along the way, looking at agreed-upon metrics, and make adjustments if necessary. Ultimately, however, your employee has to put the ball over the goal line.

If the employee seems unclear on your role, state it directly. For example: "John, I am here to support you in improving your efficiency in this area. I can be a sounding board, brainstorm ideas with you, and let you know how you are doing, but the responsibility for improvement lies with you." For the rest of the meeting with John, you must be careful not to take any action that might blur the lines of ownership of the problem and your role as a coach. Then your job is to monitor John's progress and coach him along the way. Making your role clear to your employee provides a solid boundary about who is there to offer support and facilitate improvement (you) and who has to improve (the employee).

Brainstorm and Negotiate a Solution

Imagine guiding your employee into building a step-by-step plan that not only addresses the problem, but also ensures improved future performance. You will be saved the difficult (and expensive) process of hiring and training a replacement, and you will have a motivated employee committed to successful job performance.

To accomplish this task, you must give the employee the opportunity to evaluate different solutions to the problem. The easiest way to do this is to begin a brainstorming session.

Skills Enhancement 4: Brainstorming an Action Plan

Use this exercise to brainstorm a plan of action with your employee.

Step 1: With the employee, write down the problem in objective terms.

Step 2: Write down how the problem is affecting others involved, such as the company, the team, and you, the manager.

Step 3: Spend five minutes talking with your employee about what an ideal solution would look like. Write down everything this ideal solution would have to accomplish. Try to open it up to all possibilities, even if they seem to go beyond your resources or budget.

Step 4: Take ten minutes to talk about what is necessary to go from where your employee is right now to the great solution outlined above. This may include attitude changes, skill enhancements, more time, help with prioritizing, and so on. Everything is fair game; you'll negotiate what is really possible later.

Step 5: Capture this list on paper. You'll need it to determine the agreed-upon plan.

While the potential solutions may turn out to be unreasonable or un-doable, the basis of good collaboration is a willingness to consider any-thing. Now that you have worked with the employee to talk about pos-sibilities, think about whether any of the potential solutions are practical for both the business and the employee. Consider these questions:

- Can your business afford the time and money necessary to make the plan work?
- Is the employee capable of achieving the plan?
- Are the results worth both the time and energy it will take?
- Does this really solve the problem to the satisfaction of those directly involved?

Once you have the answers to these questions, your list of realistic potential solutions will likely be much shorter. From this shorter list, you and the employee can decide which solutions work best. Be practical, and modify options if they can be made better or workable. You do not want to sponsor a plan that just won't or can't happen.

Sample Action Steps	
Issues	**Potential Action Steps**
Tardiness	For the next thirty days, check in with the manager when you arrive.
	Provide 24 hours' notice if you are going to be late.
	Arrive to meetings five minutes early.
Lack of Attention to Detail	Review each document at least three times. Make sure you take at least an hour break between checks. Mark the document each time you review it.
	Store each deliverable overnight and re-appraise it in the morning with fresh eyes.
	Create checklists of each step required to get something done. Attach the checklist to the item and physically check off each step as you complete it.
Bad Attitude	Take half a day off to evaluate and chart the pros and cons of working here. Meet tomorrow to discuss those pros and cons.
	Examine how you would characterize your attitude, whether and how you think it needs to change, and what you think would help you bring about that change. Meet the day after tomorrow to talk about your findings.
	When something about your job frustrates you, write it down. Then consider what you can do to change the situation. At the end of the week, meet with me to discuss what caused your frustrations and what we can do about it.

Sample Action Steps (continued)

Issues	Potential Action Steps
Missed Deadlines	Make a list of things you think contribute to missing your deadlines. Do you have too much to do? Do you lack the skills necessary to do the work? Are there too many things on your plate? Meet over coffee this afternoon to go over the list. Take a negotiations class to learn how to negotiate realistic deadlines. When you have an assignment, create a formal project schedule and give yourself a deadline a day or two before it is due. Allow the last day(s) for contending with unforeseen problems and error proofing.
Anger Management	Attend a course on managing your emotions in the workplace. When you feel yourself getting angry, take a fifteen-minute break to walk around the building and regain control.
Missed Sales Numbers	Build your coldcalling skills by targeting potential new clients; do so until you've acquired at least one new customer per month. Reevaluate in three months. Analyze your performance against the sales cycle to determine where your weaknesses are. Draft potential solutions to these problems and meet again next week to discuss. Write up account development plans for existing accounts. Include new sales targets and what steps you will take to achieve the targets.

Follow Up on the Action Plan

At the end of any good action plan is a brief section on how you intend to review ongoing progress, as well as a timeframe for "getting well." This doesn't have to be complicated. You could agree to meet every week for 15 minutes to go over each step of the plan and how it is going. Or you could agree to a set of measures that would indicate that the employee is back on track.

Whatever methodology you choose, make sure you follow through. Seeing the plan through to its conclusion will send the right message to the employee. Your continued commitment tells the employee that you are in it for the long haul. Moreover, the employee can feel proud and empowered when he or she meets the goals of the plan.

You also need to create a reasonable timeframe for the plan. A reasonable timeframe gives the employee the opportunity to succeed and allows the employee to go back to the job with renewed confidence in his or her ability to set performance goals and achieve them. Giving an employee too many tasks to accomplish in a short time, however, will discourage the employee and will likely result in failure.

If you follow these strategies when discussing a discipline problem with an employee, you'll walk away from the conversation having given the employee the motivation and opportunity to succeed. And with dedication, your action plan will address the issues facing you and your employee and lead to sustainable improved performance.

Smart Talk:
Smart Summary

● Before you meet with your employee, prepare for the discussion. Examine the issue from all perspectives, jot down your opening sentences, and don't assume you know the whole story. Be ready for a variety of emotional responses.

● Remember that you're there to improve the employee's workplace performance or behavior. Set the tone for the meeting by choosing an appropriate environment and using a tone of voice that conveys the gravity of the situation.

● When it's time to hear the employee's perspective, make sure you're not distracted, and focus on what the employee says—and feels. Give your employee time to process, too, even if it means awkward silences.

● Give the employee the opportunity to share new, relevant information—but don't doubt what you know. Don't allow the employee to blame others if the blame is misplaced.

● Don't walk away from a discipline discussion without an action plan. And remember—while you can provide encouragement, resources, and support, it's ultimately your employee's responsibility to solve the problem.

8

Smart Ways to Deal With Difficult Employee Reactions

The confrontation and criticism inherent in discipline can lead to unexpected—and often powerful—emotional responses from your employees. In fact, some managers avoid discipline altogether so they won't have to face these reactions. "Oh, Henry will get so mad, and his performance isn't *that* bad ..." or "Janice takes criticism so badly, there's no point talking to her about her tardiness." There is no doubt that wading into these emotional waters requires courage on your part—courage and a few of the smart strategies outlined in this chapter. Here, you will learn how to handle the most common negative reactions to discipline.

In an ideal disciplinary meeting, you point out the problem, the employee sees it as an opportunity to improve and succeed in the organization, and you both walk away from the meeting with a handshake and renewed optimism about the future. Unfortunately, that's not always what happens. Instead, some employees respond strongly—and negatively—to discipline. These negative responses typically fall into one of two categories: emotional responses and masking responses. An emotional response is a quick, often uncontrolled reaction based on the employee's immediate thoughts or feelings; a masking response is intended to deflect or protect the person's real emotions about an issue.

The most common emotional reactions to discipline include:

- **Anger.** "You have no right to say that."
- **Grief.** "I never dreamed you felt that way about me. I am crushed."
- **Anxiety.** "Oh my God, my career is ruined!"
- **Violence or threats.** "You'll be sorry you ever brought this up!"

The most common masking reactions are:

- **Denial.** "I didn't do that."
- **Silence.** "If I don't say anything, you won't be able to pin this on me."
- **Blame.** "You've got it all wrong. It wasn't me."
- **Dispassion.** "Fine, whatever."

Both types of responses can be challenging for a manager. Emotional responses involve very deep-rooted (and often extreme) feelings, while masking reactions typically signal that the employee is having a hard time processing the situation or, in the worst cases, is unwilling to accept responsibility.

These reactions can occur at any step in the discipline process, from a coaching session to the middle of what you thought was a successful improvement plan all the way to a termination meeting. Moreover, the employee may exhibit different emotions at different stages in the process, or may express more than one of these reactions at once.

That's why it's best to go in knowing what you might encounter. While these emotions can be challenging, if you know some strategies for dealing with them in the moment, you can usually work through them toward solutions.

Emotional Reactions

Sometimes, employees react very emotionally, allowing what they feel to control what they say or do. Many of these emotions, and their manifestations, feel out of place in the work environment. However, as we know deep down, the work self is intimately intertwined with the whole person. Employees who are emotionally invested in what they do are usually more passionate and dedicated to their jobs.

This means there are benefits to having an employee respond with strong emotions—it usually means the employee cares about the job, which means he or she can likely be motivated to improve. In those situations, you can often work together to direct the employee's energy into creating a solution to the problem.

Anger

Anger can be an alarming reaction to discipline. It may build gradually and explode very suddenly, often without much apparent relationship to what is actually happening in the moment. If an employee has been frustrated about a situation for a long time and is suddenly confronted with his or her responsibility for it, dormant anger can be released unexpectedly. More alarming, anger can be expressed many ways— most of which are very uncomfortable if you are on the receiving end. It may manifest itself in a raised voice, a pounded fist, angry words, or a verbal attack. At its worst, anger can become violent—a reaction that we'll discuss separately below.

But anger isn't necessarily all bad—it communicates that the employee really cares and has something significant to communicate to you. It signals that the employee is willing to lose a little control to make sure you understand.

While anger may be a potentially constructive reaction, that doesn't mean it's an acceptable one. If anger manifests itself in personal attacks or inappropriate behavior like yelling or name calling, you must immediately put an end to it. While you want to hear the employee's point of view, you must show that mutual respect and professionalism are mandatory in the work environment.

Let's look at a few smart strategies for working through a disciplinary session that is fraught with anger:

1. Slow the meeting down. Instead of plowing forward to the next point you want to make, explain to the employee that he or she needs to calm down before you can proceed. Take a moment or two to allow for this.

2. If the employee does calm down, acknowledge that you understand that he or she has something important to say, but saying it in anger is not an acceptable way to deliver the message.

3. If the employee is incapable of controlling his or her anger, or your fear grows, tell the employee that you are going to end the conversation—for now. Institute a cooldown period, most likely away from the office. Pick a time to re-engage. If the employee denies that such a meeting will be productive, commit to revisiting the issue later. Anger may be preventing the employee from seeing the situation rationally now, but that may change with time.

4. Don't compromise your safety or the safety of your team. If you're afraid that the employee's anger will erupt into violence, immediately seek help.

EXAMPLE: Pedro, a restaurant manager, decides to give Luis a verbal warning because he is not bussing the tables at his station quickly enough, even though Pedro has previously coached him on the issue. Pedro calls Luis into his office and tells him that he is still working too slowly and doesn't seem to have implemented the ideas they came up with together in their coaching session. Luis, normally even tempered, clenches his fists and turns red. "I cannot believe you are picking on me again! I am working so hard to get these tables bussed and nothing is good enough for you!"

Which of the following is an appropriate response?

- "Luis, I know this is upsetting, and I want to figure out a way we can improve this situation. Take a minute to calm down, and then let's resume the conversation."
- "Luis, anger won't help you at all here. If you don't get focused on solving this issue right away, you can bet there will be repercussions."

Here, the first response is the appropriate one. Pedro gives Luis time to calm down and an opportunity to re-engage in the discussion later, instead of making threats. Hopefully, the two will be able to have a productive conversation.

Grief

As a manager, it can be very uncomfortable when an employee is saddened or wounded by discipline. After all, your intent isn't to hurt the employee's feelings, but to help him or her succeed in the organization. But there is a positive side to grief: It shows that the employee is really invested in his or her performance and reputation. More than any other negative reaction, true grief can usually be worked out, and the employee focused on improving performance.

If your employee expresses grief—for example, by crying—it might mean one of two things: The employee is genuinely upset about having done poorly, or the employee is trying to manipulate the situation. The latter typically happens when an employee knows how to push your buttons. When an employee's grief is sincere, though, it is usually accompanied by an immediate and overwhelming reaction and continues to crop up throughout the discussion.

Either way, it is important to go into these sessions knowing how you are likely to respond to expressions of grief. If you know that tears or sadness pluck at your heartstrings and you tend to try to comfort those who are feeling sad, you may lose sight of your original purpose: To deal openly and honestly with a discipline problem that has to change if the employee is going to succeed in the organization. If you are embarrassed by tears, practice talking through the grief, even if it's just to get to the point in the discussion where you'll arrange to reschedule the meeting. You need to focus not on how the grief makes you feel, but on how to solve the problem at hand.

If an employee cries or exhibits sadness, offer a tissue if necessary, but not a shoulder to cry on. It may be tempting to make comforting statements like "It will be okay" or "Don't worry about it, things are going to be fine." However, statements like this send the wrong message: That there isn't really a problem, that the employee is not responsible for it, or that the employee's job is secure no matter what happens.

If your employee can't get past grief and into a productive discussion, try these strategies:

1. **Acknowledge the response.** Say something like "I can see how this is affecting you." Allow enough time for the employee to recover, silent time in which the employee can begin to gather his or her thoughts again. Be practical about the time allowed. If it looks like the employee is going have a hard time regaining composure, end the session and schedule a follow-up meeting.

2. **Stay focused.** Don't let the conversation shift from the problem to the employee's reaction. Focus your employee by bringing him or her back to the topic at hand and letting the employee know that you need to work through this as soon as he or she is able.

3. **Continue to maintain professionalism.** If you do so, the employee may find it easier to get his or her emotions in check.

4. **Accept that the grief might not disappear entirely.** Even if the employee has a hard time hiding all feelings of grief, the conversation can still be productive.

EXAMPLE: Using the example of Pedro and Luis above, imagine Luis instead responded to Pedro by saying, "Oh man, I really let you down. I can't believe how badly I screwed up. I just can't believe this happened." He lowers his head into his hands and covers his eyes.

How should Pedro respond?

- "Luis, I can see how badly you feel. That let's me know how important this job is to you. When you are ready, let's talk about how we can fix this problem once and for all."

- "Luis, man, please don't get upset. I didn't mean to make you feel bad. Forget it, it isn't worth getting worked up about."

Both answers have the effect of calming Luis, but only the first will actually get Luis focused on the problem at hand.

Anxiety

For some employees, the discipline process brings up feelings of inadequacy or rejection from the past. The employee may feel like a failure, or that termination of employment is inevitable. All of this can hit quickly and cause anxiety or, in the worst cases, panic. When panic or anxiety strikes, it is hard to get the employee to concentrate on the problem that necessitated the discipline in the first place.

Add to the conundrum that anxiety is catching. If you aren't nervous already, the employee's anxiety may cause you to feel a bit uneasy yourself. When that happens, employ the following strategies to get your employee (and yourself) comfortable and focused on improvement.

If your employee spirals into anxiety or panic:

1. **Slow down the meeting.** Refocus the employee on the problem at hand—not the fears in his or her head. Reiterate exactly what you are talking about, and provide adequate examples.

2. **Put the problem in the context of the full progressive discipline process.** If the employee thinks that he or she is about to be fired when that's not the case, he or she may not be prepared to think about solutions, but instead may just be anxiously waiting for the ax to fall. So be sure to tell the employee where you are in the progressive discipline continuum (but remember not to make any promises about the future—see Chapter 3).

3. **Check in frequently with your employee during the meeting.** Does he or she clearly understand the scope of what is being discussed, or has he or she blown it out of proportion? Ask simple questions like "Am I being clear?" or "Is there anything you don't understand?" or "Does this make sense to you?"

4. **Reinforce that solutions are possible.** If the employee is panicked, he or she may have a hard time thinking of ways to solve the problem.

When dealing with terminations, keep it brief. If your discussion is a termination discussion, the employee might be filled with anxiety—but you shouldn't refocus that energy on improving the problem. The situation is already beyond repair, and you don't want to get into an involved discussion that won't be fruitful. Instead, focus on closing the meeting by wrapping up logistical, and very practical, issues, such as the final paycheck, continued health coverage, and packing up.

> **EXAMPLE:** Let's go back to the example of Pedro and Luis. To open the conversation, Pedro makes his short introductory statement about the nature of the meeting. As he is talking, he sees Luis begin to drum his fingers on the tabletop. Luis's knee begins bouncing and he begins to sweat. Pedro can tell that Luis is feeling anxious.
>
> Pulling Luis out of his anxiety and back into a productive meeting is not easy. Which way improves Pedro's chances of doing so?
>
> "Luis, it's good to see that you know this is important. If this doesn't improve, it could cost you your job. Now pay attention and let's try to solve this."
>
> "Luis, I can see that this makes you anxious. The problem worries me, too, but the good news is that you have a chance to fix this before it gets worse. Do you feel like you can talk about how we can improve your bussing times, or do you need a minute?"
>
> In the second response, Pedro acknowledges the problem but focuses on the benefit of improving. He also gives Luis the opportunity to step away, if he needs to. This is much better than the slightly threatening first response, which could just make Luis more anxious.

Violence

It's unfortunate but true: Sometimes, employees react violently to workplace stress. This reaction to discipline is unacceptable—unlike other reactions, it cannot usually be overcome. A violent employee puts you and your team members at serious physical risk and leaves your company exposed to legal liability, too. If the company doesn't take action to terminate a violent employee, and that employee later harms a coworker or client, the company could be held responsible.

If an employee reacts violently or you believe violence is likely because of threatening statements, gestures, or other behaviors, try these steps:

1. **Prepare for the possibility.** If you think it's possible that an employee may be violent, let others know. Sit nearest the door so that you can get out if you need to.

2. **Have security personnel available and prepared to assist.** If your company is not big enough for a security force, make sure that you have adequate help standing by, ready to intervene if you need it.

3. **Meet with a potentially violent employee at a time when fewer coworkers will be present,** such as late in the day or at the end of the work week.

4. **Stay calm.** If the employee has not acted violently but you think he or she might, continue to listen to what he or she is saying and maintain eye contact. The employee will feel heard, which may calm him or her down, or it may allow you to discreetly seek assistance without being noticed.

5. **Get help.** If the employee has already acted violently, signal or call for help immediately and loudly. However, if the employee hasn't yet become physical, such a call for help might agitate him or her further. If possible, motion or call for help quietly, perhaps by stepping out to signal to a coworker or security personnel.

6. **Keep the situation contained.** Leave the room with the door shut until help arrives, or move the employee off the premises as quickly as possible.

7. **Report the incident.** Document it thoroughly; discuss it with your supervisor as well as your human resources department or legal counsel.

8. **Don't compromise the safety of your employees going forward.** Take extra precautionary steps to maintain safety in the workplace. You may need to notify law enforcement or your security team or to tell your employees about the situation and give them instructions on what to do if this person returns to the workplace.

Masking Reactions

Instead of acting out emotionally, some employees use defense mechanisms to mask their emotions. Noted psychotherapist Mollie Sullivan says, "People have these reactions because at some point in time, it served them really well. They have 'worked' in some way and protected this person from unpleasant situations." Of course, that can make it very hard to break through a masking response, especially if you want to turn a defensive reaction into a productive discussion.

Denial

Denial usually occurs early in the discipline process, when you first confront an employee with a problem. Instead of acknowledging the problem and focusing on the solution, the employee rejects either the existence of the problem or his or her responsibility for it. He or she may say things like "You're wrong" or "It wasn't me" or "I have no idea what you're talking about."

When someone denies ownership of the problem like this, your natural response is to try harder to make the person understand his or her responsibility. But working too hard at this can undermine your message, giving the employee control of the conversation as you try in vain to come up with the "right answer" that will get the employee to acknowledge the problem. Instead of working together to find a solution, you'll spend your time trying to convince the employee that there is a problem in the first place.

Remember: By following the smart discipline process, you'll have entered this conversation with discreet examples of the problem behavior. If the employee still isn't acknowledging responsibility after hearing what you have to say, try these steps:

1. **Go through the examples one by one.** Ask the employee, "Do you remember this happening?" or "Do you understand your role in what occurred?" Find out whether the employee sees his or her responsibility for at least part of the problem.

2. **Remember to acknowledge what the employee is saying.** Even if you disagree about the employee's level of responsibility, be sure to indicate that you hear the other perspective.

3. **Be willing to revisit the issue.** If you are given new facts and need to investigate further, say so.

4. **Change the way you say it.** Sometimes, all the employee needs to understand the problem is a few different words or phrases. Consider whether you can express the same concept another way.

5. **Frankly acknowledge the employee's denial**—it may be something he or she isn't consciously aware of. Say something like "It seems you're having a hard time acknowledging your responsibility for this problem. Why don't you take some time to think about your involvement, and what we should do going forward?" Set up a follow up date and time.

Of course, it's important that the employee acknowledge the existence of the problem. After all, how can you fix a problem that the employee doesn't believe exists or believes is someone else's responsibility? If you follow the steps above and are still not successful, you'll have to address this with the employee. You may have to craft an improvement strategy on your own, but the employee should know that the likelihood of success is much diminished without his or her commitment to acknowledging and fixing the problem.

EXAMPLE: Martha is the night shift supervisor in the children's department of a department store. Venetia is the top salesperson in her department and often works in the evenings. About once a week, the register has come up about $100 short. Martha notices that it happens only on the nights that Venetia is working. Martha monitors the situation for two additional weeks, and while she does not see Venetia take the money, she realizes that no one else has access to the register from which the money is disappearing.

Martha approaches Venetia and explains the situation. Venetia is caught completely off guard and says, "It wasn't me! There is no way I'd do anything to put my job at risk. It had to be Mike over in Men's Suits; when I take my break, he keeps an eye on the department."

Martha responds, "But Venetia, even when he's watching the floor, he doesn't have access to the register. How do you explain that?"

Venetia simply repeats, "It wasn't me."

Martha now needs to decide what to do to proceed. Which would be the most effective way to deal with Venetia's denial?

"Venetia, it sounds to me like you think Mike accessed the cash drawer while you were on your break. Is that right?"

"So Venetia, what you are saying is: This isn't your problem?"

Here, Martha recognizes that she needs to gather more information. The first option shows Venetia that Martha is really listening, and it helps Martha understand whether Venetia feels she is responsible for the problem or not. This is more effective than the second response, which just allows Venetia to deny involvement, without requiring her to explain why she's not responsible or how Mike could be involved.

Silence

Sometimes, an employee won't respond at all to discipline but will sit silently. There are many reasons for silence. Often, the employee is trying to process new or unanticipated information. The employee may feel overwhelmed, humiliated, or saddened and not know what to say. Additionally, the employee may be using silence as a "holding pattern": A time to put together a defense and respond. Both of these reasons for silence are acceptable in the disciplinary conversation, to a point. That point is determined by the length of time spent sitting quietly. If it truly looks like the employee is internally processing what you have said, give the employee enough time to do so. If the silence drags on beyond what makes sense, or it's clear that the employee is trying to avoid talking altogether, end the session with a promise to address the issue later.

In the discipline process, the least effective way to deal with silence is to fill it. If you do, you might say things that let the employee off the hook, share more information than is necessary, or suggest to the employee that you need to justify your actions. Another problem with filling the silence is that the employee doesn't have time to think about what you are saying. If the employee is just busy trying to keep up with you, he or she won't be thinking about the important points you made at the beginning of the discussion.

Dealing With Abject Silence

There is one form of silence that will require extra effort and must be specifically targeted: abject silence. You will probably recognize it when you see it—in fact, it may already sound familiar. This silence often looks like petulance and can't be broken after a reasonable time. The employee may sit with crossed arms or tightly closed lips, responding only when directly addressed and with the briefest of answers.

Abject silence is typically a form of denial. By refusing to communicate with you, the employee is refusing to acknowledge the problem and move forward to a solution. When an employee's tone, mannerisms, or body language indicate that he or she is closed to discussion, you'll have to take extra steps to overcome the silence. Begin by asking "yes or no" questions, such as "Do you remember that incident?" If the employee still won't respond, ask progressively more complicated questions like "In your eyes, what could you have done differently in that incident?" If that doesn't engage the employee, end the meeting with a promise to resume soon. Make it clear that ongoing abject silence is insubordination and cause for further discipline.

If an employee gives you the silent treatment, try these steps:

1. **Wait patiently.** The employee may feel shocked, embarrassed, or saddened. Allow the employee a moment to overcome that reaction.

2. **Respect the employee's feelings.** Tell the employee that you want to hear his or her thoughts and feelings. Don't mow over the silence—it is part of the process for the employee, and you should respect it. Remember, however, that your job is to deal with the underlying problem—the silence can't be permitted to go on forever.

3. **Meet again.** If the first meeting is unproductive, meet again. Explain to the employee that you can't get to the solution until you both acknowledge there is a problem and work together to fix it.

4. **Be firm.** While you may permit silence now, tell the employee explicitly and definitively that you expect to discuss the problem at a specific future date and time.

Silence that takes the form of self-defense can often be broken if you're willing to deal with the employee's immediate needs, instead of focusing only on the results you need to get out of the meeting. It is okay to stray a bit from your agenda if doing so may help engage the employee in the discussion and developing a solution. Be practical about how far you are willing to stray; you still have a very real issue to deal with. By expressing your commitment to the employee's success, and acknowledging that this is a hard message to hear, you may be able to break through the silence and proceed with a rich discussion.

> **EXAMPLE:** Think back to example of Martha and Venetia. What if Venetia responded with stony silence? How should Martha proceed?
>
> "Venetia, do you have anything to say? No? You leave me no choice but to terminate your employment."
>
> "Venetia, given how serious this matter is, I'm going to give you a chance to collect your thoughts. If you choose not to reply, I am going to have to move forward without your input."
>
> Actually, Martha wouldn't be completely wrong in either of these situations. But the second option recognizes that Venetia may be dealing with difficult emotions that can be overcome. If Venetia is able to process what's happening, she may eventually choose to engage in a discussion with Martha about it.

Blame

Some employees are simply unwilling to accept responsibility for a discipline problem. This often manifests itself in blame—the employee may accuse another person, or even you, for his or her failure. At its root, blame is a self-defense mechanism. When it happens, you can easily be pulled off track and sucked into a discussion you aren't prepared for. You may even begin to doubt yourself. When this happens, the employee, not you, takes control of the meeting.

When an employee lays blame on someone else, take a moment to verify what is being said. Ask a few probing questions to find out how the employee has come to this conclusion. Do the answers sound like a plausible story? Does it bear looking into further? Or does it differ too much from what you already know? After hearing the employee out, explain what you plan to do with the information.

If the employee continues to blame other people or things, try these steps:

1. **State the facts.** Ask the employee to confirm that your understanding is accurate. Use questions like "Did you see it that way?," "Do you agree that this happened?," or "Did you say that to her?"

2. **If you need to investigate further, step away.** If the employee's accusations have merit, end the session and don't deliver discipline until you know the whole story.

3. **Explain what research you've done and what conclusions you've come to.** This is where the discipline will begin—whether or not the employee is willing to participate.

4. **Don't discuss the responsibilities of others.** Even if other people are also responsible and will be disciplined, the employee needs to focus on his or her behavior, not that of others.

Dispassion

You often come to a discipline meeting only after having thought through the issues, worried about whether you've done the right thing, and committed to helping your employee improve. That's why it's frustrating when an employee responds dispassionately or refuses to engage—perhaps by acting like he or she just doesn't care or isn't interested.

Your hope is always that your employees care enough to want to work as hard as necessary to be successful, and true dispassion is a sign that an employee doesn't want to work hard. However, what initially appears to be dispassion may in fact be borne of other emotions. An employee who is hurt or embarrassed when confronted with problems may want to give you the impression that he or she "just doesn't care"—that's it's not a big deal.

In rare cases, the employee really *doesn't* care enough to work to improve the problem. You'll know because as the conversation progresses, the employee will continue to be nonresponsive. Employees who are hurt or embarrassed will likely become uncomfortable when directly confronted with the issues; perhaps avoiding eye contact with downcast eyes, mumbling, or physically withdrawing with head bowed or shoulders slumped. A dispassionate employee, on the other hand, will affect complete comfort with the situation, perhaps even meeting your eye, slouching comfortably in the chair, or allowing his or her attention to wander.

If an employee stays dispassionate and doesn't engage in the discussion, take these steps:

1. **Explain the problem.** Be very clear and have your facts in order. Ask frequent validating questions such as "Do you understand what I'm saying?" Yes or no answers are often the start of a deeper conversation.

2. **Deepen the discussion.** Start with generic questions such as "You were there that day, right?" Wait patiently for the answer, and then move on to a slightly more involved question, like "Do you remember talking to Paul about that?" Continue to ask more probing questions to get more relevant information.

3. **Stick to your agenda.** Describe what you would like to accomplish. If you are receiving no response, ask the employee how he or she would like to work towards a mutually agreeable outcome. Let the employee know that the disengagement can't continue much longer.

4. **Warn the employee of the consequences.** If the employee isn't willing to address the problem with you, whether now or in the near future, explain that you'll have no choice but to escalate discipline.

It takes a lot of energy to maintain disinterest in something that affects you a lot, which is why dispassion can usually be overcome. As we've described, it is usually a protective reaction that the employee adopts when he or she perceives something as an attack. Once the employee understands that the point of the discussion is to improve and succeed, he or she may overcome the dispassionate response.

EXAMPLE: What if, early in the discipline process, Martha had said to Venetia, "As you know, I add the register's totals each night. I have noticed that four times in the last two weeks, the register has been short $100. I've started researching this and I've discovered it is happening only on nights you work. Can you explain why?" Venetia doesn't say anything—instead, she looks down at her lap, appearing not to notice or care about the discussion.

Of the two following replies, which would most likely solicit a response?

"Venetia, I need you to reply. In fact, if you don't respond right away, I'm going to assume that you took the money."

"Venetia, do you understand what I am asking?"

While the first response may solicit a reaction from Venetia, that reaction could be an angry one. On the other hand, if Martha begins by asking Venetia whether she understands the question, Venetia has little choice but to respond with a "yes" or "no." Martha can continue to ask small, closed questions until she gets Venetia engaged in the discussion.

Dealing with employees' emotions can be a tough and confusing process. Once you've done so, however, you can focus on other issues—like setting goals and improving performance. Although you might not feel like it at the time, employees will appreciate it. Showing that you are committed to fixing problems, even when employees react emotionally, will communicate to your team that their success is important.

Smart Ways to Deal With Employee Responses: Smart Summary

- When an employee responds angrily to discipline, be prepared to slow the conversation down and walk away temporarily if needed. However, make sure that the employee understands that mutual respect is required—and if the employee acts violently or you fear violence, get help right away.

- A grieving employee is usually very invested in his or her job. With time, that grief can often be overcome. Don't allow yourself to be manipulated by it, though—that won't help you solve your problem.

- An anxious employee often simply can't hear what's being said: He or she is too concerned about what it means for the future. Do your best to focus the employee on the here and now—especially if the problem can be corrected.

- When an employee exhibits a masking reaction, there is usually a lot more going on internally. See if you can draw the employee out—but keep the discussion focused on the underlying problem, not the employee's response.

■

Smart Documentation

I f you're like most managers, you have plenty of paperwork to do. Sometimes, it might even seem like you spend more time dotting "i"s and crossing "t"s than you do dealing with the employees you supervise. But paperwork serves a very important purpose: It creates a written record of important decisions and conversations. Documenting disciplinary actions helps you prove that your actions are justified, whether to the employee, your human resources department, or a judge or jury. And of course, your written records will help you stay on top of employee problems, managing your team more successfully.

Just because documenting discipline is important doesn't mean it should take up a lot of your time, however. This chapter gives you the information you need to document employee discipline, efficiently and effectively. First, we explain the benefits of documenting your decisions. Next, we give you guidelines for creating written records that give employees the information they need to improve performance, while protecting your company legally. Finally, we'll provide a step-by-step process, including a sample form, for documenting formal disciplinary meetings, as well as some tips on documenting less formal coaching sessions and follow-up meetings.

The Benefits of Documenting Discipline

Keeping written records of your disciplinary decisions can help you do a better job of managing your employees. Documentation serves a variety of purposes: It can help you communicate with your employees, remember past disciplinary actions and decisions, and justify your decisions to others in the company or in court, should you ever be required to do so.

Of course, documentation will be absolutely crucial if your decision is ever challenged in court: It's the best proof of why discipline was necessary and what type of discipline you imposed. But documenting disciplinary issues can also help you:

- **Ensure that you and the employee are on the same page.** As you'll see below, we recommend that you share formal disciplinary documentation with the employee and secure the employee's signature of agreement or acknowledgment. While the employee may not agree that discipline was necessary, you should be able to agree on the facts—such as what happened, when, and who was involved—and collaboratively develop a plan of action.

- **Track the employee's disciplinary history.** If you supervise a lot of employees or you are faced with an employee who has recurring brushes with your company's discipline system, your records will help you remember what's already happened as you decide how to handle a current issue or how to follow up with an employee.

- **Record the employee's disciplinary history for company use.** Very few employees and managers stay in the same job at the same company forever. If you or the employee take a different position, or if you leave the company altogether, your documentation gives the company a complete record of discipline for that employee. This will give the employee's next manager the information he or she needs to handle any future problems appropriately.

- **Treat employees consistently.** To avoid the accusation that you're playing favorites—or worse, discriminating against particular employees—you must apply discipline consistently. If you have to decide what level of discipline is appropriate, documentation allows you to review how you've handled similar problems with other employees in the past. You can make sure that you're not overreacting or downplaying a problem by checking your track record. You can also assure yourself that your response is justified, if you have to escalate discipline when an employee doesn't improve.

- **Track problems on your team.** Disciplinary documentation lets you know what types of problems your employees have—and it may help you see larger patterns developing. Do you have several employees who seem to be unclear on their responsibilities? Frequent safety violations? A sexual harassment problem? Your disciplinary records will help you see the larger picture, so you can provide training, give better guidance, communicate your expectations more clearly, or take any other actions necessary to help your team improve.

- **Prove what you did and why.** When you keep good records, you'll be able to justify your discipline decisions to anyone. And sometimes, good documentation will help convince an employee (or more often, his or her lawyer) not to sue. But if you can't avoid a lawsuit, documentation will at least help you prove your side of the story. It will give you written evidence of the actions you took and your reasons. It will also show the judge or jury that you tried to help the employee improve and that the employee had notice of his or her problems.

Guidelines for Effective Documentation

Before you dive into the details of what you should include in your records, there are some basic rules you should keep in mind as you document. No matter what type of disciplinary problem you're facing, following these rules will help you draft effective, thorough documentation that will protect your company from legal trouble—and won't take up too much of your time.

Document Immediately

The best written records are contemporaneous—that is, they are created at the time of the incidents and discussions they describe. As a practical matter, you probably won't be in a position to record conversations and events as they're happening. If you wait too long to document, however, it's all too easy to forget a few of the details, especially if you're juggling a lot of different issues or responsibilities at one time. The best way to make sure your recollections are accurate and complete is to document immediately after things happen. You can't be sure you'll remember everything as clearly several months—or even several days—later.

Another important reason to create an immediate written record is to avoid suspicion that you're trying to create trumped-up charges against the employee. Even if you have perfectly innocent reasons for delaying your documentation, the employee could be suspicious of written records created after the fact, particularly if you wait until you know that you might have to fire the employee. From the employee's perspective, it might look like you are trying to justify an unfair termination.

Adopt a same-day practice. The best practice is to document events and discussions on the day they happen, if possible, but certainly within the same week. If a situation appears to be worsening rapidly, you must be especially careful to document everything immediately. Otherwise, you might have to have another disciplinary meeting with the employee before you've documented what occurred and was agreed upon in the previous meeting. You'll want to be able to show that the employee had notice of the problem and your expectations for improvement before you disciplined a second time.

Be Objective

Everything you write should be factual and objective. Personnel records are not the place for speculation, unfounded conclusions, or personal opinions. Instead, stick to what you saw, heard, or said. If you find yourself writing about what you think might have happened rather than what did happen, you've gotten off track.

This mistake is easier to make than you might think. For example, if an employee cried or yelled in a meeting, you might be tempted to write that the employee was "sad" or "angry." Instead, your documentation should indicate what the employee did or said, not what you thought it meant about his or her feelings or state of mind.

> **EXAMPLE:** Chad missed a deadline for an important assignment. He seems unhappy lately, and he's spending a lot of time on the phone rather than doing his work. Because Chad's mistake caused big problems for the company, and because he didn't give you any warning that he might miss the deadline, you decide to give him a written warning.
>
> On your first try, you write this: "Chad appears to be allowing personal problems to affect his work. He needs to get his head out of the clouds and start focusing on finishing his assignments on time."
>
> This is neither objective nor particularly descriptive. An outsider looking at it would be unable to tell what Chad did that warranted discipline. So you try again, this time sticking to what you know: "Chad missed the deadline for handing in his work on the Ascendance project. His assignment was due on Monday, May 1, 2006. Because he was late, we did not meet our May 3 deadline for presenting the project to our client. Mary Allman, our contact at Ascendance, stated

in a telephone conversation with me on May 3 that our lateness has caused them to consider using another company for future projects. Chad did not inform me ahead of time that he might not meet the deadline. I met with him on May 3 in my office. At that time, I asked him why he was late. He replied that he was swamped with other work."

What you write should clearly convey the facts, so that someone else reading it can understand what happened and why discipline was necessary. Keep in mind that many different people may read your documentation. In your company, your audience will include the employee, the human resources department, any future managers to whom the employee reports, and possibly your manager. And your records may be read by people outside the company as well: If an employee considers or takes legal action against the company, what you write may wind up in the hands of lawyers, agency investigators, judges, or jurors. You'll want them to know, just by reading the documents, that you had good reasons for the disciplinary action you took.

Avoid Legal Conclusions

Carefully select the terms you use when documenting discipline. In addition to avoiding conclusions about what an employee's thoughts or motivations are, you shouldn't draw any conclusions about what an employee's actions mean legally. That means you shouldn't use any phrases implying that the employee did something illegal, such as violating another employee's legal rights. The reason for this rule is simple: If someone later tries to hold your company legally responsible for the employee's actions, your documentation could be used as proof—against the company or even you personally.

If your company prohibits the employee's conduct, you can and should indicate that the employee violated company policy. Just steer clear of any discussion of legal violations.

EXAMPLE: Several employees complain that Doug is viewing pornographic images on his computer. Although the employees agree that Doug quickly changes screens when he realizes he is no longer alone, and no one claims that Doug has tried to show them the pictures or discuss the pictures with them, they are uncomfortable with his behavior. When you confront Doug, he admits that he has been viewing these images but says he didn't realize anyone else knew about it. He is deeply embarrassed by the incident and quickly promises that he will no longer view pornography at work.

You decide to issue Doug a written warning. In your documentation, you describe what the employees reported and how Doug responded when you talked to him. Then you state, "Because your behavior qualifies as sexual harassment, I have decided that serious disciplinary measures are in order. I am therefore giving you a written warning."

Several months later, one of the employees who complained about Doug files sexual harassment charges against the company. Her lawyer asks to see all files relating to the incident with Doug. Your company's lawyer wants to argue that, although inappropriate, Doug's conduct does not meet the legal definition of sexual harassment. The problem here is that you've already said, while writing on behalf of the company, that Doug committed sexual harassment. Although your lawyer might be able to argue around this, you've stacked the deck against your company.

Be Thorough

When you document a disciplinary action, you are creating a record for later use. That record should include all of the important facts: what happened, when, where, and so on. Of course, no manager has time to write a novel every time an employee shows up late for work or misses a production goal. But leaving out important details can create major headaches down the road:

- You might not remember exactly what happened later—for example, if you have to discipline the employee again, or review the employee's file to draft a performance appraisal.
- If the employee begins working for another manager, that manager won't know all of the facts.
- You'll be in trouble if you ever have to justify your actions to higher-ups in the company, or in court. You'll either forget what actually happened, or you'll have to say, "This important thing

happened, but for some reason I forgot to put it in my notes." Even if you're able to remember the incident, it will look less credible if you didn't make a record of it when it occurred.

EXAMPLE: Kate manages the customer service center for a software company. She fires Francis after he repeatedly fails to meet the company's productivity standards. Customer service representatives are expected to answer or return at least 15 calls per day; Francis averaged nine or ten calls per day. Reps are also expected to complete all of the paperwork for customer orders on the day the customer orders the product. Francis's paperwork was routinely two or three days late.

Francis files a discrimination lawsuit, stating that Kate singled him out for discipline because of his age (he is 55 years old). He claims that Kate told him his numbers were low but never told him how he could improve. He also says that Kate never told him about the same-day requirement for customer orders.

Kate reviews her documentation. If she finds something like "I reviewed customer service productivity requirements with Francis," with no mention of a follow-up plan, she might have a hard time disproving Francis' allegations. On the other hand, if her records say, "I expect you to complete all of the forms for customer orders on the day the orders are placed" and "I will spend one morning next week with you at your workstation; later that day, we will meet to discuss how you can shorten the time you spend on the phone with each customer," she will be able to confidently dispute his statements.

Don't Overdocument

We know, we know: We just told you to be thorough. But it's also important not to go overboard, either by formally documenting minor incidents or discussions or by going on for pages and pages about a single incident or disciplinary meeting. You probably don't have time for that kind of documentation, and it won't help your employees' performance much either. If your employees think they will be written up for every tiny misstep, they are likely to stop trying to meet your expectations—and look for another job that isn't as stressful.

This type of documentation doesn't provide much legal protection either; in fact, it can actually work against you in court. Overdocumenting minor problems will make you look like a micromanager or a nitpicker. An employee can use extensive documentation to show that you were particularly hard on him or her or that you never gave the employee a real chance to improve.

Also, the more details you write down, the easier it is to contradict yourself or get confused about what happened. If you try to remember every single thing that was said or done, you may confuse yourself or others reading the documentation, and it might be difficult to distinguish the really important facts. And these inconsistencies could give more fuel to a disgruntled employee who wants to challenge your disciplinary decisions.

Don't Make Promises

Because you want to motivate your employees to succeed, you might be tempted to offer rewards to an employee who successfully meets the goals in his or her action plan. However, you should not tell the employee that he or she will receive certain benefits for improving. Similarly, you should not promise to follow a particular disciplinary process with the employee. Either of these mistakes could tie your hands later, if the employee tries to hold you to your promise.

As we explained in Chapter 3, stating or implying that an employee will be fired only for particular types of misconduct could limit the company's right to fire that employee. And, if your documentation states that an employee will receive a promotion, raise, or other benefit for improved performance, you might have created a contract obligating the company to provide that benefit—even if the company cannot afford it or does not want to provide it.

Making promises may also send the wrong message to the employee. Instead of helping the employee understand that there is a problem, promising incentives may lead the employee to believe he or she is meeting expectations and will be given extra benefits for *exceeding* them. You want to stay focused on the disciplinary issue, ensuring the employee understands there is a problem that needs to be fixed.

EXAMPLE: Ben disciplines Jerry for roughhousing on the loading dock. Ben informs Jerry that his actions violate the company's safety rules. To give Jerry an incentive to shape up, Ben writes this in his verbal warning documentation: "You cannot violate this rule again if you wish to be promoted to Fulfillment Manager." If Jerry never roughhouses again, he might argue that he should be promoted— even if the company later decides someone else should get the job.

Explain the Effects

As we've already discussed, it's very important to communicate to the employee how his or her performance or conduct problems are affecting you, others on your team, and the company as a whole. This is the best way to convince the employee that the problem is important and must change. It also conveys respect for the employee's contribution, because people notice—and suffer—when that contribution isn't made.

To drive the point home, you should not only discuss it with the employee, but also include it in your documentation. Employees are more likely to sit up and take notice when they see, in black and white, exactly how their problems are creating more work for others, costing the company money, leading to lost customers or sales, and so on.

Always Include a Follow-Up Plan

As you know, you and the employee should always come up with a plan for improvement, including deadlines. Always include this plan in your documentation. This will remind you to check in with the employee to make sure these targets are met, and to fulfill any other obligations you have to the employee. This will also help the employee focus on what he or she needs to do, and by when, to meet your expectations.

Informal Documentation

You don't have to fill out formal paperwork every time you meet with an employee to discuss performance improvement. For example, if you have a brief coaching conversation with an employee who seems to be away from her desk frequently or turns in a report that contains a couple of typos, you shouldn't spend the time or energy to document every word you said. Similarly, if you have a quick meeting to check in with an employee whom you had to discipline, you don't have to record the meeting in great detail.

However, you should make a quick written note of these meetings for future reference. After all, what happens if that one report with typos becomes ten? You'll want to remember—and be able to show—that the incident occurred before and that you addressed it. If your first quick coaching session isn't successful, you may have to move into your company's formal discipline process—and you'll need to know and be able to show that you already spoke to the employee about the issue. Similarly, your follow-up meeting may become important if the employee later claims that it never happened or does not remember the objectives you created together to improve the problem.

What to Include

For brief meetings and conversations like these, write a short memo—a paragraph or two—summarizing the discussion. Note the date and time you spoke to the employee and the employee's response, if any. Here's a sample memo documenting a follow-up meeting with an employee who was required to take a training program:

Memo

I met with Jennifer Shiu on February 3, 2007 to find out whether she had completed her class on using Excel spreadsheets for accounting. She told me that she finished the class on January 31, and she had learned a lot of tips that she found very helpful. I asked her if she would be willing to do a brief presentation on what she learned to the bookkeeping department at our departmental meeting on February 20; she agreed to do so.

Where to Keep Informal Documentation

If your company has a procedure for handling informal documentation, follow it. Some companies require managers to create written records of coaching sessions for the employee's personnel file; others will not allow managers to place anything short of a written warning in the file.

In companies that don't have a policy on this, many managers choose not to put informal coaching memos in the employee's personnel file. Instead, it's a good idea to keep these in your office, in a separate working file for each employee or a single file for ongoing performance issues. If you later have to discipline the employee for the same problem, you can use the memo to complete the "Prior Incidents" portion of the form below.

Unlike more formal documentation, you don't have to show these "coaching logs" to the employee. In fact, the employee probably won't ever find out that you wrote yourself a note. Knowing every incident is documented might make the employee feel micromanaged and afraid of each misstep. Because so many problems can be solved at the coaching level, there's no need to make the employee feel intimidated or watched. The document is really just to remind you to monitor the situation and to give you a basis to progress in the discipline process if that becomes necessary.

 It's all discoverable.

The situation is different when more formal follow-up memos— memos that record your follow-up meetings with employees, to make sure they are carrying out the action plans developed during formal disciplinary meetings—are required. You will have to put these in the employee's personnel file. You'll want a written record showing that the employee completed any required training or courses, that you met with the employee or provided resources to the employee, or that you otherwise met the company's obligations under the employee's improvement plan. If your follow-up meeting reveals that the employee has not held up his or her end of the agreed-upon plan, you'll want a written record of that, as well. After all, you may need it to justify progressing to more serious forms of discipline.

Formal Documentation, Step by Step

This section explains exactly what information you should include in your disciplinary records. To make the process clearer, we'll be creating documentation of a written warning for Randy, a fictional employee who is having trouble meeting deadlines.

At the end of this chapter, you'll find a sample discipline form you can use. Of course, if your company has its own forms to document discipline, you should use those instead. You'll see that we prefer to address the employee directly, rather than in the third person. Again, if your company had a different practice, you should follow it.

Once the paperwork is complete and signed by both you and employee, place it in the employee's personnel file.

Heading

At the beginning of your documentation, insert the employee's name, your name, the date, and the purpose of the document—for example, a verbal or written warning. Here's the heading for Randy's written warning:

Written Warning

Date: September 10, 2007

Employee Name: Randy Clark

Manager Name: Sarah Bronson

Incident Description

Next, explain the reason you are disciplining the employee. If the employee committed misconduct, describe what happened. For poor performance, describe how the employee is falling short of company requirements or expectations. This is also the place to include information about how the employee's problem is affecting the company. Don't include information about any past incidents or problems for which you've already disciplined the employee. If it belongs in the memo, that information will go in the next section.

Randy works for a company that owns a chain of stores selling home improvement products. He missed his deadline to finish five articles on kitchen remodeling for the company's website. His manager describes it like this:

Incident Description

On August 3, 2007, I asked you to create five new articles about kitchen remodels for the company's website. As we discussed, these articles were to be descriptions of typical kitchen remodeling projects, with references and links to relevant company products. I informed you that these articles would be the prototype for a new type of website content that ties our products to a detailed description of particular projects, rather than simply listing products by category. I also informed you that I needed to have a final draft of these articles on September 8, so I could present them to our marketing team at a meeting on September 10.

On September 7, you came to my office and told me that you would not make the deadline. You told me that you had completed a draft of three articles but had not yet included references to company products. You also stated that you thought someone in marketing should handle this part of the assignment, as they are more familiar with the products than you are. You did not let me know that you might miss the deadline or that you were having any trouble with the articles until September 7.

As a result of your failure to meet this deadline, Cynthia Bradley, Russell Jenkins, and I all had to drop our other work to complete the three articles you drafted. These articles had to be changed substantially because they were not written to best utilize the company's products. We had to add products to the articles as well. Because I was able to present only three articles at the marketing meeting, we had to postpone the rollout date for this new type of content. Our department's failure to meet its goal may cause other departments to believe we are unreliable. Moreover, because the new content is expected to drive higher sales, this delay will cost the company money.

Prior Incidents

If this is not the first time the employee has had this problem, describe previous incidents here. Include any disciplinary actions or coaching sessions that occurred. Also describe the plan you and the employee came up with at that time, including any help you made available to the employee. You don't need to go into great detail here, as you've already documented the prior incident. If you kept informal documentation of earlier coaching sessions or discussions, refer back to those notes to complete this portion of the form.

Randy has already received a verbal warning for missing a previous deadline, so his manager completes this section as follows:

Prior Incidents

I have already issued you a verbal warning, on March 15, 2007, for missing a deadline. You were assigned to write a list of suggested projects store associates could discuss with customers looking for spring gardening and landscaping ideas. You missed your deadline by a week, and we were unable to present your ideas to associates at the company's quarterly meeting.

When we met to discuss this problem, you told me that you tended to wait until the last minute to complete writing projects. We agreed that you would attend a seminar on time management. We also agreed that you would outline your future writing assignments several days after receiving them, and that you would check in with me immediately if you needed help meeting a deadline. The details of this incident and our plan for improvement are in your personnel file, as is the certificate you received for participating in a seminar entitled "Time Management for Busy Employees," dated March 23, 2007.

Improvement Plan

In this section, you should first state the improvement you need to see. You should be very specific in this section, giving the employee tangible goals he or she is capable of meeting. For example, you might write,

"You must be here when your shift begins at 7:00 a.m. each morning, unless you have called in sick" or, "I need to see you at every district manager's meeting." This is far more useful to the employee than statements such as "Don't be late" or "Attend important meetings."

Next, describe the plan you and the employee have developed. Be specific about the changes you expect and the deadlines for achieving them. Again, this will help the employee understand what is expected, and it will help remind you what you should be evaluating when you revisit the issue.

Even though Randy took a time management course and has been required to submit outlines of his writing assignments, he has still missed another deadline. He and his manager agree that he needs more frequent interim deadlines to prevent him from procrastinating. Here's the plan that Randy and Sarah develop together:

Improvement Plan

Randy, you must meet your deadlines for writing assignments. When you miss your deadlines, you cause more work for me and your coworkers, and our department's reputation in the company suffers.

You have told me that you are still putting your writing assignments off until the last minute and that you are having trouble estimating how long projects will take. We have agreed that you and I will meet every Friday at 11 a.m. to discuss your writing projects. At the first meeting after I assign you a project, you will show me your outline. At subsequent meetings, you will report on your progress and show me what you have written to date. At the end of each meeting, I will tell you what I expect you to accomplish by the next meeting. I will confirm this expectation in a follow-up email to you every Friday afternoon. If you disagree with my understanding of the expectation, you have agreed to tell me immediately by the end of the day on Friday.

Employee Comments

No matter how carefully you draft your documentation, your employee may not feel that you fully or fairly captured the issue. There is no requirement that you come to consensus on what the documentation says—in fact, if you disagree with the employee's interpretation of what happened, you should stick to your version of events. Remember, you are focused on communicating the facts. Because the employee may come into the discussion with a lot of emotions, he or she may feel entirely different issues need to be addressed.

To account for this, you should leave room on the form for the employee to comment. If the employee doesn't rebut your statements, it will be very difficult for him or her to claim later that your documentation is incorrect or incomplete. If the employee takes issue with your characterization of the problem, he or she can put those concerns in writing, and the two of you can meet again to hash it out. Sometimes, the employee just needs the opportunity to "vent" to feel that both sides of the issue are accurately reflected—for instance, because the employee failed to perform as required but thinks he or she was justified in doing so.

Of course, even if the employee disputes your characterization of the problem, you'll need to know that the employee is on board about the agreed-upon solution. If the employee's written rebuttal indicates that he or she is not willing to perform the steps required by your written improvement plan, you'll know that your discipline discussion is not over. Otherwise, you're setting the employee up for failure.

Randy knows that he missed the deadline, and he agrees with the proposed action plan. However, he still thinks the project was too difficult in the first place, so he adds his two cents to the written warning:

Employee Comments

One of the reasons I missed the website deadline is because I was unable to figure out which products to feature. This isn't my responsibility; it should have been done by the marketing people.

In response to these comments, Sarah should probably have another brief meeting with Randy to discuss this issue. In this case, she could tell Randy that he must do the projects she assigns to him and that he should tell her during their first Friday meeting after a project is assigned if he thinks any part of the project is beyond his abilities. If Randy agrees to this plan, Sarah can write a brief note documenting the meeting for Randy's personnel file.

Dates, Acknowledgements, and Signatures

At the end of the form, you and the employee should sign and date it. Some employees are reluctant to sign a disciplinary form, because they believe that signing it means they agree that they deserve discipline. However, you need to have proof that the employee received a copy of the document so you can show that the employee had notice of his or her problems and the proposed resolution. Most companies get around this problem by requiring the employee only to acknowledge having received and read the document. If the employee is reluctant to sign, explain that doing so is just an acknowledgement of receipt. And if the employee wants to say anything in response, he or she should have that opportunity on the form. If the employee still refuses to sign, write a note on the document to that effect ("Delivered to the employee on September 10, 2007. Employee refused to sign the document.")

The bottom of Randy's form looks like this:

Manager: ___Sarah Bronson___ Date: September 10, 2007

I acknowledge that I have received and understand this document.

Employee: ___Randy Clark___ Date: September 10, 2007

 This form is available in Appendix A and on the enclosed CD.

Disciplinary Form

<u>Title of Form</u>
(for example, Verbal Warning, Written Warning, etc.)

Date: _____

Employee Name: _____

Manager Name: _____

Incident Description:

Prior Incidents:

Improvement Plan:

Employee Comments:

Manager: _____ Date: _____

I acknowledge that I have received and understand this document.

Employee: _____ Date: _____

Smart Documentation: Smart Summary

● **Documenting discipline has many benefits.** It ensures that you and the employee are on the same page, helps you and the company track discipline problems, helps maintain consistency, and provides proof of what you did and why.

● **The documentation you create should be understandable to anyone who reads it.** You must be clear, thorough, and factual. Be sure to include all relevant information, including dates, full names, prior incidents, and an action plan.

● **Stick to the facts.** When documenting, don't interpret the meaning of an employee's actions or word—just record those actions or words. If your documentation is based on fact, it will be hard for the employee to refute what you say.

● **Unless company policy requires otherwise, keep informal documentation in a separate file (such as a tickler log), and use it to remind yourself to follow up with employees.** If the documentation is formal and going into the employee's file, give the employee the opportunity to make comments.

● **Don't overdocument.** That means you shouldn't include information that isn't directly related to the incident you're describing. If you write down too many details, you may have a harder time distinguishing the important facts, which may be important later if you have to discuss the decision to discipline with the employee, your manager, your human resources department, or a lawyer.

Smart Collaboration: Involving the Right People at the Right Time

Sometimes, it's necessary to discuss a disciplinary issue with people in the company who are not directly involved in the situation. In particular, you'll need to talk with your manager, human resources department, and/or legal counsel to make sure you have handled an issue appropriately and legally and are marshalling all the resources necessary to ensure the employee's success. Additionally, as you work to gather all the facts, you may need to talk with other employees who have witnessed or been affected by the problem.

However, whom to tell and what to reveal can be touchy subjects. On the one hand, you want to respect the employee's privacy. On the other hand, you have a responsibility to appropriately inform certain parties and to gather all the pertinent information. This chapter will show you how to collaborate properly with others in the discipline process, while respecting the employee's privacy.

Involving Management

Often, when small problems persist or grow, you won't be the only one dealing with the discipline—you'll involve your manager, too. There are three major points in the discipline process when it may be necessary to involve your manager: when an issue has an important effect on the business, when you need an alternate perspective, or when company policy or practice dictate it.

Issues That Affect the Business

Earlier chapters explain how discipline problems affect your company, both financially and otherwise. Not only does this analysis help you figure out what level of discipline is appropriate, it also helps you determine when you should involve your manager.

If an issue has had or will have a significant financial impact on the business, you need to talk to your manager about the problem fairly quickly. What constitutes significant financial impact will vary by the size and nature of the company, but it may include lost sales, internal theft, or lost customers.

What information should you share with your manager? You probably do not need to give every detail. Instead, you only need to give a basic description of the problem, its impact, and the solution you and the employee have developed. You should also provide regular updates on the status of the action plan as it proceeds. This will assure your boss that you are on top of the issue, addressing and communicating the solutions and ensuring that the problem is getting fixed.

> **EXAMPLE:** Aaron, a sales representative, is responsible for maintaining customer relationships and ensuring that customers renew their annual subscriptions to the company's product. His numbers have been falling steadily over the past three months. Renewals are down, and so is revenue. Sharon, his manager, is concerned about his performance, as it affects not only his numbers, but hers as well. Sharon realizes that she needs to address this issue and let her boss know that she is working to fix it.
>
> Sharon sets up a meeting with Richard, her boss and the head of sales for the company. She begins by telling Richard that their sales numbers are down and that she has figured out the reason. She tells him she has set up a meeting with Aaron. Knowing that Richard has great ideas for improving renewals, she also asks him for his input. They have a productive 15-minute conversation and come up with some good ideas for bringing the numbers back up.
>
> Sharon concludes the meeting with Richard by telling him the schedule for talking with Aaron, promising to copy Richard on the action plan, and creating an ongoing agenda item of bringing Richard up to date on Aaron's progress as the plan is implemented.

In Sharon's discussion with Richard, she gave him the information he needed to feel confident that she would resolve the problem. She got him invested in Aaron's success by getting his thoughts about an effective action plan. Lastly, she has committed to keeping Richard informed, so he knows he can help redirect the process if it doesn't seem to be working.

Getting an Alternate Perspective

Sometimes, you may be unsure how to handle a disciplinary issue, or you may just need confirmation that your intended course of action is an appropriate one. Additionally, you might find it helpful just to get another opinion or idea about how you are approaching the situation. In these instances, your manager can be a perfect person to talk to. The benefits of talking to your manager include:

- **Experience.** Your manager supervises people, too—and probably has experience with many of the disciplinary issues that you face.

- **Fresh perspective.** Your manager is generally not as close to the problem as you are—and may be able to offer a fresh, and more objective, perspective. He or she may have questions or answers that you hadn't thought of.

- **Institutional knowledge.** In addition to experience managing others, your manager may know more about how the company, and other managers, have handled similar situations in the past. Your manager may also be able to tell you how the problem and your proposed solution will be viewed by others in the company.

Talking to your manager about a discipline issue has additional benefits. It guarantees that your manager won't be surprised to learn about an issue from someone else. And if you've already discussed the issue together, you'll know you have your manager's support as you carry out the discipline.

Company Policy and Practice

Even if the problem has only a minor effect on the company, and you don't feel like you need an alternate perspective, you might still need to involve your manager in a disciplinary issue. If you are required—or expected—to do so, whether by your manager, company policies, or the human resources or legal departments, you should certainly escalate the problem. Here are some examples for which you might need to bring your manager in on a disciplinary matter:

- **Company policy.** Many company policies dictate when managers must be involved—often, when a problem has escalated to a serious step in the discipline process, such as a verbal or written warning.

- **Your relationship with your manager.** If you work closely and frequently with your manager and keep him or her updated on your workload, treat the discipline process as one more business issue, and discuss it. If you don't bring it up, it may look like you are "hiding" something if and when the problem worsens and you need to involve your manager later.

- **If you have involved your human resources or legal departments.** Because the issue is taking up a significant amount of your time, you probably want to keep your manager informed about what you are working on. Additionally, chances are good that the human resources or legal department may need to raise the issue with your manager, and it's better if he or she hears it from you first.

- **Your level of experience.** If you have seen and successfully dealt with the same issue before, then chances are good you can do the same thing without more assistance. However, if the problem is new to you, and additional input would be valuable, approach your manager for help.

- **The company culture**. While some companies encourage collaborative discussion during the discipline process, others are more focused on driving results. If your company emphasizes the importance of collaboration, ask for additional input and help early in the discipline process.

If you're not sure what to do in a disciplinary situation, you should always talk to your manager. Just as you are a resource for your employees, your manager is a resource and coach for you.

Involving Human Resources

For additional help, you can and should talk to a representative of your human resources department. Human resources professionals have direct experience and training with most disciplinary issues and can counsel you on applying company policy, advise you on how to handle difficult conversations, and partner or facilitate the actual discipline process.

Applying Company Policy and Practices

At their best, company discipline policies are based on fairness and legality and will outline the steps in the company's discipline process. At worst, they are confusing, outdated, and dense with legal language and don't tell you what you really need to do. And in some cases, they just don't exist.

The good news is, there is someone in the company who can help you interpret, apply, or even work to change these policies. Your human resources department deals with these policies and practices on a regular basis. They know how the rest of the company is using them, which is important in maintaining consistent, company-wide application (see Chapter 3 for more information). They also know the ins and outs of the policy language and can decipher it for you when it seems unclear.

When your company doesn't have a written policy in place, chances are good that the company has had to deal with the same or a similar issue before, and that constitutes a practice. The human resources department is a repository of knowledge about these practices and can let you know how you should proceed based on how it's been done in the past. Again, this helps maintains consistency and fairness.

When You Don't Have a Human Resources Department

Many smaller companies operate without full-time human resources or legal help. For those of you operating in this environment, you are not without resources. For human resources help, you can consult the Society for Human Resources Management (www.shrm.org), who can either set you up with the information you need or help you find a reasonably priced consultant. SHRM has local chapters throughout the country.

For legal help, visit Nolo's website (www.nolo.com), which has information about how to find an attorney, articles and products addressing issues in employment law, and an attorney directory. If you need to hire an attorney, you may also want to ask professional colleagues for referrals.

Advising

As a manager, you may need help when you are dealing with something you have not seen before, or when you simply are not sure how to proceed. This could happen at any step in the discipline process—even if you have experience with a particular type of problem, you might not know what to do when things get worse or the employee just doesn't seem to be improving. In situations like these, your human resources department can provide advice and support, giving you the chance to test what you want to say, get feedback on how you want to proceed, and make sure your approach is consistent with company policy and practice and the law.

Human resources professionals can also role play difficult conversations, giving you a chance to practice what you will say. They can prepare you for the actual conversations by discussing potential employee reactions and how you will deal with them. They often have a good working knowledge of the overall organization, so they can help you consider how your decisions will affect the organization as a whole. Finally, many human resources professionals are trained in conflict resolution and negotiation, as well as employment law, and can help you negotiate murky legal or emotional waters.

Partnership and Facilitation

If you are a new manager, dealing with an issue that you've never experienced before, or worried about the employee's strong reaction to discipline, consider using human resources as your partner or facilitator in the disciplinary process. This involves more than just advising (although that is part of it). It typically means that you will actually have the disciplinary conversations—usually for verbal or written warnings, or even terminations—with a human resources representative in the room, acting as an "in-the-moment" coach for you or as an objective third party who facilitates the discussion. Using human resources as a partner in the discipline process will give you a safety net: They can help clarify any aspects of the process or conversation that get confused, bring up previously discussed points that you may have forgotten, and keep you from saying anything that might put the company in legal hot water.

A human resources professional can also act as a facilitator. In this role, he or she can make sure that that each party is being heard and that you are heading for a successful outcome. This is particularly useful if you have a difficult employee who sinks into silence or is known to act resentful. In this case, the human resources representative maintains objectivity and focuses on getting the issues aired on both sides of the table. This fosters collaboration and encourages the employee and manager to work together to create a successful outcome.

Of course, you need to consider how the employee might perceive having a human resources representative in the room. Involving human resources adds formality to the process. Sometimes you need that formality—for example, when giving a formal written warning. Other times, you may not want that formality—like during a coaching session. Particularly if human resources is involved early in the process, it may even tip the employee off that you do not feel that you can handle things on your own or that you need protection. This can undermine your authority with your employee and may lead him or her to believe that you are not experienced or knowledgeable enough to handle the problem.

If you are trying to decide whether to include a human resources representative in the meeting, consider these factors:

- **Does company policy require it?** If so, you should talk with the representative ahead of time, to explain why he or she needs to be involved.
- **Will the employee feel glad to have an objective listener, or embarrassed by the presence of a third party?** Obviously, this is something you can only speculate about, but if you're fairly certain that having an objective third party will help the discussion, include the human resources representative.
- **Do you need backup?** If you will better communicate your message if a third party is present, ask human resources to participate.

Involving Legal Counsel

Sometimes, you might need some help from a lawyer before you decide how to handle a discipline problem. How—and how often—you seek this help will depend on your company's structure and policies. If your company has its own legal department or in-house counsel, you might be able to just pick up the phone or walk down the hall for a quick chat. If your company uses outside counsel to handle its legal matters, you will probably need to get authorization from someone—perhaps your manager or the human resources department—to get an attorney involved. Of course, you should follow your company's procedures for when and how to involve legal counsel.

If you have the authority to decide when to consult with a lawyer, however, you should consider using it whenever you believe the company might have some legal exposure. In other words, if you have an inkling that the company might be at fault, or that pursuing discipline or terminating employment might violate the employee's legal rights, you would be wise to get some help from a lawyer as you decide how to proceed.

Consider getting some legal advice before you impose discipline or terminate employment in these situations (you can find detailed information on each of these issues in Chapter 3):

- **The employee absolutely denies the misconduct for which you are imposing discipline.** In this situation, a lawyer can help you make sure you investigated the facts thoroughly and came to the right conclusion.

- **The employee has hired a lawyer.** In this case, you know that at least one lawyer will be watching your every move—you want to make sure you have someone looking out for your legal interests, too.

- **The employee has a written or oral employment contract that restricts the company's right to fire or discipline.** You'll want to make sure you understand how to comply with that agreement.

> **EXAMPLE:** Hector is hired as the director of marketing for a large Internet service provider. The company has had trouble keeping a marketing director, so it offers Hector a three-year employment contract. The contract provides that Hector's employment can be terminated only for "good cause," which it further defines as "commission of a felony; gross malfeasance; or willful and continued failure to perform the duties of the position."
>
> Toshi is the company's vice president of sales and marketing. He believes Hector is not working out—the marketing initiatives he has rolled out have not been very successful, an advertising campaign Hector spearheaded has flopped,

and Hector's staff turnover has increased. Toshi has coached Hector, to no avail. What Toshi really wants is to replace him with someone who is more creative and better able to ignite his team's enthusiasm.

Toshi needs some legal advice. Clearly Hector hasn't committed a felony, but do his actions constitute gross malfeasance or willful and continued failure substantially to perform his duties? If Toshi doesn't have good cause to fire Hector, should he consider breaking the contract or perhaps negotiating a severance? If Toshi decides not to fire Hector, should he discipline him—and is there language he could use in his disciplinary sessions and documentation to show that the company has good cause to fire Hector under the contract? A good lawyer could help provide some answers.

- **The employee recently filed a complaint or claim with a government agency or complained within the company of illegal or unethical activity.** In this situation, disciplining or firing the employee could lead to a retaliation claim.
- **The employee recently revealed that he or she is in a protected class** (for example, the employee has recently told you that he or she has a disability or practices a particular religion).
- **You are concerned about the worker's potential for violence, vandalism, or sabotage.** This is particularly important if the worker has access to the company's high-level trade secrets or competitive information.

EXAMPLE: Roberto works for a company that makes vitamins and nutritional supplements. The company has an extensive website where it provides product information, customer testimonials, and articles on health and wellness. About one-third of the company's total product sales comes through its website. Roberto supervises the team of employees that keep the website up and running.

Roberto has already disciplined Camilla for spending work time on personal projects—another employee reported that Camilla spent a couple of hours each day on her own personal website and blog. Roberto kept an eye on Camilla and confirmed the employee's report, then gave her a written warning. During their disciplinary meeting, Camilla told Roberto that she thought he was being too harsh, and that the company should treat its technical employees better "because we are the ones who control what goes on the company's site."

A month later, Roberto notices that Camilla is still posting to her blog from work. Before deciding what to do, he reads through her blog. There, he discovers that Camilla has commented extensively on his decision to discipline her. She has also written, "This company is crazy. Don't they have any idea what kind of havoc I could cause with just a couple of keystrokes?"

Now Roberto is worried. He wants to fire Camilla, but he's concerned that she'll sabotage the website. He also has questions about her postings—can she write about the company? Can the company discipline her for it? Is it legal for her to mention him by name? Is there anything the company can do to stop her from writing about it? Again, a knowledgeable employment lawyer can help Roberto sort through the alternatives and decide what to do.

- **You are disciplining the employee for excessive absences or leave, if you are concerned that the employee's time off might be legally protected** (for example, the time off might qualify as family medical leave or protected military leave).

Involving Other Employees

Through the course of the disciplinary process, it may be necessary to talk to people who have information that is relevant or related to the problem you're dealing with. You may need to talk to people who witnessed or are affected by certain behavior or actions. And if the behavior or action was targeted at a specific person or people, you will need to let that person or those people know that you are dealing with it.

Involving Other Employees in an Investigation

Determining whom to talk to and what to say as you gather information can have a direct effect on the success of a disciplinary process. As we discussed in earlier chapters, employees often talk about what's happening in the workplace. If you cast your net too wide and involve too many people, you could severely hamper the environment in which the disciplined employee has to work. If a large group of people know about an employee's problem, it may permanently tarnish that person's reputation. This can cause an environment where it is difficult to succeed: If everyone believes that the person is a failure, the person may actually fail because he or she feels unsupported, threatened, or overwhelmed by what's happening. And of course, if you reveal too much information to too many people, a disgruntled employee might even bring a lawsuit against you, claiming defamation or invasion of privacy.

As you investigate a problem, avoid inadvertently tainting the environment by:

- **Working consciously to limit the number of people involved.** The fewer people involved, the fewer people can pass judgment on the disciplined employee. Of course, in order to be thorough and fair, you simply have to involve the pertinent people in an investigation. Just don't troll widely for information—target the people who you know have information you need.

- **Reminding the employees that you are talking to that they have an obligation to maintain confidentiality.** Reiterate the importance of confidentiality at the close of every discussion.

- **Keeping your questions as open ended as possible.** Ask only enough to get the information that you need. If you make your questions specific and closed ("yes or no" questions), you will find yourself giving out information that shouldn't be discussed. An example of this is "Did you see Rafael try to kiss Hope?" versus "Tell me about what you witnessed on Tuesday afternoon in the break room at about 3:00."

- **Keeping your disciplinary decisions private.** You will probably face more than a few questions from the employees you interview. They might want to know all the details of what happened, who was involved, and what you plan to do about it. This curiosity is natural, but you can't satisfy it. Ultimately, any discipline you decide to impose is between the disciplined employee and the company (that is, you and perhaps your manager or a human resources representative). While other employees will probably be talking about the situation, you shouldn't tell them your conclusions about the problem (in other words, what you think "really" happened) or how you decided to handle it. The most you should say is that the company is looking into the matter and will deal with it appropriately.

EXAMPLE: Vitali is the Quality Assurance Manager for a small software company. One day, Cliff, one of the QA engineers, tells Vitali about a problem with Bruce, another QA engineer. Cliff cites a recent meeting with several other members of the QA team. At the meeting, Bruce talked loudly while others were talking. He also got angry at one of the other engineers, who asked Bruce to stop interrupting. Cliff says the team has noticed that Bruce isn't finishing his work as quickly and that he seems easily upset. Cliff decided to talk to Vitali when Bruce got frustrated by a problem he was trying to work out and started cursing and throwing books and office supplies in the team's work area. Bruce then left work for the day. Cliff says that the team is concerned for Bruce, but also fearful that his increasing volatility and lack of control could lead to trouble.

Vitali knows that these allegations are serious and must be investigated. He notifies human resources and they meet to strategize about the investigation. Together they determine that Vitali should talk to the other employees who attended the meeting, as well as someone who saw Cliff's angry outburst in the work room.

Vitali meets with Andrew, the witness in the work room. He asks him, "Andrew, can you tell me what, if anything, you saw this morning in the QA work area?" Andrew replies, "Well, Bruce kind of lost it. Cliff and I were talking to each other, and Bruce suddenly started swearing at the program he was working on. He was yelling really loudly, and when we tried to find out what was going on, he started yelling and swearing at us. Then he threw some of his manuals across the room and threw his stapler and one of his speakers at the wall. At that point, I left—I was afraid of what might happen next. Cliff was trying to calm him down." Andrew then asks, "What's going to happen? Is Bruce in trouble? The whole thing was pretty weird, but it seems so out of character for him. Do you think he's having personal problems?"

Vitali responds, "I'm gathering information now about what happened. I'm also going to ask Bruce to take a day or two off while I investigate. Once I've finished my investigation and talked things over with Bruce, the company will decide how to handle the situation."

By limiting what he tells Andrew, Vitali minimizes the chance that Andrew will draw any improper conclusions. He is also taking care not to poison the investigation (or the work environment for Bruce) by sharing too much unnecessarily. At the same time, Vitali has reassured Andrew that Bruce will not be returning to work until the problem is resolved, which should alleviate Andrew's safety concerns. Vitali has given out just enough information to reassure Andrew that the company knows about the problem and will deal with it.

Communicating With Those Affected

During the course of a disciplinary action, you may also need to collaborate and communicate with people directly affected by the problem. This is particularly true when dealing with poor performance that changes the workload or work product of other team members. For example, if a project team has a member whose deliverables have been consistently substandard, and the results are affecting the whole team, then the team is going to want to know what you, the manager, are going to do about it.

The best practices for talking to employees affected by a problem are similar to those for dealing with employees during an investigation:

- Limit your conversation to the pertinent facts.
- Provide assurance that you are aware of and dealing with the situation.
- Don't give so much information that the employee can never be successful again.

When deciding how much information to share, err on the side of less rather than more.

> **EXAMPLE:** In the example of Bruce and Vitali above, the company has decided to put Bruce on a written warning as Vitali discovered that his actions were due to a personal issue at home: his wife's terminal cancer. Vitali referred Bruce to the company's employee assistance program and talked to him about rearranging his schedule for a while, so he could spend more time with his family. Vitali also arranged for Bruce to meet with a human resources representative, to find out about his right to take leave and care for his wife.
>
> What should Vitali tell the rest of the team? Only that he has spoken to Bruce and taken appropriate action. This assures the team that Vitali knows what's going on and is dealing with it. It also opens the door for team members to provide feedback should they see Bruce continue to create problems. What Vitali should not do is reveal Bruce's personal problems or explain that Bruce has received a written warning. All of this information goes beyond what the team needs to know—and revealing it could make it difficult for Bruce to do his job.

Confidentiality

If you need to discuss a problem with others in the company, you're probably painfully aware of another need: the need to maintain confidentiality, to the extent possible. After all, you don't want the employee to think you can't be trusted, and most employees would prefer not to share their disciplinary history with others who don't need to know about it. In general, that means that it's best to discuss a disciplinary issue only with those people who are directly involved or need to know. By limiting communication, you give your employee a fair chance to improve without a large number of eyes observing and passing judgment.

If you maintain confidentiality when appropriate, you will:
- establish trust between you and your employee
- limit gossip in your workplace, and
- minimize legal problems.

⚠ **Don't promise complete confidentiality.** While you want to respect the employee's privacy, you shouldn't promise the employee that you're going to keep everything confidential. There are instances when you will need to talk to others about what has been said or done. This occurs frequently when one employee accuses another of violence, harassment, or other inappropriate behavior. In those cases, you will probably have to talk to several employees—at very least, the accuser and the accused—about the allegations.

Establishing Trust

Successful discipline requires that the manager and the employee trust each other. As a manager, you must trust your employee to do all he or she can to improve. In turn, the employee must trust you to help guide the process and provide resources and encouragement when needed.

This trust can be severely undermined if the employee believes that you are talking to others inappropriately about the disciplinary process. If you have no legitimate reason to tell another person about a disciplinary issue, then don't. While your employees and coworkers may be curious, you risk serious damage to the discipline process if you undermine the employee's trust by talking to others about the problem. If you feel the need to vent or get another perspective, talk about it with an appropriate person, such as your boss.

As we discussed, there may be legitimate instances when you do need to let others know what is going on. In this case, it is a good practice to let the employee know whom you are talking to and why. This way, there is no mystery about who knows, and your employee won't be blindsided.

> **EXAMPLE:** Margot supervises a team of twelve in a large data management firm. One of her team members, Deborah, comes to her and says that Matthew, an employee from another department, has made inappropriate sexual remarks to her and has sent her inappropriate emails as well. "I really don't want him to know I told," Deborah says. "I just want him to stop."
>
> Margot knows that the matter must be investigated immediately. She tells Deborah, "I understand what you're saying, Deborah. However, I have a duty to report this to human resources and

make sure it is investigated. I will keep this confidential to the extent possible, but I am going to have to tell our human resources department, and they're going to have to talk to Matthew about the allegations. If other people witnessed these events or know anything about this, we'll need to talk to them as well. Do you understand?"

Limiting Gossip

Another reason it is important to maintain confidentiality is that it allows the employee the room to improve without being scrutinized and criticized by others. While gossip is unavoidable in the workplace, there are a few things you can do to limit it.

As the manager of the group, your own behavior is critical in letting others know what is acceptable. If you engage in gossip about discipline problems, the door is open for others to as well. Employees may have a hard time understanding the difference between sharing information on a subject and gossiping about it—which means you have to draw that line clearly. Only share information that the employee needs to know. When you're pushed for more, you can and should tell your employees no. Remember, there are many important reasons—even legal ones—to keep information private if you don't have a good reason to reveal it.

Gossip tends to die away when there is no new news on a subject. Involving only the appropriate people at the right times in the process and maintaining a steadfast tight lip about disciplinary issues will eventually quell the chatter.

Minimize Legal Problems

Keeping a disciplinary issue private will also help you avoid legal claims for defamation and violation of privacy. A disgruntled employee who believes that people are making untrue or derogatory statements may take action against a company or the individuals making the statements—including you. (See Chapter 3 for more on the legal reasons to maintain confidentiality.)

If your company has a policy addressing confidentiality, you could also put the company at risk legally if you don't follow that policy. As we discussed in Chapter 3, if you follow the policy in one situation and not another, the employee who didn't get the benefit of the policy might feel he or she wasn't treated fairly. The employee might attribute this unfair treatment to an illegally discriminatory motive on your part.

If your company has such a policy, read it carefully, and ask your human resources department or legal counsel any questions you have about how it applies.

Smart Collaboration: Smart Summary

⊙ Involve your manager in the discipline process when the problem has a significant effect on the business, you need an alternate perspective, or company policy or practice require it.

⊙ Human resources is a partner in the discipline process. Because they're usually trained and experienced, they can help you apply and navigate complex company policies and practices, advise you through the process, or partner with you in your discipline meetings.

⊙ You should work with legal counsel when the discipline process raises possible legal problems—for instance, because the employee denies misconduct resulting in discipline, has an employment contract, hires an attorney, or takes a leave that may be legally protected.

⊙ When you include other employees in the discipline process, be careful to involve only those who need to know and to share only the information necessary. Keep things as confidential as you can—it shows respect for the employee, reduces gossip in the workplace, and limits legal liability.

∎

Build Your Skills: Smart Discipline Skills

Questions

1. If you feel awkward about disciplining an employee, you should:

   a. Ask human resources to deliver the message—they have a lot of experience and will be able to communicate more clearly, anyway.

   b. Accept that it's part of the process. Discipline is awkward, but it's a necessary part of your job.

   c. Just get it over with. Sit down with the employee, say what you need to, and get out.

   d. Talk to other managers about it. Your colleagues have probably dealt with the same thing themselves.

2. Even though workplace gossip about disciplinary issues is inappropriate and wastes time, there isn't really anything you can do to prevent it.

   ☐ True   ☐ False

3. Chelsea, the manager of a clothing store, needs to discipline Evan, a supervisor, for repeatedly forgetting to lock the door to the supervisor's office at the end of his shift. Which of these is the best way to begin the conversation?

   a. "Evan, you keep leaving the door to the supervisor's office unlocked. This has got to stop immediately."

   b. "Hey, Evan! How are things going on the night shift?"

   c. "Evan, you could really get us into trouble by leaving the door to the supervisor's office unlocked. Why do you keep doing that?"

   d. "Evan, I noticed twice last week that the supervisor's office wasn't locked when I came in the morning after your shift. Can you explain why?"

4. Sy, a secretary in a college admissions office, is being disciplined for sending out letters with numerous typos to prospective students. She explains to her supervisor, Dalia, that she is making the errors because she has too many other competing tasks, and she doesn't feel like she has time to proofread the letters carefully. Which of these is the best response?

    a. "Unfortunately, Sy, that is just part of your job. You need to figure out how to get this done. Do you have any suggestions for how you can accomplish that?"

    b. "Sounds like you're feeling overwhelmed. What I hear you saying is that you don't feel you have adequate time to proofread these thoroughly. Is that right?"

    c. "I'm sorry, Sy, but I just don't agree with you. I really think you need to try and get these done, error free. What will it take?"

    d. "So what you're saying is, you're really busy so you think someone else should proofread the letters before they go out?"

5. When you deliver discipline, you should give an employee as many examples of a problem as possible.   ☐ True   ☐ False

6. When you're disciplining an employee who becomes angry, you should:

    a. Let the employee know who's in control. Anger isn't appropriate in the workplace—you need to communicate this message strongly, which may mean raising your voice if the employee's voice is raised or telling the employee it's time to walk away if he or she isn't capable of talking about things calmly.

    b. Let the employee know that his or her feelings shouldn't enter the discipline process. There's no need to get angry—it won't get you anywhere.

    c. Encourage the employee to take a break until he or she is ready to talk about it again.

    d. Try to slow the meeting down. Acknowledge the anger but tell the employee that he or she needs to calm down before you can proceed.

7. Boris needs to discipline Monica for making inappropriate and demeaning comments to a coworker, Linda. When he confronts her with the problem, Monica replies, "It wasn't me! I never said anything to Linda!" Which of these is the best response?

    a. "I know you did it, Monica. Linda told me about it, and Cory verified that it was true."

    b. "Well, I know that Linda has a tendency to exaggerate. Let me look into it."

    c. "Monica, did you tell Linda at the register last Friday, 'It doesn't take a rocket scientist' when she asked you how to change the receipt tape?"

    d. "No one's blaming you, Monica. Just tell me the truth."

8. When an employee commits misconduct that appears to be illegal, and you decide to terminate employment based on that misconduct, you should say that the employee broke the law in your termination memo.
☐ True   ☐ False

9. You should require your employee to sign your documentation, agreeing with its contents and your decision.   ☐ True   ☐ False

10. Victoria hears from four different employees that another employee, Deborah, is constantly on the phone, making personal calls to her family, who lives in London. She checks the phone records and finds that it's true, and that it's at a cost of almost $1,000. Whom should Victoria talk to about this first?

    a. Deborah.

    b. All four coworkers.

    c. Human resources.

    d. Her boss.

Answers

1. B. Sometimes it's uncomfortable or difficult to tell an employee that his or her behavior or performance isn't measuring up. If you accept that it's just part of the process, you can prepare yourself to deal with that reality. While you may want to talk about the problem with others, you should limit that to appropriate individuals like your manager, legal counsel, or human resources department—who can counsel you on how to deliver the disciplinary message. Ultimately, it's up to you—and you shouldn't deny it, even though it's awkward. Otherwise, you might have a hard time finding a collaborative solution with the employee.

2. False. Although there's nothing you can do to prohibit gossip altogether, you can limit it by involving only the appropriate people in the discipline process, keeping your employees focused on their own work, and refusing to engage in it yourself.

3. D. When you meet with an employee to administer discipline, it's a good idea to have your opening sentences prepared. In this example, Chelsea should make sure she has all the facts before telling Evan what to do. In Answer D, Chelsea makes sure she has the facts straight, but she's also focused on the problem. If she begins the conversation too informally, Evan might be confused about the purpose of the meeting. On the other hand, if she is too accusatory, Evan might shut down at the very beginning.

4. B. When you get an employee's perspective on a discipline problem, it's important to show that you're really listening and hearing what the employee is saying. You can do that by playing back what you are hearing and listening empathically. That means paraphrasing what you heard, without judgmental edits, and putting yourself in the employee's shoes. In Answer B, Dalia summarized Sy's words, which let Sy know she was really paying attention—without passing judgment. After listening this way, Dalia can engage Sy in a discussion about what to do about it.

5. False. While it's important to give the employee examples of the problem performance or behavior, it isn't necessary to have an exhaustive list. In fact, it could do more harm than good—if your examples are second-, third-, or fourthhand, or inaccurate, the employee may be so focused on the example that he or she isn't thinking about the problem and how to solve it.

6. D. If an employee is angry, you may be able to slow the meeting down. If that doesn't work, you might need to take a break—but make sure the employee understands it can't be indefinite. Choose a time to re-engage, preferably within the next day or so. You don't want so much time to pass that the employee's anger has time to fester or that you forget the important facts that led you to discipline in the first place.

7. C. In this case, Boris will be best served by going through examples of Monica's problem behavior with her. He shouldn't deny the truth of Linda's allegations or suggest that they're made up. But asking Monica to verify whether specific statements are true shows her that he's prepared and looked into the matter. She'll have a harder time dodging the questions when they're this focused.

8. False. Although you should document the facts that led you to make a discipline decision, and you should also explain what company policy it violates, you shouldn't draw legal conclusions. After all, you don't want those conclusions to be used against you—that is, you don't want to be sued for the employee's behavior and have a record of admitting that the behavior broke the law.

9. False. It's a good idea to ask the disciplined employee to sign formal documentation, but the signature need only acknowledge receipt. Requiring an employee to agree with your description can hamper the disciplinary process if the employee thinks you're being coercive; if the employee doesn't want to sign, you can just notate on the form that he or she was asked to but elected not to. Also, if you leave a blank space on the form for the employee to comment, he or she can include information you didn't record. This gives the employee the opportunity to participate in the documentation process, and it also protects you: If the employee elects not to do this but then later says your documentation was inaccurate, he or she will be hard-pressed to explain why that section of the form is blank.

10. D. Although Victoria will probably eventually discuss this with human resources and with Deborah, she should probably first discuss it with her boss. This could have significant financial impact on the company, or it could mean that she is going to have to deliver some fairly serious discipline. In either case, Victoria doesn't want her boss blindsided by hearing about the problem when the discipline is already well underway

or when human resources brings it to the boss's attention. Note that in this case, Victoria doesn't need to discuss it with the four employees who reported it: She was able to verify it independently through phone records, and she can maintain confidentiality and limit gossip by keeping it private.

■

The Disciplinary Steps

Step 1: Coaching

Sometimes, you know it's time to correct workplace behavior, but the problem isn't serious enough to warrant formal discipline like a verbal or written warning. While you want the employee to resolve the issue, you don't want to come down "too hard" or make the employee feel attacked or overwhelmed. That's where coaching comes in.

Relatively new to traditional progressive discipline, which tends to be immediately official in its approach, coaching gives you the chance to correct behaviors and actions before implementing a more serious and formal measure. For this reason, more so than the more advanced disciplinary measures in the process, coaching is an opportunity, rather than a punishment. This chapter will outline what coaching is (and is not), when and how to do it, how you know it's going well, and what to do if it's not working.

What Is Coaching?

As with sports, coaching in the workplace means offering encouragement and direction, so that the employee will accomplish the final goal. Based on your expertise, you help the employee recognize a weakness and find a way to fix it. Then you make sure that the employee is successfully improving, making adjustments if needed. While managing people involves coaching on many levels, here, we use the term "coaching" specifically in the context of progressive discipline.

One of the big benefits of coaching is that it does not confer the stigma of a formal disciplinary step, such as a verbal or written warning. As a result, the employee usually feels less threatened by coaching, and you are able to work together to correct problems quickly. This often prevents the need to go to the next measure in the progressive discipline process. Other benefits of coaching include:

- **Problems are corrected early.** Coaching allows you to address problems before they have a serious impact on the business.
- **The tone is positive.** Because coaching can be informal, it permits a less serious tone than a more advanced disciplinary measure does, emphasizing the opportunity to improve performance, rather than the consequences for failing to do so.

- **Your documentation is not as formal.** Coaching documentation does not require the same level of detail as more advanced disciplinary measures, where details are more important.
- **You create a record to move forward, if necessary.** With a history of coaching, you have solid justification—and a record of your previous efforts to help the employee improve—to move to a more serious disciplinary measure.
- **Your leadership is established.** Coaching tells your employee that you are invested in the success of your team and that you're actively leading it toward its goals.
- **Communication is improved.** Coaching gives you the opportunity to open lines of communication, preventing future misunderstandings or problems.
- **You learn about how the team is working.** Like one-on-ones, coaching sessions give you the opportunity to see how your team is working together and what roadblocks are keeping you from moving forward.

To Coach or Not to Coach?

With all the benefits of coaching, it's hard to imagine a time when it would not be appropriate. Because coaching prevents problems from growing, keeps the employee engaged, and justifies more serious measures when an employee does not improve, it is an important and valuable step to use whenever possible.

However, as we discussed in Chapter 5, there are times when a more serious disciplinary measure is warranted. You may know this immediately, or you may discover it as you try to coach the employee and meet resistance. To determine whether coaching is the right step, you should consider whether coaching can solve the problem.

Most, but not all, employee discipline problems can be addressed by coaching. Remember that it's important to impose proportionate discipline: Discipline that is directly related to the severity of the problem. Unless the problem is serious, or you've already disciplined the employee for it, it's probably appropriate to first try coaching. This notifies the employee that a problem must be fixed before it escalates and has more serious consequences for the business.

When an issue occurs repeatedly, it may indicate that more serious discipline is needed. However, don't immediately assume that if the employee repeats the same mistake that coaching just won't work. It may instead indicate that the employee needs more guidance and that you need to take additional time to discuss the issue. The employee may not understand the problem and may be repeating it unknowingly or unintentionally. Using an alternate coaching technique may also overcome that problem. (Different coaching techniques are discussed in "Types of Coaching," below.)

> **EXAMPLE:** Sandy is a dental hygienist in Dr. Brown's office. She cleans patients' teeth and has a list of daily appointments.
>
> One day, Sandy arrives to the office 20 minutes late. The first patient is kept waiting, and all Sandy's subsequent appointments run behind, too. "You really need to make it here on time," Dr. Brown tells her.
>
> Twice the next week, Sandy is behind schedule again. This time, although she is in the office on time, she is on the phone, returning patient phone calls from the day before. Dr. Brown takes Sandy aside again. This time, he explains the reason for the previous week's session. "Sandy," he says. "When you have appointments, you need to make them your first priority. That means you need to be in the office and ready to go when they arrive. If patients are kept waiting, they become frustrated and might even choose a different dental office. Do you understand?"

Because Sandy now understands the real problem—keeping patients waiting—she knows what she needs to do to correct the behavior. The additional coaching session should solve the problem. Unless she continues to run behind, no further discipline will be needed.

Types of Coaching

Coaching comes in various forms, from a simple request in the hallway to an actual sit-down session with a clear agenda. Before deciding which is appropriate for your situation, you need to understand the nature and benefits of each.

Simple Requests

Simple requests are made when an employee has tried another method of doing something, but that method hasn't been successful. Because they are very informal, you may not even realize you are coaching. Employees often respond well to this informality—most people prefer to be asked to do something, not told. As a result, simple requests often fix problems without making the employee feel bad.

Simple requests occur throughout the day: during a meeting, in casual conversation, or even via email or voicemail. You make simple requests all the time, when you ask your employees to do or try something new or different. Your comments might start with these phrases:

- "Next time, you might want to …"
- "Hey, try doing it this way …"
- "Did you consider …?"
- "Why don't you give this a try?"

Despite the informality of simple requests, it is still important that you document these incidents. You may use your calendar or tickler log to track them, jotting down a note of when you said what to whom. It can be as brief as one sentence: "Spoke with Luz about frequent interruptions during today's directors meeting." If it is written on a calendar, the date is already noted. If it is in the form of an email, you should archive it. Also write down your plans for following up or making sure the employee fixes the problem. Your notes should be clear enough that you will be able to understand them and remember the incident later, if you need to escalate to a verbal warning.

Corrective Actions

A corrective action is more directive than a simple request. You use it when you want one course of action to stop and to be replaced with another. You use phrases like:

- "Actually you can't do it that way. You need to …"
- "We need to change this. Can you please …?"

Using this language conveys a bit more urgency—that the action or behavior must change immediately.

EXAMPLE: Omar is the floor manager of a packaging plant. He oversees a large assembly line and is responsible for an output target every day. Chris is the new guy on the line.

In his second week on the floor, Chris realizes that he can save time by applying the pricing label in the upper left-hand corner instead of the upper right-hand corner, since it is closer to him. Chris makes this change and indeed sees improvement in his overall station time.

Omar is notified by the Quality Assurance inspector of the misapplication of the labels. He approaches Chris and says, "Hey Chris. Your station times are great and we're happy with your work, but I need you to change the way you are applying these labels. They've got to go in the upper right-hand corner, because we have to adhere to the design requirements."

Chris responds, "Oh, sorry, I didn't realize it was a problem. I did it because I thought I could finish applying the labels more quickly that way."

"Thanks for taking that initiative, Chris," Omar replies. "However, the design requirements are more important than the station time." Chris understands and applies the labels correctly.

Omar has provided Chris the direction he needs to solve the problem, while recognizing the value of Chris's contribution. Chris corrects the behavior, remains motivated, and will likely need no further discipline on this issue.

Coaching Sessions

While simple requests and corrective actions are appropriate for problems with quick, easy solutions, more thoughtful measures may be required when the problem is more complex or when you need input from the employee to craft a solution to the problem. In the example above, Omar knew objectively what needed to change and communicated it to Chris. But what if the problem was that Chris wasn't producing enough? Omar might have wanted to discuss with Chris why he wasn't able to meet production standards and what he needed to be able to do so.

A coaching session is like a "time out"—an opportunity to step away from the situation, communicate that change is necessary, and talk about how to make it happen. Because the session is a little more formal, you should take more time preparing what you will say and do. Set a time and date to meet with the employee to specifically discuss the issue.

> **EXAMPLE:** Jayne is a highway patrol officer. She is praised by everyone she works with for her professionalism and thoroughness. She pays close attention to detail, writes excellent incident reports, and follows up on every loose end.
>
> However, in her focus on detail and procedure, Jayne often deals abruptly with auto accident victims. Jayne's boss, Sergeant Rialto, is concerned that this could affect not only community relations, but also Jayne's ability to get good information when victims are upset. Sergeant Rialto decides that he needs to pull Jayne off the route to address the problem.
>
> Sitting down together in his office, Sergeant Rialto explains the problem: "Jayne, you've been doing really good work out there and the department appreciates it. When you are on an accident site, you are terrific at detailing the accident, getting the right people involved, and clearing the site as soon as possible.
>
> "Another important aspect of our jobs, though, is getting statements from accident victims. Sometimes, that's hard because they're so upset. You may have to spend some time calming them down. If you deal too abruptly with them, they might shut down, which could prevent us from getting the full story. I've seen you get short with accident victims. Do you see how this might affect your ability to do your job?"
>
> "You're right," Jayne replies. "I do get short with some of the victims when they have a hard time telling me what happened. What do you think I can do to make that better?"

Jayne and Sergeant Rialto are now engaged in a discussion about improving Jayne's performance on accident sites. Because the sergeant approached this situation by first praising Jayne's performance and focusing on improving (not correcting) it, Jayne is engaged in working on a solution, instead of building a defense. The sergeant will also be prepared if Jayne doesn't improve: It will be easy to explain why they would now move to the next step in the progressive discipline process.

How Do You Coach?

Now let's focus on how you actually coach. You've already decided that coaching is appropriate, so now you need to:
- prepare to talk with the employee
- meet with the employee
- document, and
- follow up.

Prepare

When you decide coaching is appropriate, there are a couple specific factors you should consider before sitting down with the employee. As with all progressive discipline measures, you should think about when and where to coach, what to say, and how the employee might react.

When and Where Is the Best Place to Coach?

Best practices would have you provide coaching as close to the actual event that precipitated it as possible. Coaching an employee through a recent event that's still fresh in both your minds is a much easier task than conjuring up memories of a past event. While this is often intuitive when you're imposing a more serious disciplinary measure, you may be tempted to put your meeting off when you're facing a minor problem. But you want to give the employee a fair shot to improve as soon as you know there's a problem—and that means raising the issue as soon as you become aware of it.

No matter which method of coaching you use, do it in a place that is not threatening for the employee. That means an environment that is confidential, but also where the employee feels comfortable. It might be in your office, in the employee's office, or over a private lunch together. Your regularly scheduled one-on-one is also a great place to engage in informal coaching. As you discuss other issues and status reports, you can work your coaching in at the appropriate time.

When you are in a coaching session, make sure the employee is comfortable and relaxed. After all, you've chosen to coach because you want the employee to engage in the process with some enthusiasm. Treating the session with too much formality could cause the employee to freeze up and become defensive.

How Will You Start the Conversation?

Although it's important to be prepared for any disciplinary discussion, you don't want to script the entire conversation in advance. When coaching, that means you should be prepared to start the conversation by putting the employee at ease but move quickly to addressing the problem and finding a solution. With more advanced disciplinary measures, communicating the import of the problem necessitates a serious tone. However, keeping a lighter and more encouraging tone when coaching may help the employee feel motivated to work with you to bring about change, instead of doing it just to avoid further discipline.

Your first couple of sentences should explain the problem, describe how it's affecting the employee's or team's performance, and end with a question designed to immediately find a solution together. Here are a few examples:

- "Thanks for meeting me here, Scott. It's nice to get out of the office every now and then. Listen, I understand that you have been having trouble getting along with Susan. In fact, I've heard that you've even raised your voice at Susan in meetings. I'm worried about what this might do to the team's morale and performance. Do you worry about this?"

- "Hey Samantha, thanks for taking the time to meet with me. You know, overall I'm really happy with your performance— you're doing a great job. And since we've added all that new responsibility, I've seen how hard you've been working to keep up. It seems like you could use some help with that. Is there anything we can do?"

- "Bob, I need to have an uncomfortable conversation with you. I value working with you, but recently, I've received some complaints. I know you're as busy as the rest of the team, but lately you've been providing incomplete information and not following up on questions until matters become urgent. Lara reported this to me on the Brody project, and Allen said it happened on the Meyers case. When this happens, it wastes everyone's time—and its hurting your working relationships. How can we tackle this problem?"

Make sure you communicate the basic problem right away. If you wait until the middle of your coaching session to finally say that there's a problem, the employee may not understand that the real purpose for the meeting is to correct a problem or may just feel blindsided. You want the employee to know right away that while the setting may be informal, the message is still important. The more coaching sessions you have, the more comfortable you will become with the process.

How Might the Employee React?

Chapter 8 gives an in-depth look at preparing for and dealing with employee responses. While each employee will respond differently, most don't respond as negatively or as strongly to coaching as to other, more serious discipline measures.

The most common reactions to coaching include:

- **Surprise.** Given that coaching is usually the first step in the discipline process, the employee may well be surprised to hear that there's a problem. Be sure to allow your employee time and space to deal with the surprise before moving on to problem solving, even if it means walking away and coming back later. Otherwise, the employee will have a hard time listening or participating.

- **Defensiveness.** Your employee may not be willing to own the issue right away and may instead blame someone else, refuse to accept your feedback, or shut down and stop talking to you at all. To work through that defensiveness, be sure that you have concrete examples of the problem and can be specific about its effect on the business.

- **Openness.** Most people really do want to improve and embrace the opportunity. Take advantage of this reaction and work together to establish a plan for improvement.

- **False assurances.** Some people will instantly agree with you and promise to immediately improve. This can be an avoidance tactic, used to try and focus your energy elsewhere. If you think the employee hasn't really heard you and committed to improvement, take some time to explain exactly what the problem is and why things need to change. Then, ask the employee what he or she will do to solve the problem. Don't settle for vague statements like "I'll take care of it" or "It won't happen again."

Dealing With Resistance

For the most part, employees are willing to improve when confronted with a discipline problem. Sometimes, however, an employee is not open to your coaching and refuses to change. Because coaching may be your first disciplinary encounter with the employee, it is often the first time you see this resistance.

There are many reasons an employee may resist coaching, including:

- The employee has been doing the job for a long time and knows the "right" way to do things.
- The employee has enjoyed great success doing things one way and sees no need to change.
- The employee disagrees with how you want to do things or believes you are not competent.
- The employee does not believe there is a problem in the first place.
- The employee does not believe there is any benefit from improving.

It's hard to recognize upfront whether an employee will be resistant to coaching, and that's why starting with coaching makes sense whenever the issue calls for it. The communication techniques discussed in Chapter 8 may help you overcome some of this resistance. If the employee's resistance prevents him or her from showing any improvement following your coaching session, you may have to take the discipline process to the next level.

Meet With the Employee

Now that you have set up the discussion, crafted your opening sentences, and considered potential responses, it's time to actually do the coaching. It's also time to listen closely to the employee's responses for information you didn't have before and to understand what caused the behavior.

Explain the Problem

Once you've started your meeting, you should provide the information the employee needs to understand the problem and develop an effective solution. If you're making a simple request or having a corrective action session, this will be a quick discussion. In a coaching session, you'll need to give more detail. You should plan to explain what the problem is (the facts), how it's affecting the company (the impact), and what the company's needs are (the goal). Then, you can determine what you and the employee need to do next (the solution).

- **The facts.** You'll need to communicate this information to the employee.
  - when the problem or incident occurred (date and time)
  - who was involved (if applicable), and
  - how you discovered the problem, including direct quotes, samples of work product, or supporting documentation.
- **The impact.** Explain how the problem affects the workplace or business and why it can't continue. For example, a problem might lead to:
  - poor teamwork
  - low productivity
  - loss of morale
  - low quality, or
  - low customer satisfaction.
- **The goal.** Be very clear about what the company needs. These are not the solutions you and the employee will come up with, but the nonnegotiable standards that must be met. For example:
  - "We need to bring in $15,000 in revenue this month."
  - "Customers must be greeted as soon as they enter the building."
  - "We can't ship this product late; it has to be done by March 1."
- **The solution.** Let the employee know that the solution is collaborative—you must find it together.

Get the Employee to Respond

While getting the employee involved in the discussion is always an important part of progressive discipline, it's particularly challenging when coaching. Because the problems you address when coaching may not be as serious as problems that require more advanced measures, your employee may have a hard time even understanding what the problem is or acknowledging that there is a problem in the first place.

On the other hand, because the problem hasn't escalated, an employee's reluctance to deal with a problem can be more easily overcome in a coaching session. If an employee isn't willing to talk in a coaching session, you can push a little harder than you might be able to if dealing with a more serious issue and work harder to get the employee engaged.

Consider the following example:

> **EXAMPLE:** Michael is the CEO of a small startup. The company plans to release a new product and is on a strict schedule to complete development in three months. Michael learns that Dan, the head of engineering, has not required his employees to focus on the product and has instead permitted them to work on less pressing projects.
>
> Michael takes Dan to lunch to discuss this. After brief small talk, Michael begins, "Dan, I am worried about something. Even though you and I went through the milestones of the project plan, and agreed on the dates that we needed to hit in order to meet the release schedule, I've been hearing that not all the engineers are focused on making that happen. Can you tell me why?"
>
> Dan replies, "I have no idea what you are talking about."
>
> Michael is ready with a few examples and the names of the engineers who are working on noncore projects. He says, "Dan, I really want to work with you in coming up with a solution to this problem. If we miss that date, the company will really suffer, and our investors will certainly question our management. Can you help me understand what's happening?"
>
> Dan softens a bit and says, "I know the company priorities. And I know my part in meeting those. You don't have to worry about me."

Michael persists, "Dan, how can we make sure that your team is focused on the same priorities? Tell me about how you communicate goals and allocate projects."

Michael stays focused in this coaching session and does not let Dan's reluctance control the conversation. By continually focusing on coming up with a solution, and giving Dan opportunities to speak, Michael eventually gets Dan to participate.

Find a Solution Together

Working with the employee to find a solution together requires creative thinking. However, when you're coaching, you have the liberty to spend more time encouraging the employee to come up with creative ideas. After all, the problem isn't as serious at this point, and it's probably the first time you've discussed the issue with the employee. That means you may be able to come up with some good ideas that can quickly solve the problem.

One way to work toward a solution is to flip roles, asking the employee what he or she would do in your position: "Betsy, if our roles were reversed, what would you suggest that I do to fix this? How long would you give me to improve?" You can also point the employee to past experience: "Betsy, have you ever seen this kind of thing before or been told that it was an issue? What did you do then?" You might even try asking the employee to play out what would happen if the problem were to continue: "Betsy, if this problem were to continue, what do you think will happen to the team or to the business? How would you reverse the trend before that happens?" By getting the employee to approach the problem in different ways, you make it easier to come up with ideas for improvement.

Document

Although documentation is a necessary part of any progressive discipline step, it can be less formal when coaching. Nevertheless, it is still important. You may need it in the future if a problem persists. For that reason, make sure you always list the most relevant facts. Documentation of simple requests or corrective actions can be a one-line sentence in your calendar or tickler log:

- "Bridgett was 10 minutes late today. Reminded her to be on time."
- "Told Carol she needed to add service revenue to her overall revenue forecast for better accuracy."

These simple reminders will help you remember what you said and when you said it, as well as give you the opportunity to see if there is a pattern of behavior emerging. If Bridgett repeats the same problem after you have coached her, you might need to move to the next level of progressive discipline; if all of your employees are having a hard time understanding customer priorities, it might be that you need to explain them more thoroughly to the whole team.

Likewise, you can use the calendar to schedule future check-ins. If the employee promises change or action, write yourself a note to discuss the employee's progress at some reasonable date in the future. If you don't think you can fit all the relevant facts into your calendar, do a more detailed coaching log or memo, like the one described below.

Because a coaching session deals with more complex issues, and it will be both harder and more important to remember the details, spend a little more time documenting this conversation. At minimum, the memo must have:

- date and time of the occurrence
- date and time of the coaching session
- a description of the issue and how it was communicated to the employee
- a brief recap of previous disciplinary history for the issue (you might have to look back at your calendar or tickler if you've coached informally)
- what the employee said or did in response, and
- the action plan, with deadlines.

These details will help refresh your memory when you want to see how an action plan is progressing, or if you need to move to another step in the progressive discipline process.

EXAMPLE: Here's how Michael, the CEO, wrote up his coaching session with Dan, who wasn't setting priorities properly for his department:

Met with Dan today, August 31, 2007, to discuss the product release. I told Dan that I'd heard Dylan was working on a database project, and that Sasha was updating the department's internal communications protocols, rather than working on the new product. I told Dan I was concerned that his group might not hit the milestones and release schedule.

Dan informed me that he had sent the team an email outlining the due dates but had not followed up and met with each team member to assign interim deadlines and establish priorities. We agreed that Dan would write up a plan by tomorrow afternoon, detailing how his team would complete the remaining work. I'll review that plan, then Dan will meet with each team member and explain the priorities and due dates. If any problems come up, Dan will discuss them with me immediately.

Follow Up

Often overlooked, following up is the most important, fruitful step in the coaching exercise. It will help you make sure that coaching is succeeding, and redirect the process when it isn't.

How will you know if coaching is successful? In some cases, it will be obvious. An employee will automatically correct behavior or improve performance, and you'll see the difference. For example, when Omar told Chris to place the labels in the upper right-hand corner, he could look at the boxes that followed to see if Chris did as he was told.

Other times, however, coaching will require ongoing evaluation. The employee may need continued feedback and praise from you. For example, in Jayne's situation, she might need to know whether her attempts to be more compassionate toward auto accident victims were successful. Because she has no objective way to measure this, she needs Sergeant Rialto to observe and then tell her what she's doing right and wrong. If he continues to do this and sees improvement each time, they'll both know that the process is working.

You may not be in direct contact with your employee every day, or you may not always see his or her work product. If that's the case, make it a part of the coaching plan to look at the employee's work product on a regular basis. If you are working with a geographically remote person, it is important to establish check-in times and discuss how the work is going. If you don't do this, you won't be able to see whether the employee is responding to your coaching.

When Coaching Is Over

If coaching is successful, you have just one step left: Document the success. If you wrote a coaching memo, add a new section briefly describing the outcome. If you are using a tickler log or your calendar, jot another one-liner noting the success.

If your employee is not responding well to coaching, and you're sure the employee has had ample opportunity to identify and correct the problem, you will need to progress to the next step in the discipline process. In the next chapter, we'll discuss how to issue a verbal warning.

 To hear a sample coaching conversation, open the audio files on the enclosed CD.

Coaching:
Smart Summary

● When you're dealing with a problem for the first time, and the problem isn't very serious, try coaching before going to more-serious disciplinary measures. Because coaching is less formal, problems can often be corrected early, and employees are less threatened by the process.

● Coaching can occur three different ways: through simple requests to change straightforward problem actions or behaviors, through corrective actions intended to have immediate effect, or through coaching sessions when problems are more serious or complex.

● If coaching isn't working, don't immediately assume it can't. It may be that your message wasn't clear to the employee, especially if you used one of the more informal coaching techniques to address the problem.

● Even though coaching is informal, it still requires documentation. You may need it to remind yourself to check in with the employee later or may need to refer to your documentation when you impose more serious discipline if coaching doesn't work.

■

Step 2: Verbal Warnings

erhaps you've had a coaching session or two with an employee, but he or she hasn't improved as expected. Or, maybe an employee has committed obvious misconduct or had a significant slip in performance that merits an immediate, more formal intervention. Either way, it's time to take progressive discipline to the next level: the verbal warning.

Giving a verbal warning is similar to a coaching session in many ways. In either case, you meet with the employee, explain the problem, make sure the employee acknowledges and understands the problem, listen to what the employee has to say about it, and work together to come up with a solution.

However, a verbal warning is also a more serious disciplinary measure, and it requires you to use—and communicate to the employee—a higher degree of formality. Although coaching is the first step in progressive discipline, the employee doesn't really enter the disciplinary system in a formal way—with official notification, documentation, and company involvement—until a verbal warning is issued. Because the problem is more serious, you will need to spend more time preparing for the meeting, conveying that the issue must be dealt with, going over why previous efforts to improve (if any) have failed, and collaboratively solving the problem. You'll also need to spend more time on documentation, and you might need to involve your human resources department or your boss.

What Is a Verbal Warning?

Sometimes called a "verbal reprimand," an "oral reminder," or something similar, a verbal warning gives the employee fair notice that there is an important problem that must be dealt with. A verbal warning is formally documented, commonly in the employee's personnel file. Even if an employee has already received coaching on a particular performance or behavior issue, a verbal warning often serves as the first true wake-up call, letting the employee know that the issue is now on the company's radar—not just a matter to be resolved between the employee and his or her manager.

When to Give a Verbal Warning

To figure out whether a verbal warning is the appropriate way to deal with a particular problem, you'll need to follow the steps outlined in Chapter 5. You'll have to review your company's policy, check in with your human resources department, consider how similar issues have been handled, and weigh how serious the problem is.

For serious misconduct, immediate termination might be the appropriate response. In contrast, many first-time performance and attendance problems are best handled in a coaching session. So where on this spectrum does the verbal warning fall? And how do you know when to use one?

A verbal warning is probably appropriate if:

- The employee has not responded to your efforts to coach a performance problem or a relatively minor conduct problem.

> **EXAMPLE:** Ken works the deli counter in a large grocery store. His manager, Clark, notices that Ken doesn't talk to the customers much. Rather than making chitchat, offering information about various items, or asking if they'd like anything else, Ken simply calls the next number and waits for the customers to tell him what they want.
>
> Clark has a coaching session with Ken, telling him that the company expects employees who interact with customers to be friendly and engaging. Clark works with Ken for an hour, demonstrating the welcoming conversation and positive demeanor he expects. By the end of the hour, Ken is chatting a bit with customers and appears to be getting the hang of things.
>
> A week later, however, Clark once again sees Ken standing silent behind the counter. Clark reminds Ken of their discussion, and Ken improves—but only temporarily. The next day, and the day after that, Clark has to keep reminding Ken to talk to the customers. Because Clark has already coached Ken and the reminders don't seem to be helping, Clark decides to issue a verbal warning. Clark hopes that having a formal disciplinary session with Ken will convey to him that his behavior must change.

If a few facts were different here or there, Clark should have chosen a different response. For example:

- If Ken had taken Clark's coaching to heart and was consistently demonstrating the kind of customer interaction Clark expected, the best response would be praise. When employees improve, you can encourage continued success with positive reinforcement, such as "Ken, I've noticed that you're really engaging the customers as we discussed, and it's having a great effect. Yesterday, Mrs. Santiago told me that she really appreciates your positive attitude and courtesy. Keep up the good work!"

- If Ken was being more friendly towards the customers but was working too slowly as a result, the best response probably would be another coaching session. Ken responded positively to the first session and probably doesn't know that his efforts to improve resulted in a different problem.

- If Ken went beyond his lack of socializing and was actually rude to the customers, a written warning might have been appropriate. Rudeness is a much more serious offense: It can lead to extreme customer dissatisfaction, and it demonstrates a major attitude problem.

• The employee has violated a company rule, but it does not appear to be deliberate or malicious, and has not caused significant harm to the company.

> **EXAMPLE:** Nguyen is a carpenter who works for a major construction company. When hired, every employee receives training in the use of safety equipment and rules for the proper operation of company machinery. The company also makes a point of enforcing these rules, so employees know that they must be followed.
>
> The site manager, Jennifer, notices that Nguyen is not wearing his safety gear when using a power saw. Because this could cause major injuries, and because of the company's position on safety violations, Jennifer decides to give him a verbal warning.

- The employee's behavior or poor performance is causing some problems for the company, but the employee seems to be unaware of the issue and genuinely interested in improvement.

> **EXAMPLE:** Marcus was recently hired as a paralegal for a large law firm. Juan, Marcus's manager, tells him that the firm is not pleased with its case management software— the software it uses to keep track of clients, billing, court dates, case data, and so on—and will soon consider some alternative programs.
>
> Marcus has used some of the other software programs and is eager to please his new boss. He decides to put together a brief comparison of the most popular programs. He asks a friend who works for another law firm to lend him the disks for that firm's software, which he loads onto his computer at work. He also downloads another program from the Internet; this program isn't available free from the software company, but he finds a pirated version on the Web. He puts together his report and shows it to Juan.
>
> At first, Juan is pleased with Marcus's initiative in preparing the report, but he quickly becomes upset when he learns how Marcus acquired the software he used to put it together. The firm's employee handbook clearly states that employees may not download software from the Internet or load programs onto their computers without the permission of the IT department. Software piracy is illegal (not to mention embarrassing for a major law firm). To remedy Marcus's error, the firm will probably have to pay for the legal right to use these programs.
>
> Juan plans to give Marcus a written warning for blatantly violating a company rule and costing the firm money. But when he sits down to talk to Marcus about the problem, Marcus says, "I wasn't going to actually use any of the programs, just look at them so I could report on their features. I thought the rule applied only to programs I was going to use as part of my job. I'm sorry I made such a stupid mistake." Although Marcus has used poor judgment, his explanation makes sense. When Juan considers the circumstances, including the fact that Marcus

only got into trouble because he was being resourceful and doing extra work, he decides to give Marcus a verbal warning instead.

How to Give a Verbal Warning

Now that you've decided a verbal warning is in order, it's time to get down to business. Like any other disciplinary measure, giving a verbal warning requires you to prepare, meet with the employee, document, and follow up. But the details are a bit different when you're using a verbal warning. You'll want to communicate that there's a real problem, but at the same time make clear that you believe the employee can and will improve. And you'll need to prepare documentation and plan to follow up in a way that's more structured than you would use for a coaching session, maximizing the employee's opportunity to succeed and creating a more detailed history that justifies your decisions and actions.

If you're dealing with a recurring problem, consider what went wrong with your coaching and how you can better bring about improvement this time around. Did you explain the problem clearly to the employee? Was your plan for improvement feasible? Why do you think the employee has failed to improve? (Of course, you can—and should—ask the employee the same question when you meet.) Did you check in with the employee to make sure he or she was on the right track?

Prepare

Begin preparing by consulting with others in the company. Many companies require managers to get some guidance from their human resources department—or from a particular higher-up in the company, such as their own manager or a company officer—if they are considering issuing a verbal warning. Some companies don't require you to check in first but require you to talk to human resources or someone else before you actually give the warning. Typically, the purpose of this type of requirement is to make sure that individual managers know how to discipline, what to say, how to document the conversation, and what to do next.

If your company doesn't require you to collaborate this way, that doesn't mean you can't. If you have any questions about whether a verbal warning is appropriate, what to say, how to deal with the employee's reactions, what types of action plans to consider, or anything else, go to your human resources department or manager. Chances are good that they can help you brainstorm the issues and develop some strategies for dealing with the problem.

Once you've done any collaboration, you're ready to plan the meeting itself. You'll need to gather necessary information, decide when and where to meet, and think through what you will say.

Gather Information

As explained in Chapter 1, you should always gather information before you meet with the employee. You'll want to make sure that you have your facts straight, so you can use those facts to successfully communicate to the employee that this is a real problem and must be corrected.

Often, you will be giving a verbal warning because your coaching efforts didn't work. In this situation, you'll need to make sure the employee understands the problem and why it must be solved. If you haven't tried coaching but have jumped to a verbal warning because the situation warrants more formal discipline, you'll need to explain why a verbal warning is appropriate. In either case, be ready with facts demonstrating the severity of the problem and the importance of immediate improvement.

- **Look at the facts.** As always, you should start by reviewing the facts of the situation that led you to decide a verbal warning was appropriate, including what actually happened, how the employee's poor performance or other problem affected the company, and so on.
- **Review past conversations.** Next, review any prior conversations you've had with the employee on this issue. If you've coached the employee, go over your notes. How often have you had to talk to the employee about this problem? What did you say about it? What was the action plan?
- **Consider what didn't work.** What specific things did the employee do or not do that caused the action plan to fail? Be prepared to discuss specifically what went wrong.

Having these facts at your fingertips will help you make your position clear—and help you evaluate the likely success of any new plans for improvement.

⚠️ **If you skipped straight to a verbal warning because the employee violated a rule or committed misconduct, review your employee handbook or other written company policies.** What does the rule require? Did the employee know about the rule or know that his or her conduct was not appropriate? What's the purpose of the rule? Being able to point to the rule and explain its importance will help you communicate why the employee's problem warrants a verbal warning—and, hopefully, help you ward off a defensive reaction.

Set Up Logistics

Now it's time to plan the meeting details: where and when you will have it and who should be there. Once you've decided that a verbal warning is in order, it's a good idea to meet with the employee right away—ideally, within a day or two of the incident you'll be discussing. Holding a meeting immediately after the incident lets the employee know that the issue is important and has captured your full attention. Also, the quicker you step in, the quicker the employee will have an opportunity to improve.

Unlike a coaching meeting, which might take only ten or fifteen minutes, you should plan at least half an hour to discuss a verbal warning. Because the employee will be facing a formal disciplinary intervention, he or she is more likely to have questions and concerns. You are also more likely to see emotional or angry reactions, which you and the employee may need some time to sort through. And, particularly if you have already coached the employee on the problem, you should budget extra time to analyze and discuss what went wrong with your previous action plan and how you can do better this time around.

Although an offsite meeting may be appropriate for a coaching session, you should stay at work to administer a verbal warning. While you want to emphasize informality in a coaching session, it's important to be more formal with a verbal warning, to demonstrate that the company is involved. If your office is private (that is, you have walls that reach to the ceiling and a door that closes), you can hold the meeting there. If not, book a conference room or another space where you can talk comfortably. If you have concerns about office gossip, you should coordinate a time and place with the employee that maximizes privacy.

If You're Managing an Offsite Employee

If you manage employees who work offsite, you may have a hard time following the suggestions above. Here are a few options for delivering a verbal warning:

Bring the employee into the office. Set up a formal meeting time and date. Even if that delays your meeting by a couple of days, it's better to have the meeting face to face.

Go to the employee's worksite. This may be feasible if the employee's location isn't very far away. Be sure that there is a private place to have your discussion, however.

If you must discipline remotely, don't do it in an email. Set up a formal phone conference, and videoconference if you can. Conduct the meeting sitting at a desk, well prepared to have the same discussion you would engage in if the employee were in the room.

Some companies require you to have a witness at formal disciplinary meetings—typically, a human resources representative or a higher-level manager. If your company is one of them, you should arrange to have the appropriate person attend. If your company doesn't require you to bring a witness, consider the pros and cons of having a third person present—these are covered in Chapter 10.

Allowing the Employee to Bring a Witness

There are two situations in which you must allow the employee to bring a witness to a disciplinary meeting:

- If your company policy states that employees may bring witnesses, then you must allow them to do so.
- If the employee is represented by a union, he or she is entitled to bring a union representative to any meeting that could lead to discipline. These rights are called "*Weingarten* rights," after the name of the U.S. Supreme Court case that created them.

If the employee asks to bring a witness or support person but you aren't required to allow it, check with your human resources department (if you have one) to find out how this type of request has been handled in the past.

There are pros and cons to allowing the employee to bring a witness. The employee might feel more comfortable—and therefore, better able to discuss the problem and possible solutions—with another person there, particularly if the employee has an emotional reaction. And allowing a witness will help the employee feel supported.

On the other hand, having an extra person in the room will probably make it more difficult to establish a rapport with the employee. If an employee brings a witness, you may also want to bring a representative from human resources, to help provide balance and perspective to the conversation.

Plan the Conversation

As always when delivering discipline, you can't script the whole discussion in advance. But you should consider how to begin the conversation and the tone you'd like to set.

Unlike a coaching session, which an employee might not even recognize as discipline, a verbal warning is a formal disciplinary step. If you've decided to issue a verbal warning, you are dealing with either a recurring problem or a first-time event that is serious enough to move past the coaching step in the disciplinary system. Either way, you should begin the conversation in a way that conveys the seriousness of the matter to the employee—without making the employee feel like he or she is under attack.

EXAMPLE: Charles supervises Peggy, who has left work early a couple of times. The first time Charles noticed that Peggy wasn't at her workstation, he sat down with her the next day for a quick reminder. She told him it wouldn't happen again. But two weeks later, Charles actually saw Peggy gathering her belongings and heading out 20 minutes before she was supposed to leave. The next day, he calls her into his office, where he plans to issue a verbal warning.

Charles is angry that Peggy has blatantly disregarded company rules and his previous efforts to coach her. As soon as she sits down, he says, "What were you doing, leaving early after I told you not to? I think I've made it clear that this is completely unacceptable, and I'm not going to let you get away with it. If this keeps up, you're going to be let go."

If Peggy responds that she left early because her husband was in a serious car accident, Charles is going to feel pretty bad. But even if Peggy doesn't have a good excuse, Charles's angry approach has essentially foreclosed any possibility of collaborative discussion. Peggy will feel that Charles has his mind made up, and it doesn't matter what she says or does. She is likely to respond defensively and will probably either clam up entirely or get angry. She might improve her attendance, at least temporarily, but her dedication to the job and the company is likely to take a sharp downturn (along with her performance, most likely). Charles has lost an opportunity to develop loyalty and improved performance and has probably made an enemy.

This would have been a better approach:

"Peggy, I asked you to meet with me today to discuss an important issue that has come up more than once: leaving work early. We talked about this a couple of weeks ago, and I thought we agreed that it wouldn't happen again. But yesterday, I saw you leaving your workstation at 4:40 in the afternoon, and you didn't return. What's going on?"

When you plan your opening sentences, remember that you want to briefly describe the problem, convey that it is serious, and mention any prior conversations about it. Here are some more examples:

EXAMPLE: "Martina, please come in and sit down. I want to talk about the way you spoke to Eric this afternoon about the Jones account. I heard you raise your voice to him and tell him that he was incompetent. I spoke to Eric about the conversation, and he told me that you said some other negative things, as well. He is upset about it, and I'm concerned. That is not how we talk to each other at this company. Tell me what happened."

"Brad, you are continuing to miss your project deadlines. We've talked about this before, and I've explained that your coworkers have to pick up the slack when you aren't finished with your work on time. We also came up with a more detailed schedule so you could complete and hand in your work a little bit at a time. However, you've been missing those interim deadlines as well. We need to get things back on track right away."

"I know that you're having a hard time arranging child care, Maurice, but you were late by more than 20 minutes twice last week. As we've discussed twice in the past month, you have to be here, on time, every day, in order to help open the store. This is a job requirement, and there are good reasons for it. We need to get this problem solved."

Save the small talk for happier times. Don't start a formal disciplinary meeting with casual chatter or questions about the employee's weekend. This will only give the employee the wrong idea about the purpose of the meeting—and could make the employee feel tricked when the real agenda is revealed. This isn't a good way to begin a conversation that you hope will be open and collaborative. Likewise, don't allow the employee to avoid the discipline discussion by sidetracking you with small talk. Say something like "I wish we could use our time today to catch up, but we are really here to address this issue." This will keep your discussion on track.

Meet With the Employee

During the meeting, you should clearly communicate what the problem is, why it's a problem, and what needs to happen next. Although the meeting will be similar to a coaching session, there are some important differences, which stem from the more formal nature of a verbal warning. Here is the basic agenda your meeting should follow (each of these steps is covered more fully below):

- State the problem.
- Review past efforts to correct, if any.
- Make sure the employee acknowledges the problem.
- Listen to the employee's explanation.
- Tell the employee that you are issuing a verbal warning.
- Develop a solution.
- Discuss next steps.

State the Problem

At the outset, tell the employee exactly why you are meeting. Explain the facts that lead you to believe there is a problem—what you saw or heard, or what was reported to you by others. Let the employee know why his or her performance, behavior, or misconduct is causing a problem for the company, and clearly state that things need to change.

> **EXAMPLE:** Steve's manager, Jerry, begins a verbal warning discussion like this: "Steve, I've asked you to meet with me today to talk about our process for managing deals. As we discussed several weeks ago, while we expect all of our account representatives to close at least three new deals each month, we also expect you to follow the processes and procedures established for implementing those deals. While your sales numbers are improving, and we want to encourage continued progress, your deal implementation memos are incomplete and often have significant errors. This means the support teams scramble around asking you to clarify what should have been clearly stated in the first place. What's more, you often don't answer their questions in a timely way, though everything you send to them is marked 'urgent.' This lack of attention to detail and process management means that the support teams spend three times the usual amount of time implementing your deals—and

it makes for bad feeling on the team. It also costs the company money, because we can't invoice until everything is satisfactorily delivered. While you are meeting the sales goals, these sales are coming at a high internal price."

Review Past Discussions

If you have already coached the employee on this issue, talk briefly about those conversations. You don't have to go into great detail—after all, the employee was at the coaching session with you. The purpose of this review is to gently remind the employee that he or she already had an opportunity to discuss and resolve the problem informally, and it didn't work. It also acknowledges that the employee didn't meet the commitments he or she made in that earlier conversation. This makes it easier for the employee to accept that a verbal warning is necessary and puts him or her in the right frame of mind to talk honestly about what happened.

> **EXAMPLE:** Jerry says, "When we talked several weeks ago about this problem, you told me that you thought it was more important to bring in deals than worry about 'mindless paperwork.' I explained then that it was vital to product delivery and asked you to reread the process handbook. We also discussed that you'd complete all deal memos fully—and if anything confused you, you were to ask me about it before you turned in the memo. I haven't heard a single question from you, but I have had continued complaints about your deal memos."

Seek the Employee's Acknowledgment

At this point, the employee will probably start talking. Before you get too involved in a conversation about what happened and why, however, it's very important to make sure that the employee understands exactly what the problem is. If the employee starts off by acknowledging the problem, you can cross this off your list. If the employee denies the problem or admits the behavior but claims that it isn't a problem or makes excuses, however, you'll need to make sure that you're both on the same page before you continue.

To do this, go back to the beginning and state the facts: what the employee did (or didn't do) and why it's a problem. If necessary, lay out the facts one by one. For example, if an employee responds to your conversation about tardiness by saying, "It's not that big of a deal—and anyway, I've hardly been late at all this month," you might respond by saying, "In fact, you were late twice last week alone—20 minutes late on Tuesday and 15 minutes late on Friday. And, as we've discussed, it is a big deal, because when you're late, you are not available to serve our customers."

> **EXAMPLE:** Steve responds to Jerry's statements by saying, "Why are you riding me so hard? My job is to bring in the business. Let the clerks do the paperwork."
>
> Jerry replies, "Steve, I'm not coming down especially hard on you. Your job isn't just to bring in the deals: It's also to manage your accounts and help the company profit from those deals. If your deal memos are incomplete, a lot of time is wasted figuring out what needs to be done, who needs to do it, and when it needs to be done. That costs the company a lot of employee time, and it also creates resentment on your team.
>
> We'll talk about why you haven't completed your deal memos correctly in a minute; first, I need to make sure that we agree about the facts. You signed four new deals this month, right?" Steve says, "Yeah, that sounds about right." Jerry responds, "And you were contacted by Claire last Friday, April 27, because the deal memo on the Briggs account was incomplete and had some incorrect information, right?" Steve agrees. Jerry continues, "Claire told me you didn't respond until the following Wednesday. Does that sound right to you?" Steve again agrees. Jerry then moves the conversation along by saying, "Okay, now that I know we're both on the same page about what actually happened, let's talk about why."

A detailed investigation can help. Sometimes, you might have to discipline an employee for behavior that you haven't witnessed firsthand, such as being rude to customers or harassing a coworker. In these situations, talking to witnesses and gathering any other evidence before you meet with the employee can help you head off a flat denial. Once the employees sees that you know (or at least, have a pretty good idea) about what happened, he or she will be less likely to stonewall.

Listen to the Employee's Explanation

Pay very careful attention to the employee's comments about what happened and why. Of course, you'll need to listen well to understand where the employee is coming from and develop an action plan to solve the problem. But you also need to make sure that a verbal warning is the appropriate disciplinary measure. You might not have the full story, or some other employee might really be to blame, which might dictate that you make the meeting a coaching session or simply a conversation. On the other hand, the incident might be worse than you feared: The employee might have done something wrong intentionally, for example, to sabotage the company or endanger a coworker.

> **EXAMPLE:** After Jerry makes sure Steve understands the problem, Steve has the chance to explain: "It takes all my energy just to bring in new clients, so the last priority on my list is filling out paperwork. You can see my new client numbers are improving but I have to tell you, not having secretarial help really handicaps me when it comes time to implement the deals. And I admit, I'm still not that comfortable with the internal process. At my old job, I just handed the deal off to administrative staff, and my numbers were great. I think that if I understood the process and technology here better, I'd have better results."
>
> Jerry responds, echoing what Steve has said to show that he's listening carefully: "I'm glad you think that you're progressing with new accounts—that's important. And it sounds like you're still having trouble making the move from selling benefit programs to selling boxed software, partly because the implementation system is new to you. Does that sound right?"

Explain the Verbal Warning

This can be the most awkward part of the conversation, but it's absolutely necessary: You must tell the employee explicitly that you are issuing a verbal warning (unless, of course, the employee has told you something that changes your mind about giving the warning). The employee needs to be on notice that he or she has entered the disciplinary system, that the issue will be documented, and that further problems could result in more serious discipline.

If you don't tell the employee that you're giving a warning, the employee might later be surprised to see the warning in his or her personnel file or to have it come up later, when it's time for bonuses, promotions, raises, and the like. What's more, it denies the employee the opportunity to improve: If the employee doesn't understand the seriousness of the problem, he or she might not understand the pressing need to immediately alter behavior.

Managers are often hesitant to announce that they're issuing a formal warning during a disciplinary meeting, because they're concerned that this will turn the employee against them and poison the rest of the conversation. But there are ways to break the news while still maintaining a positive note—for example, by emphasizing that you will continue to help the employee improve and that you hope further discussions and discipline won't be necessary.

> **EXAMPLE:** Jerry tells Steve, "I need to let you know that I'm giving you a verbal warning, based on your problem managing deals effectively. I made that decision because we've already discussed the issue and I haven't yet seen an improvement in your deal memos or your deal management generally. But I'm hopeful that we'll come up with some good ideas today that will help you understand our deal management process, so we won't have to talk about this again. In fact, I already have some ideas kicking around in my head, so let's start brainstorming on how we can resolve this problem."

Let the employee know if the warning will "expire." Many companies put a time limit on how long a verbal or written warning will remain in an employee's file. After that time has passed, the warning is removed, and the employee has a clean slate from that point forward. If your company has this type of policy, tell the employee that the warning will be removed if he or she has no further problems while the warning is active. This provides a strong incentive for improvement and lets the employee know that you really want him or her to succeed.

Develop Solutions

This is most managers' favorite part of the meeting: looking ahead to positive change in the future. Hopefully, your employee will have some ideas of what might help. Some of these ideas might be too expensive or otherwise impractical, but don't be dismissive. Instead, tell the employee why his or her idea won't work, and keep the conversation moving. Share your own ideas as well, but stay open to the employee's input. After all, the employee is the one who will ultimately have to carry out the plan, and he or she knows best what is feasible and what is not.

> **EXAMPLE:** Steve says, "I'd like to talk about solutions, too. What I'd really like is to lower my sales targets for a few months, just until I get a handle on how the deal management process works. Can we do that?" Jerry knows this is a nonstarter, and responds, "I'm afraid not, Steve. These numbers are set specifically for newer sales reps, and your coworkers are meeting them successfully. We have to come up with some ways to improve your deal management, not lower your sales goals."
>
> Steve says, "I see your point, I guess. What I really need help with is learning what the relevant information is. I want to make sure I get it in there the first time, because right now, I feel like these memos are taking up too much time. But it's really hard for me to tell what it is exactly that the support staff need from me."
>
> Jerry replies, "I can see that if you don't understand how the information is used, you won't know what to include in your memos. Have you spent a few hours listening to the customer support inbound calls, to hear the kinds of questions they get from customers?"
>
> Steve responds, "No, I haven't. I've never thought about the deals from the back end."
>
> Jerry offers, "What I'd like to do is set up a schedule, so you can spend a couple of hours with each department that helps to implement your deals. That way, you can see what information

really needs to be spelled out in your deal memos, and why it's important to manage the process very carefully. It will show you how properly managing deals really impacts their profitability, and it will give you a chance to foster better relationships with the 'back office' team. And I'd also like you to spend a couple of hours with Celia. She's our top closer and also works great with the back office."

Steve says, "That sounds great. If it's all right with you, I'd also like to show you my draft deal memos, after I've had a chance to hear from everyone else what's really important. Then you can tell me how well they meet the company's needs. Would that be okay?" Jerry agrees.

Agree On Next Steps

Once you've developed an action plan, discuss exactly what will happen next. Start by spelling out what you and the employee have committed to do. Make your action plan concrete by setting dates and specific targets for improvement. Especially if you are dealing with a recurring issue, you will want to set fairly tight deadlines and regular check-ins. If this is a recurring issue, this employee hasn't been able (or willing) to improve after notice of the problem, which means you will need to keep a closer eye on the situation.

Because you will be documenting the meeting afterward, you should also let the employee know when the paperwork will be ready. Give the employee an opportunity to read the documentation and raise any questions or concerns. It's a good idea to schedule a brief follow-up meeting the next day (assuming you can complete the paperwork by then) to review the documentation.

EXAMPLE: Jerry says, "Okay Steve, it sounds like we have a plan. I'll let the back office leads know that you'll be spending some time with them. Why don't you give me some dates and times that work for you by the end of the day, then I'll set up a schedule by the beginning of next week. After you've met with them to understand the process from their end, and you've completed another sale, you can get the draft deal memo together and we can go over it together. How does that sound?" Steve agrees to the plan.

Jerry also talks to Steve about paperwork: "As we discussed, this is a formal verbal warning, so I need to summarize our conversation in writing, for your file. As I told you, the documentation will be removed from your file after one year, as long as we don't have any further problems with this. I'll write that up by the end of the day; I'd like you to read it and make sure you agree with it. There's a space on the form for you to sign, so I know we're both on the same page. I'll email you the paperwork later today. If you'd like to talk about it after you look it over, let me know and we can talk again. If not, you can just print it out, sign it, and return it to me."

Make sure to close the meeting on a positive note. After all, you and the employee have successfully developed a solution and are both looking forward to improvement in the future. Say something like "I'm glad we talked about this and developed an action plan. I'm confident that you'll be able to follow through and get this resolved."

Don't make promises for the future. It's important to say something positive to an employee who's just received a warning: It reinforces that you want to help, are focused on what happens next, and believe in the employee. But don't take it a step further and promise a reward for improved performance (or further discipline if things don't get better). These kinds of statements might have to be followed later, even if the company can't or doesn't want to. See Chapter 3 for more information on why it's smart to avoid specific promises.

Document

After the meeting—preferably on the same day—complete your paperwork. If your company requires you to use a particular form or follow certain rules for documentation, by all means do so. If not, you can use the form we provide in Appendix A to record what happened.

Here's a sample form, which Jerry used to document his verbal warning to Steve:

Verbal Warning

Date: May 3, 2007

Employee Name: Steve Hinds

Manager Name: Jerry Martinez

Incident Description

On May 1, 2007, I received a complaint from administrative assistant Claire Stewart that your deal memo on the Briggs sale was incomplete and contained numerous errors that slowed implementation of the deal significantly. I investigated whether this was true by reviewing the deal memo (attached) and talking with the administrative staff responsible for assisting you in completing this deal.

The deal memo did not have all the information the staff needed to complete the deal. For example, the memo did not explain the shipping method or the shipping date. Additionally, the memo had errors including incorrect prices and the wrong delivery address.

On April 27, Claire tried to contact you via both email and phone to correct these errors, but you did not respond. As a result of these errors, three administrative assistants spent approximately eight extra hours trying to resolve the discrepancies. Claire also informed me that a similar problem occurred on the Edwards deal earlier in the month.

While your gross sales numbers have been improving, these errors are reducing profit margin on your deals significantly and causing extra work for other team members.

When you and I met to discuss this issue earlier today, you told me that you believed this was the responsibility of administrative staff, and that you were not comfortable with the company process.

Prior Incidents

Customer support, clerical, and fulfillment have each complained about incorrect or incomplete information on your deal memos at least three times. We discussed this in my office on April 5. At that time, I tasked you with rereading the process handbook, which you told me that you did. I also told you to ask me if you had questions about writing deal memos. Since April 5, you have not asked me any questions about deal memos.

Improvement Plan

We agreed that you will meet with each back office department and spend a couple of hours learning what information they need from you to implement your deals. You will also spend a couple of hours with Celia, who will show you one of her deal memos and explain how she decides what to include in it. You will let me know some dates and times that are good for you by tomorrow; I will set up a schedule for these visits by the beginning of next week, May 7.

We also agreed that we will review your next deal memo together. I will tell you whether that memo includes the relevant information. When you have closed your next deal, please inform me and we can schedule that review.

Manager: _____ Date: _____

I acknowledge that I have received and understand this document.

Employee: _____ Date: _____

Remember, you might need to meet with the employee again, if he or she takes issue with anything you wrote or wants to discuss things further. You'll want to secure the employee's signature, whether or not the employee adds comments to the form. You can find complete information on preparing documentation in Chapter 9.

Follow Up

What happens after you meet with the employee will make or break your action plan. Don't wait until a month or two has passed before you get involved: Check in often, offering any advice or assistance you can. Make sure that you provide the resources and other help you promised during your meeting.

You should have your calendar out as you complete your paperwork, to record important dates and commitments. For example, if you agreed to meet with the employee once a week, schedule those appointments. If you told the employee you'd make any changes—for example, by putting the employee on a particular project, giving a troublesome account to a coworker, or arranging for the employee to attend a training program—write a note to remind yourself to do it, and schedule check-ins to make sure those changes have the desired effect.

If your company removes discipline documentation from the personnel file after a certain amount of time has passed without further problems, mark that date on your calendar as well. You must keep this commitment: Chances are good that it's providing a strong incentive to your employee. If someone else (for example, the human resources department) is responsible for actually removing this documentation from the file, write yourself a note to send a reminder email a couple of days before the deadline—and check the file yourself to make sure the paperwork is no longer there.

And don't forget the power of positive reinforcement: Even if the employee doesn't turn things all the way around, it's important to praise improvement. Teachers and trainers tells us that everyone learns more quickly through praise for appropriate behavior than through punishment for doing things wrong. Look for things that you can praise, then make a point of doing it.

> **EXAMPLE:** One week after their meeting, Jerry sees Steve in the hallway and says, "Steve, I just want to let you know that Mary and Sam both made a point of telling me that they appreciated the time you took to understand how their departments functioned and you asked some good questions. I appreciate that you're taking those meetings so seriously, and I wanted to thank you for that. Here's to smooth deals in May!"

You should offer the employee praise for improvement even if he or she isn't yet performing up to your standards—but only if the employee is on an upward trajectory. This is most often an issue when dealing with performance problems: The employee's performance improves but is still short of the mark. As long as the employee is still getting better and you foresee fully acceptable performance in the near future, you should praise the improvement while noting that there's still some room for growth.

> **EXAMPLE:** In May, Steve makes his sales targets, but his revenues dip slightly. However, all his deal memos are flawless, and Steve has expressed to Jerry that he now feels more comfortable with the implementation process and more appreciative of the contribution of other staff members. He has met with Jerry a couple of times to hone his memos, and Jerry is confident that he'll keep getting better. Rather than criticizing his lowered sales numbers, Jerry tells him, "Steve, I'm happy that you understand the deal implementation process. Although your sales numbers were a little low this month, I'm confident that you'll turn that around as you get more comfortable with the implementation process and it starts taking up less of your time. Let's sit down in a couple of weeks and make sure you're still on target."

If, on the other hand, the employee doesn't seem to be improving much or at all, even after you've lived up to the commitments you made in the action plan, it's time to consider giving a written warning. Chapter 13 explains how.

 If you'd like to hear a sample verbal warning discussion, refer to the audio files on the enclosed CD.

Verbal Warnings: Smart Summary

● A verbal warning is the first "formal" step in the disciplinary process, meaning the employee is officially notified of the discipline, it is documented, and the company is involved.

● A verbal warning is appropriate when an employee hasn't responded to previous coaching efforts, an employee has violated a company rule inadvertently or unknowingly, or an employee's performance or behavior has caused problems for the company but the employee seems unaware of the issue and genuinely interested in improvement.

● A verbal warning is more formal than a coaching session. Take more time to prepare what you will say—including a review of any previous discussions on topic—and allow at least a half-hour for the discussion. The discussion should take place in a more formal setting that gives the employee privacy and communicates to the employee that the problem is serious.

● When you meet with an employee to issue a verbal warning, state the problem, review past efforts to correct it, make sure the employee acknowledges the problem, listen to the employee's explanation, tell the employee you are issuing a verbal warning, develop a solution, and discuss next steps.

● Although a verbal warning is given orally, it must be followed up by documentation that acknowledges the discipline, the reason for it, whether there were any prior incidents, and the action plan. The employee should be given a copy of the documentation and asked to sign it, acknowledging receipt.

■

13

Step 3: Written Warnings

W e all hope for the best in the disciplinary process—to have positive, productive conversations with our employees that motivate them to improve and resolve problems before they become critical. But if you're facing a problem that's ongoing, serious, or both, a written warning may be your only choice, because either company policy or common sense dictates it.

Typically, a written warning is given when an employee doesn't improve after coaching and a verbal warning. However, you may also give a written warning for a first-time problem, if the behavior or consequences are serious enough to justify a forceful response but not so serious as to call for immediate termination of employment.

Giving a written warning can be difficult. Because a written warning is—and will be viewed by the employee as—a serious disciplinary measure, you should anticipate that the employee might become defensive or emotional. Particularly if you're revisiting an issue that you and the employee have discussed before, the employee might feel more frustrated, angry, or embarrassed that there hasn't been sufficient improvement. Typically, written warnings come with some serious job consequences—such as ineligibility for merit raises and promotions or lowered performance appraisals—which can also lead to heightened emotions and anger.

And the employee might not be the only person who's upset about the situation. Because you're dealing with someone who has either committed serious misconduct or failed to improve after you've tried to help, you might be frustrated and angry yourself. This can make it tough to get down to the business at hand: communicating, clearly and objectively, why the situation is not acceptable and how it will need to change. If you're dealing with one-time, serious misconduct, you'll need to keep close tabs on the employee in the future, to make sure your written warning puts the problem in the past. If you're dealing with an ongoing problem, the action plan you develop at this stage might have to include more detail, oversight, and direction from you.

This chapter explains how to give a written warning, from start to finish. You'll learn when a written warning is appropriate, how to plan to meet with the employee, and what to say during the meeting. You'll also learn how to document the situation—that is, how to actually write your written warning—and how to follow up afterwards, to make sure that the employee stays on track.

A Written Warning Is Both a Conversation and a Document

It used to be standard practice for a written warning to simply appear on a worker's desk or locker, unaccompanied by any discussion. (Pink slips—notices that the employee had been fired—often showed up in the same, silent way.) In today's modern workplace, however, the term "written warning" generally refers both to the actual written document and to the conversation that accompanies it. Giving a written warning doesn't simply mean handing over a piece of paper—it also means explaining the warning to the employee and talking about what will happen next.

At some companies, managers are told to draft their written warning before they meet with the employee, then hand it over during the meeting. There are several problems with this approach, however:

- You can't be sure that the facts warrant a written warning until you meet with the employee and hear him or her out. If you were wrong in your assessment of the situation, you'll have to go back on what you've said, get your piece of paper back from the employee, and start all over again.

- You won't be able to include the employee's response in your documentation. Sometimes, the employee says something during your meeting that should be memorialized—such as admitting to wrongdoing or providing an explanation for poor performance.

- Once you hand over the written warning, the employee will start reading—and stop listening to you. The employee might also be upset that you decided how to handle the situation without even asking for his or her side of the story.

For all of these reasons, we recommend that you write your written warning after you meet with the employee, just like any other disciplinary documentation.

What Is a Written Warning?

A written warning is the second formal step in most progressive discipline systems (following a verbal warning) and is typically reserved for fairly serious problems. Often, a written warning affects an employee's opportunities for advancement and eligibility for merit raises, bonuses, and consideration for special projects. Because a written warning has significant consequences, it gives the employee an extra incentive to make a change for the better. If the employee can't or won't improve, it also lays the groundwork for a fair and legally defensible termination.

When to Give a Written Warning

To figure out whether a written warning is the appropriate way to deal with a particular problem, you'll need to follow the steps outlined in Chapter 5. You'll have to review your company's policy, check in with your human resources department, consider how similar issues have been handled, and weigh how serious the problem is.

Because a written warning is a severe disciplinary measure, it isn't the right response to minor problems or many first-time offenses. At the other end of the spectrum, some problems—almost always misconduct—are so serious that they justify immediate termination of employment. So when is a problem serious enough to warrant a written warning, but not so serious that the employee should be fired? Here are some examples:

- The employee has not improved a performance, attendance, or misconduct problem, even after you've provided coaching and given a verbal warning. In this situation, a written warning is appropriate; it is simply the next step in the discipline process.

    EXAMPLE: Cora answers phones at the help desk of a large company. Cora and the other customer service representatives answer basic customer questions, but they forward most calls on to other departments or outside technicians. If the customer wants to purchase a product or receive a refund, Cora or one of her coworkers processes the transaction.

    Customer service representatives are expected to answer an average of 20 calls a day, return all messages left since the previous business day, and process all paperwork for orders and refunds on the same day they are made. Cora averages about 14 calls a day and often waits several days before processing paperwork or returning customer calls.

Cora's manager had a coaching session with her and asked her to spend a morning observing a more experienced coworker handling calls. The manager also reviewed the ordering and refund paperwork with Cora, to make sure she understood what was required. When Cora didn't improve, the manager gave her a verbal warning. Because Cora said that it was hard for her to budget her time properly to get everything done, the manager sent her to a time management seminar. Cora still hasn't improved, so the manager decides to give her a written warning.

> **⚠ Make sure the employee had a fair opportunity to improve.** Before you decide to give a written warning for an ongoing problem, take a look at the action plan you came up with in your last disciplinary meeting with the employee. Were the goals you set feasible? Did you provide the resources necessary for the employee to succeed? Did you hold follow-up meetings as promised? If your review reveals flaws in the action plan, you might want to scale back and give another verbal warning—this time, with a fair and achievable action plan.

- The employee has taken an extended unexcused absence, failed to turn up at a mandatory event, or otherwise engaged in a serious and/or flagrant violation of the company's attendance rules. Typically, managers handle first-time attendance problems through coaching. If that first absence is prolonged or causes extreme hardship, however, stronger discipline might be appropriate.

  EXAMPLE: Josephine is a driver for a company that delivers documents and packages. Each driver is responsible for pickups and deliveries in a particular region. The company requires drivers to request vacation time at least three weeks in advance and requires drivers to call in before taking a sick day, so it can line up substitute drivers.

Josephine doesn't show up for work on a Wednesday. Her supervisor, Hank, calls her home; when no one answers, Hank leaves a message asking Josephine to call in right away. Josephine doesn't show up or call in until Friday afternoon, when she calls Hank and tells him that she will return to work on Monday morning. Josephine explains that she has been out of town since Tuesday evening, when her sister called from out of state and said that she had been evicted. Josephine went to help her sister find a new place to live and move into it.

Because Hank didn't know whether Josephine was coming in, he had to find a driver at the last minute for three days in a row. Some of the customers on Josephine's regular route complained about late service, and one important delivery didn't get made on time. Hank knows that Josephine understood the company's attendance policy, because he explains it to all drivers when they are hired. Even though Josephine had a compelling reason to be out, she didn't call or ask for permission. All in all, Hank decides that this conduct merits a written warning.

- The employee has committed misconduct that is serious but does not warrant termination. Examples typically include horseplay, violations of safety rules, problems dealing with customers or clients, or mistreatment of coworkers.

EXAMPLE: Dave asked Crystal, his coworker, out a month ago, but she told him she was seeing someone else. Since then, Dave has asked Crystal questions about her boyfriend, what they do together, how she feels about him, and so forth. Although they are friendly with each other, Crystal is uncomfortable about Dave's interest in her love life. When she tells him she doesn't want to talk about her relationship, Dave responds, "Why won't you tell me anything about this guy? You don't seem very excited about him; are you sure you don't want to go out with me instead?"

Claude, their manager, overhears the end of this conversation as he's walking by Crystal's cubicle. He also sees that Crystal looks upset, so he asks her to come to his office. Claude asks Crystal what's going on, and she says, "I don't want to get Dave in trouble, but he's kind of creeping me out. He asked me to go on a date with him, and when I told him I had a boyfriend, he just started in with all of these questions. I don't want to go out with him and I don't want to talk about my relationship, but he just doesn't seem to be getting the message."

After conferring with the human resources department and considering the situation carefully, Claude decides to give Dave a written warning. Discipline is clearly in order: Dave's behavior is out of line, upsetting to his coworker, and skirting close to the edge of illegality. On the other hand, Dave hasn't had any disciplinary problems before; he hasn't touched, threatened, or made crude comments to Crystal (any of which could well be grounds for immediate termination); and there's a good possibility that he doesn't understand why his behavior is inappropriate. All in all, it looks like Dave needs a serious wake-up call, and Claude decides that a written warning is the right way to deliver it. Claude also realizes that he will have to monitor the situation very carefully, to make sure Dave changes his ways.

How to Give a Written Warning

Now that you've decided to give a written warning, it's time to get started. As when you coach or give a verbal warning, you'll need to prepare, meet with the employee, document the discussion, and follow up. When you give a written warning, however, things are more formal. At this point, you're usually dealing with an employee who can't or won't meet basic standards of performance or conduct. Giving a written warning conveys that things must change if the employee wants to keep working for your company.

If you've already coached and given a verbal warning for the same behavior, you'll have to spend some time analyzing, and then discussing with the employee, why your previous action plan hasn't worked. Your first step should be to make sure that the employee had a fair chance to succeed—that is, that your action plan was clear and achievable, that you provided any resources and training you promised, and so on. Assuming the action plan was fair, you'll need to emphasize that the employee did not do as he or she agreed to do, and that this is unacceptable.

You should also spend extra time coming up with a new plan for improvement, with more frequent follow-up meetings and tight deadlines that will allow you to stay on top of the situation. Although this might feel like micro-management, you've already given the employee the opportunity to improve, and it hasn't worked. If your employee needs more involvement or direction from you in order to succeed, that's what you should provide.

If you're handling a first-time problem, the purpose of the written warning is to administer a powerful wake-up call. You must communicate why the employee's behavior was serious enough to warrant an immediate written warning and explain exactly what you expect in the future.

Prepare

Many companies require managers to get permission—from the human resources department, legal counsel, or a higher-level manager or officer—before giving a written warning. Even if your company doesn't require it, however, you should still consult with others in the company before taking action. A written warning is a serious step, and it's a good idea to get input from those who know how the company has handled similar problems in the past before moving forward, to make sure that you are acting consistently with past practice. You can also use this meeting to brainstorm about what to say during the meeting: You can practice what you plan to say and how you might react to various responses by the employee.

Once you've obtained permission—or at least some feedback—from human resources, your legal counsel, and/or your manager, plan for your meeting with the employee. As is true of other disciplinary measures, you'll need to gather necessary information, decide when and where to meet, and think through what you will say.

Gather Information

As you would before giving a verbal warning, you must get the information you need to hold a productive meeting with the employee.

You should be prepared to discuss exactly what happened, why it is a serious problem, any prior disciplinary discussions you've had with the employee, and what needs to happen going forward. You might need to investigate the facts and review your documentation from previous discussions to get ready for the conversation.

The way you prepare will depend, in part, on whether or not you have previously disciplined the employee for the same behavior.

Written Warnings for a Recurring Problem

If you are giving a written warning for an ongoing problem, you should be prepared to discuss very specifically what went wrong with the previous action plan. After all, you and the employee have already discussed this issue more than once, agreed that it's a problem, and come up with a solution that you both thought would be effective. If the employee still hasn't improved, you need to understand why.

Before you meet with the employee, you should sit down with the documentation from your previous meeting(s) and review that action plan. Think carefully about why the action plan wasn't successful and further discipline is necessary: Did the employee have the necessary resources? Did the employee follow through on the specific commitments he or she made—for example, to attend training, meet with you, hand in assignments, and so on? Did the employee improve in some areas but not others—and if so, does this indicate more clearly exactly where the weaknesses in the employee's abilities might lie?

When you give the written warning, you'll need to redouble your efforts to convince the employee that things need to change—and that the employee must commit to improving. Spend some extra time preparing to talk about how the employee's ongoing problem is affecting the company. Think through every possible impact, and make sure you have the necessary data—dollar amounts, hours lost, and so on—to make your case. Even though it may be uncomfortable, you're going to have to show the employee that the consequences for the company are simply too great to permit the problem to continue any longer.

If the employee appears to be trying hard but isn't getting any better despite your efforts to help, you might want to consider whether the employee would be more successful in another position at your company. Once you reach the written warning stage, employees who fall into this category may be starting to realize that they don't have the necessary skills and aptitudes to do the job well. In fact, some employees will raise this issue at the disciplinary meeting and ask about other positions at the company. If this happens, you'll want to be prepared to discuss the issue.

Controlling Your Emotions

If you have to give a written warning for an ongoing problem, you're probably wrestling with some tough emotions of your own. You might feel angry that the employee hasn't responded to your earlier efforts or appreciated all the time you have taken to try and resolve the problem, sad that the employee just doesn't seem to be working out, worried about backlash you might experience as a result of discipline, or insecure that you weren't sufficiently "skilled" as a manager to solve this problem already. And you probably aren't looking forward to sitting down with the employee to talk about the issue, yet again.

These are perfectly natural responses, but you can't let them dictate the tone or content of your meeting with the employee. If you speak in anger, you risk alienating the employee forever. You also make it more likely that the employee will try to take action against you, whether through poisoning your relationships with other employees, sabotage, or legal action. On the other hand, if you allow your sympathy for the employee to hold sway, you might try too hard to soften the blow. As a result, the employee might not really understand exactly what the problem is and how serious his or her situation has become, and might therefore not take advantage of this opportunity to improve.

To keep your emotions in check, focus squarely on the facts: How have the employee's problems affected the company? What did the action plan require, and how did the employee do on each item? What improvement do you need to see in each area, and by when? What resources can you offer that might help? By sticking to the facts, you should be able to avoid emotional responses that could get you into trouble.

Written Warnings for a First-Time Problem

If you have skipped straight to a written warning, that means the employee's conduct was pretty serious. Typically, managers move directly to a written warning to deal with misconduct or a serious violation of attendance rules. Especially if you have a written discipline policy or follow one in practice, you're going to have to explain to the employee why you aren't proceeding through the earlier measures in the process. At the same time, you don't need to justify your actions to the employee—remember, you're not the one who has the problem here. You're only explaining why a written warning is a logical and necessary reaction to the employee's behavior.

To prepare to discuss this with the employee, start by reviewing the rule or policy the employee violated—you'll probably want to bring a copy to the meeting. What's the purpose of the rule? Why is it important enough to enforce with a written warning? If there wasn't a written rule, but the employee's actions were contrary to common sense or company practice, be prepared to explain why that justifies the discipline you're imposing. Thinking through these issues ahead of time will help you state your reasons for discipline confidently. It will also help you deflect—or at least, shorten—arguments with the employee over the meaning or clarity of the rule, or whether it was broken.

You should also prepare to tell the employee exactly what you expect going forward, whether it's no further violations of the rule, attending antiharassment or anger management training, an apology to a coworker, or checking in with you before taking a sick or vacation day.

Arrange Logistics

Once you have gathered the necessary facts, it's time to set up the meeting itself: when and where you will hold it, and who will be there. Ideally, you should hold a written warning meeting within a day or two of learning of the incident or problem that merits discipline. Acting quickly communicates urgency: It shows the employee that this type of behavior is serious and will not be allowed to continue, and that change must be immediate. It also demonstrates to your other reports (and the rest of the company) that you are aware of the situation and taking steps to correct it. If you manage employees who are offsite, try to set up meetings either at your office or at the employee's. If that's not feasible, deliver the discipline by phone. Set up a date and administer the discipline as you would if the employee were present in the room. For more information on disciplining offsite employees, see Chapter 12.

If you are meeting to discuss an ongoing problem, you should budget 30 to 45 minutes for the meeting. You'll have to cover your previous conversations, talk about why the previous resolution didn't work, and come up with a fairly detailed plan for improvement. Because written warnings are a serious disciplinary step, you may also have to spend some extra time explaining the consequences of the written warning (on the employee's performance evaluation, merit raises, opportunities for promotion, and so on) and the reasons why you decided it was necessary to give one.

Many companies require managers to bring another person to a written warning meeting—typically, a higher-level manager or a representative from the human resources department. If your company has this type of rule, of course you must follow it. Even if your company doesn't require you to bring someone else along, you might want your manager or a human resources representative present. Although it can make it difficult to build rapport and trust with the employee, it might be a good idea if:

- **The employee doesn't seem to be getting the message that recurring behavior is a problem.** If you've already disciplined the employee and you feel that you aren't getting your message across, bringing an authority figure to the meeting conveys that the problem is serious.

- **The employee has issues with you (or vice versa).** If you think that the employee doesn't trust you, has personal problems with you, or is likely to later deny what the two of you discuss, bring a third person to serve as a witness. This also demonstrates that you are imposing discipline because the employee is causing problems for the company, not because of your own personal feelings.

- **The employee is angry or volatile.** If you think the employee may become angry or make threats, by all means bring a witness along. Having a third party present may remind the employee to act professionally and help defuse the situation. If the employee's reaction becomes dangerous, you will more readily be able to seek outside assistance.

Letting the employee bring a witness. For information on allowing the employee to have a witness at the meeting, see Chapter 12.

Hold the meeting in your office (as long as it's relatively soundproof) or a private conference room. Don't meet offsite or in a public area such as the lunchroom. You want to communicate a serious, respectful, and professional tone—and maintain control of the meeting. If you decide—or are required—to bring a human resources representative or a higher-level manager to the meeting, you could also hold it in that person's office. This might be a good idea if the employee seems to blame you for the problem or has resisted your guidance in the past—it suggests that the problem is a company problem that goes beyond you.

Plan the Conversation

As with any disciplinary measure, before you actually meet with the employee, you should think about how to start the conversation and the main points you want to cover. Because written warning discussions are often more emotionally charged, you might even want to take some notes to bring to the meeting, so you don't forget anything if the discussion becomes heated. Just don't spend so much time and energy consulting your notes that you aren't able to be fully present in your conversation with the employee.

When you give a written warning, you are dealing with a serious problem. You should start the meeting in a manner that communicates this clearly. At the same time, however, you'll want to let the employee know that you are committed to resolving the situation and to helping him or her improve, if possible. When you plan your opening sentences, remember that you want to briefly describe the problem, convey that it is serious, and mention any prior conversations about it. If you've discussed the issue before, you'll need to acknowledge what's happened or failed to happen since the last time the issue was raised, and why or how the previous action plan didn't work. Here are some examples:

- "Mike, please come in and sit down. I need to talk to you about a very serious customer complaint I received this morning. A woman named Mrs. Daglian told me that she tried to ask you a question while you were stocking the shelves and that you ignored her. When she asked you again, you interrupted her and said loudly, "I heard you the first time, lady. I'm busy—ask the front desk." Mrs. Daglian said you then turned your back on her and walked away. LeShawn was working with you at the time, and he confirmed what Mrs. Daglian said. He had to apologize for your behavior. This is not an acceptable way to treat our customers."

- "Carl, you are continuing to take long lunches and breaks, even though we've discussed this before. When we last spoke, you promised that you would keep your breaks to fifteen minutes and your lunches to half an hour, as company policy requires. But twice last week, you took breaks that were more than half an hour long each. I've already explained that this is causing resentment among your coworkers, who are putting in more work time than you and having to deal with more customers in your absence. I've looked at your numbers, and you process fewer orders than any of your coworkers. This situation needs to change, right away. The company pays you to work a full eight-hour day, and right now, we are not getting our money's worth."

- "We need to talk about your work product, Mariah. As we've already discussed, the presentations you are creating for our clients are too long, and the main points aren't emphasized adequately. Since we last discussed this issue, two salespeople have complained that they don't like using your materials, because the audience gets confused. This has a serious effect on our reputation and our brand. We've sent you to the Writing for Maximum Impact seminar, and I've spent time going over your presentations with you, but these problems aren't improving. We need to come up with a plan today that will resolve this issue once and for all."

You should anticipate that the employee might have a defensive reaction to receiving a written warning. The employee will now suffer real consequences—and may be on the verge of losing his or her job—so you may be challenged on your reasons for acting. Before the meeting, prepare to answer such a challenge with factual statements, like "Milo, I know this is not a surprise to you. You and I have met twice in the last few months to talk about missed deadlines. I sent you to a time management class, worked with you to prioritize your projects, and met with you every week to gauge your progress. As you know, the

Abbot report was a day late, and you didn't run the weekly financials until Monday. You agreed to get things in on time, and you haven't lived up to that agreement."

Meet With the Employee

As when you give a verbal warning, you'll need to state the problem, explain its impact, discuss the issue with the employee, and come up with an action plan. When you give a written warning, however, you'll need to deliver your message a bit more forcefully—and you might face more pushback from the employee.

State the Problem

Start the meeting by letting the employee know what the problem is and why it's a problem. Briefly describe the facts, then explain how the employee's behavior is affecting the company. Explicitly state that the employee's behavior is not acceptable and needs to change.

> **EXAMPLE:** Let's continue with the example involving Dave, above, the employee who wouldn't take no for an answer. After investigating, Claude calls Dave into his office and says, "Hi Dave, please sit down. I have a serious problem I need to discuss with you. As you know, I caught part of your conversation with Crystal earlier today, and what I heard bothered me. I asked Crystal about it, and she told me you had asked her out and asked her a number of questions about her boyfriend, even after she told you she didn't want to discuss it. When I asked you about this earlier, you confirmed what Crystal said. This kind of behavior is inappropriate, it's making Crystal uncomfortable, and it needs to stop."

Investigate serious misconduct. Especially if one employee reports misconduct by another, you need to investigate before you decide what to do. In this example, Claude already spoke to Dave, who agreed with Crystal's version of events. It wouldn't be fair (or legally defensible) to simply discipline Dave without hearing his side of the story. For detailed information on investigating misconduct, see Nolo's *Workplace Investigations* by Lisa Guerin, available for download at www.nolo.com.

If you're dealing with a recurring problem, think carefully about how you phrase what you say, starting with how you present the problem. If you've dealt with this issue before, either the employee didn't fully understand the problem, or the employee can't or won't fix it. If the employee didn't understand, saying the same thing again isn't going to make the problem any clearer. You may need to walk through the issues more slowly to make sure the employee gets it.

Review Past Discussions

If you're giving a written warning for an ongoing problem, briefly summarize your previous discussions with the employee on the topic. You don't have to give all of the details, but you should mention the prior conversations, restate the action plan you came up with at that time, and explain how the employee has not lived up to his or her commitment. If you've been following the progressive discipline process and documenting thoroughly, this should be pretty easy to do. Moreover, it will help the employee contextualize the discipline.

> **EXAMPLE:** Christine is giving a written warning to Sheila for continuing to hand in substandard work reports, even after being coached and receiving a verbal warning. After stating the problem and the impact it's continuing to have on the company, Christine says, "Sheila, I'm especially concerned because we've talked about this problem before. We met in March, and again last month, to talk about the weekly reports. I agreed to tell you exactly what I expect in those reports and provide detailed comments on how you can improve your work. I've lived up to those commitments, but you haven't done what you promised: hand in reports that are complete, cover all of our accounts, and provide the information the rest of the company needs to understand how our department is doing."

If you are imposing discipline for a serious first-time problem, you may not have had previous discussions with the employee. However, you should mention any workplace policies, training sessions, or announcements that demonstrate the employee's behavior was inappropriate. For example, if an employee takes several days off and doesn't call in, you could say, "The employee handbook states that you must receive permission from your manager before taking a vacation day."

Get the Employee's Acknowledgment

Before you continue, make sure the employee understands the problem and agrees with you on the basic facts. By doing this, you'll ensure that you're on the same page and talking about the same issues. You'll also set the stage for the employee to take responsibility for the problem— something that can't happen as long as the employee is arguing with you about what occurred and whose fault it was.

> **EXAMPLE:** Tanya is giving Gerard a written warning for missed deadlines. She has already told him which deadlines were missed and reviewed their prior disciplinary conversations. Gerard says, "Yeah, but I've had a lot of other things to do in the past few weeks. You can't expect me to get everything done on time. Anyway, I was hardly late."
>
> Tanya responds by saying, "As we've discussed before, Gerard, I do expect you to get your work done on time. It's an essential part of your job, and our whole department is set back when you're late. And each of your last three reports has been at least two days late; the one you just handed in was four days late, and I was unable to use it at the company meeting. We'll talk about why you're missing deadlines in a minute. For right now, I want to make sure that we agree that your reports are due each Monday afternoon, and the last three reports have been late. Isn't that correct?"

Listen to the Employee's Explanation

If the employee doesn't offer an explanation, ask for one. What the employee says will help you figure out what went wrong and why, and help you come up with an appropriate plan for improvement. Listening carefully engages the employee and shows that you're interested. It also gives the employee a chance to vent a bit, if necessary.

Listening will also help you make sure that a written warning is appropriate. After all, the employee might have had good reason for committing what looked like misconduct or may have a good excuse for an ongoing attendance or performance problem. In this situation, you might want to use a lesser disciplinary measure or forgo discipline altogether. And, of course, if the employee's actions were even worse than they appeared to be, you might want to consider a more serious response.

> **EXAMPLE:** Rob is meeting with Jonelle, who has already been coached and received a verbal warning for tardiness. Rob and Jonelle agreed, at their last meeting, that Jonelle would check in with him each morning when she arrived, before attending to anything else. This morning, Jonelle was a half-hour late checking in with Rob. Rob was in a meeting when Jonelle arrived, but he sat down with her as soon as he was finished. After reviewing their earlier agreement, Rob asked, "Why were you late this morning?"
>
> Jonelle replied, "I actually got to work a bit early, but a customer had a seizure in the lobby. I helped take care of him—you know I used to be a nurse—until the EMTs got there. I also called his wife and let her know what happened. Once he was taken away, I took a little time to clean myself up, then I came right up here."
>
> Rob realizes that Jonelle should not be disciplined for being late and thanks her for the explanation—and the customer care.

Explain the Written Warning

As with a verbal warning, you must tell the employee that you are giving a written warning. You don't want the employee to be surprised to find a written warning in the personnel file later or to be blindsided when the warning gets in the way of a promotion or raise. Explicitly stating that you are giving a written warning also reinforces the message that the situation is serious.

⚠ **Make sure the employee's performance appraisal is consistent with your reasons for discipline.** If you give an employee a written warning for poor performance, the employee's next performance appraisal should reflect the problem—that is, it should note the employee's performance difficulties and mention the written warning. If the appraisal instead gives the employee high marks for performance and suggests a merit raise, the employee will likely be confused about what constitutes good performance—and you will have trouble justifying your discipline (and a later decision to terminate employment, if it comes to that).

If company policy dictates specific consequences for receiving a written warning, explain them briefly to the employee. For example, an employee who has received a written warning might be ineligible for certain job benefits or opportunities, might not be considered for promotions or performance-based bonuses, or might receive a lower performance appraisal. Remember, it is important to impose these criteria consistently among your employees, too.

> **EXAMPLE:** "Corinne, I'm giving you a written warning for mis-handling customer checks. I decided a written warning was called for because this is the second time you haven't deposited checks on time, and this affects our cash management. I also need to tell you that a written warning makes you ineligible for an overall rating of 'exceeds expectations' on this year's performance appraisal, which could affect your eligibility for raises and bonuses, if they are offered this year. I know these are serious consequences, and I think they are justified by your actions. But I'm confident that you can solve this problem and get back on the right track."

Let the employee know if the warning will "expire." Many companies put a time limit on how long a verbal or written warning will remain in an employee's file, or how long it will continue to affect the employee's opportunities at the company. Once the warning is removed, the employee has a clean slate from that point forward. If your company has this type of policy, tell the employee that the warning will be removed if he or she has no further problems while the warning is active. This provides a strong incentive for improvement.

Develop Solutions

Now it's time to talk about how to solve the problem. If you're dealing with one-time misconduct, the solution is usually quite clear: The employee has to stop. In this situation, an employee might need some training or perhaps even a referral to your company's Employee

Assistance Program (EAP), if you have one. But there's no need to spend lots of time brainstorming ideas for the future.

> **EXAMPLE:** Back to Dave and Claude's meeting, about getting too personal with a coworker. Claude says, "Dave, this behavior needs to stop. You may not ask Crystal out on dates or ask her about her personal life. She has made clear to you that these conversations make her uncomfortable, and they cannot continue. Do you understand?"
>
> If Dave says that he understands, this portion of the meeting is over. But what if Dave responds, "You mean I can't talk to her, ever again? She and I are kind of friends. I mean, I didn't realize she was taking all of this so seriously, but it seems weird that I can never even say hello to her."
>
> Claude might say, "Dave, that isn't what I said. You can say hello to Crystal or ask how she's doing, and you can have regular conversations with her about work. What you can't do is ask her out, ask her about her boyfriend, comment about her appearance, or other things like that. Do you understand the difference?"
>
> If Dave indicates that he understands, the session has addressed the issue. If not, or if Dave continues to argue the point, Claude should probably send him to more detailed sexual harassment training.

If, on the other hand, you're dealing with an ongoing problem, you'll really need to go deep in this part of the conversation. You and the employee have already discussed this problem and come up with a solution—and it didn't work. At this point, you'll need to talk about why that happened and what needs to change in the future for the employee to improve.

> **EXAMPLE:** Melanie is a member of a cross-departmental team tasked with developing and implementing new branding for a company that makes shampoo, lotion, and other toiletries. Melanie's own department handles the product packaging. They determine what goes on the labels for various products and various markets,

contract with vendors to produce the packaging, and oversee the entire packaging process.

Carly, Melanie's boss, has heard from other team members that Melanie doesn't contribute at the meetings. Carly has met with Melanie to discuss this twice, and Melanie promised to be more actively involved in the conversation. But Melanie still hasn't spoken up. Carly decides to give her a written warning and tells her, "Melanie, if you don't give the team input from our department, they won't know how expensive various redesigns might be, how particular types of logos and verbiage might affect our costs, and so on. We already discussed this problem, and you told me you would be more vocal during the meetings, but it hasn't happened. Why haven't you played a more active role?"

Melanie responds, "You know, I really don't like Travis, who runs the meetings. I feel like he always looks down on me, and I'm self-conscious about saying anything. Also, I'm just naturally kind of shy, I guess."

Carly says, "Melanie, all of us have personal feelings about the people we work with, but you can't let that get in the way of doing your job. I need for you to represent our department at these meetings. And that requires you to speak up. Is that going to be a problem?"

Melanie at last admits, "I guess it might be, just because of my shyness. I feel weird that everyone is looking at me, and I can't remember what I want to say."

Carly responds, "It's common for people to feel fearful of speaking in front of a group. But again, you're letting that get in the way of doing your job. I'd like for you to do two things. First, before the meeting scheduled for next month, I'd like you to meet with me and go over what you plan to say at the meeting. I understand the group will be discussing color options, and you are the only one who knows what those options cost. We'll review what you want to say about it, and I'll help you iron out the kinks.

"In the meantime, I'd like you to go to a workshop on speaking in public. It's something our company representatives attend when they start here, and I think it will do you a lot of good. I'll check the schedule for upcoming workshops and sign you up. I think that will help you stop allowing this problem to hold you back at work. What do you think?"

Carly had to dig a bit to get to the real root of the problem. Before, she thought Melanie just didn't know that she should be speaking up. Then, Melanie raised Travis as a possible issue. But another aspect of the problem—Melanie's fear of speaking in public—was something that she found more difficult to admit. Once Carly understood all the causes of the problem, she was able to come up with some detailed solutions that should help Melanie feel more comfortable with this aspect of her job.

Summarize the Action Plan

End the meeting by summing up what you and the employee have agreed to. Unless you were dealing with serious misconduct—to which the resolution is typically "stop doing that"—you'll also want to set some dates and goals for improvement. Especially if you're dealing with an ongoing problem, you should make the schedule fairly tight, with frequent follow-up meetings and progress checks. This will show your employee that you're serious about needing to see immediate improvement and help you keep a close eye on the problem. If you don't see a change after giving the employee a fair chance, you know that the employee either can't or won't improve—and that it's time to consider termination.

If your company uses a performance improvement plan (PIP) or similar approach, in which the action plan is in place for a set amount of time (three or six months, for example), let the employee know how long it will last. You might say, "For the next six months, you are to complete every recap report on time. This means I have to have the finished report, with no mistakes, on my desk by Thursday afternoon. If you meet this goal for the next six months, you will be taken off the performance improvement plan and the written warning will be removed from your file."

It's best to complete your documentation right after the disciplinary meeting, while it's still fresh in your mind. You will also want to schedule another brief meeting—preferably in the next day or two—to go over the paperwork. As explained in Chapter 9, you'll want to give the employee a chance to review your written documentation and talk to you about any questions or concerns.

Try to close the meeting on a positive note. Although this can be tough to do, especially if you feel like you're dealing with the same problem over and over again, it's very valuable for the employee, who probably needs encouragement. Remember, though, not to make any promises for the future: Leave yourself (and your company) the leeway to handle future problems or achievements as you see fit when the time comes. A simple statement like "This was a productive discussion, and I think we've come up with some good ideas to resolve this situation" is fine.

Document

Once your meeting is over, it's time to actually write your written warning. If your company requires you to use a particular form or follow certain rules, by all means do so. If not, you can use the form we provide in Chapter 9 to create the written warning.

Here's a sample form, which Claude used as his written warning to Dave:

Written Warning

Date: February 12, 2008

Employee Name: Dave Costello

Manager Name: Claude Washington

Incident Description

On February 11, 2008, I overheard part of a conversation you had with Crystal Cavalier in her cubicle. I heard you questioning her about her boyfriend, then saying something like "Are you sure you don't want to go out with me instead?" I also observed that Crystal did not respond. Instead, she turned away from you and focused on her computer screen.

I called Crystal into my office and asked her what happened. She said you had asked her out and persisted in asking her questions about her relationship with her boyfriend, even after she told you she didn't want to discuss it. She confirmed that you said, "Are you sure you don't want to go out with me instead?," even though she previously turned down your request for a date. She told me that she felt very uncomfortable about your interest in her, and that she felt you were not getting the message that she does not want to have a romantic relationship with you.

When I talked to you later that same day, you confirmed that you had said these things to Crystal.

Prior Incidents

No prior reported incidents of similar behavior.

Improvement Plan

Dave, your conduct violates company policies on appropriate workplace behavior. Specifically, your conduct violates our policy on Professional Behavior (p. 23 of the Employee Handbook) and Harassment (p. 12). Your comments and requests for a date made Crystal very uncomfortable. She has stated that clearly to you, but you have persisted.

You are not to talk to Crystal about her personal life or ask her out on dates. In addition, because you seem unclear about what constitutes appropriate workplace behavior, I have scheduled you to attend a sexual harassment training workshop on February 19. Following this training, we will meet again to make sure that you understand the types of comments and behavior that are inappropriate in the workplace.

Employee Comments

Manager: _____ Date: _____

I acknowledge that I have received and understand this document.

Employee: _____ Date: _____

For help preparing documentation, see Chapter 9. For additional samples of written warnings, see Appendix B.

Follow Up

Because you are dealing with a serious problem, you should plan to check in with the employee regularly to make sure the situation is improving. You might also need to check in with others in the company. While this may seem to take an inordinate amount of time and energy, the consequences of failing to correct the problem are very serious now, and it's imperative that you do everything you can to help the employee succeed.

> **EXAMPLE:** The day after Claude meets with Dave, he calls Crystal into his office. Claude says, "I want you to know that I've spoken to Dave and told him his behavior is inappropriate. I've given him clear instructions that he may not ask you out or talk to you about your relationship. Please come to me right away if Dave says or does anything to make you uncomfortable."
>
> Notice that Claude did not tell Crystal that he gave Dave a written warning—that isn't any of Crystal's business. However, it's very important for Claude to ask Crystal to bring future problems to his attention immediately. Because harassment happens in private, this might be the only way Claude can find out whether Dave really got the message. And, now that Claude knows about Dave's behavior, the company is legally liable for any harassment Crystal suffers. If Dave continues to question Crystal inappropriately even after being disciplined and going to sexual harassment training, the company will probably have to fire him.

There's still room for positive reinforcement. Even though you're dealing with a major problem, don't forget to praise the employee if you see improvement. The employee might have a long way to go, but it's important to mark any progress in that direction. Unless you're dealing with a really bad egg, your employee probably feels pretty bad about letting you and the company down. By giving praise, you are communicating that you still support the employee and want him or her to do well.

Schedule Important Dates

After the disciplinary meeting, schedule your follow-up meetings, the employee's goals, and so on in your calendar. If you've agreed to provide training, equipment, or other resources, write yourself a note—and follow through right away. And, if your company removes written warnings from an employee's file after a certain amount of time, mark that date on your calendar. You'll want to make sure that the documentation is removed if the employee has no further problems.

When the Action Plan Is Complete

Sometimes, particularly for serious misconduct, the action plan will be as simple as "stop it." For example, if an employee left the store safe open—and full of cash and valuables—overnight, your action plan might say, "You are to check the safe each night before you leave to make sure it is closed and locked." This type of action plan doesn't have a start and end date: You don't really need to follow up unless the employee leaves the safe open again—and if that happens, termination is probably appropriate.

Other action plans call for the employee to do discrete, one-time tasks, such as attending a training seminar, getting a certification, giving an apology, or completing a report. For these plans, you should give the employee a date by which he or she must complete these items, then follow up to make sure the employee did what was required. If the employee doesn't meet one of these goals, you should meet immediately to find out why; if the employee doesn't have a good reason or excuse, it might be time to consider termination. If the employee does meet the goal, you should document that briefly.

> **EXAMPLE:** Penny gave Jessie a written warning for poor performance. Among other things, the action plan they developed required Jessie to take a class on how to use PowerPoint. Jessie took the class by the required date. Penny documents this as follows:

Date: September 25, 2007

On September 1, 2007, I gave Jessie Pitt a written warning. In his action plan, I required him to complete a training class on using PowerPoint, among other things. He was to complete this class by October 1, 2007.

    Jessie informed me today that he completed the class "PowerPoint Basics: Presentations, Graphics, and More!" on September 24. He gave me a copy of his certificate of completion (attached) as well as a syllabus from the class. I have asked him to do a brief presentation, using PowerPoint, at the next department meeting on October 15. He has agreed to do so.

Signed: *Penny Meyer*

If you put a time limit on the entire action plan, you must decide, at the end of that time, whether the employee has done as you agreed. For example, if you have a proofreader who is not catching grammatical errors, your action plan might say, "You will review each document for errors two times, with a minimum of a one-hour break between each review. Additionally, you will reduce your weekly average error rate from 4 per document to 2 per document. You and I will meet each week on Monday morning to discuss your progress." If the employee successfully completes this type of action plan, you should also write a memo to the file.

 To hear a sample written warning meeting, open the audio files on the enclosed CD.

Written Warnings: Smart Summary

● Written warnings are difficult because employees usually recognize them as a serious disciplinary measure and may become defensive or emotional. Additionally, if you've dealt with the same issue with the employee before, you might also be frustrated or angry. Control these emotions by preparing thoroughly and focusing the discussion on the problem and how to improve it.

● A written warning is usually the right response when an employee hasn't improved a problem after coaching and a verbal warning, the employee has flagrantly violated the company's attendance rules, or the employee has committed serious misconduct that does not warrant immediate termination.

● When you give a written warning, focus on creating a very detailed, thorough, and clear action plan—particularly if you've already coached or given a verbal warning. If the employee needs more involvement or direction from you to succeed, provide it.

● You should write the written warning after you've had a chance to meet with the employee and get his or her input or perspective. Complete the documentation right after the meeting, when it's still fresh in your mind. You might want to schedule another brief meeting to go over the written document with the employee.

■

Build Your Skills: The Disciplinary Steps

Questions

1. What are the three types of coaching?

2. Which of these is a common reaction to coaching?

   a. Surprise

   b. Anger

   c. Denial

   d. Blame

3. Verbal warnings don't require formal documentation—after all, they're just oral reminders to shape up. ☐ True ☐ False

4. Which of these situations probably calls for a verbal warning?

   a. For the first time, Sarah, a long-time budget analyst, shows up to work 15 minutes late.

   b. Imran, a new transfer to the mail room, violates a company policy that prohibits wearing ear plugs or headphones while operating a mail sorting machine; he'd never read the policy, though it was given to him.

   c. Pamela, a new clerk, sends the entire department's time sheets to payroll a few hours late because she misread the policy and thought they were due on the fifteenth, when actually that's the date checks are issued.

   d. Greg, a veteran supervisor, tells one of his employees, Jim, all the details of the investigation into a coworker's harassment suit.

5. Even though it may be uncomfortable, when you give a verbal warning, you should tell the employee explicitly that you are doing so.
   ☐ True ☐ False

6. When you decide to issue a written warning, how should you deliver it?

   a. Carry it to the meeting you have with the employee. Give it to the employee at the start of the meeting.

   b. Have a discussion with the employee about it, then draft the warning and place it in the employee's personnel file.

   c. Carry it to the meeting you have with the employee. Give it to the employee at the end of the meeting.

   d. Meet with the employee, then draft the written warning, send it to the employee for acknowledgment, and place it in the employee's file.

7. Because employee discipline is a serious matter, it should be delivered in a serious setting. Whenever possible, you should meet with the employee in your office.   ☐ True   ☐ False

8. Which of these steps will help you prepare for a written warning?

   a. Consult with your boss, human resources, or your legal department to get input on how similar problems have been handled in the past.

   b. Review the employee's previous disciplinary history.

   c. Think about why the previous action plan, if there was one, didn't work.

   d. All of the above.

9. In which situation might it be appropriate for you to bring a witness to a discipline meeting?

   a. You're in an informal coaching session, and you want to make the employee feel more at ease, so you grab lunch with the employee and a human resources representative the employee is friendly with.

   b. You are issuing a written warning, and it seems the employee is really resisting your guidance—in fact, the employee hasn't done anything to follow the action plan you two have outlined together.

   c. You don't feel comfortable issuing the discipline; even though company policy calls for it, the employee is your friend. You'd rather bring your boss along to deliver the tough message.

   d. You're issuing a verbal warning to an employee for an attendance policy violation. The employee was late three times in two weeks;

you've dealt with the same issue many times before and have even coached this employee about it.

10. What is the purpose of a written warning?

   a. To make sure you communicate very clearly—on paper—what the problem is, so that the employee understands it and you have a written record of it.

   b. To make sure that the employee is given a fair opportunity to improve performance or behavior.

   c. To make sure you treat employees consistently, issuing similar discipline for similar problems.

   d. All of the above.

Answers

1. The three types of coaching are simple requests, corrective actions, and coaching sessions. You make simple requests when a method of doing something hasn't been successful, and you ask the employee to try something new or different. Corrective actions are a little more serious; they occur when you tell an employee how something must be done or done differently. You can deal with more-complex problems with coaching sessions—opportunities to sit down with employees to discuss problems and find solutions together, before things get worse.

2. A. Because coaching is the first step in the disciplinary process, employees are often surprised by it. Sometimes you may need to allow the employee a little time to deal with that reaction. The more serious reactions—anger, denial, and blame—typically happen later in the process, when discipline becomes more serious.

3. False. Verbal warnings are the first formal entry into the discipline process, when the employee is made aware that discipline is happening. They need to be formally documented so that the manager will have a record of what's happened in the event that further discipline—or even termination—becomes necessary.

4. B. In this case, Imran inadvertently violated a company rule that was implemented for his own safety. Imran should have read the policy, but his failure to follow it here appears inadvertent, so a verbal warning is probably appropriate. Answers A and C probably call for coaching—the employees there have correctible problems that don't appear extremely serious. And in Answer D, Greg is creating serious problems for the company, not to mention acting extremely inappropriately and insensitively, by revealing this information. More serious discipline is probably necessary.

5. True. Even though it might be uncomfortable, when you issue a verbal warning, you should state explicitly that that's what you're doing. That way, the employee is on notice that he or she has entered the formal disciplinary system and won't be surprised to come across the documentation later.

6. D. The best way to make sure you fully capture all the facts is to meet with the employee, draft the documentation, and then ask the employee

to acknowledge that he or she received it (often in a separate, brief meeting). This ensures you hear the whole story, and that the whole story is accurately captured in the documentation, before the warning is issued.

7. False. The appropriate setting for a disciplinary discussion will vary based on the type of discipline being administered. For example, if you're going to coach an employee, it might be more comfortable to do so in an informal setting. If you and the employee need to brainstorm possible action plans, it might be appropriate to work in a neutral space, like a conference room, with a whiteboard.

8. D. In this case, all these steps will help you get ready to deliver a written warning. Talking to an appropriate third party will help you gain perspective—but make sure it's someone whom you should be talking to about the issue, not a peer or subordinate. Likewise, if you review the employee's disciplinary history, don't give undue weight to things that happened in the distant past. And finally, as you think about the former action plan and why it didn't work, think about your responsibility for that, too—not just the employee's.

9. B. When an employee resists your guidance, it may mean that you need the help or intervention of a third party. You probably wouldn't want a third party involved in an informal coaching session (Answer A), especially if it could keep the employee from understanding the purpose of the discussion: to improve behavior. And while you should definitely talk to your boss if you don't feel comfortable issuing discipline (Answer C), you can cause confusion for the employee—and appear weak or unsure of yourself—if you ask the boss to issue the discipline directly. Finally, if you're carefully following a clear company policy, and you've dealt with the issue before, you probably won't need outside assistance (Answer D).

10. D. All of the answers are benefits that result from a fair, consistent discipline system. Answer B speaks to what is probably the most basic reason to use it: You want the employee to succeed. At the same time, you will be communicating clearly to the employee, and you'll have a written record in case you have to impose further discipline or terminate employment (Answer A). You'll also be imposing consistent discipline (Answer C).

If Discipline Fails

Termination

E ven if you faithfully follow the disciplinary strategies in this book, chances are good that you'll one day be faced with a manager's least favorite task: firing an employee. The discipline and communication techniques explained in the previous chapters will help you get most employees back on track, but there will still be a few who are simply unable—or unwilling—to do the job. Whether the employee has failed to resolve an ongoing problem or has committed egregious misconduct, it's time to consider termination of employment.

This chapter explains how to decide whether it's time to fire someone and how to handle every step of the termination process. Before we get to those details, however, we should acknowledge a basic fact about terminations: They are difficult for everyone involved. The employee who is being fired will be out of work and may face financial, emotional, and family troubles as a result. As the agent of this unhappiness, you will almost certainly feel some sadness, anxiety, or even guilt about your role in the process.

Only the most hard-hearted person could avoid feeling at least a little bit bad about firing someone. But, if you find these emotions overwhelming, remember this: If you followed the strategies we've explained, you gave the employee every opportunity to improve. The employee either wasn't capable of improvement or chose not to take advantage of those opportunities. Either way, an employee who isn't able or willing to do what the job requires should not be holding that job.

You may also be concerned about how your team might react to the news that one of their coworkers has been fired. If you fear that your team will be angry or blame you for the fired employee's woes, you might be pleasantly surprised. Often, coworkers are relieved to see a problem employee go. If the employee has committed serious misconduct, coworkers aren't likely to miss the fighting, harassment, or theft. If the employee has had ongoing performance or attendance problems, coworkers have probably grown pretty tired of having to pick up the slack—and somewhat frustrated that the employee seems to have been "getting away with it," while they toil away. This generally holds true even if the employee was otherwise well liked and coworkers feel sad about the situation on a personal level.

Is It Time for Termination?

There are two scenarios when termination might be appropriate. In the first, the employee commits misconduct so serious that it's incompatible with continued employment at your company. (We list many of these firing offenses in Chapter 5.) An employee who threatens others, acts violently, makes racist comments, commits blatant sexual harassment, steals from the company, or otherwise demonstrates serious disregard for the legal rights of others or the company should be fired.

In the second scenario, the employee has a performance, attendance, or misconduct problem that you've addressed through your company's disciplinary policy. You've provided coaching and given a verbal warning and a written warning, but the situation has not improved. At this point, you know that it's time to replace the employee. An employee who either cannot or will not do what the job requires, even after several constructive interventions, is unlikely to improve at this late date.

In either situation, there are a number of factors you should consider when you're deciding whether to fire the employee. Carefully weighing each of the factors below before you take action will help you make sure that you're making the right decision—and help you minimize the possibility of legal trouble down the road. It will also help you ensure that you're being fair and impartial, rather than allowing emotions to influence your decision.

Here is a checklist that will help you make sure you've considered every angle before you fire an employee (each item is explained in more detail below):

- Make sure you know the facts.
- Check the employee's personnel file.
- Review company policies.
- Consider past statements to the employee
- Examine how other employees have been treated.
- Consider the timing.
- Get a second opinion.

What About Final Warnings?

Some companies use progressive discipline policies that give employees a final warning before firing them. The final warning might take a number of forms—it might be called a suspension, probationary period, performance improvement plan (PIP), last-chance agreement, decision-making leave, or something else. Regardless of its name, the message conveyed by the final warning is this: One more strike and you're out.

We don't think final warnings are a good idea. From a practical standpoint, an employee who has already had three chances to improve is unlikely to turn things around on the fourth try. It's far more sensible to cut your losses (in time and energy) than to keep trying to inspire improvement.

Using a final warning also creates legal risks. Because any type of final warning typically is accompanied by an explicit statement that the employee will be fired if the problem continues, it can lead the employee to believe that he or she will not be fired otherwise. That is, a final warning can undo a company's at-will rights (explained in Chapter 3). What if the employee develops another problem or improves somewhat but, you ultimately decide, not enough? What if there is a targeted layoff due to lack of work or location transfer? The language found in a typical final warning could tie the company's hands in these situations.

Don't be afraid to ask for help. Termination is the aspect of your job that's most likely to lead to legal trouble. It's also the most likely to cause you stress and emotional discomfort. The information we provide below should help alleviate your concerns, but don't hesitate to call on your human resources department or legal counsel for advice. They can help you troubleshoot your decision, consider other courses of action, practice delivering the message to the employee, and more.

Make Sure You Know the Facts

As always, your first step is to gather information. When you are terminating employment, it is especially important to get your facts straight. If there's any question about what has happened, the company must investigate and come to a conclusion. No matter how serious the offense, you must take the time to gather facts—even if you catch the employee apparently "in the act." There is always the possibility, no matter how slim, that things are not as they appear to be. And the employee might have an explanation or reason for the misconduct that is not immediately apparent.

If you are dealing with serious misconduct, you might want to put the employee on paid suspension while the investigation takes place. This will get the employee out of the workplace and give you some time to proceed carefully. For step-by-step instructions on investigating, see *Workplace Investigations*, by Lisa Guerin (available for download at Nolo's website, www.nolo.com).

⚠ Don't use unpaid investigative suspensions. If you suspend an employee while you investigate an issue, the suspension should be paid. As a practical matter, paying the employee demonstrates that you have not yet made up your mind and plan to conduct an impartial investigation. Legally, you can create problems if you suspend exempt employees—those who are not entitled to earn overtime—for reasons that are not allowed by the Fair Labor Standards Act. You might even convert these employees into nonexempt employees, which means your company would probably be faced with hefty overtime costs. It's much easier, more fair, and less expensive in the long run to suspend employees with pay while you investigate.

If you are dealing with an ongoing problem, a full-blown investigation is probably unnecessary. However, you should still take whatever steps are necessary to make sure that you understand what happened and that the employee is responsible. Once you are satisfied that you have the facts you need, move on to the next step.

EXAMPLE: Lindsey is facing termination for poor performance. Her manager, Jason, has coached and given warnings, but Lindsey has continued to spend at least an hour a day talking to friends on the phone, looking at catalogs, and otherwise goofing off. As a result, Lindsey doesn't finish her work on time.

Several weeks ago, Jason put Lindsey on a performance improvement plan (PIP) and told her that she had to meet every requirement in the plan. One of the requirements was that Lindsey finish everything assigned to her for the week before she leaves on Friday afternoon, then send Jason an email detailing every completed assignment. Jason was on a business trip last week, and he didn't get an email from Lindsey last Friday. He notices, when he arrives on Monday morning, that Lindsey's desk is littered with papers, making it look like she didn't finish everything before she left.

Jason is ready to fire Lindsey as soon as she arrives for work. But before he does, he needs to find out what happened. Of course, one possibility is that Lindsey simply blew off the PIP and left for the weekend without finishing her work. In this case, termination would be entirely appropriate. On the other hand, maybe Lindsey didn't finish her work because she had to leave early for a legitimate emergency, such as a sudden illness or a family crisis. Maybe Lindsey finished her work but couldn't send Jason an email because the computers were down. Maybe Lindsey finished most of her work but couldn't complete an assignment because she needed guidance from Jason, who was traveling on Friday afternoon when she tried to reach him. Before Jason makes a final decision, he needs to find out exactly what happened and why.

Check the Employee's Personnel File

Next, read the employee's personnel file—even if you think you already know what's in it. If you are dealing with persistent problems with performance, attendance, or conduct, these issues should be documented in the file. The employee's performance evaluations should note these deficiencies and suggest goals for improvement. There should also be notes from your disciplinary meetings with the employee.

Weigh Your Disciplinary Documentation Against Evidence of Good Performance

When you review the employee's personnel file, pretend you're a lawyer representing the employee. Are there documents you could use to show that the employee should not have been fired? If so, consult with your human resources department—or legal counsel—before proceeding.

A file that contains glowing performance appraisals, merit raises, commendations, and promotions could spell trouble—especially if they contradict your reasons for firing. An employee who is fired for poor performance should not be able to point to positive reviews and merit increases. Similarly, an employee who is fired for insubordination and attitude problems should not have a recent evaluation praising the employee's teamwork, collegiality, and willingness to go the extra mile.

Of course, if you have carefully followed the procedures outlined in this book, you will have documented the employee's problems appropriately. However, if other managers have supervised the employee, or you weren't fully aware (until reading this book) of how to use and document disciplinary measures, you might find that the file is a bit thin. In this situation, you should consult your human resources department for guidance. If, together, you conclude that the file doesn't include sufficient documentation of the problem and your efforts to help the employee improve, you might need to hold off on the termination and give the employee another, well-documented chance.

EXAMPLE: Julius is considering firing Kathy for ongoing attendance problems. Julius just took over managing Kathy's group a month ago. When he began, Marc—the team's former manager—told him that Kathy often came in late, despite his repeated conversations with her about it over the last year. Since Julius has been her manager, Kathy has continued the trend. Julius gave her a verbal warning because it has been an ongoing problem, but Kathy hasn't improved at all.

Now Julius thinks it's probably time to replace Kathy. After all, she has had an attendance problem for more than a year and has shown no signs of improvement after repeated efforts by two managers. But when he looks at Kathy's personnel file, Julius realizes that he might not be able to fire her without some legal risk. His verbal warning is in the file, but there are no other disciplinary documents. Apparently, Marc didn't keep a record of his conversations with Kathy, nor did he use the company's disciplinary system. What's more, Kathy's last appraisal rates her overall performance as "outstanding" and makes no mention of her attendance problem. After talking to the human resources director, Julius decides to give Kathy a written warning and explicitly tell her that she will lose her job if she doesn't arrive on time, every day.

If the employee has committed a single act of serious misconduct, the file probably won't contain any mention of prior problems—and that's fine. Of course, if this isn't the employee's first major blunder, you should find documentation of the prior incident(s) in the file.

Does the Employee Have a Contract?

As you review the employee's paperwork, look for a written employment contract. As explained in Chapter 3, an employment contract doesn't protect the employee from termination, but it may limit your options. The language of the contract governs when you can fire an employee. For most contracts, this means you need only have a good business reason (good cause) to end the employment relationship. However, if the company agreed to different restrictions (for example, that the employee could be fired only for committing a criminal act or for defrauding the company), consult with your human resources department or legal counsel to make sure that your reasons for firing fit within these limits.

Review Company Policies

Next, take a look at your company's employee handbook and other written policies. As you review these materials, ask yourself a few questions:

- **Did you follow the company's discipline policy?** Make sure you've followed the rules to the letter before you fire anyone.
- **Did the employee have notice that his or her behavior was a problem?** Of course, if you've been dealing with ongoing issues, your conversations and documentation have made this clear to the employee. For egregious misconduct, make sure the employee's actions are either prohibited by company policy or so obviously wrong that no explicit notice is necessary. (For more on this, see Chapter 5.)
- **Is your right to fire limited?** As explained in Chapter 3, most companies are at-will employers, which reserve the right to fire employees at any time, for any reason that is not illegal. However, companies can forfeit this right—and one common way they do is by making promises of continued employment in their employee handbooks. If you see something in your company's written policies that makes you think you might not be able to fire at will, talk to your human resources department or legal counsel.

Consider Statements Made to the Employee

Consider whether you have said anything that might have led the employee to believe he or she would be fired only for specific reasons. As you'll recall from Chapter 3, if you promise an employee continued employment or say that he or she will be fired only for certain reasons, you may have created an implied contract. In this situation, you must make sure that your decision to fire is in keeping with your earlier statements. For example, if you told an employee (before reading this book) that you would never fire someone who was doing a good job, that statement wouldn't prevent you from firing the employee for poor performance. If, on the other hand, the employee has an attendance problem but performs well when at work, your earlier statement might limit your options. If you have any concerns about prior statements you've made to an employee, consult your human resources department or legal counsel.

Consider How Others Employees Have Been Treated

In Chapter 3, we explained the importance of being consistent. A fired employee's most effective argument to a jury is that you've acted unfairly, by treating the employee differently from others who have been in the same position. An employee who makes this argument can even risk admitting misconduct or poor performance. The employee's complaint is not that he or she is perfect, but that you've come down harder on him or her than you have on others who have committed the same transgression.

Before you fire an employee, make sure that your actions are consistent with the way you've handled similar offenses or misconduct by other workers. Have you always fired for this type of behavior? Or have you given other employees another chance or helped them try to improve? Also consider how your company has handled similar problems. Is your plan to fire the employee consistent with your company's treatment of other workers with similar issues?

If you have treated other employees differently, there may be a good reason for the difference. Perhaps one person's conduct was worse, was more intractable, lasted longer, or caused the company more trouble. Make sure that your choice to fire this employee, while allowing others to remain, will make sense to a jury as a valid business decision.

Consider the Timing

If an employee recently complained of illegal activity in the workplace, such as discrimination or harassment, firing that person may lead to a retaliation claim. Firing someone shortly after he or she exercised a legal right or complained of improper or illegal activity could also lead to legal trouble. Even if you have a good reason to terminate employment, the employee might think that you are acting out of illegal motives. Similarly, if you fire someone who just told you that she is pregnant, has a disability that requires accommodation, or holds certain religious beliefs, the employee could decide that the firing and the disclosure are linked.

Of course, this doesn't mean that you can never fire someone who has a disability, for example, or that complaining of sexual harassment makes an employee "fire-proof." In this situation, however, you must make very certain that your reasons for firing are beyond reproach— and that you can show, through documentation, that the employee's problems preceded his or her protected activity. If you are considering firing an employee in these circumstances, talk to your human resources department and/or legal counsel.

Get a Second Opinion

If possible, have a second person from within your company review the decision to terminate. (Many companies require managers to have a higher-level manager or human resources representative review firing decisions.) The purpose of this review is to make sure that your decision is legitimate, reasonable, and well supported. The reviewer should consider how the termination would look to someone outside the company. The reviewer should also make sure that the decision is based on objective, work-related concerns—not favoritism, discrimination, or other subjective factors.

Ideally, the person who does this review should be removed from the situation and have no stake in the outcome, such as a human resources representative. The less contact the reviewer has had with the people involved, the more likely his or her decision will be objective.

Take the reviewer's comments seriously. If the reviewer finds that your decision could be challenged, find out the basis for the problem. Is there insufficient documentation in the file? Have other employees committing similar misconduct been retained? Was your decision colored by your dislike of the worker or—worse—by prejudice? Use the reviewer's comments to figure out how you can either salvage the employment relationship or properly document and support your decision.

Prepare for the Meeting

If you decide, after carefully considering each of the factors discussed above, that you should fire the employee, it's time to plan the termination meeting. You'll be tempted to put this off, but don't. Even though you might feel badly about having to fire someone, if you've followed the guidelines explained in earlier chapters, you also probably know that the time has come. Once the employee has demonstrated an inability or unwillingness to meet the company's expectations, it's time to cut your losses, stop spending so much time on disciplinary matters, and find someone who can do the job.

The fifteen minutes or so it takes you to break the bad news to an employee you have to fire may be the most important of the employment relationship. The way you handle this meeting could well determine whether the employee moves on to greener pastures without hard feelings or whether the employee harbors ill will towards the company that manifests itself in malicious gossip, litigation, or even violence or sabotage. It follows, then, that it's well worth spending some time planning the meeting, so you can make sure that you're ready to handle it well.

Where to Meet

If the employee has a private office, that's a good place to hold the termination meeting. The employee will be most comfortable there and won't have to take a "walk of shame" through the building after being fired. Also, you will be able to end the meeting easily, simply by leaving the room. This can be an important advantage if the employee wants to argue with you about the termination.

If you fear that the employee may become violent, however, there are some different factors to consider. In this situation, you'll want to hold the meeting in an area that is as far away from other employees as possible. You should choose a private space that is also close to a building exit, so the employee can be escorted out of the building, if necessary. You might also arrange to have security standing by, close to where you will meet but not visible to the employee.

When to Meet

There are many different theories about which day—and time of day—is best for firing an employee. Some say employees should be fired first thing Monday morning, to give them time to get on with life and ramp up their job searches right away. Others say Friday afternoon is best, because fewer employees will still be at work to see the employee leave with his or her possessions.

Our advice is to let the schedule of the employee and your workplace guide your decision. If the employee is completing an assignment on a Wednesday, it makes more sense (and is kinder) to fire that employee right away than to assign busy work just to carry the employee to a Friday termination. If you know that important customers will be in the office on Monday, it's probably better to wait until Tuesday to fire someone. Usually, there's no need to follow a hard-and-fast rule; do what makes sense.

Again, however, different considerations apply if you are firing someone from whom you fear violence or sabotage. In this situation, you'll want to fire the employee at the end of the workday and end of the workweek. You will want to get this employee out the door as soon as possible—and the fewer employees around when that happens, the better.

Who Should Attend the Meeting

Many companies require managers to bring another person—usually another manager or someone from human resources—to a termination meeting, to act as a witness. If your company doesn't require this, you should bring another company representative only if there's a good reason. Bringing someone to act as a witness could make the employee feel embarrassed and humiliated, and it's not necessary if you're dealing with a reasonable, relatively trustworthy employee.

On the other hand, if the employee has already talked about hiring a lawyer, has made threats, or had done anything else that makes you uncomfortable about handling the meeting on your own, by all means bring another company representative along.

What You Can Offer the Employee

You should anticipate that the employee will be concerned about the future. Money, benefits, continued use of company property (such as a car or laptop), finding another job—all of these issues will be front and center in the employee's mind as soon as you announce your decision.

Do any preparation necessary to find out what you can tell the employee about the following:

- **Final paychecks.** State law governs how much time a company has to hand over that final check. Some states (including California) require companies to pay a fired employee immediately; others allow several days or more. (Appendix C includes a chart with information about each state's law.) If you have to—or your company is willing to—provide the check right away, make arrangements to have it cut and bring it to your meeting.
- **Continued insurance benefits.** A federal law called the Consolidated Omnibus Budget Reconciliation Act (COBRA) requires employers that have at least 20 employees and offer health insurance

benefits to continue those benefits for a period of time after an employee quits or is fired (at the employee's expense); similar state laws apply to smaller employers. If the employee is entitled to continued benefits, talk to your human resources department to find out exactly what to tell the employee. There may also be paperwork you can give the employee that explains the issue.

- **Severance pay.** If your company will offer severance to the employee, find out what the package will be. Today, most companies don't offer severance as a matter of course but do provide some benefits to certain employees. In the case of an employee you have to fire for disciplinary reasons, you will probably be offering severance only if the company believes that the employee might have a valid legal claim against it. As a condition of receiving a severance package, an employee in this situation is typically asked to sign a release, agreeing not to sue the company in the future.

- **Company property.** Sometimes, an employee who is using company property will really be left in the lurch if he or she has to hand that property over right after being fired. To take an obvious example, an employee who drove a company car to work might have no way to get home. And certainly, an employee who has been using a company-issued cell phone or computer might need some time to buy a replacement. If it's not too much of a hardship, and you don't suspect that the employee will take advantage of the situation, it can be a very kind gesture to allow the employee to continue using company property for a short period of time. Decide how you will handle this issue ahead of time, so you can let the employee know.

- **References.** Be ready to explain your company's policy about references. This is likely to be a major concern for the employee. If your company (like many, these days) follows a strict "name, rank, and serial number" approach, let the employee know. If the company is willing to give a fuller reference in exchange for a release—a practice we recommend (see "Giving References," below)—explain the procedure and provide a form for the employee to sign.

- **Contact person.** You should decide whom the employee can contact with further questions. Often, it makes sense to provide a contact in the human resources department who can help with questions about benefits, company property, and so on. Write down this person's name and number on a piece of paper, so you can hand it to the employee during the meeting.

Giving References

There's a very good reason why many companies no longer give detailed references: They are afraid of being sued for defamation by the former employee. If the employee can prove that the employer said something false that harmed the employee's reputation, caused a prospective employer not to hire the employee, or otherwise caused the employee damage, the employee might have a viable case. Even though most employers don't—and certainly don't intend to—say things about a former employee that are not true, companies have generally decided to play it safe and just say as little as possible.

However, there are also good reasons to provide a more detailed reference. First off, it might help a fired worker find a new job more quickly, particularly if the worker had good qualities that might be a better fit for a different type of job. The sooner the employee gets a new job, the sooner he or she will be able to move on and, hopefully, get over any negative feelings about you and your company. Giving a reference will also help out your counterparts at other companies. After all, you probably call around for references when you hire. Where would you be if no one gave you any information?

Of course, you'll need to follow your company's procedures for references, if it has established some. If not, however, we think the best way to reconcile these competing interests is to give a more detailed reference, but only if the employee signs a release agreeing not to sue you or the company for anything you say. You should also let the employee know exactly what you plan to say, so the employee can decide whether to list you as a reference or not. For more tips on giving a reference safely, see *Dealing With Problem Employees*, by Amy DelPo and Lisa Guerin (Nolo).

Want more information on termination procedures? Take a look at *Dealing With Problem Employees,* by Amy DelPo and Lisa Guerin (Nolo), which includes detailed information on giving references, severance and releases, continuing insurance, and other important topics.

What You Need From the Employee

Before the employee leaves the building, you'll want to get back any company property in the employee's possession (unless you are planning to let the employee use it for a while; see "What You Can Offer the Employee," above). This includes not only things like a phone, car, or computer, but also client files, keys to the building, corporate credit cards, and long-distance telephone cards. Make a list of everything the employee might have, then bring it with you to the meeting so you can make sure you collect every item.

In addition to property, the employee might have information you need, too. Depending on the employee's position, you might want to ask about the status of various projects or accounts, find out where the employee keeps things in his or her desk or computer files, and so on. Make a list of these things, too, so you can ask the employee when you meet.

Don't go overboard. Although you are probably thinking about how the company will cover the employee's job in the future, that is not what the employee is thinking about. Don't ask too many detailed questions about work during the termination meeting. If you do, you risk appearing to be insensitive to the employee's plight—and too eager to move on. Stick to the bare minimum you need. If you absolutely need more information later, you can ask the company's contact person to get in touch with the employee and get more information.

The Termination Meeting

Now that your preparation is complete, it's time to sit down and deliver the news. No matter how carefully you plan the other aspects of the meeting, what you say and how you say it will be the most important thing to the employee. More than anything else, your words and demeanor will determine whether the employee leaves on a positive or a negative note.

Before you enter the meeting room, remember that your goal is to terminate employment, not to denigrate or hurt the employee. Choose your words carefully, and maintain your self-control. The employee might become angry or upset, but you shouldn't. Treating the employee disrespectfully at this crucial point could damage your reputation with your other employees and even prod the fired employee to take action against you and/or the company.

Remember, too, that the employee is losing a lot. Most of us look at our jobs as more than a source of income: They might also be a source of self-esteem, companionship, identity, and more. Even an employee who has had several chances to improve—and probably saw this day coming—is likely to be upset when you actually announce the termination. Don't expect the employee to make your job any easier or go out of his or her way to ease the transition.

State Your Business

It's especially important during a termination meeting to get right to the point, without any small talk or pleasantries. While you might think you are easing the blow by asking about the employee's kids or hobbies, you are really just setting both of you up for an extremely awkward transition to the real reason for the meeting.

Start the meeting by saying that you are terminating the employee's employment and why. Don't hide behind vague phrases like "We've decided to make a change" or "This might not be the best fit." The best approach is to actually say that you are terminating employment.

Don't hide behind the company. You might be tempted to distance yourself from the situation by claiming that "the company" or "senior management" made the decision to fire. In the typical discipline scenario that results in termination, this type of statement would not be entirely true: You will have been making these decisions yourself for the employees you supervise. What's more, acting as if you didn't make the decision allows the employee to believe that you might not agree with it, which can lead to suspicions about the true reasons for the termination.

This is particularly true if you take your "I'm not the bad guy" routine a step further and claim to actually disagree with the termination decision. It's much more respectful—and safer, from a legal point of view—to make it clear that you made the decision.

Don't Be Drawn Into a Debate

Sometimes, an employee will respond to being fired by trying to argue the issue. You can help avoid this by being very clear when you announce the termination, as explained above. But if the employee tries to change your mind, simply say, "I'm sorry you feel that way, but the decision is final." Don't undermine your decision by getting in an argument with the employee about whether or not termination is justified.

It's also very important to avoid responding in kind to an angry or upset employee. For example, imagine that the employee says, "I can't believe you're doing this to me! How am I going to support my family?!" If you respond with "If you really cared about your family, you wouldn't have downloaded pornography on your company PC," what happens next will be a yelling match. It's far better to say, "I'm sorry, but my decision is final. Now, let's talk about what will happen next."

You may feel sorry for the employee, which is perfectly natural. But if you've followed the procedures we've described in this book, you've already given the employee every opportunity to improve. Ultimately, the employee was not able to do the job in an acceptable way—a way that is sustainable for the health of the company. It's important to keep this in mind when you fire someone, to make sure that you don't backpedal at the last minute. Your natural instinct to feel sad for someone who's lost a job shouldn't translate into changing your mind, offering to reconsider, or saying things that will undermine the decision.

EXAMPLE: Christine manages vendor accounts for a large catering company. Unbeknownst to her manager, Christine and her husband started their own linen supply service, "Tablecloths & More," solely to provide linens to the company for its events. Christine hired "Tablecloths & More" to provide linens for every large company event and paid herself a hefty markup, well higher than what the company was paying its other linen vendors. When Lily, Christine's manager, found out about this blatant conflict of interest, she asked Christine about it. After a long, uncomfortable meeting, Christine finally admitted the scheme. After considering the factors listed above, Lily decided to fire her.

Lily goes to Christine's office, along with the director of human resources (as her company requires when an employee is fired). Lily starts the meeting this way: "Christine, I've decided to terminate your employment, effective immediately. Directing company business to your own company is a violation of company policy prohibiting conflicts of interest. I can't have someone working here who puts the interests of her own business ahead of the company's interests."

Explain What Happens Next

Once you've announced your decision (and headed off any effort to change your mind), let the employee know about anything that's coming to him or her: final paycheck, continued insurance benefits, severance (if applicable), and so on. Also, explain your company's position on references. If your company provides references and the employee is interested, talk about what you might say to a prospective employer.

EXAMPLE: Christine knew that she would probably be fired if she got caught, so she doesn't argue with Lily about her termination. Lily continues the meeting like this: "Here is your final paycheck. It covers from the first of the month until the end of the day today. We won't require you to work the rest of the day, but we are going to pay you for it. Also, I've brought some forms with me that give you the option of continuing your health insurance, if you pay the full premium. You can read those at your leisure; if you have any questions about them, you can ask Scott in Human Resources.

"Our company provides references only if the employee who's leaving signs a release agreeing not to take any action against the company for anything said by the person providing the reference. Scott can explain that to you further, if you're interested. You should know that, although there are some positive things I can say about your work, I would also have to reveal the reason you were fired."

Review Property and Paperwork

After explaining what happens next, it's time to get back company property, such as keys, phones, credit cards, and so on. If you've decided to allow the employee to use any of these items for a while, explain what will happen and how and when you will get the property back.

If the employee will have any ongoing obligations to the company, discuss those now, as well. For example, if the employee has signed a valid noncompete agreement, promising not to work for a competitor for a set period of time after leaving your company, you should bring that agreement with you and remind the employee of its terms. If the employee has had access to company trade secrets during his or her employment, you should let the employee know that he or she has an obligation not to reveal that information.

> **EXAMPLE:** Because Christine committed misconduct that involved deception and defrauding the company, Lily doesn't want to allow her to keep any company property. Lily also wants to make very sure that Christine doesn't use the company's confidential information, particularly about its clients, after she leaves. Lily starts this part of the conversation this way: "Christine, I need to get back any company property in your possession. I'll need your keys to the building, the company credit card and phone card, and your cell phone. If there are any personal numbers you need to get off your cell phone, I'll give you a few minutes to write them down now."
>
> Lily continues, "I'd also like to talk to you about your obligations to the company. As you may know, we consider information about our clients—including their names, preferences, and specifications,

and the prices we charge them for various services—to be company trade secrets. This means that you may not reveal or use this information, even after your employment here is over. If you do use this information, the company can sue you for damages. Do you have any questions about this?"

You might want to have passwords and access codes turned off during the meeting. If you fear violence, sabotage, or other angry actions against the company, you should arrange to have the employee's access to the workplace, computer and email system, phone system, company credit card accounts, and so on blocked while you are in the termination meeting. If you disable passwords, cancel accounts, and so on while the meeting takes place, you remove many opportunities for the employee to do damage. At the same time, of course, this tactic clearly demonstrates that you don't trust the employee—so use it only when warranted.

Tie Up Loose Ends

Once you've finished with all of the details, find out whether the employee has any questions. You should also explain how you will handle the employee's ongoing work.

> **EXAMPLE:** Lily tells Christine, "Tammi is going to take over your accounts until we hire someone new. Tammi will be instructed to tell any vendors who inquire that you're no longer with the company. That's the same thing I'm going to tell your coworkers.
> "Do you have any questions about anything I've said?"

Close on a Positive Note

When you've covered everything, end the meeting cordially. Give the employee the name of a contact person to call with any questions, then wish the employee good luck. Don't say anything that undermines or contradicts your decision to terminate employment, however.

EXAMPLE: Lily is rather angry at Christine, who has not only betrayed her trust but also ripped the company off. Lily also feels worried that Christine might try to take client files or other company information with her. So, Lily decides to keep her closing remarks very brief and to leave her witness behind while Christine cleans out her desk and office.

"Christine, I've asked Scott to make himself available to answer any questions that might come up later. I've written his number down for you. I'm going to leave now, to give you some time to gather your things together. Scott will be here to assist you with anything you need and to walk you out when you're ready to leave. Best of luck in the future, Christine."

Does the Employee Need an Escort?

Unless you have a legitimate fear of violence, sabotage, or theft, it's best to avoid the strong-arm tactic of having the fired employee escorted through the building by a guard. In most situations, this is simply unnecessary and is likely to embarrass and humiliate the fired worker. It could also make the rest of your team feel that you are heartless or unkind.

At the same time, however, it is a good idea to get a fired employee out of the building as soon as possible. You don't want the employee stopping at every desk to tell the sad tale of being fired. For these reasons, it's a good idea to escort the employee out yourself. Let the employee stop to say goodbye to friends along the way, and offer to help carry things to the employee's car. This is a humane approach that is also effective at getting the employee out of the building relatively quickly.

Documentation

Once you've fired the employee, the last step in the termination process is to document your decision in an internal memorandum to the employee's personnel file. The purpose of this memo is quite different from a disciplinary memo. When you document discipline, you have a number of goals: to make sure you and the employee agree on what happened and what will happen next; to memorialize your decision so the employee will know what's expected in the future; and to help the employee's future managers at the company understand what took place, to name a few. When you document a termination, your goal is simply to make a written record of what happened, so you can defend it later if necessary.

Keeping this goal in mind, your documentation should completely and accurately describe the reason or reasons you decided to terminate employment. If the employee committed a one-time serious offense, write down what happened and why it is cause for termination. Whenever possible, specify the policy the worker violated. If the worker engaged in persistent misconduct or poor performance over a period of time, specify not only the problem but also your efforts to remedy it. Write down the dates of disciplinary meetings and warnings.

Below is a sample termination memo, written by Lily from the example above.

If you have followed the advice in this book, you should already have a lot of documentation about the employee's problem and your response, if you are dealing with an ongoing problem. As a result, this memo can be fairly short and to the point—as long as it is also accurate and complete. For a one-time firing offense (such as Christine's), you might need to include a few more details.

Once the employee is gone and you've filed your termination memo, you still have one important job to do: Get yourself and your team focused on the work ahead. Chapter 15 explains how to share the difficult news with your staff, figure out the lessons you need to learn from this disciplinary experience, and move on.

Termination Memorandum

By: Lily Lamont

Date: November 13, 2007

Re: Christine Coleman

I terminated Christine Coleman's employment today. Yesterday, November 12, 2007, Martin Yarrow told me that Christine was routing work to a company she owns with her husband, "Tablecloths & Things." I looked over the vendor records for the past year and saw that Tablecloths & Things had received every contract for linens in the last four months. I also saw that we were paying Tablecloths & Things $0.50 more per tablecloth, and $0.10 more per napkin, than we paid to any other linen vendor in the past year. These higher charges added up to almost $5,000 in the last quarter.

I met with Christine this morning to talk about this. When I presented her with the facts described above, Christine admitted that she had been routing all of the company's linen contracts to the company she owned with her husband. She also admitted that she gave these contracts to her company even though other vendors were available to provide the same service for less.

Based on these facts and my conversation with Christine, I decided to terminate her employment. Christine's behavior violates our company policy on conflicts of interest. I informed Christine that her employment was terminated in a meeting this afternoon, which Scott McPhee from Human Resources also attended.

Signed: *Lily Lamont*

Dated: Nov. 13, 2007

Termination: Smart Summary

○ Termination is a serious step: It indicates that the progressive discipline process hasn't worked. For that reason, you should carefully review the facts, the employee's personnel file, company policies, past statements made to the employee, how other employees have been treated, and the timing before making the decision. You might also want to get a second opinion from an appropriate person like your manager, human resources, or your legal counsel.

○ When you prepare to meet with the employee, have administrative issues—like the final paycheck, continued insurance benefits, severance pay, the return of company property, references, and a contact person—sorted out. This will save you and the employee potential embarrassment and discomfort.

○ Your goal when documenting termination is different from your goals when documenting discipline: You simply want to make a written record of what happened, so you can defend it later if necessary. Note former discipline and also what specific policy was violated, if applicable.

○ If you feel guilty about the decision to terminate, remember this: You only got to this point because either the employee committed egregious and obviously unacceptable misconduct, or the employee was given the opportunity to improve and was unwilling or unable to do so.

Life After Discipline

Y ou're at the end of a long, arduous journey. Maybe you went through the entire progressive discipline process with the employee, coaching, encouraging, and monitoring along the way. Or perhaps, you were forced to take immediate action to deal with a really serious issue.

In either case, the progressive discipline process can take a toll on all those involved: the manager, coworkers, and even the company itself. It takes time, effort, and commitment. It can take you away from your core work, and it can be highly emotional. After the stress of disciplining and terminating the employee, you're probably just ready to wash your hands of the whole affair.

Unfortunately, it's not quite time to do that. First, you'll want to spend some time "wrapping up." This is an opportunity to learn from your experience and decide how to move forward. It's a multi-step process that requires you to:

- evaluate what went right and wrong
- communicate an appropriate amount of information to your team, and
- update other relevant people in the company, including managers and coworkers.

Conduct a Process Evaluation

Before you explain to others what happened, how you dealt with it, and how you plan to proceed, take some time to think about it privately. The discipline process stirs up all kinds of emotions: you may feel angry, defeated, or saddened by what's occurred. Taking some time alone gives you the opportunity to separate those emotions from actual events, so that you can figure out whether there is anything you, or someone else, could have done differently. In business—and discipline is no different—this step is often referred to as conducting a "post mortem."

The post mortem may well be the key to preventing future problems. It gives you a chance to reflect on what preventative steps could have been taken, what went well, and what could have been done better. If others were involved in the discipline process, it allows you to evaluate the success of each person's role—not to lay blame, but to learn and improve or eliminate these issues in the future.

The overarching question that should be ever present in the post mortem process is: *What could I have done differently?* No one is perfect, and the only person's behavior and actions you control is your own. Focus on the things you have the ability to change to make the process work better the next time around.

To do this, you can think about the following questions:

- **Did you impose discipline fairly?** That means that you made sure the discipline was proportionate to the problem, applied discipline according to company policy, and disciplined consistently for similar problems.

- **Did you communicate clearly?** At every step, the employee should have understood your expectations—what specific tasks were required, when they were required, and how they were to be accomplished. Ideally, your emotions were in check, and you kept communications as confidential and factual as possible. At the same time, you showed respect and empathy for the employee's thoughts and feelings.

- **Did you get help when you needed it?** Sometimes, you might not have known the answers or how to solve the problem. Did you ask for help when you needed it? If the employee (or you) needed help from outside sources, did you get those people involved at the appropriate juncture?

- **How do you think the employee felt?** Although most employees won't feel happy about the discipline process (and may not like you), it is important that the employee feels he or she got a fair shake.

- **What did you do right?** Make sure to think about the things that went well, so that you can repeat them in the future.

When you conduct a post mortem, you'll also want to think more specifically about opportunities you had to prevent, discover and investigate, respond to, and follow up on the problem. Next, we'll go through some of the specific questions you should ask yourself to evaluate how well you took advantage of your opportunities.

Check out the "Discipline Review Checklist." To make it easier for you to ask yourself these questions, we've included a "Discipline Evaluation Checklist" in Appendix A, and on the CD in the back of this book. You can use the checklist to brainstorm and to prepare yourself to talk about the problem with others. Although a lawsuit is unlikely, if there is one, you don't want the terminated employee privy to your innermost thoughts. For that reason, we don't recommend responding to these questions on paper. Simply use the list to collect your thoughts and help you to assess the process.

Looking at all these factors doesn't mean that you won't have any discipline problems in the future. After all, you can't force employees to behave or perform a certain way. However, you can make sure that you were not the reason the employee didn't behave or perform as expected.

Could You Have Prevented the Problem?

Hindsight is 20/20—looking back, you may be able to see exactly what you could have done to prevent the problem in the first place. It might even be recognizing that you hired the wrong person. Or it might be that there was nothing you could do—that a problem was sudden and completely unanticipated.

In trying to evaluate whether there was anything you could have done to prevent the problem, consider these questions:

- **Were you checking in with the employee?** Most employees want to succeed—but not all employees will tell you when they realize they're failing. As we discussed in Chapter 4, it's your responsibility to touch base with the employee, and that's your opportunity to see if there are any concerns that could create problems down the road.

- **Were you checking in with your team?** Remember, your team members offer information and perspectives you won't otherwise get. Sometimes, listening to what your team members have to say is the first step to heading off discipline problems. If you haven't been taking the time to sit down with your employees—saying "good morning" in the elevator doesn't count—you're probably losing the opportunity to gain some valuable information. Refer back to Chapter 4 to see if you were doing your best—sitting down with employees regularly, listening empathically, and following up when appropriate.

- **Did you make a mistake in assigning duties or tasks to the employee?** Sometimes, discipline problems occur because managers hire underqualified candidates, ignore troublesome history or experience (or the lack thereof), or give employees duties that go beyond their level of expertise. It may be that you pushed an employee into a position or duty that wasn't appropriate for that person's skill level.

Did You Recognize the Problem?

Even if you couldn't have prevented a problem, you might have been able to recognize it earlier in the process. As we've already discussed, when managers fail to recognize problems early, everyone loses. The company, the manager, and the employee waste valuable time and resources trying to undo mistakes that could have been avoided.

Sometimes, it's difficult to pinpoint exactly when you became aware of a problem. Here are some questions to ask yourself to see whether you were clued into the problem at the first opportunity:

- **Were there any signs that something wasn't right?** Often, you have indications that something might not be right—something you might only be able to describe as a "gut feeling." An employee with a performance problem may have been underqualified when you compare the job's requirements to the person's resume, or an employee with an attendance problem might have started arriving a couple of minutes late months ago, showing up later and later as weeks went by. Did you see those things at the time and take them into account? If you did, you might handle future situations differently, getting involved earlier in the process. On the other hand, if you only see those signs in retrospect, what can you do to make sure they're more visible next time?
- **Did you speak up as soon as you had reason to believe there was a problem?** Often, we don't speak up because we think a problem is "no big deal"—an employee is ten minutes late, and we don't want to make a fuss. Remember, though, that sometimes very simple conversations and coaching techniques make it possible to

nip problems in the bud. Refer back to Chapter 11 to see how you might have coached an employee through a minor problem.

Did You Respond Appropriately to the Problem?

Once you decided to deal with the problem, how did you handle it? Consider these questions:

- **Did you respond to the problem immediately?** Doing so keeps the facts fresh and relevant. Catching it early also minimizes the impact of the problem and maximizes the chance that your employee will improve.
- **Did you investigate?** It's not fair to discipline an employee until you know the whole story—and sometimes, that means a lot of investigative work on your part. This includes research, like looking at your company's relevant policies to make sure you are applying them fairly and consistently, reviewing the employee's history, and looking at how others in the company have handled the same or similar problems.
- **Did you plan?** Did you sit down and think about where you were going to meet with the employee, what you would say, and how the employee might respond? This planning allows you to make sure you get the most important points across, without getting sidetracked by the employee's emotions.
- **Did you get the right people involved?** Did you involve your manager, human resources, or legal counsel in the discipline at the right time in the process?
- **Did you work with the employee to create an action plan?** Did the employee know what was expected next? If your action plan was unclear, nonexistent, or prepared just by you, you didn't give the employee a fair shot at owning and fixing the issue.

Did You Follow Up?

After the meeting ended, what did you do to ensure the employee's continued success? Here are a couple things to consider:

- **Did you document?** Documenting does more than protect the company—and you—if there is a dispute. Documenting reminds you of important facts, including what the employee's concerns were and what you agreed to do to solve the problem.

- **Did you check in with the employee?** The employee needed to hear the message that the problem was correctible. If you weren't checking in with the employee—praising successes, offering further direction or encouragement, and voicing concerns about continued problems—you might not have provided every available resource for success.
- **Did you hold up your end of the bargain?** If there were tasks you were supposed to do in the action plan, did you do them?

Talk to Your Team

After you've spent some time evaluating what happened, you should move on to thinking about what to share with your team and how to share it. Although you have handled the discipline issue based on a thorough analysis of the facts and arrived at a fair and reasoned conclusion, most likely your team has not been privy to the whole process as it unfolded. Instead, the situation may have become fodder for gossip, and incomplete stories shared.

Change itself can be alarming for employees. William Bridges, a noted change management guru, says, "That decision (to make a change) and the first steps taken to implement it are (management's) beginning, but for the people who haven't been in the transition process up to this point, that same decision and those same steps represent an ending to the way things were."

As with any change, termination is an ending to the way things were and can cause confusion and even fear in the workplace. Your employees need some way to "catch up" in the process you have already gone most of the way through: What felt like a long process for you may feel very sudden for them. You need to communicate a delicately balanced message that employees must meet the company's expectations, without creating an environment of fear and dread.

Decide How Much to Share

When you've determined that a disciplinary issue has affected the team's morale or performance, you must take immediate steps to address it. You'll want to talk to the team about what happened, why, and where to go next—without sharing all the gory details.

Here are some of the most important issues to consider when deciding how much information to share with employees:

- **The need to know.** What your team members want to know may be very different from what they need to know. Often all a team needs to know is that an employee is no longer with the company. You may need to say only that the employee has departed and identify who will handle his or her job tasks. If more detail is needed, limit it to issues that affect the employees' ability to get their jobs done.

- **Confidentiality.** There are a couple of reasons to maintain confidentiality, when possible: It assures your team members that they will be afforded the same respect, and it avoids legal trouble, including possible defamation claims if word gets back to the former employee. (See Chapter 3 for more information about potential legal problems that can result from unnecessarily breaching confidentiality.)

- **Your role.** Although you want to assure employees that the situation was handled fairly, you don't want to spend time explaining what you did and why. This could lead you to say negative things about the employee to justify the actions you took. Those statements could get back to the employee, but they could also cause coworkers to worry about whether you'd say the same kinds of things about them.

- **Morale.** Understand that employees feel insecure about their own jobs when a coworker is terminated. Although you can't share details about the discipline, you can reiterate your commitment to disciplining fairly. If your company has a written progressive discipline policy, you can also emphasize your commitment to following that policy.

EXAMPLE: Joseph supervises a team of 12 customer service representatives in a call center. He receives a report that one of the representatives, Greg, shouted profanity at a customer on the phone. The report is verified by a telephone recording of the call.

Joseph calls Greg into his office to discuss the incident. Greg begins to yell at Joseph, calling him a liar and making obscene gestures. Joseph asks Greg to leave the office for the rest of the afternoon to cool down. Later that day, Greg calls Joseph and threatens to harm him physically. Because of the seriousness of the behavior, Joseph terminates Greg's employment immediately.

Employees have heard about Greg's behavior and threats but don't know the details. Joseph can hear his team members whispering about it. He quickly calls a team meeting and explains, "As you may have heard, Greg exhibited some inappropriate behavior today, including threats. Because of safety concerns, we had to terminate his employment. The front desk and security have been alerted that Greg is not allowed in the building, and security guards are available to escort you to your car when you leave the building. We're sorry that the situation came to this, but we hope you understand that that employee safety is a priority in this company, and we want to make sure you all feel secure.

"For now, we'll all take on a little extra work until we can find a replacement for Greg. I'll work with human resources to get the opening posted as soon as possible, hopefully this week. If you have safety concerns, please talk to me or human resources."

Decide How to Share It

Once you've decided that you need to talk to your employees, and you know what you want to say, you must decide how you will share the message. You'll have to decide:

- **When to talk to employees.** Talk to your employees as close to the end of the process as possible. Waiting two or three weeks for things to "cool down" makes you look like you are avoiding something or that you don't value your employees enough to inform them of important issues. Plus, you want to end all the speculation and chatter and get everyone focused back on the work as soon as you can.

- **Whether to talk to employees together or individually.** If the issue has affected everybody equally, talk to your employees together. In the example above, Greg's behavior was equally dangerous for everyone involved, and Joseph saved time and sent a consistent message by talking to everyone at once, while still giving the employees the opportunity to come to him individually. If the issue affects only a more limited number of employees, or might embarrass someone (for example, an employee who was sexually harassed by a coworker), you might want to talk only to the affected employees, individually. You might also choose to talk individually to employees who are more directly affected by the problem—for instance, because they will be responsible for assuming some of the former employee's duties.

- **How to respond to questions.** While it's good to communicate openly, your team also needs to know that you're going to be conscious of each employee's privacy and communicate only appropriate facts. Field questions all day long about the work going forward, but steer clear of probing questions that go beyond what the employees need to know.

Focus Your Team on the Work Ahead

While it's important to tell your team what happened so you can eliminate the mystery and intrigue, it's even more important to communicate what must happen going forward. Gathering your team and outlining the work that needs to be done will not only get your team members focused back on their jobs, it will also put the distracting issue to rest. To do this, you'll need to decide what needs to be accomplished and then focus on what steps have to occur for that to happen.

Step One: What Needs to Be Accomplished?

Before you can decide who does what and when, you'll need to know what needs to be done in the absence of the former employee. It may be that you just need to reassign his or her duties. If you aren't familiar with everything your employee did, you may need to research or discuss with individual employees what needs to get done.

However, it's also possible that other team members lost focus on their own goals as a result of the discipline process. It's inevitable that, as a manager, something had to give as you dedicated time to dealing with the discipline and termination. It may be that other employees were left spinning their wheels without a clear idea of what they should have been doing. You'll want to reevaluate where things are and do whatever's necessary to get the team back on track.

Step Two: Set Targets

Now that you know what work needs to be done, give your employees new work targets–deadlines, milestones, or measurements—to refocus them on their work. This narrow concentration will allow little time for conversing about the past. It also reaffirms that you are personally committed to the team's performance. After all, you probably haven't spent as much time managing them as you would have under normal circumstances.

> **EXAMPLE:** Louise manages a team of analysts who are responsible for implementing new record-keeping software within the company. The implementation is a multi-step process, with each team member working with a different department to implement the software by a target date. During actual implementation of the software within each department, several team members assist the member who is primarily responsible for that department, who leads the project.
>
> Chad is responsible for implementing the new system in the accounting department. As his implementation date comes closer, it becomes evident that Chad has not done the work necessary to make it happen—and in fact, has lied to Louise about his accomplishments. After much investigation and discipline, Louise terminates Chad's employment.
>
> Louise's team members were planning on helping Chad with the implementation in accounting and have set other projects aside in preparation. Louise realizes that considerable work needs to be done before Chad's project can be implemented, though. She gathers together the team that was going to help Chad and works with them to set new, more appropriate deadlines for implementing the software in accounting. She decides to keep the other teams on track, given that they were not as affected by Chad's performance.

In this example, Louise is not only focused on the practical issue of completing the software rollout in the accounting department, she is giving that team something to focus on other than Chad's termination.

When the tasks or projects you have assigned have been completed, celebrate that accomplishment. While largely symbolic, this celebration signifies to your team that you all have indeed moved on and worked together to accomplish goals despite prohibitive challenges.

Tell Others Who Need to Know

Even after you've shared the necessary information with your team, you might not be done. Although you may have involved various people in your company as you went through the disciplinary process (human resources, legal counsel, or the management team), there may be additional people who need to be involved now that the issue has been resolved. These include people who worked closely with the employee and others in the management chain.

Whom Do You Tell?

As with all communication in the disciplinary process, you should tell only others in your company who need to know about the termination. First, consider whether you need to tell people who worked closely with the employee but were outside your own team, or people who relied on his or her function to complete their own jobs. For example, a salesperson is not only a member of the sales team, but has a set of customers and support staff. If the salesperson is terminated, support staff might need to know whether that changes their job duties, or what to tell customers about the former employee.

Second, identify other managers or departments who need to know about the specific issue you've faced. While your boss has probably already gotten involved, the impact may have reached others if it has caused your team to miss deadlines or has affected the company's bottom line. In those circumstances, you may need to explain to other managers who depend on your work or those who have set company-wide goals based on your deliverables.

What Do You Say?

Just as with your own team, you want to thoughtfully communicate relevant information to the people that need to know. What you say will be dictated by your audience. An employee from another department probably only needs to know how the discipline impacts his or her job;

your boss might need to know how the details are going to affect your ability to meet goals and deadlines; and upper management may need to know only the "big picture" financial effect and plan for the future.

That means that you need to plan what you say based on your audience. To do that, be prepared to acknowledge the issue, explain the issue's impact, and outline the plan going forward.

Acknowledge the Issue

How you acknowledge the issue will be depend on your reasons for sharing the information. For example, if you are talking to an employee who worked with the terminated employee, you need share only information that relates to the working relationship—and that may mean saying very little about what actually happened.

On the other hand, if you're talking to someone up the chain of command, you will probably have to provide more detail. You should be prepared to explain how you recognized the problem and how you handled it. Those concerned with the bottom line may wonder how or why the problem escalated, but if you imposed discipline fairly, that's something you'll be able to explain.

> **EXAMPLE:** Morgan works in the office of a small architecture firm. One of her job duties is processing payroll. Once checks are issued, Libby, a mailroom employee, picks them up from Morgan and delivers them to employees.
>
> Hannah, Morgan's boss, discovers that Morgan has been making errors in the payroll. After Hannah utilizes the progressive discipline process, Morgan is unable to improve her performance. Hannah terminates Morgan's employment and assigns payroll processing to another employee, Darrin. Hannah calls Libby. She states, "Libby, I know you usually pick up paychecks from Morgan. I just wanted to let you know that Morgan's no longer with the company, and Darrin will be processing the payroll now. Please pick up the checks from him, and direct any questions you have about payroll to him as well."

Hannah has taken care to make sure that the people who work closely with Morgan are not left wondering whom they now need to work with.

Remember what you learned in your process evaluation. When you have to explain what happened to upper management, the lessons you learned in your process evaluation are handy: You can preempt most of management's concerns since you have already thought it through so well, and you can provide a thorough analysis of what you did and why. Likewise, documenting your disciplinary actions pays off here, too—you'll be able to respond to more specific questions if they arise, because you will have written down the most pertinent details.

Explain the Impact

In addition to acknowledging the issue, you're going to have to explain the impact. This will indicate to others that you've thought of a solution—not just recognized the existence of a problem.

When you're dealing with coworkers, you probably need to explain only the impact on that person's job. When dealing with higher-ups, you might have to explain the fiscal impact or how it affects your ability to meet target goals or deadlines. Again, this can often be one brief sentence such as "This has set back our product release timeline three weeks" or "Our customer satisfaction in the Southeast has declined as a result."

Outlining the plan you have put in place to recover from the discipline issue is the meat of any discussion you would have with others who work closely with your team, or the larger management team. This brief sentence should focus on the business steps you are taking to address the issue (as opposed to the disciplinary steps you took in addressing it with the individual). So if your issue was an employee with an apparent dismal attitude and your customer satisfaction in the Southeast declined as a result, you would add a sentence that says, "We have implemented a customer satisfaction recovery operation and trained each person on how to achieve it. We expect to have the issue fixed by the next reporting period." You are using a brief sentence or two to describe what's been done to address the business issue that might arise and assuring your audience that you have things under control.

EXAMPLES:

To the direct team: "As many of you know, John has left the company. I know his leaving may cause more work for some of you, but here is the plan for short-term coverage …. We also have some rebuilding work to do with John's former customers, and the plan for that is …."

To the upper management chain: "We recently let John go due to substandard performance. This will put a strain on the team in the short term, but I believe it will help the team overall in the longer term. To cover for John, I have asked Mary, Patricia, and Susan to each take one of his regions for now. To account for that new workload, I've extended their deadlines for completing the customer survey analysis. In the meantime, we will actively search for John's replacement."

To the Board of Directors: "We recently terminated an employee, John, for failure to uphold our standards of customer service. He was responsible for the loss of two long-term customers, and this may have ongoing revenue impact. I have put my top three people on the three regions that John formerly covered and directed them to rebuild these lost relationships. The overall impact to revenue will be $500,000 initially, but I expect to recoup about $300,000 of that through these focused efforts."

Moving Forward

Once you've evaluated the discipline process, focused your team on forward-looking objectives, and communicated the necessary information to others in the company, you're ready to move on. Hopefully, you've learned steps, tools, and tips that will help you either avoid or control the discipline process in the future. And you can continue to utilize the skills you've learned here to make each encounter with your employees more successful and more positive. Remember that all new concepts take practice to turn into habits, so don't let frustration or qualified success keep you from doing the right thing. Stay the course, practice discipline smartly, and watch your team flourish under your care.

■

Build Your Skills: If Discipline Fails

Questions

1. Termination of employment is usually not a manager's favorite task. What's something important about a well-run process that you should remember as you prepare yourself to give the bad news?

2. When an employee is accused of serious misconduct, and you need to investigate, it's a good idea to put the employee on an unpaid leave.

   ☐ True   ☐ False

3. On what day or at what time of day should you terminate employment?

   a. It depends on the situation and your workplace.

   b. At the beginning of the workweek.

   c. On Friday, after everyone has gone home.

   d. As soon as you're able to wrap up the employee's final projects.

4. Employees are often angry about being fired. To be safe, whenever you decide to terminate employment, you should have an employee's passwords and access codes turned off during the termination meeting.

   ☐ True   ☐ False

5. Nora is getting ready to fire Stuart for serious misconduct—he has given away several thousand dollars' worth of the company's products to friends and family for free, in violation of company policy. Which of these reasons should cause Nora to reconsider that decision?

   a. Stuart's file shows he has always been an exemplary performer; this is his first discipline problem.

   b. Stuart tells Nora when they meet that he did not know this was prohibited and thought it was "not a big deal."

   c. At the termination meeting, Stuart tells Nora that he was sexually harassed by a coworker.

   d. The prior week, Stuart complained to the human resources department that he was sexually harassed by a coworker.

6. When you have to fire an employee, what are some of the benefits of conducting a post mortem?

7. Which of these factors indicate that you could have done more to prevent a discipline problem?

    a. You didn't meet regularly with your employees.

    b. You didn't speak up as soon as you saw a problem.

    c. You didn't create an action plan with the employee.

    d. You didn't document.

8. When an employee is terminated, it's best not to say anything to coworkers—after all, you want to respect that person's privacy.

    ☐ True   ☐ False

9. What is the most important method for getting beyond a termination, as a team?

    a. Spend some time together talking about the termination and how everyone feels about it.

    b. Focus your team on the work that needs to be done by setting and meeting identified targets.

    c. Get away from the office for a team-building exercise or break.

    d. Meet regularly with your team members to reinforce the rules or expectations that the terminated employee failed to meet.

10. Chrissy had to terminate Lloyd's employment. She crafts this statement: "Lloyd is no longer with the company. From now on, when you have questions about the Stow-rite line of products, please contact Evelyn." To whom should Chrissy deliver such a message?

    a. Holly, her boss.

    b. The whole company.

    c. The customer service team who usually calls Lloyd when they need help with customer inquires about Stow-rite products.

    d. Sidney and Leny, who Chrissy knows usually eat lunch with Lloyd.

Answers

1. Remember: If you followed the strategies explained in this book, you've given the employee every opportunity to improve. The employee either wasn't capable of improvement or chose not to take advantage of those opportunities. Either way, the employee isn't willing or able to do what the job requires.

2. False. Whether called "leave" or "suspension," it's a bad idea to put an employee on an involuntary, unpaid break while you conduct an investigation into that person's conduct. While a paid suspension may be necessary—so that you can gather information without the employee's presence and make sure you know the facts—when the suspension is unpaid, it looks like you're penalizing the employee and might send the message that you've already made up your mind about the truth of the allegations. Moreover, if you suspend an exempt employee, you could run into legal wage and hour problems.

3. A. It's best to let the workplace guide your decision. However, if you fear violence or sabotage from an employee, you should terminate employment at the end of the workweek or workday and get the employee out the door as soon as you can.

4. False. Although you may wish to disable passwords, access codes, and the like if you fear violence, sabotage, or theft of company secrets, it isn't necessary in every case. In many instances, the employee will feel grief, disappointment, frustration, or humiliation—and there's no need to compound that by also making the employee feel like you don't trust him or her.

5. D. In this instance, firing Stuart after he complained of illegal activity could look like retaliation. Nora will want to talk to her human resources department or legal counsel to first make sure that the firing is beyond reproach. Here, it doesn't matter that Stuart had a great performance record (Answer A), because his problem is serious misconduct that justifies immediate termination. It's also fair to terminate Stuart for stealing the company's products even though he didn't know it violated company policy—whether because he *should* have read it because it was accessible to him, or because common sense should tell him that it's not okay to take things without paying for them (Answer B). Finally, although Nora should sit up and take notice of Stuart's claim that he was

sexually harassed (Answer C), if she'd already made and communicated the decision to terminate employment, Stuart will have a hard time arguing that her decision was made *because* of his claim.

6. The post mortem gives you an opportunity to separate your emotions from actual events so that you can figure out whether there is anything you could have done differently or better. It allows you to reflect on what preventative steps could have been taken and what you could have changed to get a different result.

7. A. While all these factors indicate steps you might have taken to help the discipline process succeed, most involve actions you could have taken *after* you knew there was a problem. However, if you'd been meeting with your employees regularly, you might have been turned on to discipline problems early on—either because the employees themselves would have told you about their problems, or because being in touch with your team would have clued you in to areas of weakness.

8. False. While you should respect the terminated employee's privacy, you will probably want to acknowledge that the employee isn't with the company any longer. After all, the termination process is a big transition point for your employees, and they may be feeling nervous or confused. It's a good idea to let them know that the employee is gone—but be tight-lipped about the details.

9. B. The best method to move beyond the termination is to get your employees focused on the work that needs to be done. This provides the opportunity for everyone to think about something other than the termination and to set and meet their own targets. Doing this sets your employees up for the opportunity to succeed—something they may badly need. Don't forget to praise them when they accomplish their goals.

10. C. In this case, Chrissy needs to tell those who used to work with Lloyd that he is no longer with the company—but that doesn't mean she needs to go into great detail. Instead, she just needs to let them know how it will affect their jobs. So here, it's probably enough to just tell them that they can now direct their calls to Evelyn.

Appendixes

Tools, Checklists, and Summaries

Sample Policy Language

Workplace Discipline

Any employee conduct that violates company rules or that, in the opinion of the company, interferes with or adversely affects our business is sufficient grounds for disciplinary action.

Disciplinary action can range from coaching to immediate discharge. Our general policy is to take disciplinary steps in the following order:

- coaching
- verbal warning(s)
- written warning(s), and
- termination.

However, we reserve the right to alter the order described above, to skip disciplinary steps, to eliminate disciplinary steps, or to create new and/or additional disciplinary steps.

In choosing the appropriate disciplinary measure, we may consider any number of factors, including

- the seriousness of your behavior
- your history of misconduct or performance problems
- your employment record
- the length of your employment with this company
- the strength of the evidence against you
- your ability to correct the behavior
- your attitude about the behavior
- action we have taken to respond to similar behavior by other employees
- how your behavior affects this company, its customers, and your coworkers, and
- any other circumstances related to the nature of the behavior, your employment with this company, and the affect of your behavior on the company.

We will give these considerations whatever weight we deem appropriate. Depending on the circumstances, we may give some considerations more weight than others—or no weight at all.

Sample Policy Language (cont'd)

Some conduct may result in immediate termination of your employment. Here are some examples:

- theft of company property
- excessive tardiness or absenteeism
- arguing or fighting with customers, coworkers, managers, or supervisors
- bringing a weapon to work
- threatening the physical safety of customers, coworkers, managers, or supervisors
- physically or verbally assaulting someone at work
- any illegal conduct at work
- use or possession of alcohol or illegal drugs at work
- working under the influence of alcohol or illegal drugs
- failing to carry out reasonable job assignments
- insubordination
- making false statements on a job application
- violating company rules and regulations, and
- discrimination or harassment.

Of course, it is impossible to compile an exhaustive list of the types of conduct that will result in immediate termination. Those listed above are merely illustrations.

You should remember that your employment is at the mutual consent of you and this company. This policy does not change that fact. This means that you or this company can terminate our employment relationship at will, at any time, with or without cause, and with or without advance notice.

As a result, this company reserves the right to terminate your employment at any time for any lawful reason, including reasons not listed above. You also have the right to end your employment at any time.

Disciplinary Form

Title of Form

(for example, Verbal Warning, Written Warning, etc.)

Date: _____

Employee Name: _____

Manager Name: _____

Incident Description:

Prior Incidents:

Improvement Plan:

Employee Comments:

Manager: _____ Date: _____

I acknowledge that I have received and understand this document.

Employee: _____ Date: _____

Discipline Evaluation Checklist

General Considerations

- Did you impose discipline fairly?
  - Was the discipline proportionate to the problem?
  - Did you apply company policy?
  - Did you discipline consistently for similar problems?
- Did you communicate clearly?
  - Did the employee know what specific tasks were required?
  - Did the employee know when each task was to be completed?
  - Did the employee understand how each task was to be accomplished?
  - Did you keep your emotions in check?
  - Did you keep your communications as factual and confidential as possible?
  - Did you respect the employee's thoughts and feelings?
- Did you get help when you needed it?
  - If you didn't know what to do or wanted a fresh perspective, did you ask your boss, human resources, or your legal department for help?
  - If the employee needed additional training, accommodation, or instruction, did you get the right people involved?
- How do you think the employee felt?
  - Did the employee feel fairly treated?
  - Did the employee feel blindsided?
- What did you do right?

Preventing the Problem

- Were you checking in with the employee?
- Were you checking in with your team?
  - Did you have regular one-on-ones?
  - Did you have team meetings?

- Did you assign appropriate tasks and duties to the employee?
  - Was the employee qualified for the job?
  - Were the tasks you assigned appropriate for the position?

Recognizing the Problem

- Were there indicators something wasn't right?
  - If yes, did you take them into account in deciding when to discipline?
  - If no, what can you do to make sure you see the indicators next time?
- Did you speak up as soon as you had reason to believe there was a problem?

Responding to the Problem

- Did you respond to the problem immediately?
- Did you investigate?
  - Did you talk to relevant people?
  - Did you research relevant company policy, the employee's disciplinary history in the company, and how others have been disciplined for similar infractions?
- Did you plan?
  - Did you think about what you were going to say and where you would meet?
  - Did you prepare yourself for the employee's responses?
- Did you work with the employee to create an action plan?

Follow Up

- Did you document?
- Did you check in with the employee?
  - Did you praise successes?
  - Did you offer further direction when needed?
  - Did you voice concern about continued problems?
- Did you complete any tasks that you agreed to in the action plan?

Skills Enhancement 1: Setting Expectations

Allow 90 minutes to two hours and gather your team in a room with a large writing area (whiteboard or paper posted on the walls). Designate a scribe who will capture everything the team comes up with (you may choose to use an outside facilitator for that task). Tell your team that you are leaving the room for 30 minutes, and during that time, they should write down every question that they can think of relating to you as a manager, such as:

- How do you prefer to communicate with your employees?
- What is your management style?
- When will we know we did a good job?
- When will we know we did a bad job?
- And so on.

You may choose to open up these questions to things your employees may want to know about you as a person—such as your favorite foods or colors or what you like to do with your free time.

After 30 minutes, re-enter the room. For the next hour or so, answer each of the questions posed by the group. If there are other important details that you want to communicate to everyone about your expectations, take the opportunity to build on the discussion and share that information.

Skills Enhancement 2: Opening Discussions

Let's take a moment to put together a few sample openings based on a few different scenarios. Take a moment to jot down how you would open the following discussions.

EXAMPLE 1: Terry needs to talk to Jill about continued errors in her reports. As the office administrative assistant, Jill is responsible for delivering accurate reports. Lately she has been forwarding reports without verifying that the sales numbers are accurate. How would you, as Terry, open the discussion with Jill?

EXAMPLE 2: Damon sends out a joke over the office intranet. While some people find the joke funny, it leaves others uneasy, as its central figures are Catholic priests. Tricia manages Damon and wants to talk to him about the boundaries of appropriate humor in the workplace. If you were Tricia, how would you open the conversation with Damon?

In the first example, Terry really needs to know the whole story. He can open the discussion in several ways. While Terry certainly knows the outcome—others in the company don't feel they can rely on the team's sales numbers–he does not know *why* Jill is making the mistakes. And while the reason for Jill's flawed reports won't change the company's need for accurate information, it may change the direction of Terry's discipline.

Based on the need to garner more information, here are a couple of potential opening lines Terry could use:

- Jill, I'd like to talk to you about inaccuracies we've been finding in the sales reports. Can you help me understand why this has been happening?
- Jill, when we don't provide accurate sales figures, others in the company feel that they can't rely on us. You've had inaccurate numbers on the reports a few times, and I'm concerned about the negative effect this is having on our team. Can you tell me how we might be able to address this together?

Skills Enhancement 2: Opening Discussions (cont'd)

In the second example above, Tricia has a difficult task. She must communicate to Damon that his joke wasn't appropriate. At the same time, she doesn't want Damon to think that a sense of humor is unappreciated. Here, the goal is not to understand what Damon was thinking, but to let him know that others might find it offensive. A few opening lines might be:

- Damon, I wanted to talk to you about the joke you sent out on the office intranet. The joke wasn't appropriate for the workplace, and some people expressed that it made them uncomfortable. When you think about the joke, do you see how that could have happened?
- Damon, I appreciate your good sense of humor, but the joke you sent wasn't appropriate. A joke that stereotypes different religious groups could really anger or offend some of your coworkers. That's one of the reasons company policy restricts use of the intranet to work-related communications—it's really not a tool to use for personal reasons. Do you understand?

Skills Enhancement 3: Choosing Tone of Voice

Consider the following examples and jot down the tone of voice that you would adopt if you were dealing with each issue:

EXAMPLE 1: Rick manages the receptionist in his law firm. She has done an exemplary job of being the "face of the firm." She is friendly and puts people at ease. Rick has noticed that she has been very down the last few days, not her normal welcoming self. He sees that she is treating people who come into the firm differently than she normally would. He decides to discuss it with her.

EXAMPLE 2: Carrie is the CFO of a major corporation. One day she is in the restroom and happens upon a woman curled in the corner of the bathroom, disheveled, sobbing, and with bruises on her wrists and arms. With some careful coaxing, Carrie learns that the woman has been physically assaulted by a coworker after she told him she would not date him any longer. Carrie comforts the woman, gets her medical help, enlists the aid of the legal and human resources departments in investigating the situation quickly and thoroughly, and is ready to sit down with the man in question.

EXAMPLE 3: Rosanne has worked with Maggie for nearly 10 years. She hired Maggie after having worked with her at two different companies. They see each other socially and their families are friendly. Lately, Maggie has been finishing projects late—an issue Rosanne has addressed with Maggie before. Maggie always replies, "Oh, you know me! I'm worth the wait!" Rosanne decides to meet with Maggie to talk about the problem.

How would you handle these situations? There is no "right" answer. The most important thing is to match your tone to the gravity of the situation. If Rick took a cold, authoritarian tone instead of a questioning tone, the receptionist might immediately feel defensive and clam up. Likewise, if Carrie were to sit down with the woman's alleged abuser and use a concerned or friendly tone instead of a stern one, it would send this

Skills Enhancement 3: Choosing Tone of Voice (cont'd)

man the message that the company does not crack down on violence in the workplace.

The example of Rosanne and Maggie is the trickiest. The women have a friendship that extends outside the office and a history of working together. Maggie is letting those lines blur as she gets coached by Rosanne and, thus, is not taking the problem seriously. It is up to Rosanne to assert her leadership position and convey to Maggie that the problem must be dealt with, despite their friendship. Her tone should be firm and professional to get this message across.

Skills Enhancement 4: Brainstorming an Action Plan

Use this exercise to brainstorm a plan of action with your employee.

Step 1: With the employee, write down the problem in objective terms.

Step 2: Write down how the problem is affecting others involved, such as the company, the team, and you, the manager.

Step 3: Spend five minutes talking with your employee about what an ideal solution would look like. Write down everything this ideal solution would have to accomplish. Try to open it up to all possibilities, even if they seem to go beyond your resources or budget.

Step 4: Take ten minutes to talk about what is necessary to go from where your employee is right now to the great solution outlined above. This may include attitude changes, skill enhancements, more time, help with prioritizing, and so on. Everything is fair game; you'll negotiate what is really possible later.

Step 5: Capture this list on paper. You'll need it to determine the agreed-upon plan.

While the potential solutions may turn out to be unreasonable or undoable, the basis of good collaboration is a willingness to consider anything. Now that you have worked with the employee to talk about possibilities, think about whether any of the potential solutions are practical for both the business and the employee. Consider these questions:

- Can your business afford the time and money necessary to make the plan work?
- Is the employee capable of achieving the plan?
- Are the results worth both the time and energy it will take?
- Does this really solve the problem to the satisfaction of those directly involved?

Once you have the answers to these questions, your list of realistic potential solutions will likely be much shorter. From this shorter list, you and the employee can decide which solutions work best. Be practical, and modify options if they can be made better or workable. You do not want to sponsor a plan that just won't or can't happen.

Build Your Skills: An Overview of Progressive Discipline

Questions

1. When dealing with an employee problem, progressive discipline requires you to follow these steps: coaching, verbal warning, written warning, and finally, termination. ☐ True   ☐ False

2. What is the main purpose of progressive discipline?

3. When disciplining an employee, you should listen to his or her side of the story, and then explain how to solve the problem.

    ☐ True   ☐ False

4. Caroline catches one of her employees, Norma, violating a company dress code. Which of these factors should she consider when deciding what level of discipline is appropriate?

    a. Norma works in the food service industry and wears open-toed shoes and shorts to work, which violates health codes.

    b. Norma has never been disciplined for her attire before.

    c. Both A and B.

    d. Neither A nor B.

5. Melissa and Alejandra are caught reading magazines and chatting on the job. Melissa has been disciplined for making personal phone calls during work time; Alejandra has no previous disciplinary history. Should their boss, Ida, impose the same discipline on each of them?

    a. Yes, because they were doing the same thing.

    b. Yes, because it isn't fair to take Melissa's previous disciplinary record into account, since it was for something different.

    c. No, because Melissa has a previous disciplinary history for a similar incident, but Alejandra doesn't.

    d. No, but only if Alejandra apologizes.

6. An at-will employee can be fired at any time, for any reason.

   ☐ True   ☐ False

7. You can create a legal contract without ever writing down an agreement or making a verbal promise.

   ☐ True   ☐ False

8. To motivate an employee with a performance problem, it's a good idea to tell the employee what disciplinary measure you'll impose next if the problem doesn't improve.

   ☐ True   ☐ False

9. What is a reasonable accommodation?

10. Dalton calls you on Monday morning to ask if he can take the morning off to wait for a contractor; his roof started leaking during a major storm over the weekend, and he needs to have it repaired right away. Although you don't have to allow him the extra time, you understand his situation and tell him that's fine. If Michael calls you to ask for the morning off because his car has broken down and he needs to get it to a mechanic and arrange alternate transportation, which of these reasons justify treating Michael differently?

    a. Dalton has worked for you for a long time, and you trust him, whereas Michael is a new employee.

    b. Michael just took twelve weeks off under the FMLA, and you want him to start catching up on the work that piled up while he was out.

    c. Michael had plenty of time to take his car to the mechanic while he was on FMLA leave.

    d. None of the above.

Answers

1. False. Although coaching, verbal warning, written warning, and termination are the typical steps in a progressive discipline policy, whether you follow this progressive pattern will depend on different factors, including your company's policy and the seriousness of the problem. For example, if an employee steals $10,000 from the company but has never been disciplined before, company policy or common sense should tell you to terminate employment, not to coach the employee.

2. The main purpose of progressive discipline is employee retention and improvement. That means you're constantly working to help your employee meet the job's requirements—not pushing that employee toward termination.

3. False. When you discipline an employee, you should make sure you know all the facts and listen to the employee's side of the story. Once you have done so, you should work *with* the employee to collaboratively find solutions together—not to tell the employee how to solve the problem.

4. C. You should determine the seriousness of a problem—and thus what level of discipline is appropriate—by considering the problem's effect, the severity of the behavior, the employee's disciplinary history, and the legality of the behavior. Here, Norma's behavior violates health codes—a legal factor Caroline will definitely want to take into account. However, she'll also want to consider the fact that Norma's never been disciplined for this behavior before—maybe she doesn't know the rule, or maybe correcting it now can prevent it from occurring again.

5. C. While it is important to administer consistent discipline for similar problems, you should also take into account the employee's unique situation when talking with the employee about the problem. Here, Melissa has already been disciplined for making personal phone calls during work time—which means she's already been caught chatting on the job. In this case, it's fair to take that into account and to impose different discipline on the two women as a result.

6. False. An at-will employee can be fired at any time, for any reason *that isn't illegal.* For example, it is illegal to fire an at-will employee because

he or she is a certain race, has complained to a government agency about illegal behavior, or has taken a legally protected leave of absence.

7. True. Sometimes, contracts can be *implied* by statements or actions. For example, a statement like "If you complete the improvement plan, you'll become a permanent employee" could be interpreted to mean that you are promising permanent employment as long as the improvement plan is carried out. This could limit your right to fire the employee if he or she has other performance problems not addressed in the improvement plan, for example.

8. False. Telling the employee what the next step is could obligate you to provide that step, even if you later decide that a more serious action should be imposed. To maximize flexibility, focus on the immediate problem and solution—not on what might happen down the line.

9. Reasonable accommodations include assistance or changes to the job or workplace that will enable an employee with a disability to do the job. If you know an employee is disabled, your company has a legal duty to provide that employee with a reasonable accommodation to accomplish his or her job duties, so long as that won't create an undue hardship for the business (for instance, because it's so expensive that it would make it difficult for the company to keep operating).

10. D. While it's perfectly acceptable to offer extra time off when it's not legally required, if you do so, you have to be prepared to offer it on an issue-by-issue basis, not an employee-by-employee basis. Here, if you're going to allow Dalton to take time off to take care of an urgent personal matter, you should allow Michael the same. And you can't penalize Michael for taking legally protected FMLA leave.

Build Your Skills: Is It Time for Discipline?

Questions

1. What are the three types of employee problems?

2. When an employee has a problem in one area that causes problems in another area, you must discipline that employee twice.

   ☐ True   ☐ False

3. Which of these will help you define your expectations of employee performance?

   a. The job description.

   b. Individual performance goals.

   c. Both A and B.

   d. Neither A nor B.

4. Esther tells Fred that she needs a report "on her desk" by Friday. On Friday at 6:30 p.m., Fred puts the report in her "in" basket. Esther is already gone for the day, and she's flying to a regional office on Monday morning—she needs the report for that trip. Since Fred didn't bring it to her until Friday evening, and he didn't email it to her, she wants to discipline him. Is discipline justified?

   a. Yes, because Fred should have known that "by Friday" meant by the close of business—5 p.m.—on Friday.

   b. Yes, because Fred should have emailed her the report.

   c. No, but only if Esther's usual practice was to receive hard copies instead of email.

   d. No, because there was no way Fred could have known that Esther expected him to email the report, if she never told him.

5. When an employee's behavior changes in a negative way, it could mean that a discipline problem is developing.

   ☐ True   ☐ False

6. It isn't fair to discipline an employee for an inappropriate action or behavior if company policy didn't prohibit it—after all, the employee had no way of knowing the behavior wasn't allowed.

☐ True ☐ False

7. In which of these situations is it probably appropriate to first coach an employee, before moving to a more serious form of discipline?

a. The employee makes some small calculation errors on a department efficiency analysis report, which goes to the department manager, the employee's boss.

b. The employee fails to show up to work or call in sick for two days in a row.

c. The employee plays a practical joke on a coworker, yanking the chair out from under her when she's about to sit down for a meeting. The coworker falls to the ground, injuring herself.

d. None of the above.

8. You should always give employees a second chance before terminating employment.

☐ True ☐ False

9. You should terminate the employment of anyone using drugs or alcohol at work.

☐ True ☐ False

10. If an employee repeats the same mistake over and over, progressive discipline requires you to escalate your response.

☐ True ☐ False

Answers

1. The three types of employee problems are performance problems, attendance problems, and misconduct.

2. False. Whether an employee needs to be disciplined for one or both problems depends on the facts of the specific situation. Usually, if you identify and fix the underlying problem, both problems will be solved. In the example in Chapter 4, Kristen spent too much time on the Internet in violation of company policy (misconduct), which meant she had a hard time getting her job done (poor performance). However, it's possible that just by disciplining her for using the Internet, her manager also solved her performance problem, because she'll now have more time to do her work.

3. C. A job's objective requirements, and individual performance goals, will help you define performance expectations. The job requirements will tell you what any person holding the position is expected to accomplish. Performance goals are just as important, however—they tell you what specific goals will nurture the employee's strengths, work on weaknesses, and build skills.

4. D. Managers commonly believe that some expectations are so obvious that they don't need to be verbalized—and then they're disappointed when employees don't meet those expectations. Here, Esther expected Fred to get her the report by the close of business Friday or to email it to her. Unless she told Fred either of these things, though, it isn't really fair to discipline him. After all, he did get the report to her by Friday—he even stayed late to do it. Esther needs to be clearer about her expectations, so Fred will have the opportunity to meet them.

5. True. When an employee exhibits a negative behavioral change, you'll want to explore why. It could mean that the employee is having a work-related problem that requires your intervention, or it could mean that the employee is having personal problems that won't affect his or her work or performance. Either way, getting involved shows the employee you care and gives you the opportunity to identify and perhaps prevent a developing problem.

6. False. Although company policies give employees guidelines for acceptable behavior, they're not the only source. Some behavior

that isn't specifically prohibited by company guidelines also justifies discipline—for example, when an employee violates the law or doesn't follow explicit instructions you've given.

7. A. Many employee performance problems can be overcome with coaching. Often coaching provides the opportunity to further educate an employee or find additional resources to help the employee get the job done. In this case, the employee's errors didn't cause too much trouble, because her boss caught them. The boss can use this opportunity to coach the employee and figure out whether additional resources are needed.

8. False. Some behavior is so egregious that it justifies immediate termination—for example, when an employee's acts endanger or damage others or the employee's misconduct involves dishonesty.

9. False. Although you can prohibit employees from drinking alcohol or using illegal drugs at work and can discipline employees for violating those rules, you must be careful when dealing with legal drugs. That's because your duty to provide reasonable accommodation to an employee with a disability may include accommodating the employee's use of drugs to accommodate the disability.

10. False. Sometimes, employees repeat the same behavior because they don't understand what you expect or why. Before escalating discipline, consider whether the rule, and its rationale, were clearly laid out for the employee.

Build Your Skills: Smart Discipline Skills

Questions

1. If you feel awkward about disciplining an employee, you should:

    a. Ask human resources to deliver the message—they have a lot of experience and will be able to communicate more clearly, anyway.

    b. Accept that it's part of the process. Discipline is awkward, but it's a necessary part of your job.

    c. Just get it over with. Sit down with the employee, say what you need to, and get out.

    d. Talk to other managers about it. Your colleagues have probably dealt with the same thing themselves.

2. Even though workplace gossip about disciplinary issues is inappropriate and wastes time, there isn't really anything you can do to prevent it.

    ☐ True   ☐ False

3. Chelsea, the manager of a clothing store, needs to discipline Evan, a supervisor, for repeatedly forgetting to lock the door to the supervisor's office at the end of his shift. Which of these is the best way to begin the conversation?

    a. "Evan, you keep leaving the door to the supervisor's office unlocked. This has got to stop immediately."

    b. "Hey, Evan! How are things going on the night shift?"

    c. "Evan, you could really get us into trouble by leaving the door to the supervisor's office unlocked. Why do you keep doing that?"

    d. "Evan, I noticed twice last week that the supervisor's office wasn't locked when I came in the morning after your shift. Can you explain why?"

4. Sy, a secretary in a college admissions office, is being disciplined for sending out letters with numerous typos to prospective students. She explains to her supervisor, Dalia, that she is making the errors because she has too many other competing tasks, and she doesn't feel like she has time to proofread the letters carefully. Which of these is the best response?

   a. "Unfortunately, Sy, that is just part of your job. You need to figure out how to get this done. Do you have any suggestions for how you can accomplish that?"

   b. "Sounds like you're feeling overwhelmed. What I hear you saying is that you don't feel you have adequate time to proofread these thoroughly. Is that right?"

   c. "I'm sorry, Sy, but I just don't agree with you. I really think you need to try and get these done, error free. What will it take?"

   d. "So what you're saying is, you're really busy so you think someone else should proofread the letters before they go out?"

5. When you deliver discipline, you should give an employee as many examples of a problem as possible.   ☐ True   ☐ False

6. When you're disciplining an employee who becomes angry, you should:

   a. Let the employee know who's in control. Anger isn't appropriate in the workplace—you need to communicate this message strongly, which may mean raising your voice if the employee's voice is raised or telling the employee it's time to walk away if he or she isn't capable of talking about things calmly.

   b. Let the employee know that his or her feelings shouldn't enter the discipline process. There's no need to get angry—it won't get you anywhere.

   c. Encourage the employee to take a break until he or she is ready to talk about it again.

   d. Try to slow the meeting down. Acknowledge the anger but tell the employee that he or she needs to calm down before you can proceed.

7. Boris needs to discipline Monica for making inappropriate and demeaning comments to a coworker, Linda. When he confronts her with the problem, Monica replies, "It wasn't me! I never said anything to Linda!" Which of these is the best response?

   a. "I know you did it, Monica. Linda told me about it, and Cory verified that it was true."

   b. "Well, I know that Linda has a tendency to exaggerate. Let me look into it."

    c. "Monica, did you tell Linda at the register last Friday, 'It doesn't take a rocket scientist' when she asked you how to change the receipt tape?"

    d. "No one's blaming you, Monica. Just tell me the truth."

8. When an employee commits misconduct that appears to be illegal, and you decide to terminate employment based on that misconduct, you should say that the employee broke the law in your termination memo.

☐ True   ☐ False

9. You should require your employee to sign your documentation, agreeing with its contents and your decision.   ☐ True   ☐ False

10. Victoria hears from four different employees that another employee, Deborah, is constantly on the phone, making personal calls to her family, who lives in London. She checks the phone records and finds that it's true, and that it's at a cost of almost $1,000. Whom should Victoria talk to about this first?

    a. Deborah.

    b. All four coworkers.

    c. Human resources.

    d. Her boss.

Answers

1. B. Sometimes it's uncomfortable or difficult to tell an employee that his or her behavior or performance isn't measuring up. If you accept that it's just part of the process, you can prepare yourself to deal with that reality. While you may want to talk about the problem with others, you should limit that to appropriate individuals like your manager, legal counsel, or human resources department—who can counsel you on how to deliver the disciplinary message. Ultimately, it's up to you—and you shouldn't deny it, even though it's awkward. Otherwise, you might have a hard time finding a collaborative solution with the employee.

2. False. Although there's nothing you can do to prohibit gossip altogether, you can limit it by involving only the appropriate people in the discipline process, keeping your employees focused on their own work, and refusing to engage in it yourself.

3. D. When you meet with an employee to administer discipline, it's a good idea to have your opening sentences prepared. In this example, Chelsea should make sure she has all the facts before telling Evan what to do. In Answer D, Chelsea makes sure she has the facts straight, but she's also focused on the problem. If she begins the conversation too informally, Evan might be confused about the purpose of the meeting. On the other hand, if she is too accusatory, Evan might shut down at the very beginning.

4. B. When you get an employee's perspective on a discipline problem, it's important to show that you're really listening and hearing what the employee is saying. You can do that by playing back what you are hearing and listening empathically. That means paraphrasing what you heard, without judgmental edits, and putting yourself in the employee's shoes. In Answer B, Dalia summarized Sy's words, which let Sy know she was really paying attention—without passing judgment. After listening this way, Dalia can engage Sy in a discussion about what to do about it.

5. False. While it's important to give the employee examples of the problem performance or behavior, it isn't necessary to have an exhaustive list. In fact, it could do more harm than good—if your examples are second-, third-, or fourthhand, or inaccurate, the employee may be so focused on the example that he or she isn't thinking about the problem and how to solve it.

6. D. If an employee is angry, you may be able to slow the meeting down. If that doesn't work, you might need to take a break—but make sure the employee understands it can't be indefinite. Choose a time to re-engage, preferably within the next day or so. You don't want so much time to pass that the employee's anger has time to fester or that you forget the important facts that led you to discipline in the first place.

7. C. In this case, Boris will be best served by going through examples of Monica's problem behavior with her. He shouldn't deny the truth of Linda's allegations or suggest that they're made up. But asking Monica to verify whether specific statements are true shows her that he's prepared and looked into the matter. She'll have a harder time dodging the questions when they're this focused.

8. False. Although you should document the facts that led you to make a discipline decision, and you should also explain what company policy it violates, you shouldn't draw legal conclusions. After all, you don't want those conclusions to be used against you—that is, you don't want to be sued for the employee's behavior and have a record of admitting that the behavior broke the law.

9. False. It's a good idea to ask the disciplined employee to sign formal documentation, but the signature need only acknowledge receipt. Requiring an employee to agree with your description can hamper the disciplinary process if the employee thinks you're being coercive; if the employee doesn't want to sign, you can just notate on the form that he or she was asked to but elected not to. Also, if you leave a blank space on the form for the employee to comment, he or she can include information you didn't record. This gives the employee the opportunity to participate in the documentation process, and it also protects you: If the employee elects not to do this but then later says your documentation was inaccurate, he or she will be hard-pressed to explain why that section of the form is blank.

10. D. Although Victoria will probably eventually discuss this with human resources and with Deborah, she should probably first discuss it with her boss. This could have significant financial impact on the company, or it could mean that she is going to have to deliver some fairly serious discipline. In either case, Victoria doesn't want her boss blindsided by hearing about the problem when the discipline is already well underway,

or when human resources brings it to the boss's attention. Note that in this case, Victoria doesn't need to discuss it with the four employees who reported it: She was able to verify it independently through phone records, and she can maintain confidentiality and limit gossip by keeping it private.

Build Your Skills: The Disciplinary Steps

Questions

1. What are the three types of coaching?

2. Which of these is a common reaction to coaching?

   a. Surprise

   b. Anger

   c. Denial

   d. Blame

3. Verbal warnings don't require formal documentation—after all, they're just oral reminders to shape up.　☐ True　☐ False

4. Which of these situations probably calls for a verbal warning?

   a. For the first time, Sarah, a long time budget analyst, shows up to work fifteen minutes late.

   b. Imran, a new transfer to the mail room, violates a company policy that prohibits wearing ear plugs or headphones while operating a mail sorting machine; he'd never read the policy, though it was given to him.

   c. Pamela, a new clerk, sends the entire department's time sheets to payroll a few hours late because she misread the policy and thought they were due on the 15th, when actually that's the date checks are issued.

   d. Greg, a veteran supervisor, tells one of his employees, Jim, all the details of the investigation into a coworker's harassment suit.

5. Even though it may be uncomfortable, when you give a verbal warning, you should tell the employee explicitly that you are doing so.

   ☐ True　☐ False

6. When you decide to issue a written warning, how should you deliver it?

    a. Carry it to the meeting you have with the employee. Give it to the employee at the start of the meeting.

    b. Have a discussion with the employee about it, then draft the warning and place it in the employee's personnel file.

    c. Carry it to the meeting you have with the employee. Give it to the employee at the end of the meeting.

    d. Meet with the employee, then draft the written warning, send it to the employee for acknowledgment, and place it in the employee's file.

7. Because employee discipline is a serious matter, it should be delivered in a serious setting. Whenever possible, you should meet with the employee in your office. ☐ True ☐ False

8. Which of these steps will help you prepare for a written warning?

    a. Consult with your boss, human resources, or your legal department to get input on how similar problems have been handled in the past.

    b. Review the employee's previous disciplinary history.

    c. Think about why the previous action plan, if there was one, didn't work.

    d. All of the above.

9. In which situation might it be appropriate for you to bring a witness to a discipline meeting?

    a. You're in an informal coaching session, and you want to make the employee feel more at ease, so you grab lunch with the employee and a human resources representative the employee is friendly with.

    b. You are issuing a written warning, and it seems the employee is really resisting your guidance—in fact, the employee hasn't done anything to follow the action plan you two have outlined together.

    c. You don't feel comfortable issuing the discipline; even though company policy calls for it, the employee is your friend. You'd rather bring your boss along to deliver the tough message.

    d. You're issuing a verbal warning to an employee for an attendance policy violation. The employee was late three times in two weeks;

you've dealt with the same issue many times before and have even coached this employee about it.

10. What is the purpose of a written warning?

a. To make sure you communicate very clearly—on paper—what the problem is, so that the employee understands it and you have a written record of it.

b. To make sure that the employee is given a fair opportunity to improve performance or behavior.

c. To make sure you treat employees consistently, issuing similar discipline for similar problems.

d. All of the above.

Answers

1. The three types of coaching are simple requests, corrective actions, and coaching sessions. You make simple requests when a method of doing something hasn't been successful, and you ask the employee to try something new or different. Corrective actions are a little more serious; they occur when you tell an employee how something must be done or done differently. You can deal with more complex problems with coaching sessions—opportunities to sit down with employees to discuss problems and find solutions together, before things get worse.

2. A. Because coaching is the first step in the disciplinary process, employees are often surprised by it. Sometimes you may need to allow the employee a little time to deal with that reaction. The more serious reactions—anger, denial, and blame—typically happen later in the process, when discipline becomes more serious.

3. False. Verbal warnings are the first formal entry into the discipline process, when the employee is made aware that discipline is happening. They need to be formally documented so that the manager will have a record of what's happened in the event that further discipline—or even termination—becomes necessary.

4. B. In this case, Imran inadvertently violated a company rule that was implemented for his own safety. Imran should have read the policy, but his failure to follow it here appears inadvertent, so a verbal warning is probably appropriate. Answers A and C probably call for coaching— the employees there have correctable problems that don't appear extremely serious. And in Answer D, Greg is creating serious problems for the company, not to mention acting extremely inappropriately and insensitively, by revealing this information. More serious discipline is probably necessary.

5. True. Even though it might be uncomfortable, when you issue a verbal warning, you should state explicitly that that's what you're doing. That way, the employee is on notice that he or she has entered the formal disciplinary system and won't be surprised to come across the documentation later.

6. D. The best way to make sure you fully capture all the facts is to meet with the employee, draft the documentation, and then ask the employee

to acknowledge that he or she received it (often in a separate, brief meeting). This ensures you hear the whole story, and that the whole story is accurately captured in the documentation, before the warning is issued.

7. False. The appropriate setting for a disciplinary discussion will vary based on the type of discipline being administered. For example, if you're going to coach an employee, it might be more comfortable to do so in an informal setting. If you and the employee need to brainstorm possible action plans, it might be appropriate to work in a neutral space, like a conference room, with a whiteboard.

8. D. In this case, all these steps will help you get ready to deliver a written warning. Talking to an appropriate third party will help you gain perspective—but make sure it's someone whom you should be talking to about the issue, not peer or subordinate. Likewise, if you review the employee's disciplinary history, don't give undue weight to things that happened in the distant past. And finally, as you think about the former action plan and why it didn't work, think about your responsibility for that, too—not just the employee's.

9. B. When an employee resists your guidance, it may mean that you need the help or intervention of a third party. You probably wouldn't want a third party involved in an informal coaching session (Answer A), especially if it could keep the employee from understanding the purpose of the discussion: to improve behavior. And while you should definitely talk to your boss if you don't feel comfortable issuing discipline (Answer C), you can cause confusion for the employee—and appear weak or unsure of yourself—if you ask the boss to issue the discipline directly. Finally, if you're carefully following a clear company policy, and you've dealt with the issue before, you probably won't need outside assistance (Answer D).

10. D. All of the answers are benefits that result from a fair, consistent discipline system. Answer B speaks to what is probably the most basic reason to use it: You want the employee to succeed. At the same time, you will be communicating clearly to the employee, and you'll have a written record in case you have to impose further discipline or terminate employment (Answer A). You'll also be imposing consistent discipline (Answer C).

Build Your Skills: If Discipline Fails

Questions

1. Termination of employment is usually not a manager's favorite task. What's something important about a well-run process that you should remember as you prepare yourself to give the bad news?

2. When an employee is accused of serious misconduct, and you need to investigate, it's a good idea to put the employee on an unpaid leave.

   ☐ True   ☐ False

3. On what day or at what time of day should you terminate employment?

   a. It depends on the situation and your workplace.

   b. At the beginning of the workweek.

   c. On Friday, after everyone has gone home.

   d. As soon as you're able to wrap up the employee's final projects.

4. Employees are often angry about being fired. To be safe, whenever you decide to terminate employment, you should have an employee's passwords and access codes turned off during the termination meeting.

   ☐ True   ☐ False

5. Nora is getting ready to fire Stuart for serious misconduct—he has given away several thousand dollars' worth of the company's products to friends and family for free, in violation of company policy. Which of these reasons should cause Nora to reconsider that decision?

   a. Stuart's file shows he has always been an exemplary performer; this is his first discipline problem.

   b. Stuart tells Nora when they meet that he did not know this was prohibited and thought it was "not a big deal."

   c. At the termination meeting, Stuart tells Nora that he was sexually harassed by a coworker.

   d. The prior week, Stuart complained to the human resources department that he was sexually harassed by a coworker.

6. When you have to fire an employee, what are some of the benefits of conducting a post mortem?

7. Which of these factors indicate that you could have done more to prevent a discipline problem?

   a. You didn't meet regularly with your employees.

   b. You didn't speak up as soon as you saw a problem.

   c. You didn't create an action plan with the employee.

   d. You didn't document.

8. When an employee is terminated, it's best not to say anything to coworkers—after all, you want to respect that person's privacy.

   ☐ True   ☐ False

9. What is the most important method for getting beyond a termination, as a team?

   a. Spend some time together talking about the termination and how everyone feels about it.

   b. Focus your team on the work that needs to be done by setting and meeting identified targets.

   c. Get away from the office for a team-building exercise or break.

   d. Meet regularly with your team members to reinforce the rules or expectations that the terminated employee failed to meet.

10. Chrissy had to terminate Lloyd's employment. She crafts this statement: "Lloyd is no longer with the company. From now on, when you have questions about the Stow-rite line of products, please contact Evelyn." To whom should Chrissy deliver such a message?

    a. Holly, her boss.

    b. The whole company.

    c. The customer service team who usually calls Lloyd when they need help with customer inquires about Stow-rite products.

    d. Sidney and Leny, who Chrissy knows usually eat lunch with Lloyd.

Answers

1. Remember: If you followed the strategies explained in this book, you've given the employee every opportunity to improve. The employee either wasn't capable of improvement or chose not to take advantage of those opportunities. Either way, the employee isn't willing or able to do what the job requires.

2. False. Whether called "leave" or "suspension," it's a bad idea to put an employee on an involuntary, unpaid break while you conduct an investigation into that person's conduct. While a paid suspension may be necessary—so that you can gather information without the employee's presence and make sure you know the facts—when the suspension is unpaid, it looks like you're penalizing the employee and might send the message that you've already made up your mind about the truth of the allegations. Moreover, if you suspend an exempt employee, you could run into legal wage and hour problems.

3. A. It's best to let the workplace guide your decision. However, if you fear violence or sabotage from an employee, you should terminate employment at the end of the workweek or workday and get the employee out the door as soon as you can.

4. False. Although you may wish to disable passwords, access codes, and the like if you fear violence, sabotage, or theft of company secrets, it isn't necessary in every case. In many instances, the employee will feel grief, disappointment, frustration, or humiliation—and there's no need to compound that by also making the employee feel like you don't trust him or her.

5. D. In this instance, firing Stuart after he complained of illegal activity could look like retaliation. Nora will want to talk to her human resources department or legal counsel to first make sure that the firing is beyond reproach. Here, it doesn't matter that Stuart had a great performance record (Answer A), because his problem is serious misconduct that justifies immediate termination. It's also fair to terminate Stuart for stealing the company's products even though he didn't know it violated company policy—whether because he *should* have read it because it was accessible to him, or because common sense should tell him that it's not okay to take things without paying for them (Answer B). Finally, although Nora should sit up and take notice of Stuart's claim that he was

sexually harassed (Answer C), if she'd already made and communicated the decision to terminate employment, Stuart will have a hard time arguing that her decision was made *because* of his claim.

6. The post mortem gives you an opportunity to separate your emotions from actual events so that you can figure out whether there is anything you could have done differently or better. It allows you to reflect on what preventative steps could have been taken and what you could have changed to get a different result.

7. A. While all these factors indicate steps you might have taken to help the discipline process succeed, most involve actions you could have taken *after* you knew there was a problem. However, if you'd been meeting with your employees regularly, you might have been turned on to discipline problems early on—either because the employees themselves would have told you about their problems, or because being in touch with your team would have clued you in to areas of weakness.

8. False. While you should respect the terminated employee's privacy, you will probably want to acknowledge that the employee isn't with the company any longer. After all, the termination process is a big transition point for your employees, and they may be feeling nervous or confused. It's a good idea to let them know that the employee is gone—but be tight-lipped about the details.

9. B. The best method to move beyond the termination is to get your employees focused on the work that needs to be done. This provides the opportunity for everyone to think about something other than the termination and to set and meet their own targets. Doing this sets your employees up for the opportunity to succeed—something they may badly need. Don't forget to praise them when they accomplish their goals.

10. C. In this case, Chrissy needs to tell those who used to work with Lloyd that he is no longer with the company—but that doesn't mean she needs to go into great detail. Instead, she just needs to let them know how it will affect their jobs. So here, it's probably enough to just tell them that they can now direct their calls to Evelyn.

Progressive Discipline Basics:
Smart Summary

○ If your company has a discipline policy, you should follow it. The techniques in this book, including planning, communication, collaboration, documentation, and follow up, can be used in conjunction with that policy. When in doubt about what to do, what your company policy requires, or whether the policy creates legal risks for the company, you should talk to your manager, human resources department, or legal counsel.

○ A carefully written discipline policy notifies employees that they'll be disciplined for violating company policy, gives managers guidance about how to apply company policy, tells employees that they'll have fair opportunity to improve the problem performance or behavior, and reserves the right to deviate from the policy when appropriate and to terminate employment at will.

○ When faced with a problem requiring discipline, you'll have to gather information, assess the severity, decide how to respond, meet with the employee, document, and follow up.

○ Discipline should be proportionate to the seriousness of the problem, considering things like the effect of the behavior, the frequency of the behavior, the employee's disciplinary history, and the legality of the employee's conduct.

Principles of Effective Progressive Discipline: Smart Summary

- The number one goal of progressive discipline is retention—not termination. That means working collaboratively with your employees to solve problems, not mechanically going through the progressive discipline steps until you terminate employment.

- Imposing proportionate discipline communicates to the employee how serious the problem is; it also tells other employees what the company expects.

- Listening to your employees is a fundamental part of the progressive discipline process. If you do all the talking, you won't understand the basis of the employee's thoughts or actions, and you'll have a hard time addressing the problem with a relevant solution.

- Today's workers expect to be treated as individuals with unique and valuable contributions to make. That's why, in the progressive discipline process, it's important to enlist the employee's help in crafting a solution.

- Progressive discipline gives you the flexibility to develop solutions relevant to individual employees and their working styles. However, at the same time, it's important to administer discipline consistently—to impose similar discipline for similar problems.

Avoiding Legal Trouble: Smart Summary

- You can terminate the employment of an at-will employee at any time, for any reason that isn't illegal. Don't undermine at-will employment or lock your company into a specific course of action by threatening or promising an employee certain steps in the discipline process.

- When you discipline, find out how others in the company have handled similar issues in the past. This helps you apply discipline consistently and objectively.

- If you grant leave to employees when it's not required by law, you must do it consistently among employees to avoid looking like you're "playing favorites" or worse, discriminating.

- Dangerous situations can create serious liability for the company, especially if not handled immediately. When an employee does something dangerous, act quickly to put a stop to it.

- Don't promise employees confidentiality, but maintain it when possible. Show your employees you respect their privacy and avoid defamation claims.

- Documenting your discipline decisions serves many purposes. It creates a written record of why you imposed discipline, the employee's response, and the plan of action you and the employee decide on. This may be very important if you ever have to justify your actions in a lawsuit.

Identifying Potential Problems:
Smart Summary

- There are three broad categories of employee problems: performance problems, attendance problems, and misconduct. Sometimes, an employee will have trouble in one of these areas, and it will affect another. In those instances, make sure your discipline addresses the root of the problem.

- If your employees don't know what your expectations are, they're likely to disappoint you. Take the time to define your expectations of performance and behavior, giving your employees full opportunity to grow and succeed.

- Communicating regularly and openly with your employees keeps you up to speed on how they're doing and gives you advance warning of possible problems. At the same time, it gives employees a sense of ownership and investment in their jobs, motivating them to succeed.

- To help spot employee problems, look for signs of trouble like declining performance, changed behavior, and tension between team members.

Deciding What Action to Take:
Smart Summary

- Before deciding to discipline, make sure the employee knew the rule that was violated, actually violated the rule without good reason to do so, and isn't protected by law from complying with the rule.

- When deciding what level of discipline is appropriate, remember that the discipline should be proportionate to the problem. Consider the effect of the problem, the frequency of the problem, the employee's disciplinary history, and the legality of the behavior.

- In most instances, when an employee first suffers from poor performance, you can begin the discipline process at the very beginning: by coaching the employee.

- Some behavior is so serious that immediate termination of employment should be considered. Typically, this is true when an employee engages in seriously inappropriate misconduct, such as violence, stalking, dishonesty, use of illegal drugs at work, or harassment.

Why Discipline Is Hard: Smart Summary

● Accept that discipline might feel awkward, for both you and the employee. Plan to acknowledge and deal with this discomfort.

● Your job isn't to be liked by all your employees—your job is to ensure your team members' success, and that may mean you have to impose consistent and fair discipline at times. Don't allow your desire or need to be liked to affect your disciplinary decisions.

● Know that employees who don't know the whole story may think you're not being fair when you decide to discipline someone. If you have all the facts, evaluate the problem thoroughly, and apply discipline consistently, you know you're being fair—even if your employees don't.

● The only way to know with certainty how an employee will react to discipline is to actually do it and experience the reaction. Prepare yourself for different possibilities, but don't delay discipline because you're dreading the reaction.

● Even though it's uncomfortable to discipline, doing so sets expectations for your team. This will motivate employees to try and meet your expectations and help limit future problems.

Smart Talk:
Smart Summary

○ Before you meet with your employee, prepare for the discussion. Examine the issue from all perspectives, jot down your opening sentences, and don't assume you know the whole story. Be ready for a variety of emotional responses.

○ Remember that you're there to improve the employee's workplace performance or behavior. Set the tone for the meeting by choosing an appropriate environment and using a tone of voice that conveys the gravity of the situation.

○ When it's time to hear the employee's perspective, make sure you're not distracted, and focus on what the employee says—and feels. Give your employee time to process, too, even if it means awkward silences.

○ Give the employee the opportunity to share new, relevant information— but don't doubt what you know. Don't allow the employee to blame others if the blame is misplaced.

○ Don't walk away from a discipline discussion without an action plan. And remember—while you can provide encouragement, resources, and support, it's ultimately your employee's responsibility to solve the problem.

Smart Ways to Deal With Employee Responses: Smart Summary

- When an employee responds angrily to discipline, be prepared to slow the conversation down and walk away temporarily if needed. However, make sure that the employee understands that mutual respect is required—and if the employee acts violently or you fear violence, get help right away.

- A grieving employee is usually very invested in his or her job. With time, that grief can often be overcome. Don't allow yourself to be manipulated by it, though—that won't help you solve your problem.

- An anxious employee often simply can't hear what's being said: He or she is too concerned about what it means for the future. Do your best to focus the employee on the here and now—especially if the problem can be corrected.

- When an employee exhibits a masking reaction, there is usually a lot more going on internally. See if you can draw the employee out—but keep the discussion focused on the underlying problem, not the employee's response.

Smart Documentation: Smart Summary

● **Documenting discipline has many benefits.** It ensures that you and the employee are on the same page, helps you and the company track discipline problems, helps maintain consistency, and provides proof of what you did and why.

● **The documentation you create should be understandable to anyone who reads it.** You must be clear, thorough, and factual. Be sure to include all relevant information, including dates, full names, prior incidents, and an action plan.

● **Stick to the facts.** When documenting, don't interpret the meaning of an employee's actions or words—just record those actions or words. If your documentation is based on fact, it will be hard for the employee to refute what you say.

● **Unless company policy requires otherwise, keep informal documentation in a separate file (such as a tickler log), and use it to remind yourself to follow up with employees.** If the documentation is formal and going into the employee's file, give the employee the opportunity to make comments.

● **Don't overdocument.** That means you shouldn't include information that isn't directly related to the incident you're describing. If you write down too many details, you may have a harder time distinguishing the important facts, which may be important later if you have to discuss the decision to discipline with the employee, your manager, your human resources department, or a lawyer.

Smart Collaboration:
Smart Summary

○ Involve your manager in the discipline process when the problem has a significant effect on the business, you need an alternate perspective, or company policy or practice requires it.

○ Human resources is a partner in the discipline process. Because they're usually trained and experienced, they can help you apply and navigate complex company policies and practices, advise you through the process, or partner with you in your discipline meetings.

○ You should work with legal counsel when the discipline process raises possible legal problems—for instance, because the employee denies misconduct resulting in discipline, has an employment contract, hires an attorney, or takes a leave that may be legally protected.

○ When you include other employees in the discipline process, be careful to involve only those who need to know and to share only the information necessary. Keep things as confidential as you can—it shows respect for the employee, reduces gossip in the workplace, and limits legal liability.

Coaching:
Smart Summary

○ When you're dealing with a problem for the first time, and the problem isn't very serious, try coaching before going to more serious disciplinary measures. Because coaching is less formal, problems can often be corrected early, and employees are less threatened by the process.

○ Coaching can occur three different ways: through simple requests to change straightforward problem actions or behaviors, through corrective actions intended to have immediate effect, or through coaching sessions when problems are more serious or complex.

○ If coaching isn't working, don't immediately assume it can't. It may be that your message wasn't clear to the employee, especially if you used one of the more informal coaching techniques to address the problem.

○ Even though coaching is informal, it still requires documentation. You may need it to remind yourself to check in with the employee later or may need to refer to your documentation when you impose more serious discipline if coaching doesn't work.

Verbal Warnings:
Smart Summary

○ A verbal warning is the first "formal" step in the disciplinary process, meaning the employee is officially notified of the discipline, it is documented, and the company is involved.

○ A verbal warning is appropriate when an employee hasn't responded to previous coaching efforts, an employee has violated a company rule inadvertently or unknowingly, or an employee's performance or behavior has caused problems for the company but the employee seems unaware of the issue and genuinely interested in improvement.

○ A verbal warning is more formal than a coaching session. Take more time to prepare what you will say—including a review of any previous discussions on topic—and allow at least a half hour for the discussion. The discussion should take place in a more formal setting that gives the employee privacy and communicates to the employee that the problem is serious.

○ When you meet with an employee to issue a verbal warning, state the problem, review past efforts to correct it, make sure the employee acknowledges the problem, listen to the employee's explanation, tell the employee you are issuing a verbal warning, develop a solution, and discuss next steps.

○ Although a verbal warning is given orally, it must be followed up by documentation that acknowledges the discipline, the reason for it, whether there were any prior incidents, and the action plan. The employee should be given a copy of the documentation and asked to sign it, acknowledging receipt.

Written Warnings:
Smart Summary

○ Written warnings are difficult because employees usually recognize them as a serious disciplinary measure and may become defensive or emotional. Additionally, if you've dealt with the same issue with the employee before, you might also be frustrated or angry. Control these emotions by preparing thoroughly and focusing the discussion on the problem and how to improve it.

○ A written warning is usually the right response when an employee hasn't improved a problem after coaching and a verbal warning, the employee has flagrantly violated the company's attendance rules, or the employee has committed serious misconduct that does not warrant immediate termination.

○ When you give a written warning, focus on creating a very detailed, thorough, and clear action plan—particularly if you've already coached or given a verbal warning. If the employee needs more involvement or direction from you to succeed, provide it.

○ You should write the written warning after you've had a chance to meet with the employee and get his or her input or perspective. Complete the documentation right after the meeting, when it's still fresh in your mind. You might want to schedule another brief meeting to go over the written document with the employee.

Termination:
Smart Summary

⦿ Termination is a serious step: It indicates that the progressive discipline process hasn't worked. For that reason, you should carefully review the facts, the employee's personnel file, company policies, past statements made to the employee, how other employees have been treated, and the timing before making the decision. You might also want to get a second opinion from an appropriate person like your manager, human resources, or your legal counsel.

⦿ When you prepare to meet with the employee, have administrative issues—like the final paycheck, continued insurance benefits, severance pay, the return of company property, references, and a contact person—sorted out. This will save you and the employee potential embarrassment and discomfort.

⦿ Your goal when documenting termination is different from your goals when documenting discipline: You simply want to make a written record of what happened, so you can defend it later if necessary. Note former disciplineand also what specific policy was violated, if applicable.

⦿ If you feel guilty about the decision to terminate, remember this: You only got to this point because either the employee committed egregious and obviously unacceptable misconduct, or the employee was given the opportunity to improve and was unwilling or unable to do so.

Sample Documentation

Sample Coaching Memo 1

To: File
From: Michael Norris
Date: August 31, 2007
Re: Dan Warburg

Met with Dan today, August 31, 2007, to discuss the product release. I told Dan that I'd heard Dylan was working on a database project and that Sasha was updating the department's internal communications protocols, rather than working on the new product. I told Dan I was concerned that his group might not hit the milestones and release schedule.

Dan informed me that he had sent the team an email outlining the due dates but had not followed up and met with each team member to assign interim deadlines and establish priorities. We agreed that Dan would write up a plan by tomorrow afternoon, detailing how his team would complete the remaining work. I'll review that plan, then Dan will meet with each team member and explain the priorities and due dates. If any problems come up, Dan will discuss them with me immediately.

Sample Coaching Memo 2

To: File
From: Eileen Wilkins
Date: December 14, 2006
Re: Grace Hernandez

Grace and I met yesterday, December 13, 2006, to talk about errors in the customer records database. I told Grace that I had received several reports from the sales team that some of the information entered in the last three months—including phone numbers and names—is incorrect. I also told Grace that these errors make it difficult for salespeople to make their calls and track sales, which results in lost time and revenue.

Grace initially denied that she was responsible for these errors but eventually agreed that she was the only one who made entries in the database during the last three months. Grace also told me that since we rented out some of our office space, she has been very busy answering phones and assisting visitors to the tenant company and has not had as much time to see to her job responsibilities.

I told Grace that our new tenant is entitled only to basic reception services under our lease, and that I would talk to them about getting their own receptionist if they were taking up too much of her time. Grace wasn't sure exactly how much time she was spending on them, so she suggested that she would keep a log of her hours for the next week. We will meet again on December 22 to review her log and come up with an action plan. In the meantime, I have authorized Grace to work up to an hour of overtime each day (if necessary) to complete her own duties. We have also agreed that Grace will double check customer information before entering it into the database. On December 22, we will also come up with a plan to review the information currently in the database for accuracy.

Sample Coaching Memo 3

To: File
From: Sergeant Rialto
Date: March 21, 2008
Re: Meeting With Jayne Thomas

I pulled Jayne off the route today to discuss her demeanor with accident victims. I told Jayne that her work has been good, particularly at detailing accidents, involving the appropriate people, and clearing the scene quickly. I also told Jayne that I have seen her deal with accident victims too abruptly, which could cause them to clam up and not provide as much detail as they otherwise might.

Jayne agreed that she is sometimes abrupt and said that she sometimes gets impatient when victims have a hard time explaining what happened. Jayne asked whether we had a class that would help her with this, but we do not. I suggested that Jayne could ride along with Janet Singh a couple of days next week and see how she handles accident victims; Jayne agreed that this would be helpful. I also told Jayne that I would observe her next few interactions with accident victims carefully and give her detailed feedback on her tone and demeanor.

Sample Verbal Warning 1

Verbal Warning

Date: May 3, 2007
Employee Name: Steve Hinds
Manager Name: Jerry Martinez

Incident Description

On May 1, 2007, I received a complaint from administrative assistant Claire Stewart that your deal memo on the Briggs sale was incomplete and contained numerous errors that slowed implementation of the deal significantly. I investigated whether this was true by reviewing the deal memo (attached) and talking with the administrative staff responsible for assisting you in completing this deal.

The deal memo did not have all the information the staff needed to complete the deal. For example, the memo did not explain the shipping method or the shipping date. Additionally, the memo had errors including incorrect prices and the wrong delivery address.

On April 27, Claire tried to contact you via both email and phone to correct these errors, but you did not respond. As a result of these errors, three administrative assistants spent approximately eight extra hours trying to resolve the discrepancies. Claire also informed me that a similar problem occurred on the Edwards deal earlier in the month.

While your gross sales numbers have been improving, these errors are reducing profit margin on your deals significantly and causing extra work for other team members.

When you and I met to discuss this issue earlier today, you told me that you believed this was the responsibility of administrative staff, and that you were not comfortable with the company process.

Prior Incidents

Customer support, clerical, and fulfillment have each complained about incorrect or incomplete information on your deal memos at

Sample Verbal Warning 1 (cont'd)

least three times. We discussed this in my office on April 5. At that time, I tasked you with rereading the process handbook, which you told me that you did. I also told you to ask me if you had questions about writing deal memos. Since April 5, you have not asked me any questions about deal memos.

Improvement Plan

We agreed that you will meet with each back office department and spend a couple of hours learning what information they need from you to implement your deals. You will also spend a couple of hours with Celia, who will show you one of her deal memos and explain how she decides what to include in it. You will let me know some dates and times that are good for you by tomorrow; I will set up a schedule for these visits by the beginning of next week, May 7.

We also agreed that we will review your next deal memo together. I will tell you whether that memo includes the relevant information. When you have closed your next deal, please inform me and we can schedule that review.

Manager: _____ Date: _____

I acknowledge that I have received and understand this document.

Employee: _____ Date: _____

Sample Verbal Warning 2

Verbal Warning

Date: July 18, 2007
Employee Name: Luis Guerrero
Manager Name: Pedro Salazar

Incident Description

On July 11, Ken Schwarz complained to me that the tables at your station often are still dirty and/or have dirty dishes on them when he seats customers. Since receiving that complaint, I have checked the entire restaurant a few times each day and have noticed that only your tables are left unbussed for more than a minute or two. When you do not bus your tables promptly, our customers have to wait longer to be seated or have to sit at tables that have not been cleaned properly. This reflects badly on all of us.

I met with you earlier today to discuss this problem. You told me that you were working as quickly as you can, and that you believe you have improved since our last discussion.

Prior Incidents

We met on June 12, 2006 to discuss this issue. At that time, I told you that I had received complaints from customers that your tables were not properly cleaned and that I had noticed that you were not bussing your tables as quickly as the other staff. We agreed that you would clear and wipe down each table within several minutes after customers leave. We also agreed that you were spending too much time hanging out with the dishwashers in the kitchen, and that your speed would improve if you waited at your station in the dining room, with the other bussers.

During the last week, I have observed that you are still spending time in the kitchen, rather than with the other bussers in the dining room. I also noticed that you do not bus tables immediately after customers

Sample Verbal Warning 2 (cont'd)

leave. During the dinner rush last Friday, for example, one of your tables was not bussed for eight minutes after the customers left.

Improvement Plan

We have agreed that I will spend 15-20 minutes with you each day for the next two weeks, observing your work and giving you feedback on how to improve. At the end of that time, I expect you to bus each table in your section within two minutes after the customer leaves.

To do your job properly, you must be at your station. Therefore, we have also agreed that you will remain at your station in the dining room at all times, unless you are on break.

Employee Comments

Manager: _____ Date: _____

I acknowledge that I have received and understand this document.

Employee: _____ Date: _____

Sample Verbal Warning 3

Verbal Warning

Date: April 18, 2008
Employee Name: Sharon Osmond
Manager Name: Ed Washington

Incident Description

On April 11, 2008, I received a complaint from June Kulau that you had pushed her to accept one of the candidates (Robert McAdams) you recruited for the product development team. June told me that she raised concerns about Robert's qualifications, but you told her she was not being creative and had to learn to "think outside the box." June also told me that you said you didn't think you'd be able to find another candidate for several months, and that she should accept Robert rather than leaving the position open. June has provided me with the email messages in which these exchanges took place.

Based on your advice, June interviewed Robert for the position. However, June learned that Robert did not meet some of the essential job requirements. He was not familiar with basic market research techniques and had no experience with children's products. He was also unaware of the "Healthy Back Packs" line of ergonomic bookbags and backpacks for kids—our bestselling, signature product in this area. Based on this, June decided that she could not hire Robert.

After hearing from June, I contacted the other managers for whom you recruit. Sam Montenegro, in the legal department, informed me that you had strongly recommended a paralegal (Duane Mitchell) several months ago, although Sam was not comfortable with Duane's limited experience. Sam told me that you said Duane had "intangibles" that made him an attractive candidate and asked him to "trust me on this one." Sam hired Duane based on your comments. To date, Duane's performance has been satisfactory, but Sam told me that he was

Sample Verbal Warning 3 (cont'd)

uncomfortable with the process because of your lack of regard for the position's advertised requirements.

We met today to discuss these issues. I informed you that your actions in recommending possibly unqualified candidates and pressuring managers to hire them could cause other departments to view the recruiters poorly. When you recommend candidates who are not qualified, we also risk making hiring mistakes, which are very costly—in time and money—to correct. These are serious issues that must be addressed immediately.

Prior Incidents

No prior incidents have been reported.

Improvement Plan

We have agreed that you will recommend only those candidates who meet the job requirements as stated in the job description. If you believe that a particular candidate warrants the manager's consideration, even though he or she does not meet every job requirement, you will write me a memo explaining why you believe the candidate should be considered before you make that recommendation to the manager.

In addition, you will copy me on your email messages to managers for the next two months. You have told me that you do not intend to pressure managers to hire your candidates, but that your enthusiasm for the candidates you find may be causing you to seem overbearing or unwilling to hear any criticism of the candidates you present. Seeing your messages will help me give you feedback on how to appropriately communicate with managers.

We will meet every Friday at 3:00 p.m. for the next two months to review your communications and candidate selections during the previous week. I will be talking to the managers with whom you worked during the week to get their feedback, and I will present this to you during

Sample Verbal Warning 3 (cont'd)

our meetings. After two months, we will decide whether to continue meeting on a weekly basis.

Employee Comments

Manager: _____ Date: _____

I acknowledge that I have received and understand this document.

Employee: _____ Date: _____

Sample Written Warning 1

Written Warning

Date: February 12, 2008
Employee Name: Dave Costello
Manager Name: Claude Washington

Incident Description

On February 11, 2008, I overheard part of a conversation you had with Crystal Cavalier in her cubicle. I heard you questioning her about her boyfriend, then saying something like "Are you sure you don't want to go out with me instead?" I also observed that Crystal did not respond. Instead, she turned away from you and focused on her computer screen.

I called Crystal into my office and asked her what happened. She said you had asked her out and persisted in asking her questions about her relationship with her boyfriend, even after she told you she didn't want to discuss it. She confirmed that you said, "Are you sure you don't want to go out with me instead?," even though she previously turned down your request for a date. She told me that she felt very uncomfortable about your interest in her, and that she felt you were not getting the message that she does not want to have a romantic relationship with you.

When I talked to you later that same day, you confirmed that you had said these things to Crystal.

Prior Incidents

No prior reported incidents of similar behavior.

Improvement Plan

Dave, your conduct violates company policies on appropriate workplace behavior. Specifically, your conduct violates our policy on Professional

Sample Written Warning 1 (cont'd)

Behavior (p. 23 of the Employee Handbook) and Harassment (p. 12). Your comments and requests for a date made Crystal very uncomfortable. She has stated that clearly to you, but you have persisted.

You are not to talk to Crystal about her personal life or ask her out on dates. In addition, because you seem unclear about what constitutes appropriate workplace behavior, I have scheduled you to attend a sexual harassment training workshop on February 19. Following this training, we will meet again to make sure that you understand the types of comments and behavior that are inappropriate in the workplace.

Employee Comments

Manager: _____ Date: _____

I acknowledge that I have received and understand this document.

Employee: _____ Date: _____

Sample Written Warning 2

Written Warning

Date: October 21, 2006
Employee Name: Melanie Cohen
Manager Name: Carly Genrette

Incident Description

On October 20, I spoke to Travis, who leads the new branding team, to find out whether you were contributing at the team's meetings. He informed me that he did not remember you saying anything during the last few meetings. I also spoke to Jenya, who confirmed that you had not contributed at these meetings.

As we have discussed previously, when you don't participate in the branding meetings, the team is deprived of our department's perspective on the pros and cons of the proposed redesigns. Because we handle all of the packaging, this means that the team might choose branding that has undisclosed costs, affects our ability to make required disclosures on the product box, negatively impacts our ability to use particular vendors, and so on. You are on the team to give our department's input on the redesign proposals; because you have not provided this input, the redesign might be more expensive or difficult to implement than necessary.

When I talked to you about this problem today, you let me know that you feel shy about speaking up at the meetings. You also told me that you are nervous and uncomfortable talking to a group and that you are concerned that Travis looks down on you.

Prior Incidents

We have discussed this problem twice before, on August 14, and again on September 30, when I gave you a verbal warning. On each occasion, I informed you that you needed to speak up at the branding team meetings. We have reviewed the type of information you should be bringing to the meeting and sharing with the team. I have also reviewed

Sample Written Warning 2 (cont'd)

your written notes from the meetings. However, you have not spoken up at these meetings.

Improvement Plan

We have agreed that you will attend a workshop on public speaking. Our company representatives attend a training class to develop the skills as public speakers. The next class begins on November 1 and lasts for six weeks. I have enrolled you in this class. The company will pay for you to attend, and we will arrange your work around the class sessions.

We have also agreed that you and I will meet before the next three meetings to review what you plan to say. At the next meeting, the team will be discussing color options for the branding, and they must have our input on cost. You will present our department's information as if you were speaking to the team, and I'll give you feedback. We will also meet after each team meeting, to review what you said and how it was received.

Employee Comments

Manager: _____ Date: _____

I acknowledge that I have received and understand this document.

Employee: _____ Date: _____

Sample Written Warning 3

Written Warning

Date: September 10, 2007
Employee Name: Randy Clark
Manager Name: Sarah Bronson

Incident Description

On August 3, 2007, I asked you to create five new articles about kitchen remodels for the company's website. As we discussed, these articles were to be descriptions of typical kitchen remodeling projects, with references and links to relevant company products. I informed you that these articles would be the prototype for a new type of website content that ties our products to a detailed description of particular projects, rather than simply listing products by category. I also informed you that I needed to have a final draft of these articles on September 8, so I could present them to our marketing team at a meeting on September 10.

On September 7, you came to my office and told me that you would not make the deadline. You told me that you had completed a draft of three articles but had not yet included references to company products. You also stated that you thought someone in marketing should handle this part of the assignment, as they are more familiar with the products than you are. You did not let me know that you might miss the deadline or that you were having any trouble with the articles until September 7.

As a result of your failure to meet this deadline, Cynthia Bradley, Russell Jenkins, and I all had to drop our other work to complete the three articles you drafted. These articles had to be changed substantially because they were not written to best utilize the company's products. We had to add products to the articles as well. Because I was able to present only three articles at the marketing meeting, we had to postpone the rollout date for this new type of content. Our department's failure to meet its goal may cause other departments to believe we are unreliable.

Sample Written Warning 3 (cont'd)

Moreover, because the new content is expected to drive higher sales, this delay will cost the company money.

Prior Incidents

I have already issued you a verbal warning, on March 15, 2007, for missing a deadline. You were assigned to write a list of suggested projects store associates could discuss with customers looking for spring gardening and landscaping ideas. You missed your deadline by a week, and we were unable to present your ideas to associates at the company's quarterly meeting.

When we met to discuss this problem, you told me that you tended to wait until the last minute to complete writing projects. We agreed that you would attend a seminar on time management. We also agreed that you would outline your future writing assignments several days after receiving them, and that you would check in with me immediately if you needed help meeting a deadline. The details of this incident and our plan for improvement are in your personnel file, as is the certificate you received for participating in a seminar entitled "Time Management for Busy Employees," dated March 23, 2007.

Improvement Plan

Randy, you must meet your deadlines for writing assignments. When you miss your deadlines, you cause more work for me and your coworkers, and our department's reputation in the company suffers.

You have told me that you are still putting your writing assignments off until the last minute and that you are having trouble estimating how long projects will take. We have agreed that you and I will meet every Friday at 11 a.m. to discuss your writing projects. At the first meeting after I assign you a project, you will show me your outline. At subsequent meetings, you will report on your progress and show me what you have written to date. At the end of each meeting, I will tell you what I expect you to accomplish by the next meeting. I will confirm

Sample Written Warning 3 (cont'd)

this expectation in a follow-up email to you every Friday afternoon. If you disagree with my understanding of the expectation, you have agreed to tell me immediately by the end of the day on Friday.

Employee Comments

One of the reasons I missed the website deadline is because I was unable to figure out which products to feature. This isn't my responsibility; it should have been done by the marketing people.

Manager: _____ Date: _____

I acknowledge that I have received and understand this document.

Employee: _____ Date: _____

Sample Follow Up 1

To: File
From: Donald Briggs
Date: February 3, 2007
Re: Jennifer Shiu

I met with Jennifer Shiu on February 3, 2007 to find out whether she had completed her class on using accounting. She told me that she finished the class on January Excel spreadsheets for 31, and she had learned a lot of tips that she found very helpful. I asked her if she would be willing to do a brief presentation on what she learned to the bookkeeping department at our departmental meeting on February 20; she agreed to do so.

Signed: *Donald Briggs*

Date: February 3, 2007

Sample Follow Up 2

To: File
From: Penny Myer
Date: September 25, 2007
Re: Jessie Pitt

On September 1, 2007, I gave Jessie Pitt a written warning. In his action plan, I required him to complete a training class on using PowerPoint, among other things. He was to complete this class by October 1, 2007.

Jessie informed me today that he completed the class "PowerPoint Basics: Presentations, Graphics, and More!" on September 24. He gave me a copy of his certificate of completion (attached) as well as a syllabus from the class. I have asked him to do a brief presentation, using PowerPoint, at the next department meeting on October 15. He has agreed to do so.

Signed: *Penny Meyer*

Date: 9-25-07

Sample Follow Up 3

To: File
From: Vitali Marcuse
Date: May 31, 2007
Re: Bruce Bohannon

On April 30, I gave Bruce Bohannon a written warning for inappropriate workplace behavior (see file). I informed Bruce that the company would not tolerate any further angry outbursts and advised him to consult the EAP program if he wanted assistance in dealing with his wife's illness.

Today, Bruce informed me that he has been meeting with one of the EAP counselors on a regular basis and plans to continue to do so. Bruce also told me that he would like to leave half an hour early each Wednesday for the next six weeks, so he can attend a support group at the hospital for partners of cancer patients. I said this would be fine; Bruce will take personal time for these absences.

Signed: *Vitali Marcuse*

Date: 5-31-07

Sample Termination 1

Termination Memorandum

By: Lily Lamont
Date: November 13, 2007
Re: Christine Coleman

I terminated Christine Coleman's employment today. Yesterday, November 12, 2007, Martin Yarrow told me that Christine was routing work to a company she owns with her husband, "Tablecloths & Things." I looked over the vendor records for the past year and saw that Tablecloths & Things had received every contract for linens in the last four months. I also saw that we were paying Tablecloths & Things $0.50 more per tablecloth, and $0.10 more per napkin, than we paid to any other linen vendor in the past year. These higher charges added up to almost $5,000 in the last quarter.

I met with Christine this morning to talk about this. When I presented her with the facts described above, Christine admitted that she had been routing all of the company's linen contracts to the company she owned with her husband. She also admitted that she gave these contracts to her company even though other vendors were available to provide the same service for less.

Based on these facts and my conversation with Christine, I decided to terminate her employment. Christine's behavior violates our company policy on conflicts of interest. I informed Christine that her employment was terminated in a meeting this afternoon, which Scott McPhee from Human Resources also attended.

Signed: *Lily Lamont*

Date: Nov. 13, 2007

Sample Termination 2

Termination Memorandum

By: Joseph Farradeh
Date: September 5, 2007
Re: Greg Johnson

I terminated Greg Johnson's employment today. This morning, Marion Samuels told me that Greg was shouting loudly on the phone in the customer service center. Marion heard him say, "Bitch, I already told you we don't have a record of that! Leave me the fuck alone."

I asked Greg to come to my office and told him that I had heard he may have used profanity with a customer earlier today. Greg immediately jumped out of his chair and screamed, "You're a liar! I never did anything like that!" He also raised the middle fingers of both hands in the direction of the call center and said, "They're all a bunch of jerks. I swear, when I find out who told you that, I'm going to deal with it."

At this point, I asked Greg to sit down immediately and summoned Tom Grady, head of security. I told Greg that he should take the rest of the day off, so I would have a chance to find out what happened. I also told him that he was not to return to work or contact any of his coworkers until he heard from me. Tom escorted Greg from the building and alerted the rest of the security team that he was not to be allowed back on company premises until further notice.

At 1:30 p.m., Greg called me. He asked what the company was planning to do, and I told him that I was still investigating. Greg said, "If you know what's good for you, you won't take someone else's word over mine. You seem like a nice enough guy, but I bet you can't handle yourself in a fight. And you never know when you might turn around and find me right behind you."

Shortly after this conversation, the IT department delivered the records of Greg's calls for the morning. The recordings confirmed that Marion

Sample Termination 2 (cont'd)

correctly heard Greg's statements and that Greg was speaking to a customer at the time.

Based on these facts, I decided to terminate Greg's employment immediately. I did so in a conference call to his home, with Tom Grady and Elizabeth Durkheim from human resources sitting in. I also told Greg that he was not to return to the building for any reason and that I had informed the local police of his threats against me.

Signed: *Joseph Faradeh*

Date: 9-5-07

Sample Termination 3

Termination Memorandum

By: Louise Salk
Date: December 10, 2007
Re: Chad Chang

I terminated Chad Chang's employment today. Chad was responsible for implementing our new record-keeping software in the accounting department. On October 15, 2007, I met with each of the analysts on the team to find out how they were progressing with their implementation milestones. During my meeting with Chad, he informed me that he was on track for our January 30 deadline. He told me that he had met with Charlotte Holmes and Jonathan McBryde about the project and given each a schedule of tasks to be completed before the rollout.

During my meetings with Charlotte and Jonathan, however, both expressed concern about Chad's project. Charlotte said that Chad didn't seem to have a clear sense of how much time the project would take and had met only two of the project milestones thus far. Jonathan said that he had never met with Chad or received any tasks from him and that he was worried about meeting the January 30 deadline.

Following these meetings, I met with Chad again. After some discussion, Chad admitted that he had not met with Jonathan and had not yet met with anyone in accounting to discuss the project. He also told me that he might be a bit further behind than he initially had reported to me. Chad also admitted that he had met only the initial two milestones, but the remaining items were not completed. I gave him a verbal warning (attached) and asked him to update me on his progress on a weekly basis.

On November 15, I gave Chad a written warning for performance (attached). In the month since our verbal warning, Chad had not met any of his project milestones. Although he had made some progress in catching up on the work he had already missed, he was falling further behind. I assigned an extra member to Chad's team and asked Chad to

Sample Termination 3 (cont'd)

come to me if he needed additional resources to meet the January 30 deadline. I continued to meet with Chad every week thereafter.

On November 29, during our weekly meeting, Chad informed me that he did not think he could meet the deadline. Chad told me that he would need at least three more team members and another month to complete the implementation in the accounting department.

During the first week of December, I met with each member of Chad's team. Charlotte informed me that Chad could not answer her questions about the project and that she was unsure how to proceed. Jonathan informed me that several employees in accounting had complained that Chad's instructions to them were not clear, and they were confused about how and when the implementation would proceed. And Corinne, whom I assigned to Chad's team two weeks earlier, told me that Chad had given her a very heavy workload, making her primarily responsible for meeting the project milestones going forward.

Based on these facts, I decided to terminate Chad's employment. I did so in a meeting earlier today, which Gail Richards also attended.

Signed: *Louise Salk*

Date: December 10, 2007

C

State Laws

State Laws Prohibiting Discrimination in Employment

State	Law applies to employers with	Private employers may not make employment decisions based on				
		Age (protected ages, if specified)	Ancestry or national origin	Disability	AIDS/ HIV	Gender
Alabama *Ala. Code §§ 25-1-20, 25-1-21*	20 or more employees	✓ (40 and older)				
Alaska *Alaska Stat. §§ 18.80.220, 47.30.865*	One or more employees	✓ (40 and older)	✓	Physical and mental	✓	✓
Arizona *Ariz. Rev. Stat. §§ 41-1461, 41-1463*	15 or more employees	✓ (40 and older)	✓	Physical	✓	✓
Arkansas *Ark. Code Ann. §§ 16-123-102, 16-123-107, 11-4-601, 11-5-403*	9 or more employees		✓	Physical and mental		✓
California *Cal. Gov't. Code §§ 12920, 12941; Cal. Lab. Code § 1101*	5 or more employees	✓ (40 and older)	✓	Physical and mental	✓	✓
Colorado *Colo. Rev. Stat. §§ 24-34-301, 24-34-401, 24-34-402, 27-10-115*	One or more employees	✓ (40 to 70)	✓	Physical, mental, and learning	✓	✓
Connecticut *Conn. Gen. Stat. Ann. §§ 46a-51, 46a-60, 46a-81*	3 or more employees	✓ (40 and older)	✓	Present or past physical, mental, or learning	✓	✓
Delaware *Del. Code Ann. tit. 19, §§ 710, 711*	4 or more employees	✓ (40 and older)	✓	Physical or mental	✓	✓
District of Columbia *D.C. Code Ann. §§ 2-1401.01, 2-1401.02, 7-1703.03*	One or more employees	✓ (18 and older)	✓	Physical or mental	✓	✓

[1] Employers covered by FLSA.

Marital status	Pregnancy, childbirth, and related medical conditions	Race or color	Religion or creed	Sexual orientation	Genetic testing information	Additional protected categories
✓ (Includes changes in status)	✓ Parenthood	✓	✓			Mental illness
		✓	✓		✓	
		✓	✓	✓	✓[1]	
✓	✓	✓	✓	✓	✓	• Gender identity • Medical condition • Political activities or affiliations
	✓	✓	✓			• Lawful conduct outside of work • Mental illness
✓	✓	✓	✓	✓	✓	Mental retardation
✓	✓	✓	✓		✓	
✓ (Includes domestic partnership)	✓ Parenthood	✓	✓	✓	✓	• Enrollment in vocational, professional, or college education • Family duties • Source of income • Place of residence or business • Personal appearance • Political affiliation • Smoker • Any reason other than individual merit

State Laws Prohibiting Discrimination in Employment (cont'd)

State	Law applies to employers with	Private employers may not make employment decisions based on				
		Age (protected ages, if specified)	Ancestry or national origin	Disability	AIDS/ HIV	Gender
Florida *Fla. Stat. Ann. §§ 760.01, 760.02, 760.10, 760.50, 448.075*	15 or more employees	✓	✓	"Handicap"	✓	✓
Georgia *Ga. Code Ann. §§ 34-6A-1 and following, 34-5-1, 34-5-2*	15 or more employees (disability) 10 or more employees (gender)			Physical or mental		✓[2]
Hawaii *Haw. Rev. Stat. §§ 378-1, 378-2*	One or more employees	✓	✓	Physical or mental	✓	✓
Idaho *Idaho Code §§ 67-5902, 67-5909*	5 or more employees	✓ (40 and older)	✓	Physical or mental		✓
Illinois *775 Ill. Comp. Stat. §§ 5/1-102, 5/1-103, 5/2-101, 5/2-102; Ill. Admin. Code tit. 56, § 5210.110*	15 or more employees One or more employees (disability)	✓ (40 and older)	✓	Physical or mental	✓	✓
Indiana *Ind. Code Ann. §§ 22-9-1-2, 22-9-3, 22-9-2-1, 22-9-2-2*	6 or more employees	✓ (40 to 70)	✓	Physical or mental (15 or more employees)		✓
Iowa *Iowa Code §§ 216.2, 216.6*	4 or more employees	✓ (18 or older)	✓	Physical or mental	✓	✓
Kansas *Kan. Stat. Ann. §§ 44-1001, 44-1002, 44-1112, 44-1113, 44-1125, 44-1126, 65-6002(e)*	4 or more employees	✓ (18 or older)	✓	Physical or mental	✓	✓
Kentucky *Ky. Rev. Stat. Ann. §§ 344.030, 344.040, 207.130, 207.150, 342.197*	8 or more employees	✓ (40 or older)	✓	Physical	✓	✓

[2] Wage discrimination only

Marital status	Pregnancy, childbirth, and related medical conditions	Race or color	Religion or creed	Sexual orientation	Genetic testing information	Additional protected categories
✓		✓	✓			Sickle cell trait
✓	✓ Breastfeeding	✓	✓	✓	✓	Arrest and court record (unless there is a conviction directly related to job)
		✓	✓	✓		
✓	✓	✓	✓	✓		• Citizen status • Military status • Unfavorable military discharge
		✓	✓			
		✓	✓		✓	
		✓	✓		✓	Military status
		✓	✓			• Smoker or nonsmoker • Occupational pneumoconiosis with no respiratory impairment resulting from exposure to coal dust

State Laws Prohibiting Discrimination in Employment (cont'd)

State	Law applies to employers with	Private employers may not make employment decisions based on				
		Age (protected ages, if specified)	Ancestry or national origin	Disability	AIDS/ HIV	Gender
Louisiana La. Rev. Stat. Ann. §§ 23:301 to 23:352	20 or more employees	✓ (40 or older)	✓	Physical or mental		✓
Maine Me. Rev. Stat. Ann. tit. 5, §§ 4552, 4553, 4571	One or more employees	✓	✓	Physical or mental		✓
Maryland Md. Code 1957 Art. 49B, §§ 15, 16	15 or more employees	✓	✓	Physical or mental		✓
Massachusetts Mass. Gen. Laws ch. 151B, §§ 1, 4	6 or more employees	✓ (40 or older)	✓	Physical or mental	✓	✓
Michigan Mich. Comp. Laws §§ 37.1201, 37.1202, 37.2201, 37.2202, 37.1103	One or more employees	✓	✓	Physical or mental	✓	✓
Minnesota Minn. Stat. Ann. §§ 363A.03, 363A.08, 181.974	One or more employees	✓ (18 or older)	✓	Physical or mental	✓	✓
Mississippi Miss. Code Ann. §§ 33-1-15						
Missouri Mo. Rev. Stat. §§ 213.010, 213.055, 191.665, 375.1306	6 or more employees	✓ (40 to 70)	✓	Physical or mental	✓	✓
Montana Mont. Code Ann. §§ 49-2-101, 49-2-303	One or more employees	✓	✓	Physical or mental		✓
Nebraska Neb. Rev. Stat. §§ 48-1101, 48-1102, 48-1001 to 48-1002, 20-168	15 or more employees	✓ (40 to 70) (Applies to employers with 25 or more employees)	✓	Physical or mental	✓	✓

Marital status	Pregnancy, childbirth, and related medical conditions	Race or color	Religion or creed	Sexual orientation	Genetic testing information	Additional protected categories
	✓ (Applies to employers with 25 or more employees)	✓	✓		✓	Sickle cell trait
	✓	✓	✓	✓	✓	• Past workers' compensation claim • Past whistleblowing
✓	✓	✓	✓	✓	✓	
✓		✓	✓	✓	✓	• Military service • Arrests
✓	✓	✓	✓		✓	• Height or weight • Arrest record
✓	✓	✓	✓	✓	✓	• Gender identity • Member of local commission • Perceived sexual orientation • Receiving public assistance
						• Military status (all employers) • No other protected categories unless employer receives public funding
	✓	✓	✓		✓	
✓	✓	✓	✓			
✓	✓	✓	✓		✓	

State Laws Prohibiting Discrimination in Employment (cont'd)

State	Law applies to employers with	Private employers may not make employment decisions based on				
		Age (protected ages, if specified)	Ancestry or national origin	Disability	AIDS/ HIV	Gender
Nevada *Nev. Rev. Stat. Ann. §§ 613.310 and following*	15 or more employees	✓ (40 or older)	✓	Physical or mental		✓
New Hampshire *N.H. Rev. Stat. Ann. §§ 354-A2, 354-A6, 354-A7, 141-H:3*	6 or more employees	✓	✓	Physical or mental		✓
New Jersey *N.J. Stat. Ann. §§ 10:5-5 to 10:5-12; 34:6B-1*	One or more employees	✓ (18 to 70)	✓	Past or present physical or mental	✓	✓
New Mexico *N.M. Stat. Ann. §§ 28-1-2, 28-1-7*	4 or more employees	✓ (40 or older) (Applies to employers with 20 or more employees)	✓	Physical or mental		✓
New York *N.Y. Exec. Law §§ 292, 296; N.Y. Lab. Law § 201-d*	4 or more employees	✓ (18 and over)	✓	Physical or mental	✓	✓
North Carolina *N.C. Gen. Stat. §§ 143-422.2, 95-28.1, 127B-11, 130A-148, 168A-3, 168A-5*	15 or more employees	✓	✓	Physical or mental	✓	✓
North Dakota *N.D. Cent. Code §§ 14-02.4-02, 14-02.4-03, 34-01-17*	One or more employees	✓ (40 or older)	✓	Physical or mental		✓
Ohio *Ohio Rev. Code Ann. §§ 4111.17, 4112.01, 4112.02*	4 or more employees	✓ (40 or older)	✓	Physical, mental, or learning		✓

[3] Employers with 15 or more employees.

Marital status	Pregnancy, childbirth, and related medical conditions	Race or color	Religion or creed	Sexual orientation	Genetic testing information	Additional protected categories
	✓	✓	✓	✓	✓	• Lawful use of any product when not at work • Use of service animal
✓	✓	✓	✓	✓	✓	
✓ (Includes domestic partner)	✓	✓	✓	✓	✓	• Predisposing genetic characteristics • Military service or status • Smoker or nonsmoker
✓ (Applies to employers with 50 or more employees)	✓	✓	✓	✓[3]		• Gender identity (employers with 15 or more employees) • Serious medical condition
✓	✓	✓	✓	✓	✓	• Lawful use of any product when not at work • Military status • Observance of Sabbath • Political activities
		✓	✓		✓	• Lawful use of any product when not at work • Military service • Sickle cell trait
✓	✓	✓	✓			• Lawful conduct outside of work • Receiving public assistance
	✓	✓	✓			

State Laws Prohibiting Discrimination in Employment (cont'd)

		Private employers may not make employment decisions based on				
State	Law applies to employers with	Age (protected ages, if specified)	Ancestry or national origin	Disability	AIDS/ HIV	Gender
Oklahoma *Okla. Stat. Ann. tit. 25, §§ 1301, 1302; tit. 36, § 3614.2; tit. 40, § 500; tit. 44, § 208*	15 or more employees	✓ (40 or older)	✓	Physical or mental		✓
Oregon *Or. Rev. Stat. §§ 659A.001 and following, 659A.303*	One or more employees	✓ (18 or older)	✓	Physical or mental (Applies to employers with 6 or more employees)		✓
Pennsylvania *43 Pa. Cons. Stat. Ann. §§ 954-955*	4 or more employees	✓ (40 to 70)	✓	Physical or mental		✓
Rhode Island *R.I. Gen. Laws §§ 28-6-18, 28-5-6, 28-5-7, 23-6-22, 12-28-10*	4 or more employees One or more employees (gender-based wage discrimina-tion)	✓ (40 or older)	✓	Physical or mental	✓	✓
South Carolina *S.C. Code Ann. §§ 1-13-30, 1-13-80*	15 or more employees	✓ (40 or older)	✓	Physical or mental		✓
South Dakota *S.D. Codified Laws Ann. §§ 20-13-1, 20-13-10, 60-12-15, 60-2-20, 62-1-17*	One or more employees		✓	Physical, mental, and learning		✓
Tennessee *Tenn. Code Ann. §§ 4-21-102, 4-21-401 and following, 8-50-103, 50-2-201, 50-2-202*	8 or more employees One or more employees (gender-based wage discrimina-tion)	✓ (40 or older)	✓	Physical or mental		✓
Texas *Tex. Lab. Code Ann. §§ 21.002, 21.052, 21.101, 21.402*	15 or more employees	✓ (40 or older)	✓	Physical or mental		✓

Marital status	Pregnancy, childbirth, and related medical conditions	Race or color	Religion or creed	Sexual orientation	Genetic testing information	Additional protected categories
		✓	✓		✓	• Military service • Smoker or nonsmoker
✓	✓	✓	✓		✓	
	✓	✓	✓			• Familial status • GED rather than high school diploma • Use of guide or service animal
	✓	✓	✓	✓	✓	• Domestic abuse victim • Gender identity or expression
	✓	✓	✓			
		✓	✓		✓	Preexisting injury
		✓	✓			
	✓	✓	✓		✓	

State Laws Prohibiting Discrimination in Employment (cont'd)

State	Law applies to employers with	Age (protected ages, if specified)	Ancestry or national origin	Disability	AIDS/ HIV	Gender
		Private employers may not make employment decisions based on				
Utah *Utah Code Ann. §§ 34A-5-102, 34A-5-106*	15 or more employees	✓ (40 or older)	✓	Follows federal law	✓	✓
Vermont *Vt. Stat. Ann. tit. 21, § 495, 495d; tit. 18, § 9333*	One or more employees	✓ (18 or older)	✓	Physical or mental	✓	✓
Virginia *Va. Code Ann. §§ 2.2-3900, 40.1-28.6, 51.5-41*	Law applies to all employers	✓	✓	Physical or mental		✓
Washington *Wash. Rev. Code Ann. §§ 38.40.110, 49.60.040, 49.60.172, 49.60.180, 49.12.175, 49.44.090; Wash. Admin. Code 162-30-020*	8 or more employees One or more employees (gender-based wage discrimination)	✓ (40 or older)	✓	Physical, mental, or sensory	✓	✓
West Virginia *W.Va. Code §§ 5-11-3, 5-11-9, 21-5B-1, 21-5B-3, 21-3-19*	12 or more employees	✓ (40 or older)	✓	Physical or mental	✓	✓[4]
Wisconsin *Wis. Stat. Ann. §§ 111.32 and following*	One or more employees	✓ (40 or older)	✓	Physical or mental	✓	✓
Wyoming *Wyo. Stat. §§ 27-9-102, 27-9-105, 19-11-104*	2 or more employees	✓ (40 or older)	✓	Not specified		✓

[4] Equal pay laws apply to employers with one or more employees

Marital status	Pregnancy, childbirth, and related medical conditions	Race or color	Religion or creed	Sexual orientation	Genetic testing information	Additional protected categories
	✓	✓	✓			
		✓	✓	✓	✓	Place of birth
✓	✓	✓	✓		✓	Use of a service animal
✓	✓	✓	✓		✓	• Hepatitis C infection • Member of state militia • Use of a trained guide dog
		✓	✓			• Smoking away from work
✓	✓	✓	✓	✓	✓	• Arrest or conviction • Lawful use of any product when not at work • Military service or status
		✓	✓			• Military service or status • Smoking off duty

Current as of February 2006

State Laws That Control Final Paychecks

State and statute	Paycheck due when employee is fired	Paycheck due when employee quits	Unused vacation pay due	Special employment situations
Alaska *Alaska Stat.* *§ 23.05.140(b)*	Within 3 working days.	Next regular payday at least 3 days after employee gives notice.	No provision.	
Arizona *Ariz. Rev. Stat.* *§ 23-353*	Next payday or within 3 working days, whichever is sooner.	Next payday.	Yes.	
Arkansas *Ark. Code Ann.* *§ 11-4-405*	Within 7 days from discharge date.	No provision.	No provision.	Railroad or railroad construction: day of discharge.
California *Cal. Lab. Code* *§§ 201 to 202, 227.3*	Immediately.	Immediately if employee has given 72 hours notice; otherwise, within 72 hours.	Yes.	Motion picture business: if fired, within 24 hours (excluding weekends & holidays); if laid off, next payday. Oil drilling industry: within 24 hours (excluding weekends & holidays) of termination. Seasonal agricultural workers: within 72 hours of termination.
Colorado *Colo. Rev. Stat.* *§ 8-4-109*	Immediately. (Within 6 hours of start of next workday, if payroll unit is closed; 24 hours if unit is offsite.) Employer decides check delivery.	Next payday.	Yes.	
Connecticut *Conn. Gen. Stat.* *Ann. § 31-71c*	Next business day after discharge.	Next payday.	Only if policy or collective bargaining agreement requires payment on termination.	
Delaware *Del. Code Ann. Tit.* *19, § 1103*	Next payday.	Next payday.	No provision.	

State Laws That Control Final Paychecks (cont'd)

State and statute	Paycheck due when employee is fired	Paycheck due when employee quits	Unused vacation pay due	Special employment situations
District of Columbia *D.C. Code Ann. § 32-1303*	Next business day.	Next payday or 7 days after quitting, whichever is sooner.	Yes, unless there is express contrary policy.	
Hawaii *Haw. Rev. Stat. § 388-3*	Immediately or next business day, if timing or conditions prevent immediate payment.	Next payday or immediately, if employee gives one pay period's notice.	No.	
Idaho *Idaho Code § 45-606; 45-617*	Next payday or within 10 days (excluding weekends & holidays), whichever is sooner. If employee makes written request for earlier payment, within 48 hours of receipt of request (excluding weekends & holidays).	Next payday or within 10 days (excluding weekends & holidays), whichever is sooner. If employee makes written request for earlier payment, within 48 hours of receipt of request (excluding weekends & holidays).	No provision.	
Illinois *820 Ill. Comp. Stat. § 115/5*	At time of separation if possible, but no later than next payday.	At time of separation if possible, but no later than next payday.	Yes.	
Indiana *Ind. Code Ann. §§ 22-2-5-1, 22-2-9-2*	Next payday.	Next payday. (If employee has not left address, (1) 10 days after employee demands wages or (2) when employee provides address where check may be mailed.)	Yes.	
Iowa *Iowa Code §§ 91A.4, 91A.2(7)(b)*	Next payday.	Next payday.	Yes.	If employee is owed commission, employer has 30 days to pay.

State Laws That Control Final Paychecks (cont'd)

State and statute	Paycheck due when employee is fired	Paycheck due when employee quits	Unused vacation pay due	Special employment situations
Kansas *Kan. Stat. Ann. § 44-315*	Next payday.	Next payday.	Only if required by employer's policies.	
Kentucky *Ky. Rev. Stat. Ann. §§ 337.010(c), 337.055*	Next payday or 14 days, whichever is later.	Next payday or 14 days, whichever is later.	Yes.	
Louisiana *La. Rev. Stat. Ann. § 23:631*	Next payday or within 15 days, whichever is earlier.	Next payday or within 15 days, whichever is earlier.	Yes.	
Maine *Me. Rev. Stat. Ann. tit. 26, § 626*	Next payday or within 2 weeks of requesting final pay, whichever is sooner.	Next payday or within 2 weeks of requesting final pay, whichever is sooner.	Yes.	
Maryland *Md. Code Ann., [Lab. & Empl.] § 3-505*	Next scheduled payday.	Next scheduled payday.	Yes, unless employer has contrary policy.	
Massachusetts *Mass. Gen. Laws ch. 149, § 148*	Day of discharge.	Next payday. If no scheduled payday, then following Saturday.	Yes.	
Michigan *Mich. Comp. Laws §§ 408.471 to 408.475; Mich. Admin. Code R. 408.9007*	Next payday.	Next payday.	Only if required by written policy or contract.	Hand-harvesters of crops: within one working day of termination.
Minnesota *Minn. Stat. Ann. §§ 181.13 to 181.14; 181.74*	Immediately.	Next payday. If payday is less than 5 days from last day of work, then following payday or 20 days from last day of work, whichever is earlier.	Only if required by written policy or contract.	Migrant agricultural workers who resign: within 5 days.
Missouri *Mo. Rev. Stat. § 290.110*	Day of discharge.	No provision.	No.	

State Laws That Control Final Paychecks (cont'd)

State and statute	Paycheck due when employee is fired	Paycheck due when employee quits	Unused vacation pay due	Special employment situations
Montana *Mont. Code Ann. § 39-3-205; Mont. Admin. Code 24.16 7521*	Immediately if fired for cause or laid off (unless there is a written policy extending time to earlier of next payday or 15 days).	Next payday or within 15 days, whichever comes first.	Yes.	
Nebraska *Neb. Rev. Stat. §§ 48-1229 to 48-1230*	Next payday or within 2 weeks, whichever is earlier.	Next payday or within 2 weeks, whichever is earlier.	Yes.	
Nevada *Nev. Rev. Stat. Ann. §§ 608.020 to 608.030*	Immediately.	Next payday or 7 days, whichever is earlier.	No provision.	
New Hampshire *N.H. Rev. Stat. Ann. §§ 275:43(III), 275:44*	Within 72 hours. If laid off, next payday.	Next payday, or within 72 hours if employee gives one pay period's notice.	Yes.	
New Jersey *N.J. Stat. Ann. § 34:11-4.3*	Next payday.	Next payday.	No provision.	
New Mexico *N.M. Stat. Ann. §§ 50-4-4 to 50-4-5*	Within 5 days.	Next payday.	No provision.	If paid by task or commission, 10 days after discharge.
New York *N.Y. Lab. Law §§ 191(3), 198-c(2)*	Next payday.	Next payday.	Yes.	
North Carolina *N.C. Gen. Stat. §§ 95-25.7, 95-25.12*	Next payday.	Next payday.	Yes, unless employer has a contrary policy.	If paid by commission or bonus, on next payday after amount calculated.
North Dakota *N.D. Cent. Code § 34-14-03; N.D. Admin. Code R. 46-02-07-02(12)*	Next payday, or 15 days, whichever is earlier.	Next payday.	Yes.	

State Laws That Control Final Paychecks (cont'd)

State and statute	Paycheck due when employee is fired	Paycheck due when employee quits	Unused vacation pay due	Special employment situations
Ohio *Ohio Re. Code Ann. § 4113.5*	First of month for wages earned in first half of prior month; 15th of month for wages earned in second half of prior month.	First of month for wages earned in first half of prior month; 15th of month for wages earned in second half of prior month.	Yes.	
Oklahoma *Okla. Stat. Ann. Tit. 40, §§ 165.1(4), 165.3*	Next payday.	Next payday.	Yes.	
Ohio *Ohio Re. Code Ann. § 4113.5*	First of month for wages earned in first half of prior month; 15th of month for wages earned in second half of prior month.	First of month for wages earned in first half of prior month; 15th of month for wages earned in second half of prior month.	Yes.	
Oregon *Or. Rev. Stat. §§ 652.140, 652.145*	End of first business day after termination (must be within 5 days if employee submits time records to determine wages due).	Immediately, with 48 hours' notice (excluding weekends & holidays); without notice, within 5 business days or next payday, whichever comes first (must be within 5 days if employee submits time records to determine wages due).	Yes.	Seasonal farm workers: fired or quitting with 48 hours' notice, immediately; quitting without notice, within 48 hours or next payday, whichever comes first.
Pennsylvania *43 Pa. Cons. Stat. Ann. §§ 260.2a, 260.5*	Next payday.	Next payday.	No provision.	
Rhode Island *R.I. Gen. Laws § 28-14-4*	Next payday.	Next payday.	Yes, if employee has worked for one full year.	

State Laws That Control Final Paychecks (cont'd)

State and statute	Paycheck due when employee is fired	Paycheck due when employee quits	Unused vacation pay due	Special employment situations
South Carolina *S.C. Code Ann. §§ 41-10-10(2), 41-10-50*	Within 48 hours or next payday, but not more than 30 days.	No provision.	Yes.	
South Dakota *S.D. Codified Laws Ann. §§ 60-11-10 to 60-11-14*	Next payday (or until employee returns employer's property).	Next payday (or until employee returns employer's property).	No.	
Tennessee *Tenn. Code Ann. § 50-2-103*	Next payday or 21 days, whichever is later.	Next payday or 21 days, whichever is later.	Yes.	Applies to employers with 5 or more employees.
Texas *Tex. Lab. Code Ann. § 61.001, 61.014*	Within 6 days.	Next payday.	Yes.	
Utah *Utah Code Ann. §§ 34-28-2, 34-28-5; Utah Admin.Code 610-3*	Within 24 hours.	Next payday.	Only if required by policy or contract.	
Vermont *Vt. Stat. Ann. tit. 21, § 342(c)*	Within 72 hours.	Next regular payday or next Friday, if there is no regular payday.	No provision.	
Virginia *Va. Code Ann. § 40.1-29(A.1)*	Next payday.	Next payday.	No provision.	
Washington *Wash. Rev. Code Ann. § 49.48.010*	End of pay period.	End of pay period.	No provision.	
West Virginia *W.Va. Code §§ 21-5-1, 21-5-4*	Within 72 hours.	Immediately if employee has given one pay period's notice; otherwise, next payday.	Yes.	

State Laws That Control Final Paychecks (cont'd)

State and statute	Paycheck due when employee is fired	Paycheck due when employee quits	Unused vacation pay due	Special employment situations
Wisconsin *Wis. Stat. Ann.* *§§ 109.01(3), 109.03*	Next payday or 1 month, whichever is earlier. If termination is due to merger, relocation, or liquidation of business, within 24 hours.	Next payday.	Yes.	Does not apply to managers, executives, or sales agents working on commission basis.
Wyoming *Wyo. Stat. Ann.* *§ 27-4-104,* *27-4-507(c)*	5 working days.	5 working days.	Yes.	

Current as of February 2006

■

How to Use the CD-ROM

T he tear-out forms in Appendix A are included on a CD-ROM in the back of the book. This CD-ROM, which can be used with Windows computers, installs files that you use with software programs that are already installed on your computer. It is *not* a stand-alone software program. Please read this appendix and the README. TXT file included on the CD-ROM for instructions on using the Forms CD.

Note to Mac users: This CD-ROM and its files should also work on Macintosh computers. Please note, however, that Nolo cannot provide technical support for non-Windows users.

How to View the README File

If you do not know how to view the file README.TXT, insert the Forms CD-ROM into your computer's CD-ROM drive and follow these instructions:

- Windows 98, 2000, Me, and XP: (1) On your PC's desktop, double click the My Computer icon; (2) double click the icon for the CD-ROM drive into which the Forms CD-ROM was inserted; (3) double click the file README.TXT.
- Macintosh: (1) On your Mac desktop, double click the icon for the CD-ROM that you inserted; (2) double click on the file README.TXT.

While the README file is open, print it out by using the Print command in the File menu.

Four different kinds of files are contained on the CD-ROM:

- A word processing (RTF) form that you can open, complete, print, and save with your word processing program (see "Using the Word Processing Files to Create Documents," below),
- Portable Document Format (PDF) forms that can be viewed only with Adobe Reader (see "Using PDF Files to Print Out Forms," below). These forms are designed to be printed out and filled in by hand or with a typewriter,
- MP3 audio files that you can listen to using your computer's media or MP3 player (see "Listening to the Audio Files," below), and

- A PowerPoint presentation (PPS) that can be viewed with Microsoft PowerPoint Viewer (see "Using the PowerPoint Presentation," below).

See below for a list of forms, their file names, and their file formats.

Installing the Form Files Onto Your Computer

Before you can do anything with the files on the CD-ROM, you need to install them onto your hard disk. In accordance with U.S. copyright laws, remember that copies of the CD-ROM and its files are for your personal use only. The form files must be installed; installing the audio files, however, is optional.

> ### Listening Without Installing
>
> If you don't want to copy 50 MB of audio files to your hard disc, you can "play" the CD on your computer. For details, see "Playing the Audio Files Without Installing," below.

Insert the Forms CD and do the following for your operating system:

Windows 98, 2000, Me, and XP Users

Follow the instructions that appear on the screen. (If nothing happens when you insert the Forms CD-ROM, then (1) double click the My Computer icon; (2) double click the icon for the CD-ROM drive into which the Forms CD-ROM was inserted; and (3) double click the file WELCOME.EXE.)

By default, all the files are installed to the \Discipline Resources folder in the \Program Files folder of your computer. A folder called "Discipline Resources" is added to the "Programs" folder of the Start menu.

If you chose to install the audio resources files, the installer will place them in the \Discipline Resources\Audio folder in the \Program Files folder of your computer. It will add a subfolder called "Audio" to the "Discipline Resources" folder described above.

Macintosh Users

Step 1: If the "Discipline Resources CD" window is not open, open it by double clicking the "Discipline Resources CD" icon.

Step 2: Select the "Discipline Resources" folder icon.

Step 3: Drag and drop the folder icon onto the icon of your hard disk.

To copy the audio files:

Step 1: If the "Discipline Resources CD" window is not open, open it by double clicking the "Discipline Resources CD" icon.

Step 2: Select the "Discipline Audio" folder icon.

Step 3: Drag and drop the folder icon onto the icon of your hard disk.

Using the Word Processing Files to Create Documents

This section concerns the files for forms that can be opened and edited with your word processing program.

All word processing forms come in rich text format. These files have the extension ".RTF." For example, the form for the Disciplinary Form discussed in Chapter 9 is in the file DisciplineForm.rtf. All forms, their file names, and their file formats are listed below.

RTF files can be read by most recent word processing programs including all versions of MS Word for Windows and Macintosh, WordPad for Windows, and recent versions of WordPerfect for Windows and Macintosh.

To use a form from the CD to create your documents, you must: (1) open a file in your word processor or text editor; (2) edit the form by filling in the required information; (3) print it out; and (4) rename and save your revised file.

The following are general instructions. However, each word processor uses different commands to open, format, save, and print documents. Please read your word processor's manual for specific instructions on performing these tasks.

Do not call Nolo's technical support if you have questions on how to use your word processor or your computer.

Step 1: Opening a File

There are three ways to open the word processing files included on the CD-ROM after you have installed them onto your computer:

- Windows users can open a file by selecting its "shortcut" as follows: (1) Click the Windows "Start" button; (2) open the "Programs" folder; (3) open the "Discipline Resources" subfolder; (4) open the "Forms" subfolder; and (5) click on the shortcut to the form you want to work with.
- Both Windows and Macintosh users can open a file directly by double clicking on it. Use My Computer or Windows Explorer (Windows 98, 2000, Me, or XP) or the Finder (Macintosh) to go to the folder you installed or copied the CD-ROM's files to. Then, double click on the specific file you want to open.
- You can also open a file from within your word processor. To do this, you must first start your word processor. Then, go to the "File" menu and choose the "Open" command. This opens a dialog box where you will tell the program (1) the type of file you want to open (*.RTF), and (2) the location and name of the file (you will need to navigate through the directory tree to get to the folder on your hard disk where the CD's files have been installed).

Where Are the Files Installed?

Windows Users: The RTF file are installed by default to a folder named \Discipline Resources\Forms in the \Program Files folder of your computer.

Macintosh Users: The RTF file is located in the "Forms" folder within the "Discipline Resources" folder.

Step 2: Editing Your Document

Fill in the appropriate information according to the instructions and sample agreements in the book. Underlines are used to indicate where you need to enter your information, frequently followed by instructions in brackets. Be sure to delete the underlines and instructions from your edited document. You will also want to make sure that any signature lines in your completed documents appear on a page with at least some text from the document itself.

Editing Forms That Have Optional or Alternative Text

Some of the forms have optional or alternate text:
- With optional text, you choose whether to include or exclude the given text.
- With alternative text, you select one alternative to include and exclude the other alternatives.

When editing these forms, we suggest you do the following:

Optional text

If you don't want to include optional text, just delete it from your document.

If you do want to include optional text, just leave it in your document. In either case, delete the italicized instructions.

Alternative text

First delete all the alternatives that you do not want to include, then delete the italicized instructions.

Step 3: Printing Out the Document

Use your word processor's or text editor's "Print" command to print out your document.

Step 4: Saving Your Document

After filling in the form, use the "Save As" command to save and rename the file. Because all the files are "read-only," you will not be able to use the "Save" command. This is for your protection. *If you save the file without renaming it, the underlines that indicate where you need to enter your information will be lost and you will not be able to create a new document with this file without recopying the original file from the CD-ROM.*

Using PDF Files to Print Out Forms

Electronic copies of useful forms are included on the CD-ROM in Adobe PDF format. You must have Adobe Reader installed on your computer to use these forms. Adobe Reader is available for all types of Windows and Macintosh systems. If you don't already have this software, you can download it for free at www.adobe.com.

All forms, their file names, and their file formats are listed below.

These forms cannot be filled out using your computer. To create your document using these files, you must: (1) open the file; (2) print it out; and (3) complete it by hand or typewriter.

Step 1: Opening PDF Files

PDF files, like the word processing files, can be opened in one of three ways.

- Windows users can open a file by selecting its "shortcut" as follows: (1) Click the Windows "Start" button; (2) open the "Programs" folder; (3) open the "Discipline Resources" subfolder; (4) open the "Forms" folder; and (5) click on the shortcut to the form you want to work with.
- Both Windows and Macintosh users can open a file directly by double clicking on it. Use My Computer or Windows Explorer (Windows 98, 2000, Me, or XP) or the Finder (Macintosh) to go to the folder you created and copied the CD-ROM's files to. Then, double click on the specific file you want to open.
- You can also open a PDF file from within Adobe Reader. To do this, you must first start Reader. Then, go to the "File"` menu and choose the "Open" command. This opens a dialog box where you will tell the program the location and name of the file (you will need to navigate through the directory tree to get to the folder on your hard disk where the CD's files have been installed).

> ### Where Are the PDF Files Installed?
>
> **Windows Users:** PDF files are installed by default to a folder named \Discipline Resources\Forms in the \Program Files folder of your computer.
>
> **Macintosh Users:** PDF files are located in the "Forms" folder within the "Discipline Resources" folder.

Step 2: Printing PDF files

Choose "Print" from the Adobe Reader "File" menu. This will open the Print dialog box. In the "Print Range" section of the Print dialog box, select the appropriate print range, then click OK.

Step 3: Filling in PDF files

The PDF files cannot be filled out using your computer. To create your document using one of these files, you must first print it out (see Step 2, above) and then complete it by hand or typewriter.

Listening to the Audio Files

This section explains how to use your computer's media player to listen to the audio files. All audio files are in MP3 format. (Most computers come with a media player that plays MP3 files.) For example, "Segment 1: Coaching Session" is in the file Segment1-Coaching.mp3. At the end of this appendix, you'll see a list of the audio files and their file names.

You can listen to files that you have installed on your computer, or you can listen without having installed the files to your hard disk. (See "Playing the Audio Files Without Installing," below).

Please keep in mind that these are general instructions—because every media player is unique, these steps may not mirror the steps you need to follow to use your player. Please do not contact Nolo's technical support if you are having difficulty using your media player.

	PRICE	CODE
Fight Your Ticket & Win in California	$29.99	FYT
How to Change Your Name in California	$29.99	NAME
Nolo's Deposition Handbook	$29.99	DEP
Represent Yourself in Court: How to Prepare & Try a Winning Case	$39.99	RYC
Win Your Lawsuit: A Judge's Guide to Representing Yourself in California Superior Court	$29.99	SLWY

HOMEOWNERS, LANDLORDS & TENANTS

	PRICE	CODE
California Tenants' Rights	$27.99	CTEN
Deeds for California Real Estate	$24.99	DEED
Every Landlord's Legal Guide (National Edition, Book w/CD-ROM)	$44.99	ELLI
Every Landlord's Guide to Finding Great Tenants (Book w/CD-ROM)	$19.99	FIND
Every Landlord's Tax Deduction Guide	$34.99	DELL
Every Tenant's Legal Guide	$29.99	EVTEN
For Sale by Owner in California	$29.99	FSBO
How to Buy a House in California	$29.99	BHCA
The California Landlord's Law Book: Rights & Responsibilities(Book w/CD-ROM)	$44.99	LBRT
The California Landlord's Law Book: Evictions (Book w/CD-ROM)	$44.99	LBEV
Leases & Rental Agreements	$29.99	LEAR
Neighbor Law: Fences, Trees, Boundaries & Noise	$26.99	NEI
Renters' Rights (National Edition)	$24.99	RENT

IMMIGRATION

	PRICE	CODE
Becoming A U.S. Citizen: A Guide to the Law, Exam and Interview	$24.99	USCIT
Fiancé & Marriage Visas (Book w/CD-ROM)	$34.99	IMAR
How to Get a Green Card	$29.99	GRN
Student & Tourist Visas	$29.99	ISTU
U.S. Immigration Made Easy	$39.99	IMEZ

	PRICE	CODE
The Executor's Guide: Settling a Loved One's Estate or Trust	$34.99	EXEC
How to Probate an Estate in California	$49.99	PAE
Make Your Own Living Trust (Book w/CD-ROM)	$39.99	LITR
Nolo's Simple Will Book (Book w/CD-ROM)	$36.99	SWIL
Plan Your Estate	$44.99	NEST
Quick & Legal Will Book (Book w/CD-ROM)	$19.99	QUIC
Special Needs Trust: Protect Your Child's Financial Future (Book w/CD-ROM)	$34.99	SPNT

FAMILY MATTERS

Always Dad	$16.99	DIFA
Building a Parenting Agreement That Works	$24.99	CUST
The Complete IEP Guide	$34.99	IEP
Divorce & Money: How to Make the Best Financial Decisions During Divorce	$34.99	DIMO
Divorce Without Court	$29.99	DWCT
Do Your Own California Adoption: Nolo's Guide for Stepparents & Domestic Partners (Book w/CD-ROM)	$34.99	ADOP
Every Dog's Legal Guide: A Must-Have for Your Owner	$19.99	DOG
Get a Life: You Don't Need a Million to Retire Well	$24.99	LIFE
The Guardianship Book for California	$34.99	GB
A Legal Guide for Lesbian and Gay Couples	$34.99	LG
Living Together: A Legal Guide (Book w/CD-ROM)	$34.99	LTK
Nolo's IEP Guide: Learning Disabilities	$29.99	IELD
Parent Savvy	$19.99	PRNT
Prenuptial Agreements: How to Write a Fair & Lasting Contract (Book w/CD-ROM)	$34.99	PNUP
Work Less, Live More	$17.99	RECL

GOING TO COURT

Beat Your Ticket: Go To Court & Win! (National Edition)	$21.99	BEYT
The Criminal Law Handbook: Know Your Rights, Survive the System	$39.99	KYR
Everybody's Guide to Small Claims Court (National Edition)	$29.99	NSCC
Everybody's Guide to Small Claims Court in California	$29.99	CSCC

	PRICE	CODE

MONEY MATTERS

Title	Price	Code
101 Law Forms for Personal Use (Book w/CD-ROM)	$29.99	SPOT
Chapter 13 Bankruptcy: Repay Your Debts	$39.99	CHB
Credit Repair (Book w/CD-ROM)	$24.99	CREP
How to File for Chapter 7 Bankruptcy	$29.99	HFB
IRAs, 401(k)s & Other Retirement Plans: Taking Your Money Out	$34.99	RET
Solve Your Money Troubles	$19.99	MT
Stand Up to the IRS	$29.99	SIRS

PATENTS AND COPYRIGHTS

Title	Price	Code
All I Need is Money: How to Finance Your Invention	$19.99	FINA
The Copyright Handbook: How to Protect and Use Written Works (Book w/CD-ROM)	$39.99	COHA
Copyright Your Software (Book w/CD-ROM)	$34.95	CYS
Getting Permission: How to License & Clear Copyrighted Materials Online & Off (Book w/CD-ROM)	$34.99	RIPER
How to Make Patent Drawings	$29.99	DRAW
The Inventor's Notebook	$24.99	INOT
Nolo's Patents for Beginners	$24.99	QPAT
Patent, Copyright & Trademark	$39.99	PCTM
Patent It Yourself	$49.99	PAT
Patent Pending in 24 Hours	$34.99	PEND
Patenting Art & Entertainment: New Strategies for Protecting Creative Ideas	$39.99	PATAE
Profit from Your Idea (Book w/CD-ROM)	$34.99	LICE
The Public Domain	$34.99	PUBL
Trademark: Legal Care for Your Business and Product Name	$39.99	TRD
Web and Software Development: A Legal Guide (Book w/CD-ROM)	$44.99	SFT
What Every Inventor Needs to Know About Business & Taxes (Book w/CD-ROM)	$21.99	ILAX

	PRICE	CODE

RESEARCH & REFERENCE

Legal Research: How to Find & Understand the Law	$39.99	LRES

SENIORS

Long-Term Care: How to Plan & Pay for It	$19.99	ELD
Social Security, Medicare & Goverment Pensions	$29.99	SOA

SOFTWARE

Call or check our website at www.nolo.com for special discounts on Software!

Incorporator Pro	$89.99	STNC1
LLC Maker—Windows	$89.95	LLP1
Patent Pending Now!	$199.99	PP1
PatentEase—Windows	$349.00	PEAS
Personal RecordKeeper 5.0 CD—Windows	$59.95	RKD5
Quicken Legal Business Pro 2007—Windows	$109.99	SBQB7
Quicken WillMaker Plus 2007—Windows	$79.99	WQP7

Special Upgrade Offer

Save 35% on the latest edition of your Nolo book

Because laws and legal procedures change often, we update our books
regularly. To help keep you up-to-date, we are extending this special
upgrade offer. Cut out and mail the title portion of the cover of your old
Nolo book and we'll give you 35% off the retail price of the New Edition
of that book when you purchase directly from Nolo. This offer is to
individuals only. Prices and offer subject to change without notice.

	PRICE	CODE
Legal Guide for Starting & Running a Small Business	$34.99	RUNS
Legal Forms for Starting & Running a Small Business (Book w/CD-ROM)	$29.99	RUNSF
LLC or Corporation?	$24.99	CHENT
The Manager's Legal Handbook	$39.99	ELBA
Marketing Without Advertising	$20.00	MWAD
Music Law (Book w/CD-ROM)	$39.99	ML
Negotiate the Best Lease for Your Business	$24.99	LESP
Nolo's Guide to Social Security Disability (Book w/CD-ROM)	$29.99	QSS
Nolo's Quick LLC	$29.99	LLCQ
The Performance Appraisal Handbook	$29.99	PERF
The Small Business Start-up Kit (Book w/CD-ROM)	$24.99	SMBU
The Small Business Start-up Kit for California (Book w/CD-ROM)	$24.99	OPEN
Starting & Running a Successful Newsletter or Magazine	$29.99	MAG
Tax Deductions for Professionals	$34.99	DEPO
Tax Savvy for Small Business	$36.99	SAVVY
Whoops! I'm in Business	$19.99	WHOO
Working for Yourself: Law & Taxes for Independent Contractors, Freelancers & Consultants	$39.99	WAGE
Working With Independent Contractors (Book w/CD-ROM)	$29.99	HICI
Your Crafts Business: A Legal Guide (Book w/CD-ROM)	$26.99	VART
Your Limited Liability Company: An Operating Manual (Book w/CD-ROM)	$49.99	LOP
Your Rights in the Workplace	$29.99	YRW

CONSUMER

	PRICE	CODE
How to Win Your Personal Injury Claim	$29.99	PICL
Nolo's Encyclopedia of Everyday Law	$29.99	EVL
Nolo's Guide to California Law	$24.99	CLAW

ESTATE PLANNING & PROBATE

	PRICE	CODE
8 Ways to Avoid Probate	$19.99	PRAV
Estate Planning Basics	$21.99	ESPN

CATALOG
...more from Nolo

BUSINESS	PRICE	CODE
Business Buyout Agreements (Book w/CD-ROM)	$49.99	BSAG
The CA Nonprofit Corporation Kit (Binder w/CD-ROM)	$69.99	CNP
California Workers' Comp: How to Take Charge When You're Injured on the Job	$34.99	WORK
The Complete Guide to Buying a Business (Book w/CD-ROM)	$24.99	BUYBU
The Complete Guide to Selling a Business (Book w/CD-ROM)	$24.99	SELBU
Consultant & Independent Contractor Agreements (Book w/CD-ROM)	$29.99	CICA
The Corporate Records Handbook (Book w/CD-ROM)	$69.99	CORMI
Create Your Own Employee Handbook (Book w/CD-ROM)	$49.99	EMHA
Dealing With Problem Employees	$44.99	PROBM
Deduct It! Lower Your Small Business Taxes	$34.99	DEDU
Effective Fundraising for Nonprofits	$24.99	EFFN
The Employer's Legal Handbook	$39.99	EMPL
Essential Guide to Federal Employment Laws	$39.99	FEMP
Form a Partnership (Book W/CD-ROM)	$39.99	PART
Form Your Own Limited Liability Company (Book w/CD-ROM)	$44.99	LIAB
Home Business Tax Deductions: Keep What You Earn	$34.99	DEHB
How to Form a Nonprofit Corporation (Book w/CD-ROM)—National Edition	$49.99	NNP
How to Form a Nonprofit Corporation in California (Book w/CD-ROM)	$49.99	NON
How to Form Your Own California Corporation (Binder w/CD-ROM)	$59.99	CACI
How to Form Your Own California Corporation (Book w/CD-ROM)	$34.99	CCOR
How to Write a Business Plan (Book w/CD-ROM)	$34.99	SBS
Incorporate Your Business (Book w/CD-ROM)	$49.99	NIBS
Investors in Your Backyard (Book w/CD-ROM)	$24.99	FINBUS
The Job Description Handbook	$29.99	JOB

Prices subject to change.

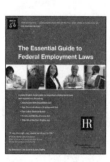
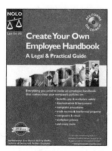

Listening to Audio Files You've Installed on Your Computer

There are two ways to listen to the audio files that you have installed on your computer.

- Windows users can open a file by selecting its "shortcut" as follows: (1) Click the Windows "Start" button, (2) open the "Programs" folder, (3) open the "Discipline Resources" subfolder, (4) open the "Audio" subfolder, and (5) click the shortcut to the audio segment you want to hear.
- Both Windows and Macintosh users can open a file directly by double clicking it. Use My Computer or Windows Explorer (Windows 98, 2000, Me, or XP) or the Finder (Macintosh) to go to the folder in which you installed or copied the CD-ROM's files. Then, double click the MP3 file you want to hear.

Where Are the Audio Files Installed?

Windows Users: MP3 files are installed by default to a folder named \Discipline Resources\Audio in the \Program Files.

Macintosh Users: MP3 files are located in the "Discipline Audio" folder.

Playing the Audio Files Without Installing

If you don't want to copy 50 MB of audio files to your hard disc, you can "play" the CD on your computer. Here's how:

Window users

Step 1: Insert the Forms CD to view the "Welcome to Nolo's Discipline Resources CD" window. (If nothing happens when you insert the Forms CD-ROM, double click the My Computer icon, double click the icon for the CD-ROM drive into which the Forms CD-ROM was inserted, and double click the file WELCOME.EXE.)

Step 2: Click "Listen to Audio."

Mac users

Step 1: Insert the Forms CD. If the "Nolo's Discipline Resources CD" window does not open, open it by double clicking the "Nolo's Discipline Resources CD" icon.

Step 2: Open the "Discipline Audio" folder by double clicking the "Discipline Audio" icon.

Step 3: Double click the audio file you want to hear.

Using the PowerPoint Presentation

"Present.pps," a presentation intended for use in staff training, is included on the CD-ROM in Microsoft's PowerPoint Show (PPS) format. You must have Microsoft PowerPoint or PowerPoint Viewer installed on your computer to use this file. PowerPoint Viewer is available for Windows and Macintosh systems. If you don't already have this software, you can download PowerPoint Viewer for free at http://www.microsoft.com/downloads.

All files and their file formats are listed below.

Step 1: Opening the Presentation

The PowerPoint presentation, like the word processing files, can be opened one of three ways.

- Windows users can open a file by selecting its "shortcut" as follows: (1) Click the Windows "Start" button; (2) open the "Programs" folder; (3) open the "Discipline Resources" subfolder; and (4) click the shortcut to "Present.pps."
- Both Windows and Macintosh users can open a file directly by double clicking on it. Use My Computer or Windows Explorer (Windows 9x, 2000, Me, or XP) or the Finder (Macintosh) to go to the folder you created and copied the CD-ROM's files to. Then, double click the specific file you want to open.
- You can also open a PPS file from within PowerPoint Viewer. To do this, you must first start PowerPoint Viewer. Then, go to the "File" menu and choose the "Open" command. This opens a dialog box where you will tell the program the location and

name of the file (you will need to navigate through the directory tree to get to the folder on your hard disk where the CD's files have been installed). If these directions are unclear, you will need to look through Power Point Viewer's help—Nolo's technical support department will not be able to help you with the use of PowerPoint Viewer.

Where Is the PowerPoint File Installed?

Windows Users: The PowerPoint file is installed by default to a folder named \Discipline Resources\PowerPoint in the \Program Files folder of your computer.

Macintosh Users: The PowerPoint file is located in the "PowerPoint" folder within the "Discipline Resources" folder.

Step 2: Viewing the Presentation

To progress through the presentation, simply left click anywhere on the screen. To return to a previous screen or the beginning of the presentation, or to end the presentation, right click and select the appropriate option from the drop down menu.

List of Files Included on the Forms CD-ROM

Form in rich text format (RTF)	File Name
Disciplinary Form	DisciplineForm.rtf
Forms in Adobe Reader PDF format	File Name
Discipline Evaluation Checklist	Checklist.pdf

Build Your Skills: An Overview of Progressive Discipline	Overview.pdf
Build Your Skills: Is it Time to Discipline?	Time.pdf
Build Your Skills: Smart Discipline Skills	Smart.pdf
Build Your Skills: The Disciplinary Steps	Steps.pdf
Build Your Skills: If Discipline Fails	Fail.pdf
Skills Enhancement: Setting Expectations	Expect.pdf
Skills Enhancement: Opening Discussions	Discuss.pdf
Skills Enhancement: Choosing Tone of Voice	Tone.pdf
Skills Enhancement: Brainstorming an Action Plan	Action.pdf
Forms in MP3 format	**File Name**
Segment 1: Coaching Session	Segment1-Coaching.mp3
Segment 2: Verbal Warning Session	Segment2-VerbalWarning.mp3
Segment 3: Written Warning Session	Segment3-WrittenWarning.mp3
Interview With Margie Mader-Clark	Interview-Mader-Clark.mp3
Interview With Lisa Guerin	Interview-Guerin.mp3
File is in PowerPoint format	**File Name**
PowerPoint Show	Present.pps

Index

C

D

U

V

W

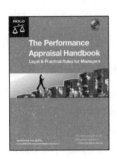